A New Star-Rating System & Other Exciting News from Frommer's!

In our continuing effort to publish the savviest, most up-to-date, and most appealing travel guides available, we've added some great new features.

Frommer's guides now include a new **star-rating system.** Every hotel, restaurant, and attraction is rated from 0 to 3 stars to help you set priorities and organize your time.

We've also added **seven brand-new features** that point you to the great deals, in-the-know advice, and unique experiences that separate travelers from tourists. Throughout the guide, look for:

Finds	Special finds—those places only insiders know about
Fun Fact	Fun facts—details that make travelers more informed and their trips more fun
Kids	Best bets for kids—advice for the whole family
Moments	Special moments—those experiences that memories are made of
Overrated	Places or experiences not worth your time or money
Tips	Insider tips—some great ways to save time and money
Value	Great values—where to get the best deals

We've also added a **"What's New"** section in every guide—a timely crash course in what's hot and what's not in every destination we cover.

Here's what the critics say about Frommer's:

Frommer's®

Munich & the Bavarian Alps

4th Edition

by Darwin Porter & Danforth Prince

WILEY

Wiley Publishing, Inc.

About the Authors

Veteran travel writers **Darwin Porter** and **Danforth Prince** have written numerous best-selling Frommer's guides, notably to Germany, France, Italy, England, and Spain. Porter, who was bureau chief for the *Miami Herald* when he was 21, wrote the first Frommer's guide to Germany and has traveled extensively in the country. Prince, who began writing with Porter in 1982, worked for the Paris bureau of the *New York Times*.

Published by:

Wiley Publishing, Inc.

909 Third Ave.
New York, NY 10022

ISBN 0-7645-6712-8
ISSN 1090-2325

Editor: Kendra L. Falkenstein
Production Editor: M. Faunette Johnston
Cartographer: Elizabeth Puhl
Photo Editor: Richard Fox
Production by Wiley Indianapolis Composition Services

Front cover photo: Hacker-Pschorr Beer Hall during Munich's Oktoberfest.
Back cover photo: View of Bavaria's Hohenschwangau Castle.

For information on our other products and services or to obtain technical support, please contact our Customer Care Department within the U.S. at 800-762-2974, outside the U.S. at 317-572-3993 or fax 317-572-4002.

Wiley also publishes its books in a variety of electronic formats. Some content that appears in print may not be available in electronic formats.

Manufactured in the United States of America

5 4 3 2

Contents

List of Maps   vii

What's New in Munich & the Bavarian Alps   1

1 The Best of Munich & the Bavarian Alps   3

1 Frommer's Favorite Munich & Bavarian Alps Experiences 4

2 Best Hotel Bets 8

3 Best Restaurant Bets 10

2 Planning Your Trip to Munich & the Bavarian Alps   13

1 Visitor Information 13

Destination: Germany—Red Alert Checklist 14

2 Entry Requirements & Customs 14

3 Money 15

The U.S. Dollar, the British Pound & the Euro 16

4 When to Go 16

Munich Calendar of Events 17

5 Health & Insurance 18

6 Tips for Travelers with Special Needs 19

7 Getting There 22

8 Escorted Tours, Package Deals & Special Interest Vacations 24

9 Planning Your Trip Online 26

10 Getting Around 28

11 Recommended Books 30

Fast Facts: Munich 30

3 Getting to Know Munich   35

1 Orientation 35

Neighborhoods in Brief 37

2 Getting Around 41

4 Where to Stay   43

1 Central Munich 44

2 Schwabing 58

3 Olympiapark 59

4 Haidhausen 59

5 Bogenhausen 60

6 Untermenzing 60

7 Obermenzing 61

8 Neuhausen 61

9 Nymphenburg 62

10 Near the Airport 62

5 Where to Dine   64

1 Restaurants by Cuisine 64

2 Central Munich 67

3 Near the Südbahnhof 83

4 Near the Isar, South of the Center 84

5 Schwabing 84

6 Bogenhausen/Prielhof 87
7 Denning 88
8 Grünwald 88
9 Nymphenburg 88

10 Obermenzing 89
11 Cafes 89
12 Beer Gardens 90

6 Exploring Munich 93

Suggested Itineraries 93
1 Exploring the City Center 94
Saving on Sightseeing 94
2 Palaces & Major Museums 95
3 The Great Churches 105
4 More Attractions 107
*Looks Like a Soup Tureen
But Isn't* 110

5 Parks, Gardens & the Zoo 111
6 The Olympic Grounds 112
Munich's Soccer Craze 112
7 Especially for Kids 114
8 Sightseeing Tours 115
9 Activities &
Outdoor Pursuits 116
Moon Over Munich 117

7 Munich Strolls 119

*Walking Tour 1:
The Historic Center* 119
*Walking Tour 2: Exploring West of
Marienplatz* 124

Walking Tour 3: Schwabing . . .127

8 Shopping 131

1 The Shopping Scene 131

2 Shopping A to Z 131

9 Munich After Dark 141

1 The Performing Arts 141
2 The Club & Music Scene 143
*Wenches, Knaves & Medieval
Delicacies* 146

3 The Bar & Cafe Scene 146
4 Beer Halls 149
5 Gay & Lesbian Clubs 151

10 Side Trips from Munich 153

1 Dachau Concentration
Camp 153
2 Starnbergersee 154
3 Tegernsee 157

4 Ammersee 160
5 Bad Tölz 162
6 Freising 166

11 The Bavarian Alps 168

1 Exploring the Region
by Car 169
2 National Park
Berchtesgaden 172

3 Berchtesgaden 173
Springtime for Hitler 178
4 Bad Reichenhall 180
5 Chiemsee 183

The Fairy-Tale King 186

6 Bad Wiessee 186

7 Garmisch-Partenkirchen 190

8 Exploring the Alps 197

*The Natural World
of the Alps* 200

9 Oberammergau 201

10 Mittenwald 207

11 Neuschwanstein &
Hohenschwangau 210

A Rococo Masterpiece 211

Appendix A: Munich in Depth   214

1 History 101 214

Dateline 214

The Notorious Lola Montez ...224

2 Munich's Architecture: From the
Baroque to the 21st Century ...228

3 A Taste of Bavaria 231

Appendix B: Useful Terms & Phrases   233

1 Glossary 233

2 Menu Terms 234

Index   237

General Index 237

Accommodations Index 243

Restaurant Index 244

List of Maps

Munich & the Bavarian Alps   5

Munich Neighborhoods   38

Central Munich
Accommodations   46

Central Munich Dining   68

Central Munich Attractions   96

The Deutsches Museum   99

The Residenz   101

Nymphenburg   105

Walking Tour 1:
The Historic Center   121

Walking Tour 2:
West of Marienplatz   125

Walking Tour 3: Schwabing   129

Munich & Environs   155

The Bavarian Alps   171

Garmisch-Partenkirchen   191

The Alps Around Garmisch   199

An Invitation to the Reader

In researching this book, we discovered many wonderful places—hotels, restaurants, shops, and more. We're sure you'll find others. Please tell us about them, so we can share the information with your fellow travelers in upcoming editions. If you were disappointed with a recommendation, we'd love to know that, too. Please write to:

Frommer's Munich & the Bavarian Alps, 4th Edition
Wiley Publishing, Inc. • 909 Third Ave. • New York, NY 10022

An Additional Note

Please be advised that travel information is subject to change at any time—and this is especially true of prices. We therefore suggest that you write or call ahead for confirmation when making your travel plans. The authors, editors, and publisher cannot be held responsible for the experiences of readers while traveling. Your safety is important to us, however, so we encourage you to stay alert and be aware of your surroundings. Keep a close eye on cameras, purses, and wallets, all favorite targets of thieves and pickpockets.

New! Frommer's Star Ratings & Icons

Every hotel, restaurant, and attraction listing in this guide has been ranked for quality, value, service, amenities, and special features using a star-rating scale. In country, state, and regional guides, we also rate towns and regions to help you narrow down your choices and budget your time accordingly. Hotels and restaurants in the Very Expensive and Expensive categories are rated on a scale of one (highly recommended) to three stars (exceptional). Those in the Moderate and Inexpensive categories rate from zero (recommended) to two stars (very highly recommended). Attractions, towns, and regions are rated according to the following scale: zero stars (recommended), one star (highly recommended), two stars (very highly recommended), and three stars (must-see).

In addition to the rating system, we also use seven icons to highlight insider information, useful tips, special bargains, hidden gems, memorable experiences, kid-friendly venues, places to avoid, and other useful information:

| Finds | Fun Fact | Kids | Moments | Overrated | Tips | Value |

The following abbreviations are used for credit cards:

AE American Express	DISC Discover	V Visa
DC Diners Club	MC MasterCard	

FROMMERS.COM

Now that you have the guidebook to a great trip, visit our website at **www.frommers. com** for travel information on nearly 2,500 destinations. With features updated regularly, we give you instant access to the most current trip-planning information available. At Frommers.com, you'll also find the best prices on airfares, accommodations, and car rentals—and you can even book travel online through our travel booking partners. At Frommers.com, you'll also find the following:

- Online updates to our most popular guidebooks
- Vacation sweepstakes and contest giveaways
- Newsletter highlighting the hottest travel trends
- Online travel message boards with featured travel discussions

What's New in Munich & the Bavarian Alps

MUNICH ACCOMMODATIONS
The Bavarian capital is bursting forth with new and restored hotels. For complete information on Munich's accommodations, see chapter 4, "Where to Stay."

Admiral (© **089/216-350**), a government-rated four-star property has opened between the Deutsches Museum and the Isar River. Elegant furnishings and top-rate comfort are its hallmark.

One of Munich's newest family-run hotels is **Asam Stadthotel** (© **089/230-9700**), lying in a restored pre-war hotel building. Accommodations facing the garden in the rear or in one of the bedrooms with a "decadently large" private bathtub are preferred.

A family favorite, **Hotel Mirabell** (© **089/549-1740**), has opened within walking distance of the Hauptbahnhof. Clean, comfortable, and affordable bedrooms are spread across six floors.

Another recent discovery, **Hotel St. Paul** (© **089/5440-7800**) is one of the city's most affordable and agreeable hotels, with handsomely furnished bedrooms and a great buffet breakfast.

For motorists who don't want to stay in the congested inner city, **Mercure München Königin Elisabeth** (© **089/126-860**) is just 15 minutes from the center and has much going for it, including excellent rooms, a Biergarten, and a health center.

Relatively undiscovered, **Hotel-Pension Mariandl** (© **089/534-108**) is a small Bavarian hotel of both charm and character. It's in a neo-Gothic town house built at the turn of the 20th century, just a 10-minute walk from the grounds where Oktoberfest is held.

MUNICH RESTAURANTS   An array of excellent restaurants in various price ranges have opened in Munich, which now competes with Berlin as the culinary capital of Germany. For complete information on Munich's restaurants, see chapter 5, "Where to Dine."

Bistro Cézanne (© **089/391-805**), in the Schwabing district, brings the charm and flair of Paris to this sector of Munich.

Its name, **Der Tisch** (© **089/557-154**), is minimalist, meaning "the table," but this little bistro, with its international cuisine, has become one of the most fashionable places to eat in Munich. The cooking is divinely contemporary and is a delight to behold—for example, pike-perch on a mound of cabbage sprinkled with a beet-flavored pink sauce.

A major new rendezvous point in Munich is **Café am Beethovenplatz** (© **089/5440-4348**), which you can patronize as a cafe or a full-fledged restaurant. At the grand piano in the center, music (not just works composed by Beethoven) is played. The bustling place is very middle European—its savory food a combination of Bavarian and international styles.

The new hangout for the *literati* and others in Munich is **Café Dukatz in the Literaturhaus** (℃ **089/291-9600**), decorated with memorabilia of the writer Oskar Maris Graft (1894–1967). Many of the movers and shakers in German publishing come here during the day to "drink books" and order from the well-prepared international menu.

At long last, Munich has a good Jewish restaurant: **Cohen's** (℃ **089/280-9545**), which is like those that thrived in Munich before the rise of Hitler. The wine comes from Israel, and many of the dishes are familiar to those who frequent New York delis: gefilte fish, bagels with smoked salmon, and chopped chicken liver.

A new and amusing food oddity is **Erstes Münchner Kartoffelhaus** (℃ **089/296-331**), or the "House of Potatoes." The spotlight here is on the lowly spud, which is sometimes treated imperially, with platters fit for a king when they are served with the likes of smoked salmon or fresh shrimp.

MUNICH ATTRACTIONS Munich is a new city built over the old (after World War II), and it is filled with both ancient and modern treasures. For complete information on Munich's attractions, see chapter 6, "Exploring Munich."

The city's newest museum, and in some respects, one of its greatest museums, the **Pinakothek der Moderne** (℃ **089/23805-118**), opened in the fall of 2002. This is one of the world's largest museums devoted to the visual arts of the 19th and 20th centuries, featuring a vast display of some of Germany's best fine and applied arts. This is Munich's answer to London's Tate Gallery or Paris' Pompidou Museum.

THE BAVARIAN ALPS   Stretching from Munich to the Austrian border, the fir-clad Bavarian Alps are a land of summer flowers, shimmering alpine lakes, and half-timbered houses. For complete information on the Bavarian Alps, see chapter 11, "The Bavarian Alps."

Accommodations   The big news blowing through the windswept Alps is that the American-based Intercontinental chain is constructing a luxury hotel in Obersalzberg, the former site of Hitler's Alpine command post. (Hitler's Berghof, where he lived with his mistress, Eva Braun, was destroyed in 1945.)

The architects and builders of the hotel claim that in no way will the site or the resort be turned into a shrine for the neo-Nazi movement. In other words, vendors won't be allowed to sell Third Reich souvenirs.

The site of the former holiday mansion of Herman Göring, commander of the Luftwaffe, will become a golf course. None-too-happy Jewish leaders have had their concerns eased somewhat since a Documentation Center, recently opened nearby, reveals how the Nazi top brass at this mountaintop retreat planned the destruction of the Jews and other minorities within Europe.

Restaurants   Prien is the liveliest resort on Chiemsee, which is one of the most beautiful lakes in the Bavarian Alps. On the western bank of the lake, **Restaurant Mühlberger** (℃ **08051/966-888**) has opened. Its savory Continental cuisine (menu items reflect a diversity of regional culinary conditions) has made it a hit around the lake, much frequented by visitors and locals alike.

The Best of Munich & the Bavarian Alps

Sprawling **Munich (München),** home to some 1.3 million people, is the capital of Bavaria, and one of Germany's major cultural centers (only Berlin outranks it in terms of museums and theaters). It's also one of Germany's most festive cities, and its location, at the foot of the Alps, is idyllic.

Thomas Mann, a longtime resident of Munich, wrote something about the city that might have been coined by an advertising agency: "Munich sparkles." Although the city he described was swept away by two world wars, the quote is still apt. Munich continues to sparkle, drawing temporary visitors and new residents like a magnet from virtually everywhere.

Some of the sparkle comes from its vitality. With its buzzing factories, newspapers and television stations, and service and electronics industries, it's one of Europe's busiest and liveliest places. More subtle is Munich's amazing ability to combine Hollywood-type glamour and stylish international allure with its folkloric connections. Few other large cities have been as successful as Munich in marketing folklore, rusticity, and nostalgia for the golden days of yesteryear, yet this rustic ambience coexists with the hip and the avant-garde, high-tech industries, and a sharp political sense. This is what lends the city such a distinctive flair.

As Americans migrate to New York or San Francisco to seek opportunity and experience, so Germans migrate to Munich. Munich is full of non-Bavarians. More than two-thirds of the German citizens living in Munich have come from other parts of the country, and tens of thousands are expatriates or immigrants from every conceivable foreign land. Sometimes these diverse elements seem unified only by a shared search for the good life.

Outsiders are found in every aspect of Munich's life. The wildly applauded soccer team, FC Bayern München, is composed almost entirely of outsiders—Danes, Belgians, Swedes, Prussians—and the team was trained by a Rhinelander throughout its spate of recent successes. The city's most frequently quoted newspaper mogul (Dieter Schröder) and many of the city's artistic movers and shakers are expatriates, usually from North Germany. What's remarkable is the unspoken collusion of the whole population in promoting Bavarian charm, despite the fact that real dyed-in-the-wool Bavarians risk becoming a distinct minority in their own capital.

Virtually everyone has heard the city's many nicknames—"Athens on the Isar," "the German Silicon Valley," and "Little Paris." But none seems to stick. More appropriate is a more ambivalent label—"the secret capital of Germany."

Munich's self-imposed image is that of a fun-loving and festival-addicted city—typified by its Oktoberfest. This celebration, which began as a minor sideshow to a royal wedding in 1810, has become a symbol of the city itself.

Redolent with nostalgia for old-time Bavaria, it draws more than 7 million visitors each year. For these 16 days every fall, raucous hordes cram themselves into the city to have a good time.

Oktoberfest is so evocative, and so gleefully and unashamedly pagan, that dozens of places throughout the world capitalize on its success by throwing Oktoberfest ceremonies of their own. These occur even in such unlikely places as Helen, Georgia, where citizens and merchants reap tidy profits by wearing dirndls and lederhosen, playing recordings of the requisite oompah-pah music, and serving ample provisions of beer in oversize beer steins. No one has ever marketed such stuff better than Munich, but then, few other regions of Europe have had such alluring raw material from which to draw.

A somewhat reluctant contender for the role of international megalopolis, Munich has pursued commerce, industry, and the good life without fanfare. You get the idea that in spite of its economic muscle and a roaring GNP, Munich wants to see itself as a large agrarian village, peopled by jolly beer drinkers who cling to their folkloric roots despite the presence on all sides of symbols of the high-tech age.

Underneath this expansive, fun-loving Munich is the reality of an unyielding, ongoing conservatism and resistance to change, both religious and political. But as a symbol of a bold, reunited Germany forging a new identity for the 21st century, Munich simply has no parallel. As such, it continues to exert a powerful appeal.

1 Frommer's Favorite Munich & Bavarian Alps Experiences

• **Socializing at the Biergarten:** If you're in Munich anytime between the first sunny spring day and the last fading light of a Bavarian-style autumn, you might head for one of the city's celebrated beer gardens (*Biergarten*). Our favorite is Biergarten Chinesischer Turm (p. 91) in the Englischer Garten. Traditionally, beer gardens were tables placed under chestnut trees planted above storage cellars to keep beer cool in summer. Naturally, people started to drink close to the source of their pleasure, and the tradition has remained. It's estimated that, today, Munich has at least 400 beer gardens and cellars. Food, drink, and atmosphere are much the same in all of them. See the "Beer Gardens" section of chapter 5 for more recommendations.

• **Enjoying Munich's World-Class Music:** The city is home to outstanding classical music; notable are the Bavarian State Opera (p. 142) and the Munich Philharmonic (p. 142). Prices are affordable and the selection is diverse. The season of summer concerts at Nymphenburg Palace (p. 103) alone is worth the trip to Munich.

• **Nude Sunbathing in the Englischer Garten:** On any summery sunny day, it seems that half of Munich can be seen letting it all hang out. The sentimental founders of this park with their romantic ideas surely had no idea they were creating a public nudist colony. Even if you don't want to take it all off, you can still come here to enjoy the park's natural beauty. See p. 111.

• **Exploring the Zugspitze:** There is no grander and more panoramic alpine view in all of Bavaria than that which can be enjoyed by ascending the Zugspitze, the tallest mountain peak in Germany, separating the German and Austrian

Munich & the Bavarian Alps

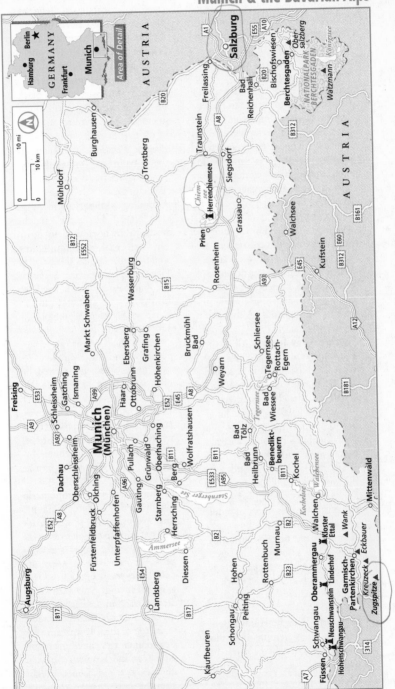

frontiers. A playground for hikers in summer, the mountain range becomes a snowfield for winter skiers, who enjoy slopes beginning at 2,610m (8,700 ft.). Once you've scaled the heights, you'll feel on top of the world. See p. 118.

- **Snacking on Weisswurst:** Munich's classic "street food" is a "white sausage" made of calf's head, veal, and seasoning, about the size of a hot dog. Smooth and light in flavor, it is eaten with pretzels and beer—nothing else. Weisswurst etiquette calls for you to remove the sausage from a bowl of hot water, cut it crosswise in half, dip the cut end in sweet mustard, then suck the sausage out of the casing in a single gesture. When you learn to do this properly, you will have become a true Münchner. See "A Taste of Bavaria," in appendix A for more on Weisswurst.

- **Getting Away from It All at the Hirschgarten:** For a glimpse of what Munich used to be like, flee from the tourist hordes and traffic to the Hirschgarten or "Deer Meadow." A "green lung" between Donnersberg Bridge and Nymphenburg Park, the area has been a deer park since 1791. In 1890, the largest beer garden in the world was built here, seating 8,000 drinkers. The Hirschgarten remains Munich's most tranquil retreat, a land of towering oaks, chestnuts, and beeches, attracting those with a love of the great outdoors—and especially those who like to pack a picnic lunch or enjoy an open-air game of chess. See p. 111.

- **Exploring Trendy Haidhausen:** Tourists rarely venture into this district on the right bank of the Isar River. For decades it was known as a blue-collar and low-rent district of Munich. However,

hippies and artists, in the 1970s, created a cross-cultural scene that made Haidhausen, not Schwabing, the hip place to hang out. Today, it is the place to see and be seen—especially if you're a *Schicki-Micki* (a club-going Bavarian yuppie), a person who dresses only in black, or one of the *Müeslis* (European granolas). The place to go is one of the bars or cafes around Pariser Platz or Weissenburger Platz. Take the S-bahn to Ostbahnhof or Rosenheimerstrasse and get with it! See p. 37.

- **Attending Oktoberfest:** It's called the "biggest keg party" in the world. Münchners had so much fun in 1810 celebrating the wedding of Prince Ludwig to Princess Therese von Sachsen-Hildburghausen that they've been rowdying it up ever since for 16 full days between September 21 and October 6. The festival's tent city is at the Theresienwiese fairgrounds, and the Middle Ages lives on as oxen are roasted on open spits, brass bands oompahpah you into oblivion, and some 750,000 kegs of the brew are tapped. There are even tents where *Bierleichen* (beer corpses) can recover from drunkenness, listening to soothing zither music. See chapter 9.

- **Seeking R&R at Olympiapark:** Site of the 1972 Olympic Games, this 296-hectare (740-acre) park and stadium is a premier venue for various sporting events and concerts. You can swim in one of the pools, and you'll find all the jogging tracks and gyms your heart desires, even an artificial lake. To cap off your visit, take the elevator to the top of the Olympiaturm for a panoramic view of Munich and a look at the Bavarian Alps. In summer, free rock concerts blast from the amphitheater, Theatron, by Olympic Lake. See p. 112.

- **Going from Vie de Bohème to Schicki-Micki in Schwabing:** In fin-de-siècle (turn of the 20th century or Belle Epoque) Munich, Schwabing was the home of the avant-garde. Artists, writers, poets, and musicians of the era, including Thomas Mann, called it home. *Jugendstil* (Art Nouveau), the Blue Rider painters, and Richard Wagner made this area the cultural capital of Europe before 1914. A revival came in 1945, as new cultural icons such as Rainer Werner Fassbinder arose. Schwabing lives on, although today it's gentrified and populated by fashion editors and models, along with what have been called "swinging aristocrats." Although you might come here to walk in the footsteps of Wassily Kandinsky or to see where Paul Klee or Rainer Maria Rilke lived and worked, you'll also get exposure to Schicki-Mickies. Walking, strolling, shopping, and people-watching are the chief activities today. At some point, find a chair at **Café Roxy** (p. 128), 48 Leopoldstrasse, and watch the parade go by. See p. 37.

- **Soaking Up the Wittelsbach Lifestyle:** Just northwest of the city center lies Nymphenburg Palace, begun in 1664, an exquisite baroque extravaganza surrounded by a 198-hectare (495-acre) park dotted with lakes, pavilions, and hunting lodges. It was the summer home of the Bavarian rulers. We prefer to visit in either summer, when outdoor concerts are on, or spring, when the rhododendrons are in bloom. Go inside the palace for a look at the painted ceiling in the Great Hall. In such works as *Nymphs Paying Homage to the Goddess Flora,* Bavarian rococo reached its apogee. See p. 103.

- **Spending an Afternoon in the Botanischer Garten:** If you're not a plant lover, you'll be converted here. Laid out between 1909 and 1914 on the north side of Nymphenburg Park, it's one of the most richly stocked botanical wonders in Europe. You can wander among the 16 hectares (40 acres) and some 15,000 varieties of plants; a highlight is the alpine garden with rare specimens. In late spring, the heather garden is a delight. See p. 111.

- **Checking Out Market Day at Viktualienmarkt:** The most characteristic scene in Munich is a Saturday morning at this food market at the south end of the Altstadt. Since 1807, Viktualienmarkt has been the center of Munich life, dispensing fresh vegetables, fruit from the Bavarian countryside, just-caught fish, dairy produce, poultry, rich grainy breads, moist cakes, and farm-fresh eggs. Naturally, there's also a beer garden here. There's even a maypole and a statue honoring Karl Valentin (1882–1948), the legendary comic actor and filmmaker. Even more interesting than the market produce are the stallholders themselves—a few even evoke Professor Higgins's "squashed cabbage leaf," Eliza Doolittle. See p. 111.

- **Rafting Along the Isar:** Admittedly, it doesn't rival the Seine in Paris, but the Isar is the river of life in Munich. If you can't make it for a country walk in the Bavarian Alps, a walk along the left bank of the Isar is an alternative. Begin at Höllriegelskreuth and follow the scenic path along the Isar's high bank. Your trail will carry you through the Römerschanze into what Münchners call

"The Valley of the Mills" (Mühltal). After passing the Bridge Inn (Brückenwirt), you will eventually reach Kloster Schäftlarn, where you'll find—what else?—a beer garden. After a mug, you'll be fortified to continue along signposted paths through the Isar River Valley until you reach Wolfrathausen. Instead of walking back, you can board a raft made of logs and "drift" back to the city, enjoying beer and often the oompah-pah sound of a brass band as you head toward Munich. See p. 117.

- **Taking a Dip at Müller's Public Baths:** Müllersches Volksbad, at Rosenheimer Strasse I (S-bahn to Isartor), is one of the most magnificent public baths in all of Germany. This is no dull swimming pool but a celebration of grandeur fin-de-siècle style. Karl Hocheder designed this Moorish/Roman spectacle between 1897 and 1901, an era of opulence. When the baths opened, they were hailed as the most modern baths in all of Europe, surpassing anything but those in Budapest. Completely renovated, the baths today have a "gentlemen's pool" with barrel vaulting and a "ladies' pool" with domed vaulting. There are also sweat baths and individual baths for those who like to let it

all hang out—but in private. Alas, the *Zamperlbad,* or doggie bath, in the basement, is no more.

- **Spending a Night at the Hofbräuhaus:** Established in 1589 by Duke Wilhelm V to satisfy the thirst of his court, the Hofbräuhaus is not only the city's major tourist attraction but also the world's most famous beer hall, seating more than 4,000 drinkers. In 1828, the citizens of Munich were allowed to drink "the court's brew" for the first time, and it turned out to be habit-forming. A popular song, "In München Steht ein Hofbräuhaus," spread the fame of the brewery. To be really authentic, you drink in the ground-floor *Schwemme* where some 1,000 beer buffs down their brew at wooden tables while listening to the sounds of an oompah-pah band. More rooms, including the *Trinkstube* for 350, are found upstairs, and in summer, beer is served in a colonnaded courtyard patio with a lion fountain. The waitstaff, in Bavarian peasant dress, appears carrying 10 steins at once. Pretzels are sold on long sticks, and white *Radis* (radishes) are cut into fancy spirals. The Hofbräuhaus is where the good life of Munich holds forth. See p. 149.

2 Best Hotel Bets

For complete hotel information for Munich, see chapter 4, "Where to Stay."

- **Best Historic Hotel: Kempinski Hotel Vier Jahreszeiten München** (© 800/426-3135 in the U.S.) is one of the most famous hotels in the world—the lineage of this hostelry stretches back to 1858. Maximilian II himself took a personal interest in the hotel's

establishment, even going so far as to aid its founder financially. The Walterspiel family brought it to worldwide prominence, and over the years it's entertained the greats and near-greats. See p. 44.

- **Best for Business Travelers:** The **München Park Hilton** (© 800/445-8667 in the U.S.) is a modern 15-story structure, completely geared to welcome the business traveler and provide all needed services. It is close to many corporate headquarters and has the best conference facilities of any hotel in the city. Actually, the hotel was an office block until pressed into service as a hotel for the 1972 Olympics. After business is concluded, you can unwind at the hotel's health club. See p. 49.

- **Best for a Romantic Getaway: Romantik Hotel Insel Mühle** (ⓒ **089/8-10-10**), constructed around a 16th-century mill, is a romantic choice with its antique decor and its rooms with sloping garretlike ceilings. It is known for its old-world restaurant with massive beams and a wine cellar. Though far removed from the hustle and bustle, it's only 9.5km (6 miles) west of Munich's Marienplatz. See p. 60.

- **Best Trendy Hotel:** The **Mandarin Oriental** (ⓒ **089/29-09-80**), small and deluxe, in a neo-Renaissance building, is the choice of visiting celebrities, including fashion models, dress designers, and the media elite. Its discreet style and formal elegance make it the right address for those who don't want to be "too obvious"—that is, by staying at one of the lavish, bigger hotels. See p. 45.

- **Best Lobby for Pretending You're Rich: Bayerischer Hof & Palais Montgelas** (ⓒ **800/223-6800** in the U.S.) is a real old-fashioned European formal hotel with a deluxe lobby filled with English and French furniture and oriental rugs. It's been called the "living room" of Munich. "Meet you in the lounge of the Bayerischer Hof" is often heard. As hotels go, there's no more impressive place to go for a drink. See p. 44.

- **Best for Families: Four Points Hotel München Olympiapark** (ⓒ **089/35-75-10**) is right at Europe's biggest sports and recreation center and rents many triple rooms that are ideal for families. It's among the most modern and best-kept places in the city, and your child will enjoy meeting some of the sports heroes who often stay here. At Olympiapark, the entire family can use the sports facilities, including a large Olympic-size swimming pool. See p. 51.

- **Best Moderately Priced Hotel:** Built as a private villa at the turn of the 20th century, **Hotel Olympic** (ⓒ **089/231-89-0**) has been converted into a hip, attractive, and affordable hotel. Rooms are minimalist, all white, and stylish. See p. 53.

- **Best Budget Hotel: Uhland Garni** (ⓒ **089/54-33-50**), a family run place, is one of the most inviting of the small hotels of Munich. Behind a facade with summer geraniums, it welcomes you into rooms converted from grand apartments built a century ago. It's also a good choice for families as many units contain bunk beds for children. See p. 57.

- **Best B&B: Gästehaus Englischer Garten** (ⓒ **089/3-83-94-10**), close to the Englischer Garten and its summer nudes, is an oasis of charm and tranquility in fashionable Schwabing. An ivy-covered former private villa, it offers attractively furnished rooms; those in the annex are really small apartments with tiny kitchenettes. When the weather's right, breakfast is served in the rear garden. See p. 58.

- **Best Service: Eden-Hotel-Wolff** (ⓒ **089/55-11-50**) employs one of the most thoughtful staffs in

Munich. Although hotels like the Bayerischer Hof (p. 44) offer state-of-the-art service, the attentive, efficient, unhurried yet down-to-earth English-speaking staff here gets the job done just as well, anticipating all your needs. See p. 45.

- **Best Location: Hotel An der Oper** (© 089/2-90-02-70) is in the virtual heart of Munich. Stay here and you'll be just steps away from the central Marienplatz. Moments after leaving the hotel, you can be shopping along the Maximilianstrasse or exploring the traffic-free malls just steps from the Bavarian National Theater, and all for a reasonable price. See p. 51.

- **Best Health Club: München Marriott Hotel** (© 800/228-9290 in the U.S.) has the best-equipped fitness center of any hotel in Munich—a swimming pool almost 13.5m (45 ft.) long, whirlpools, hydrojets, a solarium, and state-of-the-art exercise equipment. There's also a *Kosmetik-Kabine* for beauty treatments and massages, plus separate saunas for men and women. Residents of the Marriott use the club for free; nonresidents pay 15€ for a day pass. See p. 58.

- **Best Hotel Pool:** The state-of-the-art indoor pool at the **Arabella Sheraton Grand Hotel** (© 089/9-26-40) is on the 22nd floor, offering not only views, but its own waterfall. Although many hotels in Munich have swimming pools, none compete with this choice. And that's not all—you get five whirlpools, along with two mixed saunas (open to both men and women), and a trio of steam rooms inspired by ancient Rome, each ideal for après-swim (after your swim). This hotel is in the verdant suburb of Bogenhausen, only seven subway stops from the center of town. See p. 60.

- **Best Spa Hotel:** The great curative spa of Bad Reichenhall is the finest and best-equipped in the Bavarian Alps. Reigning supreme here is its best hotel, **Steigenberger Axelmannstein** (© 800/223-5652 in the U.S.), which is set in lovely gardens of 3 hectares (7½ acres). Its spa equipment is always kept in the finest condition, and its bedrooms, cuisine, and on-site entertainment make it one of the great discoveries of Bavaria. See p. 181.

3 Best Restaurant Bets

For complete restaurant information for Munich, see chapter 5, "Where to Dine."

- **Best Alltime Favorite: Boettner's** (© 089/22-12-10). One of Munich's most enduring restaurants has made a spectacular comeback, albeit in a new location. In business since 1901, Boettner's offers a cuisine that is better than ever, and still uses only top-quality ingredients like lobster and fresh white truffles. Housed in a Renaissance structure in the center of Munich, the restaurant has a cuisine lighter than in the past but still featuring those rich old Bavarian favorites for those who want to indulge. See p. 67.

- **Best Spot for a Romantic Dinner: Grünwalder Einkehr** (© 089/6-49-23-04) lets you escape from the urban sprawl of Munich to a "green lung" retreat 13km (8 miles) south of the city center. In a 200-year-old former private home in a rustic setting, you can feast on French-inspired dishes that include many Gallic favorites. It's truly the best place around to get away from it all. See p. 88.

- **Best Spot for a Business Lunch: Mark's Restaurant** (✆ 089/290980), in the deluxe Rafael hotel, is the chic business luncheon spot of Munich. The movers and shakers of the Bavarian capital gather in the informal lobby-level setting of Mark's Corner to make the big deal. Menu items change according to the season and the inspiration of the chef, and, as you dine, you can practically feel euros changing hands. See p. 71.

- **Best Spot for a Celebration: Kay's Bistro** (✆ 089/2-60-35-84) is number one on the see-and-be-seen circuit. Sophisticated and chic, it's also lots of fun. It's filled nightly with a glamorous clientele who like not only good food but a festive restaurant in which to celebrate their latest deal, marriage, or divorce (whatever). The decoration is always changing based on the season, but the French and international cuisine remains eternally alluring. See p. 70.

- **Best Wine List: Geisel's Vinothek** (✆ 089/55-13-71-40), in the Hotel Excelsior, is the best spot in Munich for a taste of the grape. Dedicated to Bacchus, this deliberately unpretentious choice has one of the city's finest collections of Italian, French, Austrian, and German wines—all sold by the glass. You can also order Italian cuisine here. See p. 78.

- **Best Value: Palais Keller** (✆ 089/2-12-09-90) offers the most bang for your euro, although it's housed in the cellar of one of the most elegant hotels in Munich. Its well-prepared cuisine of Bavarian and German dishes is priced about the same as far less desirable beer halls and *Weinstuben* nearby. Let a smiling waitress in a frilly apron introduce you to *Tafelspitz* here, the fabled boiled beef dish. See p. 80.

- **Best for Kids: Mövenpick Restaurant** (✆ 089/5-45-94-90) is right in the heart of Munich and is decorated with a whimsical theme; different rooms are devoted to different cuisines, everything from the Longhorn Corner for Texas-style steaks to Grandma's Kitchen for some old-fashioned cookery. Kids like to come here for a full meal of just *Rösti,* those fabled Swiss fried potatoes. See p. 74.

- **Best Continental Cuisine: Tantris** (✆ 089/36-19-59-0), in Schwabing, serves the city's most refined cuisine, a treat to the eye as well as the palate. Chef Hans Haas is one of the top chefs of Germany and is forever sharpening his culinary skills as he wines and dines the celebrated people of Europe. Nothing in Munich equals the service, flavors, and delight found here. See p. 84.

- **Best French Cuisine: Bistro Terrine** (✆ 089/28-17-80) has food that tastes so authentically French that you'll think you're back in Lyon. Menu items are often more inventive than the Belle Epoque atmosphere of this Art-Nouveau bistro in Schwabing implies. The menu changes with the seasons—for example, in autumn, nuggets of venison might appear with hazelnut-flavored gnocchi and port wine sauce. See p. 85.

- **Best Italian Cuisine: Buon Gusto** (✆ 089/29-63-83) is an elegant choice for Italian cuisine, the finest in Munich, where the competition grows increasingly stiff. A rustic-looking bistro with an open kitchen, this restaurant's chefs are masters of Italian cookery, especially the simple but flavorful dishes of Tuscany. Pasta dishes—each homemade and succulent—are meals unto themselves. See p. 72.

- **Best Seafood: Austernkeller** (© 089/ 29-87-87) prepares not only the freshest oysters in town but also an array of delectable seafood selections that range from mussels to clams and sea snails to the wonderful lobster Thermidor. The kitsch collection of plastic lobsters shouldn't put you off: The food is far more worthy than the decor. See p. 70.
- **Best Bavarian Cuisine: Nürnberger Bratwurst Glöckl am Dom** (© 089/29-52-64) is Munich's coziest restaurant. Here you can enjoy Bavarian cuisine so authentic that it's hardly changed since the turn of the 20th century (the restaurant opened in 1893). Bavarians, often looking as stern as one of the Dürer prints on the wall, come here for all their favorite dishes—just like grandmother made a hundred years ago. See p. 80.
- **Best Late-Night Dining: Käfer am Hofgarten** (© 089/2-90-75-30) has a hip dining scene that goes until 3 in the morning on weekends. It's a fashionable French bistro with amazingly reasonable prices, and you can enjoy an international array of food, inspired by every place from America to Thailand. See p. 79.
- **Best Outdoor Dining: Locanda Picolit** (© 089/396447), an Italian restaurant in the heart of Schwabing, offers an outdoor terrace in summer with a view over a garden that's one of the most evocative in Munich. The place suggests a Mediterranean world.

Menu items change with the season, and you can enjoy the agrarian bounty of Italy while doing some people-watching and soaking up the fresh breezes blowing across Munich at the same time. See p. 86.

- **Best People-Watching: Graffunder** (© 089/29-24-27), is on Marienplatz, the virtual heart of Munich, and here you can take in the passing parade while enjoying a selection of French and Italian wines sold by the glass. Platters of food ranging from simple snacks to more elaborate concoctions are also served. But it's the landmark square of Marienplatz itself, the very center of the city's festive life, that's the real attraction. See p. 79.
- **Best Picnic Fare: Alois Dallmayr** (© 089/2-13-51-00) offers not only the best picnic fare in Munich, but the best in Germany. With the food you can gather up here, you could even invite the queen of England for lunch in the Englischer Garten. One of the world's most renowned delis, this supermarket of goodies has elegant selections like foie gras, but it also offers more democratically priced (and mundane) fare. See p. 71.
- **Best Newcomer:** On Lake Chiemsee, called the Bavarian Sea, **Restaurant Mühlberger** (© 08051/966-888), has opened in the resort town of Prien, and has quickly become acclaimed as one of the best restaurants in Bavaria. Many residents of Munich drive here just to dine on a refined, sophisticated cuisine, coming from a kitchen filled with imaginative chefs where only first-rate ingredients are used. See p. 185.

2

Planning Your Trip to Munich & the Bavarian Alps

This chapter covers everything you need to know to make trip-planning a snap, from when to go to how to shop for the best airfare. Browse through it to get started and make sure you've touched all the bases.

1 Visitor Information

VISITOR INFORMATION

TOURIST OFFICES Before you go, you'll find a German National Tourist Office in **New York** at 122 E. 42nd St., 52nd Floor, New York, NY 10168 (© **800/637-1171** or 212/661-7200); in **Toronto** at 2 Bloor St. Suite 3330, Toronto, ON M4W 3R8 (© **416/967-3381**); and in **London,** PO Box 2695, London W1A 3TN (© **020/7317-0908**).

Nearly all larger towns and all cities in Germany have tourist offices. The **German National Tourist Board** headquarters is at Beethovenstrasse 69, 60325 Frankfurt am Main (© **069/21-23-8800**).

OUR FAVORITE GERMAN WEBSITES

If you open a site that's in German, look for the little British or American flag, or for the word *English* on some, but not all, to see the pages in English.

- The German National Tourist Board site (www.germanytourism.de) gives you an online tour of several cities, and highlights attractions. You can also access facts on weather, transportation, events, and so forth. A new, related site (www.visits-to-germany.com) designed especially for United States travelers lets you design and price specific itineraries and vacation packages.

- The Hotelguide Germany IHA Hotel Association (www.hotels-germany.com) lets you book a room at any of more than 750 German hotels through their site. Conduct a search according to location and amenity preferences, or check out the page of special offers for accommodations conducive to family travel, cultural activities, sports, biking, special events, or last-minute travel.

- Get started on the appealing, if daunting, task of eating in Germany with the help of the Gastro scout.com site (www.eat-germany.net). Search for a schnitzel-filled gasthaus or other eatery by city, price, ethnicity, child-friendliness, wheelchair accessibility, or any of a slew of other criteria. Recommendations are also given on this site.

- The Munich Tourist Office site (www.munich-tourist.de) offers information about the city's history, economy, places of interest (museums, parks, churches, and so on), and accommodations. There's also an entire section devoted to Oktoberfest.

Destination: Germany—Red Alert Checklist

- Citizens of EU countries can cross into Germany for as long as they wish with a picture ID. Citizens of other countries must have a passport.
- Did you pack your camera and an extra set of camera batteries and purchase enough film? If you packed film in your checked baggage, did you invest in protective pouches to shield film from airport X-rays?
- Do you have a safe, accessible place to store money?
- Did you bring emergency drug prescriptions and extra glasses and/or contact lenses?
- Do you have your credit-card PINs?
- Did you leave a copy of your itinerary with someone at home?

- The **Munich Portal** (www.perob.com) brings "details of the culture of Munich, where to stay, what to eat, where to find information" and much more "to a global audience."

2 Entry Requirements & Customs

ENTRY REQUIREMENTS

Every U.S., Canadian, British, and Australian traveler entering Germany must hold a valid passport. You won't need a visa unless you're staying longer than 3 months. Once you've entered Germany, you won't need to show your passport again at the borders of the European Union countries of Belgium, France, Italy, Luxembourg, the Netherlands, Portugal, or Spain. Safeguard your passport in an inconspicuous, inaccessible place like a money belt. If you lose your passport, visit the nearest consulate of your native country as soon as possible for a replacement. It is always a good idea to have a photocopy of your passport (stored separately from it) to expedite replacement.

CUSTOMS

WHAT YOU CAN BRING INTO GERMANY In general, items required for personal and professional use or consumption may be brought in to Germany duty-free and without hassle. No duty is levied for a private car, provided that it is reported. You can also bring in gifts duty-free up to a total value of 180€.

The following items are permitted into Germany duty-free from non-EU (European Union) countries: 200 cigarettes; 1 liter of liquor above 44 proof, or 2 liters of liquor less than 44 proof, or 2 liters of wine; 50 grams of perfume and 0.25 liters of eau de cologne; 500 grams of coffee; and 100 grams of tea. From EU countries the duty-free limits are higher: 300 cigarettes; 1.5 liters of liquor above 44 proof, or 3 liters of liquor less than 44 proof, or 4 liters of wine; 75 grams of perfume and 0.375 liters of eau de cologne; 750 grams of coffee; and 150 grams of tea. Duty-free allowances are authorized only when the items are carried in the traveler's personal baggage.

WHAT YOU CAN TAKE HOME For information, **U.S. citizens** should contact the **U.S. Customs Service,**

1300 Pennsylvania Ave. NW, Washington, DC 20229 (© **877/287-8867**) and request the free pamphlet *Know Before You Go.* It's also available on the Web at www.customs.gov. (Click on "Traveler Information," then "Know Before You Go.")

For a clear summary of **Canadian** rules, write for the booklet *I Declare,* issued by the **Canada Customs and Review Agency** (© **800/461-9999** in Canada, or 204/983-3500; www.ccra-adrc.gc.ca).

Citizens of the U.K. should contact HM Customs & Excise at © **0845/010-9000** (from outside the U.K., 020/8929-0152), or consult their website at www.hmce.gov.uk for information.

For information, **Australian citizens** should contact the **Australian Customs Service** by calling © **1300/363-263** or logging on to www. customs.gov.au.

Citizens of New Zealand can have most of their questions answered in a free pamphlet available at New Zealand consulates and Customs offices: *New Zealand Customs Guide for Travellers, Notice no. 4.* For more information, contact New Zealand Customs, The Customhouse, 17–21 Whitmore St., Box 2218, Wellington (© 04/473-6099 or 0800/428-786; www.customs.govt.nz).

3 Money

Munich is an expensive city. Although prices in Germany are high, you generally get good value for your money. Hotels are usually clean and comfortable, and restaurants generally offer good cuisine and ample portions made with quality ingredients. Trains are fast and on time, and most service personnel treat you with respect.

Many people come to Germany just for winter sports. The most expensive resorts are places like Garmisch-Partenkirchen. However, if you avoid the chic places, you can enjoy winter fun at a moderate cost. Some of the winter spots in the Bavarian Alps that haven't been overrun by the beautiful people give you great value for your money. And prices in a village next to a resort are often 30% lower than at the resort itself.

In Germany, many prices for children (generally defined as ages 6–17) are considerably lower than for adults. And fees for children under 6 are often waived entirely.

THE EURO

The **euro,** the new single European currency, became the official currency of Germany and 11 other participating countries on **January 1, 1999.** The euro went into general circulation on **January 1, 2002.** Over a maximum 2-month transition period, German mark banknotes and coins were withdrawn from circulation. The symbol of the euro is a stylized E: €. Its official abbreviation is "EUR."

It's a good idea to exchange at least some money—just enough to cover airport incidentals and transportation to your hotel—before you leave home, so you can avoid the less-favorable rates you'll get at airport currency exchange desks. Check with you local American Express or Thomas Cook office or your bank to see if you can exchange your home currency for euros there. American Express cardholders can order foreign currency over the phone at © **800/807-6233.**

It's best to exchange currency or traveler's checks at a bank, not a currency exchange, hotel, or shop. Note the rates and ask about commission fees; it can sometimes pay to shop around and ask the right questions.

The U.S. Dollar, the British Pound & the Euro

In January of 2002, the largest money-changing operation in history led to the deliberate obsolescence of many of Europe's individual national currencies, including the German mark. In its place was substituted the euro, a currency based on the fiscal participation of a dozen nations of Europe.

For American Readers: At this writing, 1 euro equals approximately 89 US cents, and 1 US dollar equals approximately 1.12€.

For British Readers: At this writing, Great Britain still uses the pound sterling, with 1 euro equaling approximately 70 pence, and £1 equaling approximately 1.43€.

Note: The relative value of the euro fluctuates against the US dollar, the pound sterling, and most of the world's other currencies, and its value might not be the same by the time you actually travel to Germany.

ATMS

ATMs worldwide are linked to a network that most likely includes your bank at home. **Cirrus** (✆ **800/424-7787;** www.mastercard.com) and **PLUS** (✆ **800/843-7587;** www.visa.com) are the two most popular networks; call or check online for ATM locations at your destination. Be sure to check the daily withdrawal limit before you depart and ask whether you need a new PIN for use in Germany. Keep in mind that many European ATMs won't allow you to withdraw money from savings accounts, so be sure to transfer any funds you'll need to your checking account before leaving home.

CREDIT CARDS

Credit cards are invaluable when traveling. They are a safe way to carry money and provide a convenient record of all your expenses. Keep in mind that though credit cards are widely accepted throughout Germany, they're still not accepted quite as commonly as in the U.S., especially in smaller towns.

You can also withdraw cash advances from your credit cards. At many banks, you don't even need to go to a teller; you can get a cash advance at the ATM if you know your PIN.

Almost every credit-card company has an emergency 800-number that you can call if your wallet or purse is stolen. The company may be able to wire you a cash advance off your credit card immediately, and in many places, can deliver an emergency credit card in a day or two. **Citicorp Visa's** U.S. emergency number is ✆ **800/645-6556;** 813/623-1709 in Canada. **American Express** cardholders and traveler's check holders should call ✆ **800/233-5439** for all money emergencies. **MasterCard** holders should call ✆ **800/307-7309.**

4　When to Go

CLIMATE

In Bavaria and in the Alps, it can sometimes be very cold in winter, especially in January, and very warm in summer, but with cool, rainy days even in July and August. Spring and fall are often "stretched out." In fact, we've enjoyed many a Bavarian-style "Indian summer" until late in October. The most popular tourist months are May to October, although winter travel to the alpine ski areas is becoming increasingly popular.

Munich's Average Daytime Temperature & Days of Rain

	Jan	Feb	Mar	Apr	May	June	July	Aug	Sept	Oct	Nov	Dec
Temp. (°F)	33	35	40	50	60	65	70	73	65	50	39	33
Temp. (°C)	1	2	4	10	16	18	21	23	18	10	4	1
Days rain	19	16	19	19	21	24	18	17	18	15	17	18

HOLIDAYS

The following public holidays are celebrated in Bavaria: January 1 (New Year's Day), January 6 (Epiphany), Easter (Good Friday and Easter Monday), May 1 (Labor Day), Ascension Day (10 days before Pentecost, the 7th Sunday after Easter), Whitmonday (day after Whitsunday/Pentecost), Corpus Christi (10 days after Pentecost), August 15 (Feast of the Assumption), October 3 (Day of German Unity), November 1 (All Saints Day), November 17 (Day of Prayer and National Repentance), and December 25 and 26 (Christmas).

MUNICH CALENDAR OF EVENTS

For details on the following observances, consult the Munich Tourist Bureau at the Hauptbahnhof (© 089/2-33-03-00).

January

Fasching (Carnival). Pre-Lenten revelry characterizes this weeks-long bash, with a whirl of colorful parades and masked balls. Special events are staged at the Viktualienmarkt. The celebration culminates on Fasching Sunday and Shrove Tuesday. January 7 to Shrove Tuesday, usually 4 to 6 weeks, depending on the dates of the Lenten season. For specifics, contact the Munich Tourist Bureau.

February

Munich Fashion Week. The latest and often most elegant parades of fashion are staged throughout the week at various venues strewn across the city. Mid-February.

March

Starkbierzeit. The "strong beer season" provides serious beer drinkers with a fresh crop to tide them over until Oktoberfest. Just 1 pint of one of the dense brews churned out specifically for the season (beginning the 3rd Fri of Lent and lasting 2 weeks) ought to satiate most buzz seekers. Beers with the suffix of "-ator" (Salvator, for example) were created to be consumed at Lent. This dalliance from the strict fasting rules of Lent was approved by the Pope long ago: When he tasted what Münchners were drinking, he found it unpleasant enough to think the people could drink it and not break their fast. (What he didn't realize was that the beer had traveled considerably to get to him, which is why it was bad!) The tradition continues today.

April/May

Auer Dult. An old Munich tradition, Auer Dult is a colorful 8-day flea market fair that occurs three times a year. Prize antiques and vintage junk await the keenest eyes and most disciplined bargain hunters. Merchants set up shop on the Mariahilfplatz on the last Saturday in April (Maidult), the end of July (Jakobidult), and the end of October (Herbst Dult).

Corpus Christi street processions (street parades with dressed-up horses, a carried statue symbolizing Christ, girls dressed in white, a canopy, priests, and other functionaries) are seen all around the region on the Thursday following the eighth Sunday after Easter; the exact date changes annually.

June

Munich Film Festival. This festival isn't as popular as the February International Film Festival in Berlin, but it draws a serious audience. Late June.

Tollwood. This summer music festival, originated by environmentalists, honors the free spirit of jazz, blues, and rock from the third week in June through the first week of July in Olympia park. Ask at the Munich TouristBoard.

July

Jakobidult (see Auer Dult, under April, above).

Opera Festival and **Munich Summer of Music.** The Munich Philharmonic Orchestra's Summer of Music and the Bavarian State Opera Festival highlight the work of Munich's prodigal son, Wagner, and other masters including Mozart, Orff, Mahler, and Strauss. Contact the Munich Tourist Board for details. Month-long.

Christopher Street Day. The big day for the estimated 100,000 gay men and lesbians who live in the city attracts people from across Bavaria. This fun-filled parade, with its outrageous costumes, is one of the largest such events in Europe. It is named after the street in New York's Greenwich Village that was the site of the 1960s Stonewall Riots, said to have launched the gay liberation movement. July 15.

Tollwood (see June).

August

Olympiapark Sommerfest. This well-attended summer festival near Coubertin Platz is an outdoor musical scene that ranges from classical music to rock and jazz, along with productions staged in the park's open-air theater. Admission is free. For details, call ℂ **089/30-67-24-14.**

September

Oktoberfest. Germany's most famous beer festival takes place mostly in September, despite the name. Hotels are packed, and the beer and revelry flow on the Theresienwiese, where gigantic tents that can hold as many as 6,000 beer drinkers are sponsored by local breweries. It lasts from the middle of September to the first Sunday in October.

October

Herbst Dult (see Auer Dult, under April, above).

Oktoberfest (see September).

November

Christkindlmarkt. Every evening at 5:30pm, classic Christmas music bellows throughout the Christmas market on seasonally lit Marienplatz. You may even catch a glimpse of the *real* St. Nick. Traditionally runs from the end of November to Christmas Eve.

5 Health & Insurance

TRAVEL INSURANCE AT A GLANCE

Since Germany for most of us is far from home, and a number of things could go wrong—lost luggage, trip cancellation, a medical emergency—consider the following types of insurance.

Check your existing insurance policies before you buy travel insurance to cover trip cancellation, lost luggage, medical expenses, or car-rental insurance. You're likely to have partial or complete coverage. But if you need some, ask your travel agent about a comprehensive package. The cost of travel insurance varies widely, depending on the cost and length of your trip, your age and overall health, and the type of trip you're taking.

For information, contact one of the following popular insurers:

- **Access America** (℗ 800/284-8300; www.accessamerica.com)
- **Travel Guard International** (℗ 800/826-1300; www.travelguard.com)
- **Travel Insured International** (℗ 800/243-3174; www.travelinsured.com)
- **Travelex Insurance Services** (℗ 800/228-9792; www.travelex-insurance.com)

MEDICAL INSURANCE

Most health-insurance policies cover you if you get sick away from home—but check, particularly if you're insured by an HMO. With the exception of certain HMOs and Medicare/Medicaid, your medical insurance should cover medical treatment—even hospital care—overseas. However, most out-of-country hospitals make you pay your bills up front, and send you a refund after you've returned home and filed the necessary paperwork.

If you require additional insurance, try one of the following companies:

- **MEDEX International,** 9515 Deereco Rd., Timonium, MD 21093-5375 (℗ **888/MEDEX-00**

or 410/453-6300; fax 410/453-6301; www.medexassist.com).
- **Travel Assistance International** (℗ **800/821-2828;** www.travelassistance.com), 9200 Keystone Crossing, Suite 300, Indianapolis, IN 46240 (for general information on services, call the company's Worldwide Assistance Services, Inc., at ℗ **800/777-8710**).

The cost of travel medical insurance varies widely. Check your existing policies before you buy additional coverage. Also, check to see if your medical insurance covers you for emergency medical evacuation. If you have to buy a one-way same-day ticket home and forfeit your nonrefundable round-trip ticket, you may be out big money.

THE HEALTHY TRAVELER

German medical facilities are among the best in the world. If a medical emergency arises, your hotel staff can usually put you in touch with a reliable doctor. If not, contact your embassy or consulate; each one maintains a list of English-speaking doctors. Medical and hospital services aren't free, so be sure that you have appropriate insurance coverage before you travel. The water is safe to drink throughout Germany; however, do not drink the water in mountain streams, regardless of how clear and pure it looks.

6 Tips for Travelers with Special Needs

TIPS FOR TRAVELERS WITH DISABILITIES

Germany is one of the better countries for travelers with disabilities. In all the large cities, there are excellent facilities. The local tourist offices can issue permits for drivers to allow them access to handicapped parking areas. Older, smaller towns may pose more of a problem, however, especially where the streets are cobblestone.

In any case, a disability shouldn't stop anyone from traveling. There are more resources out there than ever before.

AGENCIES/OPERATORS

- **Flying Wheels Travel** (℗ 800/535-6790; www.flyingwheelstravel.com) offers escorted tours and cruises that emphasize sports and private tours in minivans with lifts.

- **Access Adventures** (© 716/889-9096), a Rochester, New York–based agency, offers customized itineraries for a variety of travelers with disabilities.
- **Accessible Journeys** (© 800/TINGLES or 610/521-0339; www.disabilitytravel.com) caters specifically to slow walkers and wheelchair travelers and their families and friends.

ORGANIZATIONS

- **The Society for Accessible Travel and Hospitality** (© 212/447-7284; fax 212-725-8253; www.sath.org) offers a wealth of travel resources for all types of disabilities and informed recommendations on destinations, access guides, travel agents, tour operators, vehicle rentals, and companion services. Annual membership costs $45 for adults; $30 for seniors and students.

PUBLICATIONS

- **Mobility International USA** (© 541/343-1284; www.miusa.org) publishes *A World of Options,* a 658-page book of resources, covering everything from biking trips to scuba outfitters, and a biannual newsletter, *Over the Rainbow.* Annual membership is $35.
- **Twin Peaks Press** (© 360/694-2462) publishes travel-related books for travelers with special needs.

GAY & LESBIAN TRAVELERS

Gay nightlife in Munich is busy and friendly. Homosexuality in Germany is generally accepted, especially among young people. However, in Catholic Bavaria's rural countryside, attitudes can be intolerant. The legal minimum age for consensual sex is 18. For information about the gay and lesbian scene in Bavaria, contact **Sub Info. Laden** in Munich at Mullerstrasse 43 (© 089/2-60-30-56).

Before you go, you may want to pick up a copy of *Frommer's Gay & Lesbian Europe.* It doesn't specifically include Munich but has an information-packed chapter on Berlin with general information on Germany. Otherwise, you can order such international guides as *Spartacus* and *Odysseus,* both of which are often sold at newsstands in Germany. A leading publication for gay men is the glossy German magazine, *Männer,* available at street kiosks and in gay clubs.

The **International Gay & Lesbian Travel Association (IGLTA)** (© 800/448-8550 or 954/776-2626; fax 954/776-3303; www.iglta.org), with around 1,200 members, links travelers with appropriate gay-friendly service organizations or tour specialists. It offers quarterly newsletters, marketing mailings, and a membership directory. Most members are gay or lesbian businesses, but individuals can join for $200 yearly, plus a $100 administration fee for new members. Members are kept informed of gay and gay-friendly hoteliers, tour operators, and airline and cruise-line representatives. Contact the IGLTA for a list of its member agencies, who will be tied into IGLTA's information resources.

AGENCIES/OPERATORS

- **Above and Beyond Tours** (© 800/397-2681; www.abovebeyondtours.com) offers gay and lesbian tours worldwide and is the exclusive gay and lesbian tour operator for United Airlines.
- **Now, Voyager** (© 800/255-6951; www.nowvoyager.com) is a San Francisco–based gay-owned and operated travel service.

PUBLICATIONS

- ***Out and About*** (© 800/929-2268 or 415/644-8044; www.outandabout.com) offers guidebooks and a newsletter 10 times a year packed with solid information on the global gay and lesbian scene.

- *Spartacus International Gay Guide* and *Odysseus* are good, annual English-language guidebooks focused on gay men, with some information for lesbians. You can get them from most gay and lesbian bookstores, or order them from **Giovanni's Room** bookstore, 1145 Pine St., Philadelphia, PA 19107 (© **215/923-2960;** www.giovannisroom.com).
- *Gay Travel A to Z: The World of Gay & Lesbian Travel Options at Your Fingertips,* by Marianne Ferrari (Ferrari Publications; Box 35575, Phoenix, AZ 85069), is a very good gay and lesbian guidebook series.

SENIOR TRAVEL

Mention the fact that you're a senior citizen when you first make your travel reservations. Most airlines and many hotels offer discounts for seniors. In most cities, people over the age of 60 qualify for reduced admission to theaters, museums, and other attractions, as well as discounted fares on public transportation.

AGENCIES/OPERATORS

- **Grand Circle Travel** (© **800/221-2610** or 617/350-7500; www.gct.com), offers package deals for the 50-plus market, mostly of the tour-bus variety, with free trips thrown in for those who organize groups of 10 or more.
- **Elderhostel** (© **877/426-8056;** www.elderhostel.org), arranges study programs for those aged 55 and over (and a spouse or companion of any age) in the U.S. and in more than 80 countries around the world. Most courses last 5 to 7 days in the U.S. (2–4 weeks abroad), and many include airfare, accommodations in university dormitories or modest inns, meals, and tuition.
- **Interhostel** (© **800/733-9753;** www.learn.unh.edu/interhostel), organized by the University of New Hampshire, also offers educational travel for seniors. On these escorted tours, the days are packed with seminars, lectures, and field trips, with sightseeing led by academic experts. **Interhostel** takes travelers 50 and over (with companions over 40), and offers 1- and 2-week trips, mostly international.
- **Elder Travelers,** 1615 Smelter Ave., Black Eagle, MT 59414; (www.eldertravelers.com), aids those who are more than 50 years old, like to travel and to meet people. Their stated purpose is to provide members with "zero cost lodging" anywhere in the world, including Germany, as senior citizens are hooked up with their counterpart hosts in the lands in which they travel. For $40 annually, subscriptions are given to their informative newsletter, which provides links to the best travel data sites worldwide. For more information on this unique group, seek them out at www.eldertravelers.com.
- **Vantage Deluxe World Travel,** 90 Canal St., Boston, MA 02114 (© **800/322-6677,** or 617/878-6000), for some 2 decades has taken thousands of mature travelers on out-of-the-extraordinary travel experiences in various European countries, including Germany. Travel is on luxurious river cruises and fully escorted land tours. Groups are deliberately kept small. For more details, contact www.vantagetravel.com/trips/landTours.asp.

PUBLICATIONS
- *101 Tips for the Mature Traveler* is available from Grand Circle

Travel (© **800/221-2610** or 617/
350-7500; fax 617/346-6700).
• *The 50+ Traveler's Guidebook*
(St. Martin's Press).

• *Unbelievably Good Deals and
Great Adventures That You
Absolutely Can't Get Unless
You're Over 50* (Contemporary
Publishing Co.).

7 Getting There

BY PLANE
Most airlines price fares seasonally.
During peak season, the summer
months, flights to Munich are at their
most expensive. Excluding the Christmas holidays, winter months offer the
lowest fares. This fits in fine with
those who wish to go skiing in the
Bavarian Alps. Shoulder season is
inbetween.

THE MAJOR AIRLINES
Direct flights to Munich from North
America are offered almost exclusively
on Lufthansa. On most airlines flying
to Germany from North America,
connections to Munich must be made
through Frankfurt, Düsseldorf, or
another gateway city.

Lufthansa (© **800/645-3880;** 01/
803-803-803; www.lufthansa.com),
the German national carrier, operates
the most frequent service. Lufthansa
has an alliance with **United Airlines**
and **Air Canada** to provide seamless
air service to Germany and other parts
of the globe from North America.
Dubbed "Star Alliance," the union
allows cross-airline benefits, including
travel on one or all of these airlines on
one ticket and frequent-flyer credit to
the participating airline of your
choice.

Air Canada (© **888/247-2262;**
www.aircanada.ca), **American Airlines** (© **800/443-7300;** www.aa.
com), **Continental Airlines** (© **800/
231-0856;** www.continental.com),
Delta Airlines (© **800/241-4141;**
www.delta.com), **United Airlines**
(© **800/241-6522;** www.val.com),
and **US Airways** © **800/428-4322)**
all fly daily to Germany.

From the U.K., **British Airways**
(© **0845/773-3377** U.K.; www.
british-airways.com), **Lufthansa**
(© **0845/773-7747** in the U.K.), and
British Midland (© **0870/607-0555**
in London, or 0345/554-554 in the
U.K.) fly regularly to major German
cities.

FLYING FOR LESS: TIPS
FOR GETTING THE BEST
AIRFARE
Passengers within the same airplane
cabin are rarely paying the same fare.
Passengers who can book their ticket
long in advance, who can stay over
Saturday night, or who are willing to
travel on a Tuesday, Wednesday, or
Thursday after 7pm, will pay a frac-
tion of the full fare. Here are a few
other easy ways to save.

• **Consolidators,** also known as
bucket shops, are a good place to
find low fares. Consolidators buy
seats in bulk from the airlines and
then sell them back to the public
at prices usually below even the
airlines' discounted rates. Their
small ads usually run in Sunday
newspaper travel sections. And
before you pay, request a confirmation number from the consol-
idator and then call the airline to
confirm your seat. Be aware that
bucket shop tickets are usually
nonrefundable or rigged with stiff
cancellation penalties, often as
high as 50% to 75% of the ticket
price. Protect yourself by paying
with a credit card rather than cash.
Keep in mind that if there's an airline sale going on, or if it's high
season, you can often get the same

> **Tips Cancelled Plans**
>
> If your flight is cancelled, don't book a new fare at the ticket counter. Find the nearest phone and call the airline directly to reschedule. You'll be relaxing while other passengers are still standing in line.

---

or better rates by contacting the airlines directly, so do some comparison shopping before you buy. Also check out the name of the airline; you may not want to fly on some obscure airline, even if you're saving $10. And check whether you're flying on a charter or a scheduled airline; the latter is more expensive but more reliable. **Council Travel** (© 800/226-8624; www.counciltravel.com) and **STA Travel** (© 800/781-4040; www.statravel.com) cater especially to young travelers, but their bargain-basement prices are available to people of all ages. **The TravelHub** (© 888/AIR-FARE; www.travelhub.com) represents nearly 1,000 travel agencies, many of whom offer consolidator and discount fares. Other reliable consolidators include **FlyCheap.com** (© 800/FLY-CHEAP; www.1800flycheap.com); **TFI Tours International** (© 800/745-8000 or 212/736-1140; www.lowestairprice.com), which serves as a clearinghouse for unused seats; or "rebators" such as **Travel Avenue** (© 800/333-3335; www.travelavenue.com) and the **Smart Traveller** (© 800/448-3338 in the U.S. or 305/448-3338), which rebate part of their commissions to you.

- Search **the Internet** for cheap fares. Great last-minute deals are available through free weekly e-mail services provided directly by the airlines.
- Join a travel club such as **Moment's Notice** (© 718/234- 6295; www.

moments-notice.com) or **Sears Discount Travel Club** (© 800/433-9383, or 800/255-1487 to join; www.travelersadvantage.com), which supply unsold tickets at discounted prices. You pay an annual membership fee to get the club's hot-line number. Of course, you're limited to what's available, so you have to be flexible.

- Join **frequent-flier clubs.** It's best to accrue miles on one program, so you can rack up free flights and achieve elite status faster. But it makes sense to open as many accounts as possible, no matter how seldom you fly a particular airline. It's free, and you'll get the best choice of seats, faster response to phone inquiries, and prompter service if your luggage is stolen, your flight is canceled or delayed, or if you want to change your seat.

BY TRAIN

British Rail runs four trains a day to Germany from Victoria Station in **London**, going by way of the Ramsgate-Ostend ferry or jetfoil. Two trains depart from London's Liverpool Street Station, via Harwich-Hook of Holland. Most trains change at Cologne for destinations elsewhere in Germany. Tickets can be purchased through British Rail travel centers in London (© 877/677-1066 in the U.K. or 0845/748-4950). Train journeys can be lengthy. Travel from London to Munich, depending on the connection, can take from 18 to 22 hours; it's often cheaper to fly than to take the train.

From **Paris** several trains depart throughout the day for points east, fanning out across eastern France to virtually every part of Germany. The most glamorous of these is the **Orient Express,** which departs from the Gare de l'Est around 6pm, arriving in Munich around 3am. For railway information on the French rail lines, call ✆ **01-55-62-18-00.** Likewise, trains depart from throughout Austria, Italy, Holland, Denmark, and the Czech Republic for all points in Germany, interconnecting into one of the most efficient, and densely routed, rail networks in the world. For information and timetables prior to your departure, call **Rail Europe** at ✆ **800/ 3EURAL;** www.raileurope.com.

From Switzerland, the **Bavaria** (✆ **01-57-22-22**) leaves Zürich at 7:30am daily, reaching Munich at 11:52am.

TRAVEL BY BUS (COACH)

You can travel by bus to Germany's major cities from London, Paris, and many other cities in Europe. The continent's largest bus operator is **Eurolines,** 52 Grosvenor Gardens, London SW1W 0AU (✆ **020/7730-8235;** www.eurolines.com), which operates out of Victoria Coach Station in Central London. In Paris, Eurolines, 28, avenue du Général-de-Gaulle, 93541 Bagnolet (✆ **08/36-69-52-52;** Métro: Gallieni), is a 35-minute subway ride from the center. For information about Eurolines in Germany, contact Deutsche Touring (Eurolines Stadtbüro), Am Römerhof 17, 60426 Frankfurt am Main (✆ **069/7-90-32-40**). Eurolines does not maintain a U.S.-based sales agent, but many travel agents can arrange for a ticket on the bus lines that link Europe's major cities.

8 Escorted Tours, Package Deals & Special Interest Vacations

Before you start your search for the lowest airfare, you may want to consider booking your flight as part of a travel package such as an escorted tour or a package tour. What you lose in adventure, you'll gain in time and money saved when you book accommodations, and maybe even food and entertainment, along with your flight.

PACKAGE TOURS FOR INDEPENDENT TRAVELERS

Package tours are not the same thing as escorted tours. With a package tour, you travel independently but pay a group rate. Packages usually include airfare, a choice of hotels, and car rentals, and packagers often offer several options at different prices. In many cases, a package that includes airfare, hotel, and transportation to and from the airport will cost you less than just the hotel alone would have, had you booked it yourself. That's because packages are sold in bulk to

tour operators—who resell them to the public at a cost that drastically undercuts standard rates.

ESCORTED TOURS (TRIPS WITH GUIDES)

Escorted Tours are structured group tours, with a group leader. The price usually includes everything from airfare to hotels, meals, tours, admission costs, and local transportation.

RECOMMENDED ESCORTED TOUR OPERATORS

American Express Travel (✆ **800/ 941-2639** in the U.S. and Canada) is one of the biggest tour operators in the world. Its offerings are comprehensive, and unescorted customized package tours are available, too.

Caravan Tours (✆ **800/227-2826;** www.caravantours.com) offers tours of southern Germany and Austria, many of which begin and end in Berlin. Accommodations are at the better hotels, and rates include everything except airfare. **Collette Vacations** (℃ **800/832-4656;** www.collette vacations.com) has an Alpine Countries tour that covers southern Germany, Austria, and Switzerland.

Two companies offer super-deluxe tours (with prices to match). **Abercrombie & Kent** (℃ **800/323-7308** or 630/954-2944; www.abercrombie kent.com) provides group tours to various areas of Germany and will customize them to suit your needs. **Travcoa** (℃ **800/992-2003;** www.travcoa. com) offers top-of-the-line coach tours, such as a 16-day tour of Ludwig's castles and the Romantic Road, which begins in Munich and ends in Strasbourg, France.

SPECIAL INTEREST VACATIONS

Himalayan Travel, 8 Berkshire Place, Danbury, CT 06810 (℃ **800/225-2380;** 800/743-2349; www.himalayan travelinc.com) has a variety of German adventure trips, including hiking, walking, trekking, and cycling tours of such areas as the Black Forest, Bavaria, and King Ludwig's Trail. The tours are self-guided, and luggage is transported by van from one hotel to the next. Rates include accommodations in two- and three-star hotels and some meals, but not airfare.

Europe Express, 1940 116th Ave. NE, Bellevue, WA 98004 (℃ **800/ 426-3615;** www.europeexpress.com), offers a variety of self-guided walking and biking tours as well as cross-country skiing trips throughout Germany. It covers such areas as the Black Forest and King Ludwig's Trail, and will customize your trip if you wish.

BIKING

Pedaling through the Bavarian countryside is the way to go for many visitors. You can bike through green valleys and past rivers, such as the Danube, while enjoying rural landscapes and life in German villages.

Allgemeiner Deutscher Fahrrad-Club, P.O. Box 107747; Hellerallee 23, 28077, Bremen (℃ **0421/34-62-90**), offers complete information on biking in Germany. For more information on touring Germany by bike, see "Getting Around," later in this chapter.

For the past 2 decades, **Classic Adventures,** P.O. Box 143, Hamlin, NY 14464 (℃ **800/777-8090** or 585/ 964-8488); fax 585/964-7297 has offered bike tours of such areas as the Romantic Road. **Euro-Bike and Walking Tours,** P.O. Box 990, DeKalb, IL 60115 (℃ **800/321-6060,** or 815/758-8851; fax 815/758-8822; www.eurobike.com), has a full range of bicycling and walking tours of Bavaria, as well as a 9-day biking tour of Germany, Switzerland, and France. The upscale outfitter **Butterfield & Robinson,** 70 Bond St., Suite 300 Toronto, ON, Canada M5B 1X3 (℃ **800/678-1147,** or 416/864-1354; fax 416/864-0541; www.butterfield. com), offers a new biking trip along the Romantic Road and along the banks of the Main, Tauber, and Neckar rivers.

Dozens of companies in Britain offer guided cycling tours. One of the best is the **Cyclists Touring Club,** 69 Meadrow, Godalming, Surrey GU7 3HS (℃ **01483/417-217;** www.ctc. org.uk). It charges £27 ($40.50) a year for membership.

HIKING & MOUNTAIN CLIMBING

These sports are popular in the German uplands. It's estimated that there are more than 80,000 marked hiking and mountain-walking tracks in the country. The **Verband Deutscher Gebirgs- und Wandervereine,** Wilhelmshöher Alle 157–159, 34121 Kassel (℃ **0561/938-730**), services the trails and offers details not only about trails but also about shelters, huts, and addresses of hiking associations in the various regions. The

Deutsche Alpenverein, Von-Kahr-Strasse 2–4, 80997 Munich (© **089/14-00-30**), owns and operates 50 huts in and around the Alps that are open to all mountaineers. This association also maintains a 15,000km (9,300-mile) network of alpine trails.

The best **alpine hiking** is in the Bavarian Alps, especially the 1,235m (4,060-ft.) Eckbauer, on the southern fringe of Partenkirchen. The tourist office will supply hiking maps and details (see chapter 11). Another great place for hiking is **Berchtesgaden National Park,** Kurgarten, Maximilianstrasse 1, Berchtesgaden (© **08652/22-07**), bordering the Austrian province of Salzburg (p. 172). This park also offers the best-organized hikes and will hook you up with various groups offering hikes.

MOTORCYCLING

Guided motorcycle tours through Bavaria are the specialty of **Beach's Motorcycle Adventures,** 2763 W. River Pkwy., Grand Island, NY 14072 (© **716/773-4960**; www.beachs-mca.com). Two- to three-week tours on BMW bikes begin and end in Munich, with accommodations at small hotels and inns. Maps are provided, as well as information and suggestions for sightseeing and independent cruising along the way.

WINTER SPORTS

More than 300 winter-sports resorts operate in the German Alps and wooded hill country such as the Harz Mountains and the Black Forest. In addition to outstanding ski slopes, trails, lifts, jumps, toboggan slides, and skating rinks, many larger resorts also offer ice hockey, ice boating, and bobsledding. Curling is very popular as well, especially in upper Bavaria. The Olympic sports facilities at Garmisch-Partenkirchen enjoy international renown, as do the ski jumps of Oberstdorf and the artificial-ice speed-skating rink at Inzell. More than 250 ski lifts are found in the German Alps, the Black Forest, and the Harz Mountains. Information on winter-sports facilities is available from local tourist bureaus and the offices of the German National Tourist Board (see "Visitor Information," earlier in this chapter).

Garmisch-Partenkirchen (see chapter 11) is Germany's most famous winter sports center. Set in beautiful alpine scenery, this picturesque resort is close to Zugspitze, Germany's highest mountain. A mountain railway and a cable car can take you to the peak. In the town itself is the Olympic Ice Stadium, built in 1936, and the Ski Stadium, which has two jumps and a slalom course. Skiers of every level will be satisfied with the slopes on the mountain above the town. For information, contact the **Verkehrsamt** on Richard-Strauss-Platz (© **08821/18-0700**).

9 Planning Your Trip Online

Researching and booking your trip online can save time and money. Then again, it may not. It is simply not true that you always get the best deal online. Most booking engines do not include schedules and prices for budget airlines, and from time to time you'll get a better last-minute price by calling the airline directly, so it's best to call the airline to see if you can do better before booking online.

On the plus side, Internet users today can tap into the same travel-planning databases that were once accessible only to travel agents—and do it at the same speed. Sites such as **Frommers.com, Travelocity.com, Expedia.com,** and **Orbitz.com** allow consumers to comparison shop for airfares, access special bargains, book flights, and reserve hotel rooms and rental cars.

But don't fire your travel agent just yet. Although online booking sites offer tips and hard data to help you bargain shop, they cannot endow you with the hard-earned experience that makes a seasoned, reliable travel agent an invaluable resource, even in the Internet age. And for consumers with a complex itinerary, a trusty travel agent is still the best way to arrange the most direct flights to and from the best airports.

Still, there's no denying the Internet's emergence as a powerful tool in researching and plotting travel time. The benefits of researching your trip online can be well worth the effort.

Last-minute specials, such as weekend deals or Internet-only fares, are offered by airlines to fill empty seats. Most of these are announced on Tuesday or Wednesday and must be purchased online. They are only valid for travel that weekend, but some can be booked weeks or months in advance. Sign up for weekly e-mail alerts at airline websites or check megasites that compile comprehensive lists of last-minute specials, such as **Smarter Living** (smarterliving.com) or **WebFlyer** (www.webflyer.com).

Some sites, such as Expedia.com, will send you **e-mail notification** when a cheap fare becomes available to your favorite destination. Some will also tell you when fares to a particular destination are lowest.

TRAVEL-PLANNING & BOOKING SITES

Keep in mind that because several airlines are no longer willing to pay commissions on tickets sold by online travel agencies, these agencies may either add a $10 surcharge to your bill if you book on that carrier—or neglect to offer those carriers' schedules.

The list of sites below is selective, not comprehensive. Some sites will have evolved or disappeared by the time you read this.

- **Frommer's** (www.frommers.com) is an excellent travel-planning resource. We're a little biased, of course, but we think you'll find the travel tips, reviews, monthly vacation giveaways, and online-booking capabilities thoroughly indispensable. Among the special features are our popular **Message Boards,** where Frommer's readers post queries and share advice (sometimes even our authors show up to answer questions); **Frommers.com Newsletter,** for the latest travel bargains and inside travel secrets; and Frommer's **Destinations Section,** where you'll get expert travel tips, hotel and dining recommendations, and advice on the sights to see for more than 2,500 destinations around the globe.
- **Travelocity** (www.travelocity.com or www.frommers.travelocity.com) and **Expedia** (www.expedia.com) are among the most popular sites, each offering an excellent range of options. Travelers search by destination, dates, and cost.
- **Orbitz** (www.orbitz.com) is a popular site launched by United, Delta, Northwest, American, and Continental Airlines. With this site, you're granted access to the largest data bank of low rates, airline tickets, rental cars, hotels, vacation packages, and other travel products. You get, among other offerings, available fares from more than 450 airlines.
- **Qixo** (www.qixo.com) is another powerful search engine that allows you to search for flights and accommodations from some 20 airline and travel-planning sites (such as Travelocity) at once. Qixo sorts results by price.
- **Priceline** (www.priceline.com) lets you "name your price" for airline tickets, hotel rooms, and rental cars. For airline tickets, you

can't say what time you want to fly—you have to accept any flight between 6am and 10pm on the dates you've selected, and you may have to make one or more stopovers. Tickets are nonrefundable, and no frequent-flier miles are awarded.

10 Getting Around

BY TRAIN

Before leaving for Germany, you can get complete details about the **German Federal Railroad** and the many plans it offers, as well as information about Eurailpasses, at Rail Europe (© **800/848-7245;** www.raileurope. com).

BY CAR

British travelers who want to bring their own cars over should see "Getting There," earlier in this chapter.

Competition in the European car-rental industry is fierce. All the big U.S. car-rental companies, including Avis, Budget, and Hertz, are represented in Germany. You can make reservations and do comparison shopping by calling their toll-free numbers in the United States: **Avis** (© **800/ 331-1212;** www.avis.com), **Budget** (© **800/527-0700;** https://rent.drive budget.com), and **Hertz** (© **800/654- 3131;** www.hertz.com). You can also call **Kemwel Holiday Autos** (KHA) at © **800/678-0678** (www.kemwel. com) and **Auto Europe** at © **800/ 223-5555** (www.autoeurope.com). All the major car-rental companies offer competitive rates that tend to be more attractive if you reserve your car from North America between 1 day and 2 weeks in advance of your departure. Promotional rates offered by car-rental corporations should be researched to ensure the best value.

It's important to understand the many legal and financial implications of auto insurance before you complete your initial paperwork. A collision-damage waiver (CDW) is an optional insurance policy that can be purchased when you sign a rental agreement. For an extra fee, the rental agency agrees to eliminate all but a small percentage of your financial responsibility for liability and collision damage in case of an accident. If you don't have a CDW and do have an accident, you'll usually pay for all damages, up to the cost of actually replacing the vehicle if the accident is serious enough.

The large car-rental companies offer clients the option of either automatically including the CDW as part of the rental price or forgoing it in favor of the insurance that sometimes applies automatically through your credit- or charge-card company. Certain companies, including American Express and Diners Club, agree to reimburse card users for the deductible in the event of an accident, so many renters may chose to waive the cost of the extra CDW. However, although the card issuers will usually reimburse the renter for the cost of damages, this happens several weeks after the accident, when certain documents have been completed. Unless there's a big enough credit line associated with your card, you may be required to pay cash on the spot (sometimes a large sum).

Regardless of the insurance-related options you select, cars with automatic transmission cost more in Europe than cars without it. Although all major companies allow dropoffs within Germany at no extra charge, Budget generally offers the most reasonable rates for dropoffs outside Germany.

Some travelers prefer the convenience of prepaying their rental in dollars before leaving on their trip. In such circumstances, an easy-to-understand net price (which includes the CDW, all taxes, airport surcharges, and—in some cases—additional personal accident insurance) is quoted and prepaid at least 14 days before departure by credit or charge card. The main benefit to those who opt for this is a somewhat more streamlined rental process, a price structure that is easier to understand, and an ability to avoid unpleasant surprises caused by sudden unfavorable changes in currency exchange rates. Remember, however, that if you opt to prepay, and if your plans change, you'll have to go through some rather complicated paperwork (and in some cases, the payment of a penalty of around $25) for changes or cancellation of any of these prepaid contracts.

GASOLINE   Gasoline is readily available throughout Germany, and service stations appear frequently along the Autobahns. The cheapest gasoline is at stations marked SB-TANKEN (self-service), but remember that gas will always be much more expensive than in the U.S. A liter (about ¼ gal.) costs .75€ to 2€. Gasoline pumps labeled BLEIFREI offer unleaded gas.

DRIVING RULES   In Germany, you drive on the right side of the road. Both front-seat and back-seat passengers are required to wear safety belts. Children cannot ride in the front seat.

Easy-to-understand international road signs are posted, but U.S. travelers should remember that road signs are in kilometers, not miles. In congested areas, the speed limit is about 50 kmph (around 30 mph). On all other roads except the Autobahns, the speed limit is 100 kmph (about 60 mph).

In theory, there is no speed limit on the Autobahns (in the left, fast lane), but many drivers going too fast report that they have been stopped by the police and fined on the spot. So reasonable caution is recommended here, for safety if not other reasons. A German driver on the Autobahn can be a ferocious creature, and you may prefer

the slow lane. The government recommends an Autobahn speed limit of 130 kmph (80 mph).

Note: Drinking and driving is a very serious offense in Germany. Therefore, be sure to keep any alcoholic beverages in the trunk or some other storage area. Avoid even the appearance of drinking alcohol while driving.

BREAKDOWNS/ASSISTANCE
The major automobile club in Germany is **Automobilclub von Deutschland (AvD),** Lyoner Strasse 16, 60329 Frankfurt (© **069/6-60-60**). If you don't belong to it and have a breakdown on the Autobahn, call from an emergency phone. These are spaced about a mile apart. On secondary roads, go to the nearest phone and call © **01802/22-22-22** (**Deutscher Automobil Club—ADAC**). In English, ask for "road service assistance." Emergency assistance is free, but you pay for parts or materials.

MAPS   The best maps, available at all major bookstores throughout Germany, are published by **Michelin,** which offers various regional maps. Other good maps for those who plan to do extensive touring are published by **Hallweg.**

DRIVER'S LICENSES   American and Canadian drivers, and those from EU countries, need only a domestic license to drive, but it's recommended that you carry an international driver's permit in case of an accident or other problems. Both in Germany and throughout the rest of Europe, you must also have an international insurance certificate, known as a green card (*carte verte*). Any car-rental agency will automatically provide one of these as a standard part of the rental contract, but it's a good idea to double-check all documents at the time of rental, just to be sure that you can identify the card if asked by border patrol or the police.

11 Recommended Books

If you're a hiker and plan extensive touring in the Bavarian Alps, a useful guide is **Walking in the Bavarian Alps** by Grant Bourne (published by Sabine Kroner-Bourne). All the most intriguing trails are highlighted, and the walks or hikes range from easy to difficult. The book describes 57 walks, covering such places as the Tegernsee and Berchtesgaden, along with varying recommendations for alpine hut stopovers.

For background and understanding of the German experience, any of the works by Thomas Mann (1875–1955) are recommended. Mann moved to Munich after the death of his father, where he sharpened his skills as editor of the satirical magazine *Simplicissimus* from 1898 to 1899. He remained in Munich until 1933, becoming one of Germany's celebrated writers (*Buddenbrucks,* 1901; *Death in Venice,* 1925; *The Magic Mountain,* 1927). He won the Nobel Prize for literature in 1929. In 1933, wary of the emerging National Socialists, he embarked upon a lecture tour in France and Switzerland, and from abroad he protested the Nazis loudly in essays entitled "Europe, Beware." Naturalized in the United States in 1944, he eventually returned to Europe, but not to Germany, in 1952, settling at Kilchberg on Lake Zurich. If you're politically minded, *Munich and Memory: Architecture, Monuments, and the Legacy of the Third Reich* by Gabriel David Rosenfeld (University of California Press), explores the fascinating saga of Munich's postwar architectural reconstruction and social de-Nazification. Especially intriguing is the behind-the-scenes looking at the clearing of both "rubble and rabble" from the German landscape.

A fun read for everyone is *The Beer Drinker's Guide to Munich* by Larry Hawthorne and Eliska Jezkova (Freizeit Publishers). This is an entertaining guide to the best watering holes in the beer-drinking capital of the world. You're taken on a tour of 70 of the city's finest Biergartens and beer halls, along with a selection of pubs and late-night spots. You'll also learn the history behind some of these beer halls such as the world-famous Hofbräuhaus.

Making its appearance in 2002, the latest work on "mad king" Ludwig is called *Ludwig II of Bavaria: A King's Passion for Castles* by Rolf Toman (published by Konemann). For more information on him, see "Exploring the Lake," under section 2, "Starnbergersee," in chapter 10, beginning on p. 155 or "The Fairy-Tale King" box in chapter 11, beginning on p. 186.

Bavaria's most fascinating courtesan was Lola Montez, mistress of King Ludwig I. See the box, "The Notorious Lola Montez" in Appendix A. Her fascinating tale lives on in *Lola Montez: A Life* by Bruce Seymour (Yale University).

The intriguing story of the history behind the Eagles Nest, once the vacation retreat of Hitler, is explored in the book, *Battle for Hitler's Eagles Nest,* by Leo Kessler (Severn House Publishers).

 FAST FACTS: Munich

American Express Your lifeline back to the States might be American Express, Promenadeplatz 6 (𝄐 **089/29-09-00**), which is open for mail pickup and check cashing Monday to Friday from 9am to 5:30pm and Saturday from 9:30am to 12:30pm. Unless you have an American Express card or traveler's checks, you'll be charged 1€ for picking up your mail. There are no ATMs at American Express, but across the street, at Deutsche Bank, Promenadeplatz 1, there are several available 24 hours.

Business Hours Most **banks** are open Monday to Friday 8:30am to 12:30pm and 1:30 to 3:30pm (many stay open to 5:30pm on Thurs). Most **businesses** and **stores** are open Monday to Friday 9am to 6pm (many stay open to 8 or 9pm on Thurs) and Saturday 9am to 2pm. On *langer Samstag* (the 1st Sat of the month) stores remain open until 6pm. Some (very few, actually) stores in Munich observe a late closing on Thursday, usually 8 or 9pm.

Car Rentals See "Getting Around," above.

Climate See "When to Go," earlier in this chapter.

Consulates See "Embassies & Consulates," below.

Currency See "Money," earlier in this chapter.

Currency Exchange You can almost always get a better rate at a bank than at your hotel. American Express traveler's checks are best cashed at the local American Express office (see above). On Saturday and Sunday, or at night, you can exchange money at the Hauptbahnhof exchange, Bahnhofplatz, which is open daily from 6am to 11:30pm.

Dentists For an English-speaking dentist, go to Klinik und Poliklinik für Kieferchirurgie der Universität München, Lindwurmstrasse 2A (📞 **089/ 51-60-29-11**), the dental clinic for the university. It's always open for emergencies; for less urgent cases the doctors are available daily from 8am to noon and from 12:30 to 3pm.

Doctors The American, British, and Canadian consulates as well as most hotels keep a list of recommended English-speaking physicians.

Driving Rules See "Getting Around," earlier in this chapter.

Drug Laws Penalties for illegal drug possession in Germany are severe. You could go to jail or be deported immediately. Caveat: Drug pushers often turn their customers in to the police.

Drugstores See "Pharmacies," below.

Electricity In most places, the electricity is 220 volts AC, 50 cycles. Therefore, a transformer will be needed for U.S. appliances. Many leading hotels will supply one when asked. Otherwise, bring your own.

E-Mail Head for the **Times Square Online Bistro** in the Hauptbahnhof, Bayerstrasse side (📞 **089/55-08-8000**). They have 16 computer workstations, a bistro, and bar, and are open daily 7am to 1am.

Embassies & Consulates Offices representing various foreign governments are located in Munich. A **United States** Consulate is at Königstrasse 5, D-80539 München (📞 **089/2-88-80**). A Consulate General Office for the **United Kingdom** is located at Bürkleinstrasse 10, D-80538 (📞 **089/21-10- 90**). **Canada** maintains a consulate at Tal 29, D-80331 (📞 **089/2-19-95-70**). The **Australian** government does not maintain an office in Munich, but if you should need assistance, contact their consulate in Berlin at Uhland- strasse 181-183 D-10623 (📞 **030/8-80-08-80**). **New Zealand**'s embassy is also in Berlin, Friedrichstrasse 60 (📞 **030/20-62-10**).

Emergencies For emergency medical aid, phone ℂ **192-22**. Call the police at ℂ **110**, or the fire department at ℂ **112**. These are free calls.

Fax Head for any of the many hole-in-the-wall kiosks labeled DEUTSCHE TELEKOM. These include locations on the Marienplatz and in the Haupt-bahnhof. Deutsche telecom phone cards are available in denominations of 6.50€ to 30€. You can use these to operate self-service fax machines.

Holidays See "When to Go," earlier in this chapter.

Hospitals Munich has many hospitals. Americans, British, and Canadians can contact their consulates for a recommendation of a particular hospi-tal. For emergency medical service, call ℂ **192-22**; for private Medical Service at your domicile, call **089/260-206-60**.

Language Many Germans speak English, and English is usually spoken at major hotels and restaurants as well as in principal tourist areas. Never-theless, a good phrasebook to carry with you is *Berlitz German for Trav-ellers,* available in most big bookstores in the United States.

Laundry/Dry Cleaning A good dry-cleaning establishment is **Paradies Reiningung,** Octtingenstrasse 29 (ℂ **089/22-34-65**). Look in the Yellow Pages under either *Wascherei* or *Waschsalon* for a coin-operated laundry near your hotel.

Liquor Laws As in many European countries, the application of drinking laws is flexible. Laws are enforced only if a problem develops or if deco-rum is broken. Officially, someone must be 18 to consume any kind of alcoholic beverage in Germany, although at family gatherings, wine or schnapps might be offered to underage imbibers. For a bar or cafe to request proof of age of a prospective client is very rare. Drinking and driving, however, is treated as a very serious offense.

Luggage Storage/Lockers Facilities are available at the Hauptbahnhof on Bahnhofplatz (ℂ **089/99-66-32**), which is open daily from 6am to 11pm.

Mail To mail a letter on the street, look for a painted-yellow mailbox. The cost to send an airmail letter to the United States or Canada is 1.50€ for the first 5 grams (about ⅕ oz.) and 1€ for postcards. All letters to the United Kingdom cost .55€. To mail a package, go to one of the larger post offices in Munich (see "Post Office," below).

Newspapers/Magazines The *International Herald Tribune* is the most widely distributed English-language newspaper in the city. You can also find copies of *USA Today* and the European editions of *Time* and *Newsweek.*

Pharmacies For an international pharmacy (*apotheke)* where English is spoken, go to International Ludwig's Apotheke, Neuhauserstrasse 11 (ℂ **089/2-60-30-21**; U-bahn/S-bahn: Marienplatz), in the pedestrian shop-ping zone. It's open Monday to Friday from 9am to 8pm and Saturday from 9am to 4pm. There's always a pharmacy open 24 hours in every neighborhood. Every apotheke has a sign in its window indicating where to find the nearest one staying open (it changes from night to night).

Police Throughout the country, dial ℂ **110** for emergencies. This call is free.

Post Office The **Postamt München** (main post office) is across from the Hauptbahnhof, at Bahnhofplatz 1 (© **089/599-0870**). If you want to have your mail sent to you, have it addressed Poste Restante, Postamt München, Bahnhofplatz 1, 80074 München, for general delivery. Take along your passport to reclaim any mail. The office is open Monday to Friday 7am to 8pm, Saturday 8am to 4pm, and Sunday 9am to 3pm. There are no longer fax, phone, or telex facilities available in the post office.

Radio The BBC World Service broadcasts to Munich, as does the American Forces Network (AFN), which you can hear on 1197 AM. English news broadcasts are presented frequently on the Bavarian Radio Service (Bayerischer Rundfunk).

Restrooms Use the word *Toilette* (pronounced twa-*leht*-tah). Restrooms may be labeled "WC," or "H" (for *Herren,* men) and "F" (for *Frauen,* women). The center of Munich has several clean, safe, and well-kept public facilities. You can also patronize the facilities at terminals, restaurants, bars, cafes, department stores, hotels, and pubs.

Safety Munich, like all big cities, has its share of crime, especially pickpocketing and purse- and camera-snatching. If necessary, store valuables in a hotel safe. Most robberies occur in the much-frequented tourist areas, such as the areas around the Hauptbahnhof, which can be dangerous at night, and the Marienplatz, where tourists gather. Many tourists lose their valuables when they carelessly leave clothing unprotected as they join the nude sunbathers in the Englischer Garten.

Taxes As a member of the European Union, Germany imposes a tax on most goods and services known as a **value-added tax (VAT),** or in German, *Mehrwertsteuer.* Nearly everything is taxed at 15%, including vital necessities such as gas and luxury items such as jewelry. VAT is included in the prices of restaurants and hotels. Note that goods for sale, such as cameras, also have the 15% tax already factored into the price; but the listed prices of services, such as getting a mechanic to fix your car, don't include VAT, so an extra 15% will be tacked on to the bill. Stores that display a "Tax Free" sticker will issue you a Tax-Free Shopping Check at the time of purchase. When leaving the country, have your check stamped by the German Customs Service as your proof of legal export. You can then get a cash refund at one of the Tax-Free Shopping Service offices in the major airports and many train stations, even at some of the bigger ferry terminals. Otherwise, you must send the checks to Tax-Free Shopping Service, Mengstrasse 19, 23552 Lübeck, Germany. If you want the payment to be credited to your bankcard or your bank account, mention this. There is no airport departure tax in Germany.

Telephone/Telex/Fax The **country code** for Germany is **49.** To call Germany from the United States, dial the international access code 011, then 49, then the city code (**Munich's city code is 89**), then the regular phone number. *The phone numbers listed in this book are to be used within Germany; when calling from abroad, omit the initial 0 in the city code.*

If you're within Germany but not in Munich, use **089.** If you're calling within Munich, simply leave off the code and dial only the regular phone number. Local and long-distance calls may be placed from coin-operated public telephone booths. The unit charge is .15€. More than half the phones in Germany require an advance-payment telephone card from Telekom, the German telephone company. Phone cards are sold at post offices and newsstands, costing 6€ and 25€. Rates are measured in units rather than minutes. The farther the distance, the more units are consumed. For example, a 4-minute call to the United States costs 41 units. All towns and cities in Germany may be dialed directly by using the prefix listed in the telephone directory above each local heading. Telephone calls made through hotel switchboards can double, triple, or even quadruple the charge; so try to make your calls outside your hotel.

German phone numbers are not standard and come in various formats. In some places, numbers have as few as 3 digits. In cities, one building's number may have 5 digits whereas the phone next door might have 9 digits. Germans also often hyphenate their numbers differently. But since all the area codes are the same, these various configurations should have little effect on your phone usage once you get used to the fact that numbers are inconsistent and vary from place to place.

To call the U.S. or Canada from Germany, dial 01, followed by the country code (1), then the area code, and then the number. Alternatively, you can dial the various telecommunication companies in the States for cheaper rates. From Germany, the access for **AT&T** is ✆ **0800-888-00-10;** for **MCI** ✆ **0800-888-8000;** and for **Sprint** ✆ **0800-888-0013. USA Direct** can be used with all telephone cards and for collect calls. The number from Germany is ✆ **01-30-00-10. Canada Direct** can be used with Bell Telephone Cards and for collect calls. This number from Germany is ✆ **01-30-00-14.**

Television   There are two national TV channels, ARD (Channel 1) and ZDF (Channel 2). Sometimes these stations show films in the original language (most often English). The more expensive hotels often have cable TV, with such channels, in English, as CNN.

Time Zone   Germany operates on Central European time (CET), which means that the country is 6 hours ahead of eastern standard time (EST) in the United States and 1 hour ahead of Greenwich mean time (GMT). Summer daylight saving time begins in Germany in April and ends in September—there's a slight difference in the dates from year to year—so there may be a period in early spring and in the fall when there's a 7-hour difference between EST and CET. Always check if you're traveling during these periods—especially if you need to catch a plane.

Tipping   If a restaurant bill says *Bedienung,* that means a service charge has already been added, so just round up to the nearest euro. If not, add 10% to 15%. Round up to the nearest euro for taxis. Bellhops get 1€ per bag, as does the doorman at your hotel, restaurant, or nightclub. Room-cleaning staffs get small tips in Germany, but tip concierges well who perform some special favor such as obtaining hard-to-get theater or opera tickets. Tip hairdressers or barbers 5% to 10%.

3

Getting to Know Munich

Munich is a lively place all year long—fairs and holidays seem to follow one on top of the other. But this is no "oompah" town. Here you'll find an elegant and tasteful city with sophisticated clubs and restaurants, wonderful theaters, and the finest concert halls.

One of Europe's most visited cities, Munich is full of monuments and fabulous museums. A place with memories of yesterday, both good and bad, it is very much a city living in its present. Today, with some 1.3 million inhabitants, 16% of whom are foreigners, Munich is the third largest city in Germany. It is also the German's first choice as a place to live, according to various polls. It is a major economic center for north–south European trade and for high-tech microelectronics and other industries. It also has a huge publishing center and a burgeoning number of film studios.

A city of art and culture, and Germany's largest university town, Munich is a place to have fun and enjoy the relaxed lifestyle, the friendly ambience, and the wealth of activities, nightlife, sights, and events.

1 Orientation

ARRIVING

BY PLANE The **Franz-Josef-Strauss International Airport** (© 089/97-52-13-13), opened in 1992, is a state-of-the-art facility that lies 29km (18 miles) northeast of central Munich at Erdinger Moos. Facilities include parking garages, car-rental centers, restaurants, bars, cafes, money-exchange kiosks, lockers, and luggage-storage facilities. A second terminal is slated to open sometime in 2003.

S-bahn (© 089/414-243-44) trains connect the airport with the Hauptbahnhof (main railroad station) in downtown Munich. Departures are every 20 minutes for the 40-minute trip. The fare is 8€; Eurailpass holders ride free. A taxi into the center costs about 50€. Airport buses, such as those operated by Lufthansa, also run between the airport and the center.

If you're going to rent or pick up a car at the airport, see "Getting Around," later in this chapter for more information.

BY TRAIN Most trains arrive at Munich's main rail station, the **Hauptbahnhof**, on Bahnhofplatz, one of Europe's largest stations. Located near the city center and the trade fairgrounds, it contains a hotel, restaurants, shopping, car parking, and banking facilities. All major German cities are connected to this station. Some 20 daily trains connect Munich to Frankfurt (trip time: 3¾ hr.), and 23 to Berlin (trip time: 6¾ hr.). The rail station is connected with the **S-bahn** rapid-transit system, a 418km (260-mile) network of tracks, providing service to various city districts and outlying suburbs. For S-bahn information, call ☎ **089/4142-43-44.** The **U-bahn** (subway) system serving Munich is also centered at the rail station. In addition, buses fan out in all directions from here.

BY BUS   Munich has long-distance bus service from many German and European cities. Depending on their point of origin, buses depart from the section of the Hauptbahnhof called the West-Wing Starnberger Bahnhof, or from the Deutsche Touring Terminal on Arnulfstrasse 3, about a block away. For information about connections, tariffs, and schedules, call Deutsche Touring GmbH at ☎ **089/54-58-70-11.** Regional service to towns and villages within Bavaria can be arranged through Oberbayern Autobus, Heidemann-Strasse 220 (☎ **089/32-30-40**), or DER, Landshuher Allee (☎ **089/120-4242**).

VISITOR INFORMATION

Tourist information is available at the Franz-Josef-Strauss airport in the central area (☎ **089/97-59-28-15**), as soon as you step off the plane. It's open Monday to Saturday from 8:30am to 10pm and Sunday from 1 to 9pm. The main tourist office, **Fremdenverkehrsamt,** at the Hauptbahnhof, Bahnhofplatz 2 (☎ **089/2-33-03-00;** www.muenchen-tourist.de), is found at the south exit opening onto Bayerstrasse. It's open Monday to Saturday 9am to 8pm and Sunday from 10am to 6pm. You can pick up a free map of Munich, and the Fremdenverkehrsamt will also reserve rooms for you. You will find another branch of the Tourist Information Office in Marienplatz inside the Neues Rathaus, open Monday to Saturday 10am to 8pm and Sunday 10am to 4pm.

CITY LAYOUT

Munich's **Hauptbahnhof,** or rail station, lies just west of the town center and opens onto Bahnhofplatz. From there you can take Schützenstrasse to one of the major centers of Munich, **Karlsplatz,** nicknamed *Stachus,* (see p. 124 for the story). Many tram lines converge on this square. From Karlsplatz, you can continue east along the pedestrians-only Neuhauserstrasse and Kaufingerstrasse until you reach **Marienplatz,** which is located deep in the **Altstadt (Old Town)** of Munich.

From Marienplatz you can head north on Dienerstrasse, which will lead you to Residenzstrasse and finally to **Max-Joseph-Platz,** a landmark square, with the Nationaltheater and the former royal palace, the Residenz. East of this square runs **Maximilianstrasse,** the most fashionable shopping and restaurant street of Munich, containing the prestigious Kempinski Hotel Vier Jahreszeiten München. Between Marienplatz and the Nationaltheater is the **Platzl** quarter, where you'll want to head for nighttime diversions; here you'll find some of the finest (and also some of the worst) restaurants in Munich, along with the landmark Hofbräuhaus, the most famous beer hall in Europe.

North of the old town is **Schwabing,** a former bohemian section whose main street is Leopoldstrasse. The large, sprawling municipal park grounds, the **Englischer Garten,** are due east of Schwabing.

MAIN ARTERIES & STREETS

The best-known street in Munich is the **Maximilianstrasse,** the most fashionable shopping avenue and one of the city's busiest east–west arteries. Other major east–west thoroughfares include **Kaufingerstrasse** and **Neuhauserstrasse.** Both are major shopping avenues in the core of the Altstadt's pedestrian zone. Two of Munich's great 19th-century avenues, **Ludwigstrasse** and **Brienner Strasse,** stretch toward the district of Schwabing. Ludwigstrasse was designed to display the greatness of the kingdom of Ludwig I and is bordered on both sides by impressive neoclassical and neo-Romanesque buildings.

Odeonsplatz, on the southern end of Ludwigstrasse, was established to celebrate the Bavarian kingdom. **Leopoldstrasse** begins on the northern side of Ludwigstrasse and continues through Schwabing. The last of the 19th-century boulevards to be constructed was **Prinzregentstrasse,** lying between Prinz-Carl-Palais and Vogelweide-platz. Along the Prinzregentstrasse at no. 7 is the residence of the prime minister of Bavaria.

FINDING AN ADDRESS/MAPS   Locating an address is relatively easy in Munich, as even numbers run up one side of a street and odd numbers down the other. In the Altstadt, "hidden" squares may make finding an address difficult; therefore, you may need a detailed street map, not the more general maps handed out for free by the tourist office and many hotels. The best ones (containing a detailed street index) are published by Falk, and they're available at nearly all bookstores and at many newsstands. These pocketsize maps are easy to carry and contain a detailed street index at the end.

NEIGHBORHOODS IN BRIEF

Altstadt This is the historic part of Munich, the site of the original medieval city. The Altstadt is bounded by the Sendlinger Tor ("Tor" means gate) and Odeonsplatz to the north and the south, and by the Isartor and Karlstor to the east and west. You can walk across the district in about 15 minutes.

The hub is Marienplatz, the town's primary square, with its Rathaus (Town Hall). In the Middle Ages, Marienplatz was the scene of many jousts and tournaments as well as public entertainment like executions. Today, it is brimming with mimes, musicians, and street performers. The square is also the site of many festivals and political rallies and is the traditional stopping and starting place for parades and processions. Included in the Altstadt district is the Fussgänger (pedestrian) Zone, home to many of Munich's elegant shops.

Haidhausen This district is home to Gasteig, the city's primary cultural, educational, and conference center. The modern complex houses the city library and the Munich Philharmonic Orchestra. Its various theaters and lecture halls play host to a variety of events, principally musical and theatrical performances. The district is also a lively, trendy nightlife center.

Lehel Just east of the Altstadt, this district is part of the original planned expansion of the city that occurred in the latter years of the 19th century. The area is mainly residential and is noted for its fine neo-Renaissance architecture.

Ludwigstrasse One of Munich's great monumental avenues, this street was originally designed for King Ludwig I as a street worthy of his kingdom. The buildings in the southern section of the street adhere to a strict neoclassical style, whereas the architecture in the northern sector is neo-Romanesque. The overall effect is that of uniformity.

Maximilianstrasse The equivalent of New York's Fifth Avenue, Maximilian-strasse is Munich's Golden Mile. Planned as a showcase for King Maximilian II's dominion, it has architecture in what is known as Maximilianic style, an eclectic combination of styles with an emphasis on Gothic. Here you find

Munich Neighborhoods

the city's most elegant and expensive boutiques, restaurants, and hotels. Visitors can browse through stores like Armani, Hermès, and Bulgari. Along with numerous chic hotels and restaurants, the street is also home to the Museum of Ethnology and the overpowering monument to the king, the Max-monument. The street is the primary connector from the Altstadt to the suburbs of Lehel and Haidhausen.

Olympiapark Host to rock and pop concerts as well as other performances, this residential and recreational area was the site of the 1972 Olympics, which is remembered for the terrorist attack by the Arab "Black September" group against Israeli athletes. The 1972 Munich Olympic Games were meant to show the world the bold new face of a radically rebuilt Munich, showcasing the premises of the innovative Olympic City. The Black September Arab terrorists, however, had different plans. They managed to slip into the compound housing the athletes from Israel and, before the day was over, had slaughtered a total of 11 of Israel's finest athletes. A storm of protest was raised around the world. The games were virtually ruined, and Munich's bright new image was shattered (their police force seemed to make mistake after mistake), and dank memories of the Holocaust were revived at a time when Germany, and Munich specifically, was trying to forget its recent past and show the world that it had moved into a brighter and happier future. For more information, see p. 113.

Located northwest of the city center, this enormous development is practically a city unto itself. It has its own post office, railway station, elementary school, and even its own mayor. The top level of the enormous television tower is the best place to view Munich and its vicinity.

Nymphenburg Located just northwest of the city center is the Nymphenburg Palace and Park, the original home of the Wittelsbach rulers. The baroque palace is home to the famous Nymphenburg porcelain museum and factory. Adjoining the palace is a vast expanse of lakes and gardens.

Schwabing This area, in the city's northern sector, was once (in the 1920s and then, again, after World War II and into the 1950s) a center of bohemian life, much like New York's Greenwich Village, and like Greenwich Village, it has gentrified into a locale for lawyers, producers, and other professionals, as well as a hangout for university students and a lively nightlife scene. At the turn of the 20th century, it was the place where the city's leading artists, actors, poets, musicians, and writers lived or gathered. Many famous literary figures have called Schwabing home, including Thomas Mann. Here you'll find the city's finest examples of Art Nouveau architecture. Leopoldstrasse makes almost a straight axis through its center. The Englischer Garten forms its eastern border, the Studentenstadt is to its north, and Olympiapark and Josephsplatz mark its western border.

Arabellapark The city's ultramodern commercial and industrial quarter, northeast of the city center, is home to several large international companies. Its glass and concrete buildings have become an outstanding feature of Munich's skyline.

Bogenhausen Located just northeast of the city center near Arabellapark, this area, like Schwabing, has many excellent examples of Art Nouveau architecture. Once the district where the prosperous had their homes, Bogenhausen is now home to numerous galleries, boutiques, and restaurants.

Brienner Strasse Designed as part of the development of the Maxvorstadt during the reign of Maximilian I, this street was home to the aristocratic families and wealthy citizens of Munich. Today it is the location of many galleries and luxury shops.

Maxvorstadt Launched as a planned expansion of the city by King Maximilian I, today the area draws its character from the many facilities of the University of Munich. The area is teeming with student bars, bookshops, and galleries.

Westpark This 71-hectare (178-acre) park, laid out for the fourth International Garden Show, is full of extensive lawns, playgrounds, and ponds. The park is complete with two beer gardens, several cafes, and a lakeside theater that hosts outdoor concerts during the summer months. Also located in the park is the Rudi Sedlmayer Sports Hall, one of Munich's premier venues for large rock concerts.

2 Getting Around

The best way to explore Munich is by walking. In fact, because of the vast pedestrian zone in the center, many of the major attractions can only be reached on foot. Pick up a good map and set out.

BY PUBLIC TRANSPORTATION

It's easy to explore the heart of Munich on foot, and the many attractions in the environs can be reached by Munich's excellent public transportation system.

The city's rapid-transit system is preferable to streetcars and certainly to high-priced taxis. The same ticket entitles you to ride the **U-bahn** and the **S-bahn,** as well as **trams** (streetcars) and **buses.** The U-bahn, or Untergrundbahn, is the line you will use most frequently; the S-bahn, or Stadtbahn, services suburban locations.

At the transport hub, Marienplatz, U-bahn and S-bahn rails crisscross each other. It's possible to use your Eurailpass on S-bahn journeys, as it's a state-owned railway. Otherwise, you must purchase a single-trip ticket or a strip ticket for several journeys at one of the blue vending machines positioned at the entryways to the underground stations. If you're making only one trip, a **single ticket** will average 2€, although it can reach as high as 8€ to an outlying area.

A more economical option is the **strip ticket,** called *Streifenkarte* in German. It's good for several rides and sells for 9€. A trip within the metropolitan area costs you two strips, which are valid for 2 hours. In that time, you may interrupt your trip and transfer as you like to any public transportation (including trams and buses, which usually take over where the U-bahn comes to an end), as long as you travel in one continuous direction. When you reverse your direction, you must cancel two strips again. Children 6 to 14 use the red *Kinder-streifenkarte,* costing 3.50€ for five strips; for a trip within the metropolitan area, they cancel only one strip. Children over the age of 15 pay adult fares. A **day ticket** for 4.50€, called a *Tageskarte,* is also a good investment if you plan to stay within the city limits. If you'd like to branch out to Greater Munich—that is, within an 80km (50-mile) radius—you can purchase a day card for 10€. For public transport information, dial © **089/21-03-30.**

A Map Note

See the inside back cover of this guide for a full-color map of Munich's U-bahn and S-bahn systems.

BY TAXI

Cabs are relatively expensive—the average ride costs 2.50€, plus an additional 1.50€ per kilometer. In an emergency, call ✆ **089/2-16-10,** or 089/19410 for a radio-dispatched taxi.

BY CAR

Though the major car-rental companies have easy-to-spot offices at the airport, if you're already in Munich and plan on making excursions into the Bavarian countryside, it's often more convenient to rent a car in the city center instead of trekking out to the airport. Car-rental companies are listed under *Autover-mietung* in the Yellow Pages of the Munich phone book and usually have at least one English-speaking employee. Companies include **Avis,** Nymphenburger Strasse 61 (✆ **089/12-60-00-20**), and **Sixt Autovermietung,** Einsteinstrasse 106 (✆ **089/418-0050**). Both also have branches at Munich's railway station.

Because of heavy traffic, don't attempt to see Munich itself by car. And beware if your hotel doesn't have parking. Parking garages tend to be expensive, often 13€ to 23€ per night.

See p. 28 for more on renting cars, German driving rules, and other important car-related information.

BY BICYCLE

The tourist office sells a pamphlet called *Radl-Touren für unsere Gäste,* costing only .50€. It outlines itineraries for touring Munich by bicycle.

One of the most convenient places to rent a bike is **Aktiv-Rad,** Hans-Sachs-Strasse 7 (✆ **089/26-65-06**), near the U-bahn station at Frauenhoferstrasse. It's open Monday to Friday from 9:30am to 1pm and 2 to 6pm, and Saturday from 9:30am to 1pm. Charges are 11€ to 20€ for a full day.

One of the most convenient places to rent a bike is **Radius Bikes** in the Hauptbahnhof near track 32 (✆ **089/596-113**). It's open from May to mid-October daily 10am to 6pm (Sat and Sun in July and Aug 9am–8pm). During March and April the store will be open only with good weather (call first). Closed November to February. Depending on the bike, rentals cost from 14€ to 18€ per 24-hour period. A deposit of 50€, either cash or credit card, is required. You can also rent a bike at **Mike's Bike Tour** (p. 115) for about 15€ for a 24-hour rental.

4

Where to Stay

Finding a room in Munich is comparatively easy, but tabs tend to be high. Bargains are few and hard to find—but they do exist.

If you arrive in town without a hotel reservation, go to the **Munich Tourist Information Office** on Platform 2 at the Hauptbahnhof (© **089/ 233-03-00;** www.muenchen-tourist. de), where general information about Munich and its attractions is also available; it's open Monday to Saturday 9am to 8pm and Sunday 10am to 6pm. Here, the English-speaking personnel, maintaining access to more than 300 hotels (jointly containing around 35,000 beds), will come to your rescue. Tell them what you can afford and they'll pick a suitable hotel within that price range. There's no charge for the reservation, but you must give them a 10% down payment on the room, an amount that will eventually be deducted from your final hotel bill.

Be sure to get a receipt as well as a map with instructions on how to reach the place they've booked for you. Keep your receipt. If you don't like the room, go back to the tourist office and they'll try to find you another lodging.

Frankly, we find that this reservations service is most appropriate for travelers arriving at Munich's railway station without a reservation—the last-minute arrangements it can make, especially during periods when many hotels are full—can be very useful. But they'll also arrange reservations weeks or months in advance of your arrival, without charge, if you want them to.

Written correspondence describing your parameters and your needs should be addressed to Landeshauptstadt München, Fremdenverkehrsamt, Sendlingerstrasse 1, D-80331 München. The organization can also be reached through the phone number of the tourist office itself (see above) or through their direct line (© **089/233- 96555**), by fax at 089/233-30133, or by e-mail through their website www. muenchen-tourist.de. *Note:* Whereas the tourist office itself remains open at the hours noted above, the division that arranges room reservations maintains hours as follows: Monday to Thursday from 9am to 5pm and Friday 9am to 3pm.

Advance Reservations Citi Incoming, Riemerstrasse 360 (Postfach 140163), D-80451 München (© **089/ 940-099-91;** fax 089/940-099-81; citi-incoming@t-online.de), is the best place to go if you want not only to book a hotel room but also to arrange for an Avis rental car or Grey Line sightseeing tour. The service is free and, although this company works with hotels on a commission basis, it guarantees that travelers never pay more than they would if they made the bookings themselves. In some cases, Citi Incoming can even get you a better rate than off-the-street bookings because hotels make special offers to travel agencies. Guaranteed bookings can easily be made by phone or fax. The company provides this service for other areas of Germany as well, and for neighboring countries such as Austria and Switzerland. They'll even provide you with road maps. Both long-term bookings and last-minute requests are handled. Hours are Monday to Friday from 9am to 5pm.

All hotels raise their prices for Oktoberfest and for various trade fairs. Some hotels announce their rates in advance, while others prefer to wait until the last minute to see what the market will bear. In general, prices during the festival rise about 15% or more. Prices listed under hotel reviews below are for non-Oktoberfest stays. For the most up-to-date information, you'll need to call the specific hotel where you'd like to stay.

1 Central Munich

VERY EXPENSIVE

Bayerischer Hof & Palais Montgelas ★★★   The Bayerischer Hof hotel and the 17th-century Palais Montgelas combine to form a Bavarian version of New York's Waldorf-Astoria. This establishment has been the beneficiary of lavish sums of money's worth of improvements and is now better than ever, a rival even of the front-ranking Kempinski Hotel Vier Jahreszeiten (see below). It's been a favorite ever since King Ludwig I used to come here to take a bath (the royal palace didn't have bathtubs back then). Rooms range from medium to extremely spacious. The decor ranges from Bavarian provincial to British country house chintz. Many beds are four-posters. The large bathrooms have a private phone and plenty of shelf space, with a tub-and-shower combination. Palais Montgelas has 20 of the most upscale rooms as well as conference and banqueting rooms.

Promenadeplatz 2–6, 80333 München. ℂ **800/223-6800** in the U.S., or 089/2-12-00. Fax 089/2-12-09-06. www.bayerischerhof.de. 399 units. 271€–399€ double; 1,089€ suite. AE, DC, MC, V. Parking 19€. Tram: 19. **Amenities:** Restaurant; bar; nightclub; pool; sauna; room service; massage; babysitting; laundry. *In room:* TV, minibar, hair dryer, safe.

Kempinski Hotel Vier Jahreszeiten München ★★★   This grand hotel is not only the most elegant in Munich, but it's also Germany's most famous and distinctive, and among the finest in the world. Its tradition stretches back to 1858. Rooms and suites—which have hosted royalty, heads of state, and famed personalities from all over the world—combine the charm of days gone by with modern luxuries. The antique-style beds feature fine linen on sumptuous mattresses. The large bathrooms are equipped with all sorts of special treats, including luxurious robes and a tub-and-shower combination. The windows opening onto Maximilianstrasse are double-glazed.

Maximilianstrasse 17, 80539 München. ℂ **800/426-3135** in the U.S., or 089/2-12-50. Fax 089/21-25-27-77. www.kempinski.com. 316 units. 285€–385€ double; from 590€ suite. AE, DC, MC, V. Parking 20€. Tram: 19. **Amenities:** Restaurant; bar; pool; sauna; solarium; room service; massage; babysitting; laundry/dry cleaning. *In room:* A/C, TV, dataport, minibar, hair dryer, safe.

Königshof ★★   In the heart of Munich, the lively, personalized Königshof overlooks the famous Karlsplatz (*Stachus*) and the old part of the city, where it opened in 1862. The proprietors, the Geisel family, maintain its legend. As a mansion hotel, it attracts an extremely upmarket clientele but does not match the Mandarin Oriental (see below) as a premier address. The hotel offers traditional comforts plus up-to-date facilities. All its sleekly styled rooms have soundproofing and picture windows as well as well-maintained bathrooms with shower-tub combinations. There are interesting shopping and sightseeing streets nearby.

Karlsplatz 25, D-80335 München. ✆ **800/44-UTELL** in the U.S., or 089/55-13-60. Fax 089/5513-6113. www.excelsior-muenchen.de/. 87 units. 260€–350€ double; 380€–650€ suite. AE, DC, MC, V. Parking 15€ in 180-car underground garage. S-bahn: S3, S7, or S8 to Karlsplatz. Tram: 19. **Amenities:** Restaurant; bar; sauna; room service; babysitting; laundry/dry cleaning. *In room:* A/C, TV, minibar, hair dryer, safe.

Mandarin Oriental ★   One of Munich's smaller hotels is also one of its most posh. Only the Kempinski Hotel Vier Jahreszeiten München and the Bayerischer Hof (see above) outclass this sophisticated and luxurious winner. The stylish and elegant wedge-shaped 1880s building combines neo-Renaissance, neoclassical, and Biedermeier touches. It's located within sight of the Frauenkirche at Marienplatz. A marble staircase sweeps upward to the very comfortable, large rooms, each with specially crafted furniture or original antiques. Bathrooms are well appointed, each with a tub-and-shower combination.

Neuturmstrasse 1, 80331 München. ✆ **089/29-09-80.** Fax 089/22-25-39. www.mandarinoriental.com. 73 units. 330€–420€ double; from 530€ suite. AE, DC, MC, V. Parking 19.50€. U-bahn/S-bahn: Marienplatz. Tram: 19. **Amenities:** 2 restaurants; bar; pool; room service; babysitting; laundry. *In room:* A/C, TV, minibar, hair dryer, safe.

EXPENSIVE

Admiral ★★   In the vicinity of the Deutsches Museum (p. 98) and the Isar River, this is a government-rated four-star deluxe hotel. In a tranquil location, its rooms are spread over six floors. The furnishings are elegant, the comfort top rate, and the bathrooms tiled and of a good size, each with a tub and shower combination. The bedrooms to request are those with a small balcony opening onto the hotel gardens. As a thoughtful touch, each room is supplied with a basket of fresh fruit. The breakfast buffet is one of the most generous we've seen in Munich—even the jams are homemade. And in summer, fresh Bavarian fruit is a regular feature.

Kohlstrasse 9, D-80469 München. ✆ **089/216-350.** Fax 089/293-674. www.hotel-admiral.de. 33 units. 170€–190€ double. Rates include breakfast. AE, DC, MC, V. Parking 12€. Bus: 52, 56. **Amenities:** Bar; room service; babysitting; laundry/dry cleaning. *In room:* TV, minibar, hair dryer, iron, safe.

Arabella Westpark-Hotel ★   A 10-story, government-rated four-star member of the Arabella chain, this hotel is personalized and intimate, and its bedrooms were completely renovated in 1996. Although not as fresh as they were back then, they are still well maintained and range from midsize to spacious, with tiled bathrooms with tub-and-shower combination. Bedrooms come in three different grades, prices based on altitude (the higher, the more expensive), decor, and the presence of robes. The more expensive rooms evoke a country house aura in their decor. The cheaper rooms are on the lower three floors and are the most time worn but are still sufficiently comfortable. The location on the western side of Munich is near the fairgrounds where the Oktoberfest is staged. The steel-and-glass structure is very typical of the 1980s, and is a bit too institutional for our tastes, attracting EU business clients and a lot of tour groups. Nonetheless, it has a well-trained staff and a lively atmosphere.

Garmischer Strasse 2, D-80339 München. ✆ **089/5-19-60.** Fax 089/51-96-649. www.arabellasheraton.de. 258 units. 150€–185€ double; 215€–300€ suite. Rates include breakfast. AE, DC, MC, V. Parking 15€. U-bahn: U4 or U5 to Heimeran Platz. **Amenities:** Restaurant; bar; pool; room service; laundry/dry cleaning. *In room:* A/C, TV, minibar, hair dryer, safe.

Eden-Hotel-Wolff ★★   If you must stay in the train station area, this is your best bet, despite the fact that it's often booked by groups. The austere stone-clad facade of the Eden-Hotel-Wolff does not reveal the warmth of the interior

Central Munich Accommodations

Admiral **34**
Adria **46**
Advocat **38**
Am Markt **33**
Arabella Sheraton
  Grand Hotel **48**
Arabella Westpark
  Hotel **18**
Asam Stadthotel **30**
Bayerischer Hof &
  Palais Montgelas **7**
Biederstein **50**
Bristol München **24**
Carlton Hotel **49**
City Hotel **10**
Domus **47**
Eden-Hotel-Wolff **6**
Erzgiesserei Europe **2**
Europäischer Hof **12**
Excelsior **9**
Exquisit **23**
Forum Hotel München **35**
Four Points Hotel
  München Central **15**
Gästehaus Englischer
  Garten **51**
Germania **27**
Holiday Inn Munich
  City North **1**
Hotel An der Oper **43**
Hotel Barack **20**
Hotel Concorde **41**
Hotel Leopold **1**
Hotel Mayer **13**
Hotel Mirabell **25**
Hotel Palace **45**
Hotel Pension
  Am Siegestor **52**
Hotel Pension Beck **39**
Hotel Pension Mariandl **21**
Hotel Pension
  Schmellergarten **20**
Hotel Schlicker **20**
Hotel St. Paul **16**
InterCity Hotel
  München **11**
Jedermann **14**
Kempinski Hotel Vier
  Jahreszeiten München **44**
King's Hotel **5**
Königshof **8**
Königswache **3**
Kraft Hotel **22**
Kurpfalz **15**
Mandarin Oriental **42**
Mark **26**
Mercure München
  Königin Elisabeth **4**
München Marriott Hotel **50**

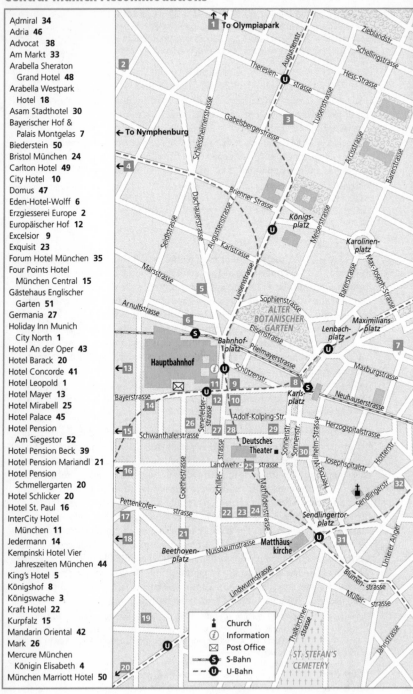

To Olympiapark

← To Nymphenburg

Hauptbahnhof

Königs-
platz

ALTER
BOTANISCHER
GARTEN

Bahnhof-
platz

Karls-
platz

Lenbach-
platz

Maximilians-
platz

Deutsches
Theater

Sendlingertor-
platz

Matthäus-
kirche

Beethoven-
platz

ST. STEFAN'S
CEMETERY

✝ Church
ⓘ Information
✉ Post Office
Ⓢ S-Bahn
-Ⓤ- U-Bahn

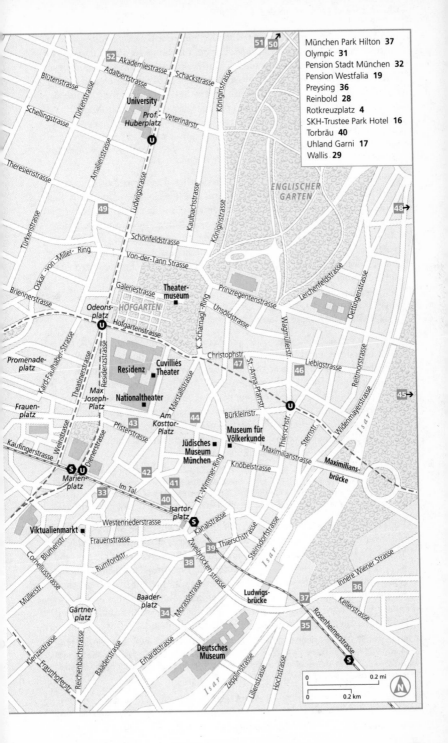

München Park Hilton **37**
Olympic **31**
Pension Stadt München **32**
Pension Westfalia **19**
Preysing **36**
Reinbold **28**
Rotkreuzplatz **4**
SKH-Trustee Park Hotel **16**
Torbräu **40**
Uhland Garni **17**
Wallis **29**

ENGLISCHER
GARTEN

Blütenstrasse
Adalbertstrasse
Akademiestrasse
Schackstrasse
Königinstrasse
University
Prof.-
Huberplatz
Veterinärstr.
Schellingstrasse
Türkenstrasse
Amalienstrasse
Ludwigstrasse
Kaulbachstrasse
Theresienstrasse
Türkenstrasse
Oskar - von -Miller- Ring
Schönfeldstrasse
Von-der-Tann Strasse
Brennerstrasse
Galeriestrasse
Theater-
museum
Prinzregentenstrasse
Lerchenfeldstrasse
Oettingenstrasse
Odeons-
platz
HOFGARTEN
Hofgartenstrasse
K. Scharnagl -Ring
Unsöldstrasse
Christophstr.
Wagmüllerstr.
Promenade-
platz
Kardt-Faulhaber-Strasse
Theatinerstrasse
Residenzstrasse
Residenz
Cuvilliés
Theater
St-Anna-Parrstr.
Liebigstrasse
Reitmorstrasse
Max
Joseph-
Platz
Nationaltheater
Marstallstrasse
Isar
Frauen-
platz
Weinstrasse
Theatinerstrasse
Pfisterstrasse
Am
Kosttor-
Platz
Bürkleinstr.
Thierschstr.
Sternstr.
Widenmayerstrasse
Maximilians-
brücke
Kaufingerstrasse
Marien-
platz
Museum für
Völkerkunde
Maximilianstrasse
Jüdisches
Museum
München
Knöbelstrasse
Im Tal
Th.-Wimmer-Ring
Isartor-
platz
Viktualienmarkt
Westenriederstrasse
Kanalstrasse
Thierschstrasse
Steinsdorfstrasse
Isar
Frauenstrasse
Blumenstr.
Rumfordstr.
Zweibrückenstrasse
Cornelliusstrasse
Baader-
platz
Morassistrasse
Ludwigs-
brücke
Innere Wiener Strasse
Müllerstr.
Gärtner-
platz
Erhardtstrasse
Kellerstrasse
Rosenheimerstrasse
Klenzestrasse
Reichenbachstrasse
Baaderstrasse
Deutsches
Museum
Zeppelinstrasse
Lillenstrasse
Hochstrasse
Fraunhoferstr.
Isar

0   0.2 mi
0   0.2 km

N

47

decoration or the comfort this hotel has. The interior is richly traditional, with chandeliers and dark-wood paneling. A few of the rooms are small, but most are spacious, and all are tastefully furnished in a decor that runs the gamut from extremely modern to rustic. Bathrooms are large, each with a tub and shower. Some units are hypoallergenic, with special beds and a private ventilation system. The staff is among the best, most efficient, and helpful in Munich.

Arnulfstrasse 4–8 (opposite the train station), 80335 München. ℭ 089/55-11-50. Fax 089/55-11-55-55. www.ehw.de. 210 units. 169€–289€ double; 368€ suite. 1 child up to age 6 stays free in parents' room. Rates include buffet breakfast. AE, DC, MC, V. Parking 14€. U-bahn/S-bahn: Hauptbahnhof. **Amenities:** Restaurant; bar; car rental; laundry/dry cleaning. *In room:* TV, minibar, hair dryer.

Excelsior Hotel ✸ This solidly comfortable, government-rated four-star hotel (which is not a member of any chain) near the city's main railway station prides itself on its restored facade, a pale gray exterior that replicates its original turn-of-the-20th-century design, which was destroyed in wartime bombings. Last renovated in 1991, the hotel's bedrooms are quite spacious, outfitted in a tasteful and conservative style. All units contain bathrooms with shower-tub combinations. Overall, this is a low-key, discreet, highly Europeanized hotel with a resolute lack of glitter.

Schutzenstrasse 11, D-80335 München. ℭ 089/55-13-70. Fax 089/55-13-71-21. www.excelsior-muenchen. de. 113 units. 190€ double; 210€–225€ suite. AE, DC, MC, V. Parking 11€. U-bahn: Hauptbahnhof. **Amenities:** Restaurant; room service; laundry/dry cleaning. *In room:* TV, minibar, hair dryer.

Forum Hotel München ✸ After the Arabella Sheraton Grand (p. 60), this is Munich's largest hotel. It's two subway stops east of the Marienplatz in a congested neighborhood near the Isar River, not far from the Gasteig Center (p. 143) and the Deutsche Museum (p. 98). An 11-story concrete structure, it offers a handsome, busy, and cosmopolitan environment much favored by business travelers and airline personnel. Guest rooms are all well maintained and have bathrooms with shower-tub combinations. Rated four stars by the government, it's the kind of place that shows bustling, international Munich at its most efficient, but not necessarily at its most charming.

Hochstrasse 3, D-81669 München. ℭ 089/4-80-30. Fax 089/4-48-82-77. www.interconti.com. 580 units. 200€–310€ double; 250€–390€ suite. During weekend periods of low demand, promotional rates of 110€ sometimes available Fri–Sun. AE, DC, MC, V. Parking 16€. S-bahn: Rosenheimer Platz. **Amenities:** 2 restaurants; bar; sauna; salon; pool; room service; laundry/dry cleaning. *In room:* A/C, TV, minibar, hair dryer, safe.

Hotel Concorde ✸ Set on a quiet side street, a few minutes' walk from some of the most frequently visited attractions in town, this efficiently-managed hotel has six floors, an elevator, and was renovated in 1996. Its desirable location and its proximity to both the British and American consulates draw a large number of diplomats. Bedrooms have modern, somewhat bland styling, with large, comfortable beds, angular contemporary furnishings, and well-kept bathrooms mostly with shower-tub combinations. Although there are no dining or bar facilities on-site, many restaurants are in the neighborhood.

Herrnstrasse 38, D-80539 München. ℭ 089/22-45-15. Fax 089/2-28-32-82. www.concorde-muenchen.de. 71 units. 128€–190€ double; 154€–220€ suite. Rates include buffet breakfast. AE, DC, MC, V. Closed Dec 22–Jan 7. Parking 11€. U-bahn: U3 or U6 to Isartorplatz; then a 3-min. walk to the hotel. **Amenities:** Lounge; laundry/dry cleaning. *In room:* TV, minibar, hair dryer.

Intercity-Hotel München ✸ This government-rated four-star hotel was once a late-19th-century Jugendstil showplace at the southern precincts of Munich's main railway station. Blasted apart during World War II and rebuilt in a bland angular style, its modern interior retains only hints of its Art Nouveau origins. If you're a railway buff, you may be disappointed that you won't be able to watch trains arriving or departing, but that's overcome by the fact that bedrooms are soundproofed against noise, and are comfortable, contemporary, and suited to the needs of international travelers. As a concession to Munich's unending obsession with folklore, a few of the hotel's bedrooms have Bavarian-style rustic furnishings. All units contain well-kept bathrooms with shower units.

Bayerstrasse 10, D-80335 München. © **089/54-55-60**. Fax 089/54-55-66-10. www.intercity-hotel.de. 200 units. 142€ double; 167€ suite. AE, DC, MC, V. Parking 10€. U-bahn or S-bahn: Hauptbahnhof. **Amenities:** Restaurant; bar; room service; massage; babysitting; laundry/dry cleaning. *In room:* TV, minibar, hair dryer.

King's First Class Hotel ⭐   The interior of King's Hotel (a 4-min. walk from the Hauptbahnhof) sports the most traditional Bavarian decor of any of the many government-rated four-star hotels in Munich. The seven-story building looks, from the outside, like a modern town house, but inside, carved headboards, flowered fabrics, and rich paneling offer a pleasant contrast to the 20th-century anonymity of the area around the city's main railway station. Built in 1987, the hotel was named after a German family that prides itself on the English spelling of its name. Some suites have tiny kitchens and almost all have well-kept bathrooms with shower units.

Dachauer Strasse 13, D-80335 München. © **089/55-18-70**. Fax 089/55-18-73-00. www.kingshotel.de. 90 units. 160€–195€ double; 210€–280€ suite. Some weekends, depending on bookings (Fri–Sun), 105€ double. AE, DC, MC, V. U-bahn: Hauptbahnhof. **Amenities:** Breakfast room; bar; sauna; babysitting; laundry/dry cleaning. *In room:* A/C, TV, minibar, hair dryer, safe.

München Park Hilton ⭐⭐   This sleek, 15-story tower in verdant Tivoli Park was transformed into a hotel from an office complex at the time of the 1972 Olympics. A government-rated five-star hotel, it lies between the Englischer Garten (p. 111) and the Isar River, in a neighborhood close to the headquarters of many giant corporations. Because of that, traffic can sometimes make access for motorists a bit difficult. It's one of Munich's two Hiltons (the other, government-rated four-star München City Hilton, is less plush and has no swimming pool). Bedrooms here have floor-to-ceiling picture windows, balconies affording a distant view of the Alps, well-kept bathrooms containing shower-tub combinations and monochromatic color schemes.

Am Tucherpark 7, D-80538 München. © **800/445-8667** in the U.S., or 089/3-84-50. Fax 089/38-45-25-88. www.hilton.com. 479 units. 230€ double; from 480€ suite. Rates include breakfast. AE, DC, MC, V. Parking 15€. U-bahn: U3 or U6 to Giselastrasse. Bus: E54 from Schwabing. **Amenities:** Restaurant; bar; pool; fitness center; sauna; Jacuzzi; room service; babysitting; laundry/dry cleaning. *In room:* A/C, TV, minibar, hair dryer, safe.

Torbräu ⭐   The foundations of this government-rated four-star hotel in the heart of historic Munich date from the 15th century. Although many vestiges of its folkloric exterior attest to the hotel's distinguished past, the bedrooms are modern and are reasonably comfortable. All units have well-kept bathrooms, mostly with shower-tub combinations. In all, the place is a lot more charming than many of its bandbox-modern competitors.

Tal 41, D-80331 München. © **089/24-23-40**. Fax 089/24-234-235. www.torbraeu.de. 92 units. 160€–250€ double. Rates include breakfast. AE, MC, V. Parking 10€. Closed 1 week at Christmas. U-bahn: Isartor. **Amenities:** 3 restaurants; bar; room service; babysitting; laundry/dry cleaning. *In room:* A/C, TV, hair dryer, safe.

MODERATE

Adria   Adria has an inviting, friendly atmosphere. The lobby sets the stylish contemporary look, and guest rooms are furnished with armchairs or sofas, small desks, and well-kept bathrooms with shower-tub combinations. Breakfast, a buffet with waffles, cakes, homemade rolls, health-food selections, and even sparkling wine, is served in the garden room. On Sunday, smoked salmon is an added treat.

Liebigstrasse 8a, D-80538 München. ✆ **089/29-30-81.** Fax 089/22-70-15. 47 units. 112€–130€ double. Rates include buffet breakfast. AE, MC, V. Free parking. Closed Dec 23–Jan 6. U-bahn: U4 or U5. Tram: 20. **Amenities:** Laundry/dry cleaning. *In room:* TV, minibar, hair dryer.

Advokat Hotel   This hotel occupies a six-story apartment house originally constructed in the 1930s. Its stripped-down, streamlined interior borrows in discreet ways from Bauhaus and minimalist models. One Munich critic said the rooms look as if Philippe Starck had gone on a shopping binge at Ikea. The result is an aggressively simple, clean-lined, and artfully spartan hotel with few facilities, except each room comes with a well-equipped, compact bathroom, mainly with both tub and shower. The German government gives it three stars. The Advokat lies around the corner from its more upscale neighbor, the Hotel Admiral, with which it shares management, but whose rooms cost 30€ more, double occupancy, per category. There's no restaurant on the premises and no particular extras to speak of other than a cozy in-house bar and a delightful rooftop breakfast. But the prices are reasonable, and the staff is helpful.

Baaderstrasse 1, 80469 München. ✆ **089/21-63-10.** Fax 089/21-63-190. www.hotel-advokat.de. 50 units. 165€–185€ double; from 195€ suite. Rates include breakfast. S-bahn: Isartor. **Amenities:** Breakfast room; bar. *In room:* TV, minibar.

Asam Stadthotel ★ *(Finds)*   One of Munich's newest family-run hotels, Asam lies in a well-restored pre-war building. Its bedrooms are large and airy, and each one is nicely appointed with comfortable, modern pieces. We prefer the accommodations facing the rear garden, with its view of the greenery and the steeples of old churches. Some of the bathrooms contain "decadently large" bathtubs, and each also comes with a shower.

Josephspitalstrasse 3, D-80331 München. ✆ **089/230-9700.** Fax 089/230-097-097. www.hotel-asam.de. 33 units. 159€–174€ double, 158€–271€ double. AE, DC, MC, V. U-bahn: Sendlinger Tor. **Amenities:** Restaurant; bar; gym; room service; babysitting; laundry/dry cleaning. *In room:* TV, minibar, hair dryer, safe.

City Hotel   This six-story hotel was built in 1972, not far from Munich's main railway station. Positioned midway between three- and four-star status by the local tourist authorities, it manages to combine coziness with a modern and efficient design and is a pleasant contrast to the congestion that's the norm all around it. Bedrooms are unfussy, uncomplicated, and blandly comfortable. All units contain bathrooms with shower units. No meals are served other than a buffet breakfast, although there's a simple beer-hall-style restaurant on the building's street level that's popular with the crowd from the many offices and businesses nearby.

Schillerstrasse 3a, D-80336 München. ✆ **089/55-80-91.** Fax 089/5-50-36-65. 65 units. 86€–127€ double. AE, DC, MC, V. Parking 8€. U-bahn: Hauptbahnhof. **Amenities:** Breakfast room; lounge; laundry/dry cleaning. *In room:* A/C, TV, minibar, hair dryer.

Erzgiesserei Europe   This clean, comfortable, and well-managed government-rated three-star hotel is less expensive than it probably could be. It was designed in a postmodern style in 1984, but its mansard roof and arched, balconied windows suggest turn-of-the-20th-century architecture. It's in a working-class residential neighborhood, a short subway ride from more interesting haunts. Bedrooms are small but comfortable, with modern furniture; some overlook the carefully landscaped inner courtyard that offers cafe service. All units have well-kept bathrooms with shower-tub combinations. On the premises is a restaurant decorated in a style of old-fashioned German nostalgia.

Erzgiessereistrasse 15, D-80335 München. ℂ **089/12-68-20.** Fax 089/1-23-61-98. www.top-hotels.de/ erzeurope. 106 units. 110€ double; 255€ suite. Rates include breakfast. AE, DC, MC, V. Parking 10€. U-bahn: U1 to Steiglmaierplatz. **Amenities:** Restaurant; bar; room service; laundry/dry cleaning. *In room:* TV, minibar, hair dryer.

Four Points Hotel München Central
Managed by a well-respected middle-bracket German hotel chain, this government-rated three-star, five-floor hotel was built in the 1960s but has been renovated many times since then. It's about a 5-minute walk from the *Messegelände* (trade fair) and the Oktoberfest grounds. Everything is modern, often attractively so, and some rooms have balconies. All units contain well-kept bathrooms with shower-tub combinations. Other than simple bar snacks and a generous morning buffet, there's no food served, but many dining options are nearby.

Schwanthalerstrasse 111, D-80339 München. ℂ **089/51-08-30.** Fax 089/51-08-38-00. www.arabella sheraton.de. 102 units. Sun–Thurs 145€–180€ double; Fri–Sat 115€ double. AE, DC, MC, V. Parking 10€. Closed 2 weeks at Christmastime. Tram: 18 or 19. **Amenities:** Bar; sauna; laundry/dry cleaning. *In room:* TV, minibar, hair dryer.

Hotel An der Oper
This five-floor hotel, built in 1969, is superbly located for sightseeing or shopping in the traffic-free malls, and it's just steps from the Bavarian National Theater (p. 142). In spite of its basic decor, there are touches of elegance. Rooms, which range from small to medium, have double-glazed windows, a small sitting area with armchairs, and a table for those who want breakfast in their rooms. Bathrooms tend to be small, but are well organized and come mainly with just a shower.

Falkenturmstrasse 11 (just off Maximilianstrasse, near Marienplatz), 80331 München. ℂ **089/2-90-02-70.** Fax 089/29-00-27-29. www.hotelanderoper.de. 68 units. 145€–180€ double. Rates include buffet breakfast. AE, MC, V. Parking 15€ nearby. Tram: 19. **Amenities:** Breakfast room; lounge; room service. *In room:* TV, minibar, hair dryer.

Hotel Biederstein *(Finds)*
Near the Englischer Garten, this B&B is a charmer and a new addition on the Munich hotel scene. Newly renovated, it is decorated with designer-style modern furnishings in the minimalist style and is operated by the same people who run Gästehaus Englischer Garten, one of the most charming and heavily booked small inns of Munich. The hotel rents bikes to its guests to ride through the English Garden. Bedrooms are spacious and comfortable with neat tiled bathrooms with shower only. A first-rate breakfast is served on the terrace.

Keferstrasse 18, 80802 München. ℂ **089/3899970.** Fax 089/389997389. 34 units. 95€–136€ double, 132€–190€ suite. V. Parking 8€. U-bahn: Münchner Freiheit. **Amenities:** Breakfast terrace; room service for breakfast; laundry. *In room:* TV.

Hotel Brack
For Oktoberfest devotees, this is one of the best choices, as it lies only a 5-minute walk from the festival grounds. It is a good location at any time of the year, however, as it lies south of the center but convenient to much of the city's allure. Lying on a broad, tree-lined avenue, it offers small to midsize bedrooms, each well equipped with such extras as a radio alarm clock, dataport,

and soundproof windows. Most accommodations also contain safes, along with good-size private bathrooms with tub and shower. The breakfast buffet is rich and varied at this family-run place with a helpful staff who go out of their way to accommodate you, including help in arranging tickets for cultural performances.

Lindwurmstrasse 153, D-80337 München. ℂ **089/747-2550.** Fax 089/7474-5599. www.hotel-brack.de. 50 units. 107€–174€ double. Extra bed 17€. Rates include buffet breakfast. AE, DC, MC, V. U-bahn: Poccistrasse. **Amenities:** Breakfast room; laundry/dry cleaning. *In room:* TV, dataport, hair dryer, safe.

Hotel Carlton   Employees at this hotel are quick to point out that this Carlton has virtually nothing in common with those grand Carltons in, say, Cannes. But despite that, they take pride in their maintenance of this five-floor arts-conscious hotel. The small but cozy bedrooms are outfitted with copies of Italian faux-baroque furniture and soft pastel colors. All units have well-kept bathrooms with shower-tub combinations. The hotel is a short walk from the clubs and restaurants of Schwabing, and draws a clientele that appreciates an ambience that's just funky and irreverent enough to be fun. Six of the bedrooms have private balconies.

Fürstenstrasse 12, D-80333 München. ℂ **089/28-20-61.** Fax 089/28-43-91. 49 units. 112€ double. Rates include breakfast. AE, DC, MC, V. Parking 10€. U-bahn: U3 or U6 to Odeonsplatz. **Amenities:** Sauna; laundry/dry cleaning. *In room:* TV, minibar, hair dryer, safe.

Hotel Domus   The name of this sleekly modern, five-story hotel might suggest a university dormitory, which it certainly isn't. Although it's rather large, it has some of the aspects of a private home. It's near the Englischer Garten (p. 111)—not so close to the historic area as the Torbräu (see above)—but parking is easier, a fact that endears it to many of its regular clients. On weekends, it draws visitors from other parts of Europe on a sightseeing binge; on weekdays, the place has a high percentage of business travelers. Guest rooms are tastefully furnished in appealing monochromatic earth tones, and to help with an undisturbed night's sleep, the hotel pays special attention to the quality of its carpeting and doors. All rooms have neatly-kept bathrooms with shower-tub combinations. There's also an exceptionally well-presented breakfast buffet.

St.-Anna-Strasse 31, D-80538 München. ℂ **089/22-17-04-08.** Fax 089/2-28-53-59. 45 units. 128€–152€ double; 135€–175€ suite. Rates include breakfast. AE, DC, MC, V. Parking 9€. U-bahn: U4 or U5 to Lehel. **Amenities:** Breakfast room; laundry/dry cleaning. *In room:* TV, minibar, hair dryer.

Hotel Exquisit ★   One of the most appealing hotels in the Sendlinger Tor neighborhood lies behind a wine-colored facade on a quiet residential street that seems far removed from the heavy traffic and bustle of the nearby theater district. Built in 1988, it has a paneled lobby whose focal point is a lounge that gets busy around 6 or 7pm. Staff is unusually pleasant, offering a genuine welcome and ushering you up to rooms that are spacious and comfortably furnished. About half overlook an ivy-draped garden, others look over the street. Bathrooms are efficient, with adequate shelf space and a tiled shower unit.

Pettenkoferstrasse 3, D-80336 München. ℂ **089/55-19-900.** Fax 089/55-199-499. www.augustiner-restaurant.com. 50 units. 120€–180€ double, 185€ suite. Rates include breakfast. AE, DC, MC, V. U-bahn: Sendlinger Tor. **Amenities:** Breakfast room; bar; sauna; solarium; room service; private garden. *In room:* TV, minibar, hair dryer.

Hotel Germania   This well-administered government-rated three-star contender was built after wartime damage reduced the vicinity of the railway station to rubble. The boxy, sedate building is not a particularly inspired architectural statement—this is very much a functional hotel geared to busy traffic from business travelers and sightseers. The cost is relatively reasonable and the rooms, although not plush, are superior to those of other comparable three-star hotels in the same neighborhood. All units come with well-maintained bathrooms equipped with shower-tub combinations. There's also an Italian restaurant on the premises.

Schwanthalerstrasse 28, D-80336 München. ☏ **089/59-04-60.** Fax 089/59-11-71. 97 units. 100€–160€ double. Rates include breakfast. AE, MC, V. Parking 10€. U-bahn or S-bahn: Hauptbahnhof. **Amenities:** Restaurant; bar. *In room:* TV.

Hotel Mirabell   Those seeking a reasonably priced hotel in the very center of town might check into this midsize, family-operated hotel that lies in the vicinity of the Hauptbahnhof. It is especially sought out by families because it rents a trio of small apartments. Now well into a quarter-century of operation, the hotel is frequently renovated as needed and immaculately kept. Bedrooms are midsize and comfortable, spread across six floors. The furnishings are contemporary, most often in pale woods with pastel prints. Bathrooms are generous in size, each with a tub and shower combination.

Landwehrstrasse 42, D-80336 München. ☏ **089/549-1740.** Fax 089/550-3701. www.book-a-hotel-in-munich.com/en/hotel/hotels/mirabell/index.html. 65 units, 3 apartments. 95€ double, 115€–128€ apartment. Rates include breakfast. AE, DC, MC, V. Parking 8€. U-bahn: Hauptbahnhof. **Amenities:** Bar; room service; babysitting; laundry/dry cleaning. *In room:* TV, hair dryer.

Hotel Olympic ⭐   Built as a private villa around 1900, this hotel represents one of Munich's most appealing conversions of an antique building into a hip and attractive hotel. The lobby occupies a high-ceilinged, Victorian vestibule that retains many of the original details. Breakfast is served in a very large, graciously proportioned dining room where memories of the grand bourgeoisie of the Industrial Revolution still seem to permeate the woodwork. Rooms are minimalist and all white, much more modern than the ground-floor reception areas, but comfortable and well engineered. Most of the midsize bathrooms come with shower only. The hotel has earned an increasing number of gay clients recently, thanks to its location within a neighborhood that's loaded with gay bars and hangouts.

Hans Sachs Strasse 4, D-80469 München. ☏ **089/231-89-0.** Fax 089/231-89-199. www.hotel-olympic.de. 38 units. 130€ double; 150€ suite. Rates include breakfast. AE, DC, MC, V. U-bahn: Sendlinger Tor. **Amenities:** Breakfast room; lounge; room service. *In room:* TV, minibar.

Hotel Reinbold   A no-nonsense, no-frills hotel, within a 3-minute walk of the railway station, the Reinbold delivers what it promises: clean, decent rooms and efficient, polite service. It's a boxy-looking structure of six concrete-and-glass stories, most recently renovated in 1996. Bedrooms are compact, monochromatic, and pleasantly (but not lavishly) furnished, and contain well-kept bathrooms with shower-tub combinations. No meal other than breakfast is served, but there are many restaurants in this busy neighborhood.

Adolf-Kolping-Strasse 11, D-80336 München. ☏ **089/55-10-40.** Fax 089/55-10-49-05. 63 units. 140€ double; 285€ suite. Rates include breakfast. AE, DC, MC, V. Parking 10€. U-bahn or S-bahn: Hauptbahnhof. **Amenities:** Bar; room service; laundry/dry cleaning. *In room:* TV, minibar, hair dryer.

Hotel St. Paul ⭐ *Value*   A recent discovery by us is one of the most agreeable and affordable hotels in town. Heinz Maresch is the host with the most, welcoming you into his haven of comfort and charm with well-sized and handsomely-furnished bedrooms, each with a well-maintained private bathroom with tub and shower combo. This place should be better known. We especially like his food selection for breakfast, with eggs prepared as you like them upon request and a tantalizing array of yogurts, fruits, juices, and cereals. The hotel lies on the western border of Munich center, near the Oktoberfestwiese, within easy reach of the U-bahn.

St-Paul-Strasse 7, D-80336 München. ☎ **089/5440-7800.** Fax 089/534-652. www.munich-info.de/hotels/info/Hotel-St-Paul_en.html. 40 units. 92€–168€ double. AE, MC, V. Free parking. U-bahn: Theresienwiese. **Amenities:** Bar; babysitting; laundry/dry cleaning. *In room:* TV, hair dryer, safe.

Kraft Hotel   One of the most appealing things about this simple, government-rated three-star hotel is its location in the heart of the Altstadt, within a few minutes' walk of the Sendlingertorplatz (the southwest corner or junction of the Altstadt) and a 5-minute walk from the main railway station. Architecturally, it's not very appealing, in the style of boxy architecture so widespread in Munich after World War II, but bedrooms are streamlined and efficiently designed, usually with some built-in furniture. All units have bathrooms with shower units. There's no restaurant on the premises, but many dining options are within a short walk.

Schillerstrasse 49, D-80336 München. ☎ **089/59-48-23.** Fax 089/5-50-38-56. 39 units. 95€–110€ double. Rates include breakfast. AE, DC, MC, V. Parking 10€. U-bahn: Sendlingertorplatz. **Amenities:** Breakfast room; lounge; laundry/dry cleaning. *In room:* TV, hair dryer.

SKH-Trustee Parkhotel   In a verdant residential neighborhood at the edge of Munich's fairgrounds and Oktoberfest site, this three-story hotel evokes an upscale apartment building. Flowers and plants festoon its balconies, and its blue-and-red bedrooms, with views over a nicely landscaped courtyard, are larger than you might expect. Each well-kept and tastefully furnished unit has floor-to-ceiling windows that flood the interior with sunlight. All rooms have bathrooms with shower-tub combinations. An English-speaking staff is able to give advice about diversions within the city. The hotel contains a bistro that's open daily for lunch and dinner, plus a conference room.

Parkstrasse 31, D-80339 München. ☎ **089/51-99-50.** Fax 089/51-99-54-20. 35 units. 120€–190€ double. Rates include breakfast. AE, DC, MC, V. Parking 9€. U-bahn: U1 to Schwanenthalerhöhe. **Amenities:** Bar; room service; babysitting; laundry/dry cleaning. *In room:* TV, minibar, hair dryer, safe.

INEXPENSIVE

Am Markt   This popular, though not luxurious, Bavarian hotel stands in the heart of the older section. Owner Harald Herrler has maintained a nostalgic decor in the lobby. Behind his reception desk is a wall of photographs of friends or former guests, including the late Viennese chanteuse Greta Keller. As Mr. Herrler points out, when you have breakfast here, you're likely to find yourself surrounded by opera and concert artists; the hotel is close to where they perform. Rooms are quite small, but modern and neat. Mattresses are well worn but comfortable. All units have sinks with hot and cold running water.

Heiliggeistrasse 6, 80331 München. ☎ **089/22-50-14.** Fax 089/22-40-17. 32 units, 12 with bathroom. 66€ double without bathroom; 87€–92€ double with bathroom. Rates include continental breakfast. Parking 8€. S-bahn: Marienplatz. **Amenities:** Breakfast room; lounge; room service. *In room:* TV.

Europäischer Hof   This nine-story hotel opposite the Hauptbahnhof still has the chapel that served its original inhabitants, an order of Catholic nuns, when it was built back in 1960. Now run by the Sturzer family, the establishment offers simple but clean accommodations, some of which overlook an inner courtyard. Most rooms have some built-in furniture; all have double-glazed windows for soundproofing. All also have well-kept bathrooms mostly with shower-tub combinations. Despite its dreary location, the hotel is clean and well managed, with cozy touches. Breakfast is the only meal served, although a likable Italian restaurant occupies part of the building's street level.

Bayerstrasse 31, D-80335 München. ⓒ 089/55-15-10. Fax 089/55-15-12-22. www.heh.de. 153 units. 96€– 167€ double. Rates include breakfast. AE, DC, MC, V. Parking 9.50€. U-bahn or S-bahn: Hauptbahnhof. **Amenities:** Bar; laundry/dry cleaning. *In room:* TV, minibar, hair dryer, safe.

Hotel Bristol München   Built around 1960, in a four-story format that includes a boxy-looking facade and a tiny reception area, this is an easy-to-live-in hotel with kindly management. Quieter rooms in back overlook a sheltered courtyard. Each has a tiny balcony and efficient but comfortable furnishings, plus a neatly organized and compact bathroom in tile containing a shower unit.

Pettenkoferstrasse 2, D-80336 München. ⓒ **089/54-82-22-0.** Fax 089/59-14-51. www.bristol-muc.com. 57 units. 87€–97€ double. Rates rise to 150€ during trade fairs. Rates include breakfast. AE, DC, MC, V. U-bahn: Sendlinger Tor. **Amenities:** Breakfast room; lounge; room service. *In room:* TV, minibar, hair dryer.

Hotel Jedermann *Value* *Kids*   Those in awe of the high prices of Munich hotels find comfort here. The Jenke family has deftly run this pleasant, cozy spot since 1961. Its central location and good value make it a desirable choice, especially for families (cribs and cots are available). The old-fashioned Bavarian rooms are generally small, but cozy and comfortable, each with a shower-only bathroom. A generous breakfast buffet is served in a charming room.

Bayerstrasse 95, 80335 München. ⓒ **089/54-32-40.** Fax 089/54-32-4111. www.hotel-jedermann.de. 52 units, 47 with shower and toilet. 49€–74€ double without bathroom; 67€–149€ double with bathroom; 95€–160€ triple with bathroom. Rates include buffet breakfast. MC, V. Parking 6.15€. 10-min. walk from Hauptbahnhof (turn right on Bayerstrasse from south exit). **Amenities:** Breakfast room; lounge; room service. *In room:* TV, safe.

Hotel Pension Am Siegestor *Value*   Simplicity itself, this little boarding house spreads itself across a trio of floors in a turn-of-the-20th-century town house near the Siegestor (Victory Arch) landmark monument. (The arch was built in the mid–19th century as a monument to honor the Bavarian Army and was based on the architectural concept of Rome's Arch of Constantine.) The location is ideal for those who want to be in the university sector west of the fabled English Garden and north of the Hofgarten. A hotel has operated at this location for half a century. Take the rickety elevator to the check-in area on the fourth floor.

Bedrooms are filled with old-fashioned furnishings, although some are more modernized. Everything depends on your room assignment. Accommodations don't have bathrooms, but the corridor plumbing is generally adequate, and you rarely have to wait in line while clad in your bathrobe. The most nostalgic bedrooms are on the top floor. These are small, intimate, and cozy rooms resting under beamed ceilings. You'll feel old Munich if you stay here. There are no amenities.

Akademeistrasse 5, D-80799 München. ⓒ **089/399-550.** Fax 089/343-050. 20 units. 56€ double. No credit cards. U-bahn: Universität. *In room:* No phone.

Hotel-Pension Beck ★ *Value*   In the increasingly chic Lehel sector, close to the Englischer Garten (p. 111) and other attractions, such as the Deutsches Museum (p. 98), this address is carefully passed around by in-the-know travelers on a budget. Rooms ranging from midsize to spacious are found in a stately town house. The owner extends a hearty welcome to her guests and is especially friendly to her English-speaking visitors. She's filled her establishment with fine carpeting, comfortable beds, pinewood pieces of furniture—all in all, a bright Bavarian ambience. Most of her accommodations don't have private bathrooms, although the hallway bathrooms are more than adequate in most cases. Don't expect a lot of amenities.

Thierschstrasse 36, D-80538 München. ℂ **089/220-708.** Fax 089/220-925. www.bst-online.de/pension. beck. 44 unit, 7 with shower. 45.50€ double without bathroom, 69€ double with bathroom. MC, V. U-bahn: Lehel. Tram: 7. **Amenities:** Breakfast room. *In room:* TV, no phone.

Hotel-Pension Mariandl ⭐ *Finds*   Relatively undiscovered, this is a small Bavarian hotel of charm and character. It is housed in a turn-of-the-20th-century neo-Gothic town house that has retained the aura of a bygone age. When the American forces overran Munich in May of 1945, this mansion was commandeered to be hastily converted into the Femina, now part of post-war history because it became the first night club to open after the war. The high-ceilinged bedrooms are spacious and comfortably furnished, alongside private bathrooms with both tub and shower. The hotel lies about a mile from the main rail station for Munich yet is only a 10-minute walk from the grounds of Oktoberfest. On the ground floor is the Café am Beethovenplatz, where guests order breakfast. That's about it for amenities, however.

Goethestrasse 51, D-80336 München. ℂ **089/534-108.** Fax 089/5440-4396. www.hotelmariandl.de. 28 units. 70€–110€ double. Rates include buffet breakfast. **Amenities:** Restaurant/cafe. *In room:* No phone.

Hotel-Pension Schmellergarten *Value*   After a successful renovation, this little hotel is now one of the best value inns of Munich, ideal for frugal travelers and popular with young people. The hotel lies on the fringe of central Munich, just a 10- to 15-minute walk to the real heart of the city, although you can also rely on public transportation. Hotel-Pension Schmellergarten is just a short walk from the Oktoberfest grounds, and the subway station is only around the corner from the front door. Rooms are small but comfortably furnished with fresh, crisp linens adorning the beds and reproductions of modern artwork hanging on the white walls. Guests meet fellow guests in the tidy little breakfast room, a friendly oasis.

Schmellerstrasse 20, D-80337 München. ℂ **089/773-157.** Fax 089/725-6886. kuhn@germanynet.de. 56€–72€ double. Rates include continental breakfast. No credit cards. Free parking. U-bahn: Poccistrasse. **Amenities:** Breakfast room. *In room:* TV, hair dryer.

Hotel Schlicker *Finds*   In spite of its location between a McDonald's and a Burger King, this is a hotel of charm and tradition, with a pedigree going back to 1544. With a stay here you are in the heart of Munich, just steps away from the landmark Marienplatz and around the corner from our favorite food market in Germany, Viktualienmarkt. Only the breakfast room suggests that this place was once an ancient inn: The rest of the hotel is modernized. This friendly, inviting hotel is run by the Mayer family, a tradition since 1897. Bedrooms are comfortable and traditional, each midsize and they come with a tiled, midsize bathroom with shower and tub.

Tal 74, 80331 München. ℂ **089/2428870.** Fax 089/296059. www.hotel-schlicker.de. 69 units. 105€–156€ double, 180€–215€ suite. AE, DC, MC, V. Parking 10€. U-bahn: Marienplatz. **Amenities:** Breakfast room; room service for breakfast. *In room:* TV.

Hotel Wallis   Unpretentious, uncomplicated, and comfortable, this government-rated three-star hotel's Bavarian-inspired interior is warmer and cozier than you'd imagine after a look at its angular post-war exterior. Bedrooms are relatively small, but they were renovated in 1995 and are furnished in a simplified version of alpine-village style. All units contain well-kept bathrooms with shower-tub combinations. Only breakfast is served, but many worthwhile restaurants are within a short walk. The staff is polite and helpful to newcomers navigating their way around the city.

Schwanthalerstrasse 8, D-80336 München. ⓒ **089/59-16-64.** Fax 089/5-50-37-52. www.muenchen-hotel. de. 54 units. 93€ double. AE, DC, MC, V. U-bahn: Karlsplatz. **Amenities:** Bar; babysitting; laundry/ dry cleaning. *In room:* TV, minibar (in some).

Kurpfalz   This family-owned hotel lies in the center of Munich in a 1927 building that has been renovated and altered many times over the years. Twelve minutes by foot from the main rail station, it is very affordable for such a central location. Luxurious it's not, although all of its rooms are clean, comfortable, and rather functionally furnished, graced in part with reproductions of Bavarian country pieces. Bedrooms are midsize for the most part, each coming with a tub and shower combination. The fair grounds for Oktoberfest lie within a 10-minute walk of the hotel, and there are many wine taverns, restaurants, and bars in the neighborhood. The breakfast buffet served each morning is extensive and varied.

Schwanthalerstrasse 121, D-80339 München. ⓒ **089/540-9860.** Fax 089/540-98811. 44 units. 60€–155€ double. Rates include breakfast buffet. AE, MC, V. Parking 8€. U-bahn: Sendlinger Tor. **Amenities:** Bar; laundry/ dry cleaning. *In room:* TV, hair dryer.

Pension Stadt München   One of the simplest and least expensive places to stay in downtown Munich is positioned one floor above street level in an old-fashioned building near the city's most important square. It attracts a heavy percentage of backpackers and gay men and women. No meals are served other than breakfast. Bedrooms are anonymous-looking, and clean, albeit a bit battered and utterly without decorative accessories. Each has a sink and shower, although the WCs are shared facilities accessible via the corridors.

Dultstrasse 1, D-80331 München. ⓒ **089/26-34-17.** Fax 089/26-75-48. 4 units (all with shower, none with WC). 70€ double. Rates include breakfast. AE, MC, V. U-bahn: Marienplatz. **Amenities:** Restaurant; bar; room service; laundry/dry cleaning. *In room:* TV, minibar, hair dryer.

Pension Westfalia ★ *(Value*   This four-story town house, originally built in 1895, near Goetheplatz is one of Munich's best pensions. It faces the meadow where the annual Oktoberfest takes place. Rooms are rather functional, and short on extras, but are well maintained, each with a small shower-only bathroom. Owner Peter Deiritz speaks English. Parking is free on the street when available.

Mozartstrasse 23, 80336 München. ⓒ **089/53-03-77.** Fax 089/5-43-91-20. www.pension-westfalia.de. 19 units, 14 with bathroom. 52€ double without bathroom; 65€–75€ double with bathroom. Rates include buffet breakfast. MC, V. U-bahn: Goetheplatz. Bus: 58. **Amenities:** Breakfast room; lounge. *In room:* TV (only in 3 rooms).

Uhland Garni ★★ *(Finds*   The century-old Uhland could easily become your home in Munich. In a residential area, the stately town mansion, built in the Art Nouveau style, stands in its own small garden, a 10-minute walk from the Hauptbahnhof. The Uhland has an inviting neo-Renaissance front turned to the street, and its windows are filled with flower boxes of geraniums in summer. Before the Hauzenberg family converted it into a small hotel in the early 1960s, each floor of the building was a single stately apartment. Improvements now include the installation of dataports in each accommodation and a computer in the little living room where you can surf the Web. The bedrooms, ranging from small to medium, are individually decorated in a combination of Bavarian and contemporary design, with many thoughtful extras. Some open onto tiny balconies, and one even has a heated waterbed. All units contain bathrooms with shower-tub combinations. This place is a good choice for families; some rooms have bunk beds provided for children.

Uhlandstrasse 1, 80336 München. ✆ **089/54-33-50.** Fax 089/54-33-52-50. www.hotel-uhland.de. 25 units. 80€–160€ double. Rates include buffet breakfast. AE, DC, MC, V. Free parking. Bus: 58. **Amenities:** Breakfast room; lounge; room service. *In room:* TV, dataport, minibar, hair dryer.

2 Schwabing

EXPENSIVE

München Marriott Hotel ★★   Marriott's usual postmodern style fits appropriately into this verdant setting along the northern tier of Schwabing. Built in 1990, about 4km (2½ miles) north of Munich's historic core, it offers a well-designed, Americanized venue whose German staff welcomes travelers from throughout Europe. Bedrooms are standard and identical, but the lobby is one of the most appealing in Schwabing, with blond wood, marble, potted plants, and sunlight streaming in from all sides. All units have well-kept bathrooms with shower-tub combinations. We always enjoy working out here because the fitness facilities are among the best of any hotel in town.

Berliner Strasse 93, D-80805 München. ✆ **800/228-9290** in the U.S., or 089/36-00-20. Fax 089/3600-2200. www.marriott.com. 348 units. 130€–220€ double; from 275€ suite. During selected nonpeak weekends 115€ double. AE, DC, MC, V. Parking 15€. U-bahn: U6 to Nord Friedhof. **Amenities:** Restaurant; bar; pool; health club; sauna; room service; babysitting; laundry/dry cleaning. *In room:* A/C, TV, minibar, hair dryer, safe.

MODERATE

Hotel Leopold ★ *Finds*   The core of this unusual hotel is a Jugendstil villa that was built as a private home in 1924. A modern annex is connected to the original house by a glass-sided passageway, and there's a garden area that belonged to the original house. It's close to an exit road from the Autobahn Nürnberg-Würzburg-Berlin, which gives the place the atmosphere of a suburban motel with plentiful parking. Despite the verdant setting, however, the hotel lies only four subway stops from the Marienplatz (p. 94), and the Englischer Garten (p. 111) is only a few minutes' walk away. Public areas have traditional Bavarian motifs. Rooms in the old section have been modernized to make them equivalent to rooms in the new section, and all have been made as soundproof as possible. All units have well-kept bathrooms with shower units.

Leopoldstrasse 119, D-80804 München-Schwabing. ✆ **089/367061.** Fax 089/3604-3150. 90 units. 128€ double. Rates include breakfast. AE, DC, MC, V. Parking 1.50€ per day uncovered or 2.50€ per day covered. U-bahn: U3 or U4 to Münchner Freiheit. **Amenities:** Restaurant; bar; health club; sauna; room service; massage; laundry/dry cleaning. *In room:* TV, minibar, hair dryer.

INEXPENSIVE

Gästehaus Englischer Garten ★★ *Kids*   This oasis of charm and tranquility, close to the Englischer Garten, is one of our preferred stopovers in Munich. The decor of the small to medium rooms has been called "Bavarian grandmotherly"; furnishings include genuine antiques, old-fashioned but exceedingly comfortable beds, and Oriental rugs. Bathrooms with showers are small and not one of the hotel's stronger features, but their maintenance is first-rate. Fifteen units are across the street in an annex; these are small apartments, each with a bathroom and a tiny kitchenette. Try for room 10, 20, 30, or 90. In fair weather, breakfast is served in a rear garden.

Liebergesellstrasse 8, 80802 München-Schwabing. ℂ **089/3-83-94-10**. Fax 089/38-39-41-33. 25 units, 20 with bathroom. 68€–78€ double without bathroom; 88€–109€ double with bathroom. Breakfast 8.50€ extra. AE, MC, V. Parking 5.10€. U-bahn: Münchner Freiheit. **Amenities:** Breakfast room; lounge; room service; private garden. *In room:* TV, minibar.

3 Olympiapark

EXPENSIVE

Four Points Hotel München Olympiapark ★★ *Kids*   Near the stadium, right at Europe's biggest sports and recreation center, this hotel will appeal to families who want to be near all the major sports action. Its guest rooms are among the most modern and best kept in the city, and sports heroes, both European and American, often stroll casually through the lobby. There's no need to drive into the city center: The U-bahn will whisk you there in minutes.

Helene-Mayer-Ring 12, D-80809 München. ℂ **089/35-75-10**. Fax 089/357-51755. www.arabellasheraton. com. 105 units. 150€–185€ double; from 200€ suite. Rates include breakfast. AE, DC, MC, V. Parking 12€. U-bahn: U2 or U3 to Olympia Centrum. **Amenities:** Restaurant; bar; room service; laundry/dry cleaning. *In room:* TV, minibar (in some), hair dryer.

MODERATE

Holiday Inn Munich City-North   This hotel, with its twin eight-story towers, was built to house visitors to the 1972 Olympics. It's near the Olympic Stadium (p. 112), about 5km (3 miles) north of the historic center. As a member of the deluxe upper tier of the Holiday Inn chain, it offers lots of features to attract guests. The lobby is stylish, and bedrooms are outfitted with big, carefully soundproofed windows and contemporary, uncontroversial furnishings. Rooms on the upper floor, facing south, benefit from views of the city and the faraway Alps; others overlook the suburbs and the urban sprawl surrounding Munich's northern tier. All units have well-kept bathrooms with shower-tub combinations.

Leopoldstrasse 194, D-80804 Munich. ℂ **800/465-4329** in the U.S., or 089/38-17-90. Fax 089/38-17-98-88. www.muenchen.holidayinn-queens.de. 365 units. 195€–395€ double; 295€–400€ suite. During selected weekends, 125€ double with breakfast included. AE, DC, MC, V. Parking 15€. U-bahn: U3 or U6 to Münchner Freiheit. **Amenities:** 2 Restaurants; 2 bars; pool; sauna; room service; babysitting; laundry/ dry cleaning. *In room:* A/C, TV, minibar, hair dryer.

4 Haidhausen

VERY EXPENSIVE

München City Hilton ★   The München City Hilton lies beside the Deutsches Museum and the performing arts center, Gasteig. This low-rise hotel, designed with red brick, shimmering glass, and geometric windows, is reminiscent of a Mondrian painting. Munich's historic center is an invigorating 25-minute walk across the river. Rooms contain modern adaptations of Biedermeier furniture and plush carpeting. The well-stocked bathrooms contain shower-tub combinations and luxurious robes.

Rosenheimerstrasse 15, 81667 München. ℂ **800/455-8667** in the U.S. and Canada, or 089/4-80-40. Fax 089/48-04-48-04. www.hilton.com. 481 units. 116€–395€ double; from 495€ suite. AE, DC, MC, V. Parking 15€. S-bahn: Rosenheimer Platz. **Amenities:** Restaurant; bar; cafe; room service; babysitting; laundry/dry cleaning. *In room:* A/C, TV, minibar, hair dryer.

EXPENSIVE

Preysing ★ *Finds*   If you want a quiet location and don't mind a hotel on the outskirts, consider the Preysing, located across the Isar near the Deutsches Museum. (A short tram ride will bring you into the center of the city.) When you first view the building, a seven-story modern structure, you may feel we've misled you. However, if you've gone this far, venture inside for a pleasant surprise. The hotel's style is agreeable, with dozens of little extras to provide homelike comfort. Fresh flowers are everywhere, the furnishings have been carefully selected, and fresh fruit is supplied daily. The spacious bathrooms have showertub combinations and deluxe toiletries. The staff is also very thoughtful.

Preysingstrasse 1, 81667 München. © **089/45-84-50.** Fax 089/45-84-54-44. 76 units. 160€–212€ double; 250€–390€ suite. Rates include breakfast. AE, DC, MC, V. Parking 12€. Tram: 18. **Amenities:** Breakfast room; lounge; pool; whirlpool; sauna; solarium; room service; babysitting; laundry. *In room:* A/C, TV, minibar, hair dryer.

5 Bogenhausen

EXPENSIVE

Arabella Sheraton Grand Hotel ★★ This is the largest hotel in Munich, set in the northern suburb of Bogenhausen, about seven subway stops from downtown Munich. This is a hotel that's hard to ignore, towering as it does 22 stories above the surrounding northern suburbs. On the top floor is Munich's most dramatic swimming pool: You get not only panoramic views of the city and the Bavarian countryside, but a waterfall as well. Rooms have been recently upgraded, and though still standardized, show a bit of style in their pine furnishing and striped fabrics, and many have balconies opening onto panoramic views. All units have well-maintained bathrooms with shower-tub combinations.

Arabellastrasse 6, D-81925 München. © **089/9-26-40.** Fax 089/92-64-86-99. www.arabellasheraton. com. 653 units. 205€ double; from 600€ suite. AE, DC, MC, V. Parking 15€. U-bahn: U4 to Arabellapark. **Amenities:** Restaurant; bar; pool; health club; sauna; room service; babysitting; laundry/dry cleaning. *In room:* A/C, TV, minibar, hair dryer, safe.

Hotel Palace ★ It's tasteful, it's restrained, it's perfectly mannered, and it's very, very aware of how prestigious a stay here can really be. One of Munich's newest hotels, it's sought out by performers at the nearby theaters and concert halls as a peaceful and nurturing address in Bogenhausen, a stylish residential neighborhood east of Munich's medieval core. Originally built in 1986 as an office building, it was later transformed into a hotel. Public areas are streamlined and contemporary, graced with elaborate hyper-modern balustrades on travertine-sheathed staircases. Rooms are immaculate and upscale, and each comes with a luxurious bathroom with tub-and-shower combination.

Trogerstrasse 21, D-81675 München. © **089/41971-0.** Fax 089/41971-819. www.dpmu.de. 72 units. 260€–320€ double; 340€–1,050€ suite. AE, DC, MC, V. U-bahn: Prinzregentumplatz. **Amenities:** Restaurant; bar; health club; sauna; steam room; room service; laundry. *In room:* A/C, TV, minibar, hair dryer, safe.

6 Untermenzing

MODERATE

Romantik Hotel Insel Mühle ★★ *(Finds)* Until 1985, this 16th-century stone-sided mill in an isolated position beside the Würm (a tributary of the Isar), was left to ruin and decay. The present-day restoration has retained part of the mill's 1506 construction. Although the hotel's reputation is based mainly on its atmospheric restaurant; its guest rooms provide a charming alternative to Munich's many large, modern hotels. The decor and design of each room is different—some have sloping garretlike ceilings—but all have thick carpets, attractive upholstery, and stylish accessories. Each also has a well-kept bathroom with a shower-tub combination.

The real beauty of the place can be seen in the massive beams of the dining room and in the mellow brick vaults of the wine cellar. There's also a plank-covered wharf where parasols shield diners from the midday sun. The cuisine features well-prepared Bavarian and Continental dishes.

Von-Kahr-Strasse 87, D-80999 München-Untermenzing. ✆ **089/8-10-10.** Fax 089/8-12-05-71. 37 units. 116€–128€ double; from 128€ suite. Rates include breakfast. DC, MC, V. Free parking. S-bahn: Pasing, then bus 76. **Amenities:** Dining room; lounge; room service; babysitting; laundry/dry cleaning. *In room:* TV, hair dryer.

7 Obermenzing
MODERATE
Jagdschloss ⭐ In the tree-filled tony suburb of Obermenzing, this century-old *Jagdschloss* (hunting lodge) is a delicious retreat that allows you to enjoy some Bavarian country life while still being close to the attractions of Munich. The country house aura, enhanced by various Bavarian artifacts, recaptures the flavors of the past, although you'll still find all the comforts of today. Much of the stucco and original paneling from the former Jagdschloss remain. You open your bedroom window onto a wooden balcony with boxes of geraniums to welcome another day. It's like a setting for a play called *Springtime in Bavaria.*

Bedrooms are snug and cozy, with comfortable furnishings and midsize bathrooms with tub and shower. You won't have to go into Munich at night, since you can stay right at the hotel, enjoying its summer Biergarten or restaurant. The kitchen serves regional specialties and the waitstaff runs around in *Lederhosen.*

Alte Allee 21, D-81245 München-Obermenzing. ✆ **089/820-820.** Fax 089/8208-2100. www.weber-gastronomie.de. 23 units. 106€ double. Rates include breakfast. MC, V. S-bahn: Pasing. **Amenities:** Restaurant; biergarten; babysitting; laundry/dry cleaning. *In room:* TV, hair dryer, safe.

8 Neuhausen
MODERATE
Mercure München Königin Elisabeth This is a chain hotel that lies 5 minutes by public transportation from the city center, in Neuhausen, south of Olympiapark. If you don't demand traditional styling, it has a lot going for it, especially its amenities that range from a bar as well as a Biergarten to several health club facilities such as a hot tub and a steam room. The bedrooms are newly refurbished, and are medium in size with tiled bathrooms with a tub and shower combination. A hair dryer can be borrowed in the lobby, which also contains a safe for guests. If you don't want to go into the city at night for amusement, you'll find a lively bar on site. It costs extra, but the hotel's breakfast buffet is one of the most generous in the area, almost enough fortification for the entire day.

Leonrodstrasse 79, D-80636 München. ✆ **089/126-860.** Fax 089/1268-6459. www.pannonia-hotels.com. 79 units. 125€ double. Children under 12 stay free in parents' room. AE, DC, MC, V. Parking 9.20€. U-bahn: Eonrodplatz. **Amenities:** Bar; biergarten; gym; sauna; laundry/dry cleaning. *In room:* TV, minibar.

Rotkreuzplatz This is an unheralded little Munich hotel known to some frugal Germans who check in when visiting the capital. Lying only 5 minutes by subway from the heart of Munich, it is easy to reach, opening onto one of the city's landmark squares. An efficient manager and staff operate this little family business, giving you a warm Bavarian welcome. Their bedrooms are completely modernized and comfortable, ranging from small to midsize, each with a tiled bathroom with either shower or bathtub. Breakfast is included in the price of your room, but it's taken at a nearby cafe. Don't expect a lot of special services or amenities. If your needs are not too demanding, you'll get a good bed for the night and much comfort.

Rotkreuzplatz 2, D-80634 München. ℂ **089/139-9080**. Fax 089/166-469. www.hotel-rotkreuzplatz.de/ flash/hr_e.htm. 56 units. 100€–148€ double. Rates include continental breakfast. AE, DC, MC, V. Parking 6€. U-bahn: Rotkreuzplatz. *In room:* TV, hair dryer, safe.

9 Nymphenburg

INEXPENSIVE

Kriemhild *(Kids)*   This is one of the best choices for visitors with kids in tow, as it lies in the suburb of Nymphenburg, one of the most famous attractions of Munich, known for its beautiful gardens and leafy parks. From the front door of this well-run establishment, you and the children can walk over to the entrance to Schloss Nymphenburg (p. 103). For dad, there is also nearby Hirschgarten Park, site of the biggest Biergarten in Europe. The government-rated three-star hotel is run exceptionally well with an accommodating staff. Everything is fresh and immaculately kept, including the shower-only bathrooms. The more spacious rooms contain a corner sofa, which can be converted for use as a three- or four-bed family room. In the morning, there's an elaborate buffet breakfast, and at night you can drink beer or wine in a cozy Bavarian-styled Guntherstube.

Guntherstrasse 16, D-80639 München. ℂ **089/171-1170**. Fax 089/1711-1755. www.kriemhild.de. 18 units. 94€–98€ double, 114€–128€ suite. AE, MC, V. Tram: 16 or 17. S-bahn: Laim. **Amenities:** Breakfast room; bar. *In room:* TV, minibar, hair dryer.

10 Near the Airport

EXPENSIVE

Kempinski Hotel Airport München *(★★)*   When it was built between the runways of Munich's airports in 1993, it was noted as the most architecturally innovative airport hotel in Europe. Partially owned by Lufthansa, it was designed by a Chicago-based architect of German descent, Helmet Jahn, with a four-story shimmering glass and steel exterior and an interior design whose colorful, postmodern accents ward off the monochromatic landscape of the surrounding airport. Despite its proximity to runways, the hotel's guest rooms are soothing and silent, the result of effective soundproofing. Each unit has a well-maintained bathroom with a shower-tub combination. A soaring lobby contains a subtropical garden with palms and has views over one of Europe's busiest airports.

Terminalstrasse 20, D-85356 München. ℂ **800/426-3135** in the U.S., or 089/9-78-20. Fax 089/97-82-26-10. www.kempinski-airport.de. 389 units. 210€–345€ double. AE, DC, MC, V. Parking 7.50€. U-bahn: Airport. Free shuttle to and from the airport. **Amenities:** Restaurant; 2 bars; pool; health club; sauna; Jacuzzi; room service; massage; laundry/dry cleaning. *In room:* A/C, TV, minibar, hair dryer, safe.

MODERATE

Arabella Sheraton Airport *(★)*   Far better than your often bleak standard airport hotel, this three-floor, red-roofed hotel, a 5-minute shuttle bus ride from the airport, is filled with grace notes such as top quality tea or coffee for the in-room beverage makers, deluxe toiletries, voice mail, and so on. A first-class hotel surrounded by greenery, it attracts a lot of international business travelers, plus tourists wishing to be near the airport for a fast getaway the following morning. The architect conceived of the Arabella as a Bavarian country house property. Bedrooms are generous in size and filled with amenities. Because the hotel offers six different types of bedrooms, from rather simple, functional doubles, to elaborate, spacious executive rooms, the Arabella attracts everybody from the frugal spender to the business client on a fat expense account. The staff is most helpful. The hotel lies 35 minutes by transportation (provided by a hotel van) to the center of Munich.

Freisingerstrasse 80, D-85445 Schwaig. (℃) **089/9272-2750**. Fax 089/9272-2800. www.arabellasheraton.de. 168 units. 60€–265€ double, 161€–348€ suite. Children 12 and under stay free in parents' room. AE, DC, MC, V. Free shuttle to airport and city center. **Amenities:** Restaurant; bar; pool; sauna; room service; babysitting; laundry/dry cleaning. *In room:* A/C, TV, dataport, minibar, coffeemaker, hair dryer, safe.

Golden Tulip Hotel Olymp 🛪   This family-run hotel offers a classic coziness and a degree of Bavarian charm. Its rich ambience comes from its use of woods such as cherry and walnut and its handmade carvings and antique paintings. In warm weather, guests sit on the terrace enjoying drinks, retreating in winter to the snug fireplace. Bedrooms are midsize to spacious and are furnished with smart, modern styling, each coming with a tiled, well-maintained private bathroom with a tub and shower combination. Under a wood-beamed ceiling, the restaurant serves a blend of Bavarian specialties and international dishes. The hotel is easily accessible to all major highways such as the A9 (Exit 69) leading into Munich, and is only a few minutes' ride from the international airport.

Wielandstrasse 3, D-85386 München-Eching. (℃) **089/327-100**. Fax 089/32710-112. www.hotel-olymp-munich.de. 99 units. 115€ double, 135€ suite. Rates include breakfast. AE, DC, MC, V. Free parking. Free shuttle to and from the airport. **Amenities:** 3 restaurants; bar; pool; sauna; room service; laundry/dry cleaning. *In room:* A/C, TV, minibar, hair dryer, safe.

5

Where to Dine

Munich is one of the very few European cities that has more than one Michelin-rated "three-star" restaurant, and some of its sophisticated eating places are among the finest anywhere. This is the place to practice *Edelfress-welle* (high-class gluttony) as there are many local specialties in Munich as well as first-class international cuisines. The classic local dish, traditionally consumed before noon, is *Weisswurst,* herb-flavored white-veal sausages blanched in water.

It is said that Münchners consume more beer than people in any other German city. Bernd Boehle once wrote: "If a man really belongs to Munich he drinks beer at all times of the day, at breakfast, at midday, at teatime, and in the evening, of course, he just never stops." The place where every first-time visitor heads for at least one eating and drinking fest is the Hofbräuhaus am Platzl. It's described on. p. 149.

1 Restaurants by Cuisine

AMERICAN
  Hard Rock Cafe
    (Central Munich, $$, p. 73)

ASIAN
  Hunsinger's Pacific ⊛
    (Central Munich, $$, p. 74)

AUSTRIAN
  Nymphenburger Hof
    (Nymphenburg, $$, p. 88)

BAVARIAN
  Am Marstall ⊛⊛ (Central
    Munich, $$$, p. 70)
  Asam Schlössel (Near the Isar,
    $$, p. 84)
  Bamberger Haus (Schwabing,
    $, p. 91)
  Biergarten Chinesischer Turm
    (Central Munich, $, p. 91)
  Café Am Beethovenplatz
    (Central Munich, $, p. 76)
  Donisl (Central Munich,
    $, p. 78)
  Erstes Münchner Kartoffelhaus
    (Central Munich, $, p. 78)

Gaststätte zum Flaucher
    (Central Munich, $, p. 91)
  Grüne Gans (Central Munich,
    $$, p. 73)
  Hackerhaus (Central Munich,
    $, p. 79)
  Halali (Central Munich,
    $$, p. 73)
  Hirschgarten (Nymphenburg,
    $, p. 91)
  Hundskugel (Central Munich,
    $, p. 79)
  Nürnberger Bratwurst Glöckl
    Am Dom ⊛⊛ (Central Munich,
    $, p. 80)
  Palais Keller ⊛⊛ (Central Munich,
    $, p. 80)
  Pfistermühle (Central Munich,
    $$, p. 74)
  Ratskeller München
    (Central Munich, $$, p. 75)
  Spatenhaus (Central Munich,
    $$, p. 75)
  Spöckmeier (Central Munich,
    $, p. 81)

Key to Abbreviations: $$$$ = Very Expensive $$$ = Expensive $$ = Moderate $ = Inexpensive

Straubinger Hof (Central Munich,
$, p. 81)
Tattenbach (Central Munich,
$, p. 82)
Weichandhof (Obermenzing,
$, p. 89)
Weinbauer (Schwabing, $, p. 87)
Weinhaus Neuner
(Central Munich, $$, p. 76)
Weisses Bräuhaus
(Central Munich, $, p. 82)
Zum Alten Markt
(Central Munich, $$, p. 76)
Zum Aumeister (Freimann,
$, p. 92)
Zum Dürnbräu
(Central Munich, $, p. 83)
Zum Hofer (Central Munich,
$, p. 83)

BEER GARDENS

Bamberger Haus (Schwabing,
$, p. 91)
Biergarten Chinesischer Turm
(Central Munich, $, p. 91)
Gaststätte zum Flaucher
(Central Munich, $, p. 91)
Hirschgarten (Nymphenburg,
$, p. 91)
Zum Aumeister (Freimann,
$, p. 92)

CAFES

Café Glockenspiel
(Central Munich, $, p. 89)
Café Luitpold (Central Munich,
$, p. 89)
Guglhopf (Central Munich,
$, p. 90)
Ruffini (Neuhausen, $, p. 90)
Schlosscafé im Palmenhaus
(Nymphenburg, $, p. 90)

CHINESE

Grüne Gans (Central Munich,
$$, p. 73)

CONTINENTAL

Alois Dallmayr ★★
(Central Munich, $$, p. 71)
Bar-Restaurant Morizz
(Central Munich, $$, p. 72)

Gästhaus Glockenbach ★★★
(Südbahnhof, $$$$, p. 83)
Hunsinger's Pacific ★
(Central Munich, $$, p. 74)
Mark's Restaurant ★
(Central Munich, $$$, p. 71)
Restaurant Lenbach ★
(Central Munich, $$, p. 75)
Times Square Online Bistro
(Central Munich, $, p. 82)

FRENCH

Am Marstall ★★
(Central Munich, $$$, p. 70)
Bistro Cézanne ★ (Schwabing,
$$, p. 85)
Bistro Terrine ★★
(Schwabing, $$$, p. 85)
Graffunder ★★ (Central Munich,
$, p. 79)
Grünwalder Einkehr ★★
(Grünwald, $$, p. 88)
Käfer am Hofgarten
(Central Munich, $, p. 79)
Tantris ★★★ (Schwabing,
$$$$, p. 84)

GERMAN

Andechser am Dom
(Central Munich, $, p. 76)
Bogenhauser Hof
(Bogenhausen/Prielhof,
$$, p. 87)
Deutsche Eiche (Central Munich,
$, p. 77)
Käfer-Schänke
(Bogenhausen/Prielhof,
$$, p. 87)
Palais Keller ★★ (Central Munich,
$, p. 80)
Pfalzer Weinprobierstube ★
(Central Munich, $, p. 80)
Zum Burgerhaus (Central Munich,
$, p. 82)

INTERNATIONAL

Asam Schlössel (Near the Isar,
$$, p. 84)
Bamberger Haus (Schwabing,
$, p. 91)
Bar-Restaurant Morizz
(Central Munich, $$, p. 72)

Boettner's ★★★ (Central Munich, $$$$, p. 67)

Bogenhauser Hof (Bogenhausen/Prielhof, $$, p. 87)

Café Am Beethovenplatz (Central Munich, $, p. 76)

Café Dukatz in the Literaturhaus ★ (Central Munich, $, p. 77)

Der Tisch ★★ (Central Munich, $$, p. 72)

Donisl (Central Munich, $, p. 78)

Garden Restaurant ★ (Central Munich, $$$$, p. 67)

Grüne Gans (Central Munich, $$, p. 73)

Hunsinger's Pacific ★ (Central Munich, $$, p. 74)

Käfer-Schänke (Bogenhausen/Prielhof, $$, p. 87)

Kay's Bistro ★★ (Central Munich, $$$, p. 70)

Mövenpick Restaurant ★ (Central Munich, $$, p. 74)

Park-Café Kitchen (Central Munich, $, p. 80)

Restaurant Königshof ★ (Central Munich, $$$$, p. 67)

Restaurant Vier Jahreszeiten ★ (Central Munich, $$$$, p. 70)

Spatenhaus (Central Munich, $$, p. 75)

Tantris ★★★ (Schwabing, $$$$, p. 84)

Zum Alten Markt (Central Munich, $$, p. 76)

ITALIAN

Alba ★ (Bogenhausen/Prielhof, $$, p. 87)

Buon Gusto (Talamonti) ★ (Central Munich, $$, p. 72)

Casale (Denning, $$$, p. 88)

Der Katzlmacher ★ (Schwabing, $$, p. 85)

Geisel's Vinothek (Central Munich, $, p. 78)

Graffunder ★★ (Central Munich, $, p. 79)

Käfer am Hofgarten (Central Munich, $, p. 79)

La Galleria ★ (Central Munich, $$$, p. 71)

La Mucca (Schwabing, $$, p. 86)

Locanda Picolit ★ (Schwabing, $$, p. 86)

Spago (Schwabing, $$, p. 86)

JAPANESE

Sushi & Soul (Central Munich, $, p. 82)

JEWISH

Cohen's (Central Munich, $, p. 77)

MEDITERRANEAN

Garden Restaurant ★ (Central Munich, $$$$, p. 67)

Restaurant Lenbach ★ (Central Munich, $$, p. 75)

MEXICAN

Sausalito's (Schwabing, $, p. 86)

PALATINATE

Pfalzer Weinprobierstube ★ (Central Munich, $, p. 80)

RHENISH

Weisses Bräuhaus (Central Munich, $, p. 82)

SEAFOOD

Austernkeller ★ (Central Munich, $$$, p. 70)

SWISS

Mövenpick Restaurant ★ (Central Munich, $$, p. 74)

THAI

Bar-Restaurant Morizz (Central Munich, $$, p. 72)

TUSCAN

Buon Gusto (Talamonti) ★ (Central Munich, $$, p. 72)

VEGETARIAN

Café Am Beethovenplatz (Central Munich, $, p. 76)

Prinz Myshkin (Central Munich, $, p. 81)

2 Central Munich

VERY EXPENSIVE

Boettner's ✹✹✹ INTERNATIONAL   Long featured in this guide, Boettner's—in business since 1901 when it first opened as a tea and oyster shop—thrives at a new location where it has kept its old devotees but also gained new and younger fans. The restaurant today is housed in Orlandohaus, a Renaissance structure in the very heart of Munich. Culinary fans from yesterday will recognize its wood-paneled interior, which was dismantled and moved to the new site. If anything, the cookery seems better than ever—at least it's lighter and more refined. Try the lobster stew in a cream sauce and almost any dish with white truffles. Pike balls appear delectably in a Chablis herb sauce, and succulent lamb or venison also appears enticingly in a woodsy morel sauce. Desserts are as sumptuous as ever. The French influence is very evident, as are many traditional Bavarian recipes.

Pfisterstrasse 9. © **089/22-12-10.** Reservations recommended. Main courses 25€–32€. AE, DC, MC, V. Mon–Sat 11:30am–2:30pm and 6–9:30pm. U-bahn: Marienplatz.

Garden Restaurant ✹ INTERNATIONAL/MEDITERRANEAN   This showcase restaurant within one of the showcase hotels of Munich looks like a miniature pastel-colored palace. It's set in a solemnly hushed room filled with blooming plants off the otherwise bustling hotel lobby. Upscale food is served to a cosmopolitan crowd. Menu items are about as cultivated and esoteric as you can find in Munich. Examples include thin noodles with strips of quail and mushroom sauce; a "land and sea" salad—a bouquet of greens accented with lobster meat and calves' liver; a soup of exotic mushrooms in puff pastry; and filet of beef stuffed with goose liver and fresh mushrooms. Despite the elaborate menu, one of the most sought-after dishes is filet of Dover sole in lemon-butter sauce, served simply but flavorfully with fresh spinach and boiled potatoes. Desserts are appropriately lavish, and wine choices are among the most varied in Munich.

In the Bayerischer Hof Hotel, Promenadeplatz 2–6. © **089/21200.** Reservations recommended. Main courses 19€–30€; fixed-price lunch 30€; fixed-price dinner 50€. AE, DC, MC, V. Daily noon–3pm and 6–11:30pm. Tram: 19.

Restaurant Königshof ✹ INTERNATIONAL   This still remains one of the grand hotel dining rooms of Munich. The Geisel family has made major renovations to the dining room, with its oyster-white panels of oak, polished bronze chandeliers, silver candelabra, and porcelain. The waiters are polite and skilled. The chefs here are highly inventive and their food (always made with extremely fresh ingredients) reflects this passion. If available, try the foie gras with sauternes, loin of lamb with fine herbs, curried breast of duck, lobster with vanilla butter, or sea bass supreme.

In the Hotel Königshof, Karlsplatz 25 (Am Stachus). © **089/55-13-60.** Reservations required. Main courses 22€–35€; fixed-price menu 75€–97€. AE, DC, MC, V. Daily noon–2:30pm and 6:30–10pm. U-bahn/S-bahn: Karlsplatz/Stachus. Tram: 19.

⟮*Tips* Tipping

If a restaurant bill says *Bedienung*, that means a service charge has already been added.

Central Munich Dining

Alba **42**
Alois Dallmayr **54**
Am Marstall **50**
Andechser am Dom **32**
Asam Schlössl **71**
Austernkeller **61**
Bamberger Haus **21**
Bar-Restaurant
  Morizz **70**
Biergarten
  Chinesischer Turm **46**
Bistro Cézanne **42**
Bistro Terrine **41**
Boettner's **53**
Bogenhauser Hof **47**
Bon Gusto
  (Talamonti) **60**
Café Am
  Beethovenplatz **6**
Café Dukatz in the
  Literaturhaus **34**
Café Glockenspiel **27**
Café Luitpold **37**
Casale **47**
Cohen's **40**
Der Katzlmacher **44**
Der Tisch **12**
Deutsche Eiche **68**
Donisl **29**
Erstes Münchner
  Kartoffelhaus **62**
Garden Restaurant **17**
Gasthaus
  Glockenbach **2**
Gaststätte zum
  Flaucher **71**
Geisel's Vinothek **7**
Graffunder **28**
Grüne Gans **65**
Grünwalder Einkehr **1**
Guglhupf **30**
Hackerhaus **24**
Halali **39**
Hirschgarten **11**
Hundskugel **23**
Hunsiger's Pacific **15**
Käfer's am
  Hofgarten **36**
Käfer-Schanke **48**
Kay's Bistro **67**
La Galleria **57**
La Mucca **13**
Lenbach **18**
Locanda Picolit **45**
Mark's Restaurant **59**
Mövepick Restaurant **19**
Nürenberger Bratwurst
  Glockl am Dom **33**
Nymphenburger Hof **4**

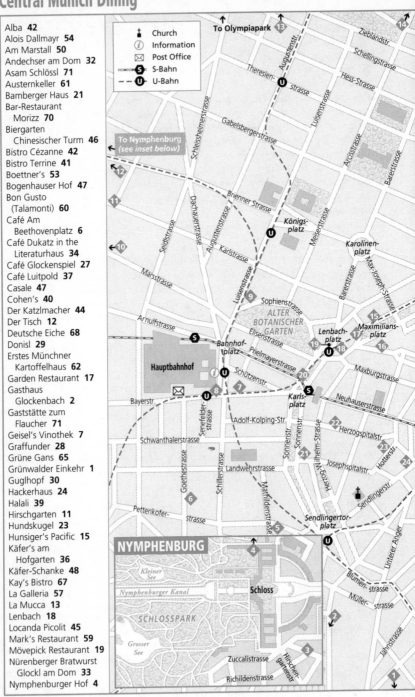

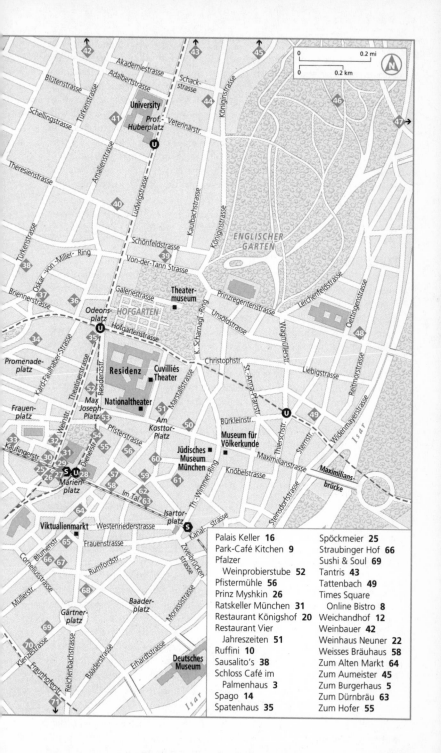

Palais Keller **16**	Spöckmeier **25**
Park-Café Kitchen **9**	Straubinger Hof **66**
Pfalzer	Sushi & Soul **69**
Weinprobierstube **52**	Tantris **43**
Pfistermühle **56**	Tattenbach **49**
Prinz Myshkin **26**	Times Square
Ratskeller München **31**	Online Bistro **8**
Restaurant Königshof **20**	Weichandhof **12**
Restaurant Vier	Weinbauer **42**
Jahreszeiten **51**	Weinhaus Neuner **22**
Ruffini **10**	Weisses Bräuhaus **58**
Sausalito's **38**	Zum Alten Markt **64**
Schloss Café im	Zum Aumeister **45**
Palmenhaus **3**	Zum Burgerhaus **5**
Spago **14**	Zum Dürnbräu **63**
Spatenhaus **35**	Zum Hofer **55**

Restaurant Vier Jahreszeiten ✦ INTERNATIONAL Restaurant Vier Jahreszeiten is in a quiet and elegant location within walking distance of the opera house. The atmosphere is dignified and refined, the service extremely competent, and the food prepared along classic French lines with many imaginative variations, including Asian influences. The menu changes every 4 to 6 weeks, but appetizers are likely to include mushroom soufflé served with artichoke-cream sauce, freshly made vegetable soup flavored with pesto, or turbot encased in basil-flavored crust. For a main course, try breast of Bresse chicken with scampi, flavored with a ginger sauce; or roast medallions of venison with cherry-pepper sauce. Another specialty is blanquette of veal and lobster. Desserts include strawberries Walterspiel or, for two, tangerine soufflé served with foamy vanilla sauce.

In the Kempinski Hotel Vier Jahreszeiten München, Maximilianstrasse 17. ℭ **089/2-12-50.** Reservations required. Main courses 22€–40€; 3-course fixed-price menu 45€. AE, DC, MC, V. Daily noon–1:30am. Tram: 19.

EXPENSIVE

Am Marstall ✦✦ BAVARIAN/FRENCH At first, the two cuisines, a combined Gallic/German wedding, seem like a mismatch. But after more and more of our Munich friends continually raved about this place, we made a visit and are now convinced that it's a marriage made in culinary heaven. The fashion and business worlds of Munich often converge here at night to enjoy the chef's specialties, which include goose liver in puff pastry or a simply perfect red bass with a bouillabaisse sauce and an accompaniment of tortellini with artichokes. The duck breast in a honey-thyme sauce is reason enough for a visit. The pre-salé lamb is bred and fattened in the windswept meadows of Brittany, bordering the sea. In autumn, many Munich gourmets come here to partake of the venison captured in the forests of Bavaria. Am Marstall isn't cheap, nor is it terribly expensive. Everything is prepared with loving care. Lunchtime fills up with ritzy, often demanding shoppers who rarely leave this bistro unsatisfied. As one diner told us, "If Munich didn't have a place like this, we'd have to invent it."

Maximilianstrasse 16. ℭ **089/2916-5511.** Reservations required. Jacket and tie for men. Main courses 13€–29€. AE, MC, V. Tues–Sat noon–2pm and 6–10pm. U-bahn: Marienplatz.

Austernkeller ✦ SEAFOOD This "oyster cellar" is a delight to both visitors and locals. You get the largest selection of oysters in town here, and many gourmands make an entire meal just of Austernkeller's raw oysters. Others prefer them elaborately prepared—for example, oysters Rockefeller. A delectable dish to start is the shellfish platter with fresh oysters, mussels, clams, scampi, and sea snails. Or you might begin with a richly stocked fish soup or cold hors d'oeuvres. French meat specialties are offered, but most guests prefer the fish dishes—no other chef in Munich can make a lobster thermidor as good as that served here.

The restaurant, under a vaulted ceiling, has a refined atmosphere, and it makes successful attempts at genuine elegance, but because of a collection of everything from plastic lobsters to old porcelain, the decor comes off as a bit kitsch. No matter, the service is attentive, and you're sure to enjoy your meal.

Stollbergstrasse 11. ℭ **089/29-87-87.** Reservations required. Main courses 18.50€–30€. AE, DC, MC, V. Daily 5pm–1am. Closed Dec 23–26. U-bahn: Isartorplatz.

Kay's Bistro ✦✦ INTERNATIONAL It's fun, media-hip, and schmaltzy, with a clientele that's either blatantly gay or very, very tolerant. Every month or so, the decor is redefined, based on glittering themes that have included

Carnival in Rio, Grace and the Grand Prix of Monaco, Chinatown, "Hooray for Hollywood," and—when we happened to drop in—New York City, when accessories included shopping bags from Bloomingdale's and plastic replicas of the Statue of Liberty. Even the background music is carefully calibrated to go with the theme of the moment. The place is fun, campy, and favored by celebrities who have included disco diva Gloria Gaynor. The cuisine changes frequently, but is light, urbane, flavorful, and sometimes named after pop icons, such as Indian-style chicken breast "Diana Vreeland." Drinks include, among others, Louisiana milk punch and an almost psychedelic Velvet Underground.

Utzschneiderstrasse 1. © 089/2-60-35-84. Reservations required. Main courses 17.50€–20€. AE, MC, V. Daily 7pm–3am. U-bahn/S-bahn: Marienplatz.

La Galleria ★ ITALIAN   This is one of the most appealing of the several Italian restaurants in Munich's center and the one that takes the greatest risks with experimental Italian cuisine. It's a few blocks east of the Marienplatz, with a modern and brightly colored setting and modern paintings. Service is gracious, and the menu changes with the availability of ingredients and the inspiration of the chefs. Examples include poached sea wolf with fresh vegetables in fennel sauce; an aromatic guinea fowl scented with lavender; filet of sole with a velvety eggplant mousse; homemade spaghetti with white Italian truffles; herb-flavored risotto with chunks of lobster and braised radicchio (the best such dish we've ever had in Munich); and roasted soft-shell crabs with a light onion sauce. Dessert might include a smooth zabaglione served with pears marinated in port wine.

Lederestrasse 2, at Sparkassenstrasse. © 089/29-79-95. Reservations recommended. Main courses 15€–22€; fixed-price dinner 45€–50€. AE, DC, MC, V. Mon–Sat noon–3pm and 6–11:30pm. Closed Aug 10–30. U-bahn/S-bahn: Marienplatz.

Mark's Restaurant ★ CONTINENTAL   This restaurant, in the prestigious Mandarin Oriental, is appropriately elegant with an impeccably trained staff. If you come here, don't ask to meet a chef named Mark (the place was named after the owner's son), and expect different venues at lunch and dinner. Lunch is served in a small, cozy enclave off the lobby, Mark's Corner, and is usually limited to a fixed-price menu favored by businesspeople. Dinners are swankier and more elaborate; they're served one floor above street level in a formal dining room that overlooks a monumental staircase and the lobby below. On Monday night only, the formal dining room is closed, and dinner is in the relatively informal lobby level setting of Mark's Corner.

Menu items change according to the season and the inspiration of the chef. Many dishes are somewhat experimental but still succeed beautifully. Examples include kohlrabi soup with strips of ham, guinea fowl in mustard sauce with herbs, wild salmon with red and green lentils, halibut with fennel sauce, a ragout of fish in puff pastry with balsamic vinegar and herbs, and breast of free-range chicken with curried vinaigrette (sometimes served as a salad).

In the Mandarin Oriental, Neuturmstrasse 1. © 089/290980. Reservations recommended. Fixed-price lunch in Mark's Corner 35€; fixed-price dinner in Mark's Restaurant 60€; main courses in Mark's Restaurant 21€–35€. AE, DC, MC, V. Daily noon–2pm and 6:30–11pm. U-bahn/S-bahn: Marienplatz.

MODERATE

Alois Dallmayr ★★ CONTINENTAL   Alois Dallmayr, which traces its history back to 1700, is the most famous delicatessen in Germany. After looking at its tempting array of delicacies from around the globe, you'll think you're lost in a millionaire's supermarket—and in fact, Dallmayr has been a purveyor to many royal courts. Here, near the Rathaus, you'll find Munich's most elegant consumers, looking for that "tinned treasure," perhaps Scottish salmon, foie gras, English biscuits, wines and spirits, as well as out-of-season fresh produce.

The upstairs dining room serves a subtle German version of Continental cuisine, owing a heavy debt to France. The food array is dazzling, ranging from the best herring and sausages we've ever tasted to such rare treats as perfectly vine-ripened tomatoes flown in from Morocco and papayas from Brazil. The famous French poulet de Bresse (this Bresse chicken is identified throughout Europe as the most flavorful and tender chicken anywhere), beloved of gourmets, is also shipped in. The smoked fish is a taste sensation, and the soups are superbly flavored, especially the one made with shrimp. If you're dining alone, you might prefer to sit at the counter. This bustling restaurant is crowded at lunchtime.

Dienerstrasse 14–15. ℂ **089/2-13-51-00.** Reservations required. Main courses 13€–35€; fixed-price menus 30€ for 3 courses, 40€ for 4 courses. AE, DC, MC, V. Mon–Wed 9:30am–7pm, Thurs–Fri 9:30am–8pm, Sat 9am–4pm. Tram: 19.

Bar-Restaurant Morizz   CONTINENTAL/INTERNATIONAL/THAI

This is the hippest gay restaurant in Munich. As estimated by the staff, it has a 70% gay male clientele; lesbian women and gay-friendly straights make up the rest of the clientele. Part of the space is devoted to a sprawling, attractive bar with a private clublike atmosphere where red leather chairs, mirrors, and an impeccably trained staff emulate a Paris hotel bar of the 1920s. You can enjoy at least 40 single-malt whiskies, a dozen single-barrel bourbons, and a wide array of unusual wines. No one will mind if you decide to eat at the bar, or never move from its premises, but the adjacent dining room offers an appealing combination of international and Continental food, prepared by a central-European staff whose interpretation of Thai cuisine is especially enjoyable. Examples include a *Vorspeisen-teller* (a plate of appetizers, similar to the Italian antipasti) of mixed Thai specialties, and some fans find the lemongrass soup almost addictive. Continental cuisine includes veal preparations, fresh fish, pastas, and salads (a platter-size version is garnished with strips of confit of duckling).

Klenzestrasse 43. ℂ **089/2-01-67-76.** Reservations recommended. Main courses 8€–18€. MC. Sun–Thurs 7pm–2am, Fri–Sat 7pm–3am. U-bahn: Fraunhoferstrasse.

Buon Gusto (Talamonti) ★ ITALIAN/TUSCAN   Devotees claim that this

is the finest Italian restaurant in Munich. Its interior features two dining areas: a simple, rustic-looking bistro overlooking an open kitchen and a more formal dining room. Menu items and prices are identical in both areas. Owned and managed by an extended family, the Talamontis, whose members are likely not to speak English, the site emphasizes fresh ingredients, strong and savory flavors, and food items inspired by the Italian provinces of the Marches and Tuscany. Delectable examples include ravioli stuffed with mushrooms and herbs, roasted lamb with potatoes, lots of different forms of scallopini, and fresh fish served simply, with oil or butter and lemon. The various risottos are especially flavorful. During Oktoberfest and trade fairs, the place is mobbed.

Hochbrückenstrasse 3. ℂ **089/29-63-83.** Reservations recommended. Main courses 21€–25€. AE, MC V. Mon–Sat 11am–midnight. U-bahn or S-bahn: Marienplatz.

Der Tisch ★★ INTERNATIONAL   Its minimalist name, "the table," doesn't

suggest the allure of this bistro, one of the best and most fashionable in Munich. You can stop in for a pre-dinner beer at the Münchner Löwenbräu brewery and beer hall across the street before heading to this 36-seat dining room. Presented on a clipboard, the daily-changing menu is eclectic and well chosen, always created from market-fresh ingredients. The cookery is resolutely contemporary—start with the eggplant mousse with a perfectly balanced tomato vinaigrette or something simpler: tuna flavored with tomato sauce and accompanied by olives and capers. The main courses are always imaginative and satisfying, especially the pike-perch over cabbage, sprinkled with a beet-flavored pink sauce. In autumn, opt for venison in a red wine sauce.

Maxvorstadt, Nymphenburger Strasse 1. ✆ 089/557-154. Reservations required. Main courses 10€–17€. AE, DC, MC, V. Mon–Fri 11:30am–3pm and 6pm–midnight. U-bahn: Stiglmeier Platz.

Grüne Gans BAVARIAN/CHINESE/INTERNATIONAL   If you're visiting Viktualienmarkt (p. 139)—and we suggest that you do—this is a small and intimate dining room that's a good reliable choice for food in the area. After looking at all the delectable foodstuffs that the people of Munich purchase, you will have whetted your appetite. "The Green Goose" stands ready to tempt you with a range of dishes, most of which are Bavarian, although the chefs dip less successfully into both an international cuisine, with a selection of some Chinese dishes tossed in for fun. The Bavarian pork dishes are the most recommendable, although you might want to begin with one of the fresh salads purchased directly from the market nearby.

The soups are excellent, especially the cream of chervil soup we recently sampled. Many good sausages are offered along with some beef specialties. They also do excellent calf's kidneys in a velvety smooth sauce made with freshly chopped tarragon. Many people in show business patronize this bustling little tavern, as the pictures on the walls testify.

Am Einglass 4. ✆ 089/266-228. Reservations recommended. Main courses 14€–20€. No credit cards. Mon–Sat 5pm–1am. U-bahn: Marienplatz.

Halali BAVARIAN   Little has changed here since the place was first decorated around 1900, and very few of the staff or its clients would ever want change. The setting is baronial, devoted to a Teutonic version of the Hunt, as its name (which translates into something akin to "Tally-Ho") suggests. Amid high ceilings, solid archways, and a collection of stags' horns, you can order flavorful traditional dishes, including the specialties of the house, terrine of venison and *Blutwurst* (blood sausage). These might be followed with filet of venison in wine sauce and succulent versions of grilled Bavarian duck, guinea fowl, or pheasant served in either Beaujolais or cranberry sauce, depending on the whim of the chef. Also recommended are ravioli, stuffed with goose meat and mushrooms or with a mixture of ricotta and Fontina cheese; fried salmon with champagne sauce; and gratin of turbot served with mushrooms and white asparagus. A traditional, popular dessert is a warm apple tart with vanilla sauce. Everything is prepared with a definite style and flair. You get very good value here.

Schönfeldstrasse 22. ✆ 089/28-59-09. Reservations recommended. Main courses 12€–20€. Fixed-price lunch 21.50€; fixed-price dinner 46€. AE, MC, V. Sun–Fri noon–2pm, Sat 6–10pm. U-bahn: Odeonsplatz.

Hard Rock Cafe *Kids* AMERICAN   This international chain member packs them in for its bar grub. Like all Hard Rocks around the world, it's filled with memorabilia, with artifacts or representations of everybody from Eric Clapton to Madonna. If you've ever dined at a Hard Rock, expect the same here, the usual array of juicy burgers, fajitas, and steaks served with tasty sides in giant portions. Their homemade-style meatloaf will make you think you're back in Kansas again, though their pasta bolognese could use a lot of improvement. You come here for the fun, the diversion, and the amusement more than the food, however.

Platz 1. ℂ **089/242-9490.** Reservations not required. Main courses 7.50€–15€. AE, MC, V. Sun–Thurs noon–1am; Fri–Sat noon–2am. S-bahn: Marienplatz.

Hunsinger's Pacific ★ *Value* ASIAN/CONTINENTAL/INTERNATIONAL
This restaurant is the creative statement of one of the city's most innovative young chefs, Werner Hunsinger. Despite the name, don't expect the menu to be devoted exclusively to Pacific Rim cuisine. Fish is the premier item here—often flown in from Pacific waters just hours after it's caught. Preparation is based on classic French-inspired methods, but many of the innovative flavors come from Malaysia (coconut milk), Japan (wasabi), Thailand (lemongrass), and India (curry). You could begin with a tuna carpaccio with sliced plum, fresh ginger, and lime. Main courses include a succulent version of bouillabaisse with aioli, which you might follow with cold melon soup garnished with a dollop of tarragon-flavored granita. Fried monkfish in the Malaysian style and turbot in chile and ginger sauce are evocative of Hawaii. One of the best things about this place is that it has relatively low prices for food that is superior to some of its more expensive competitors.

Maximiliansplatz 5 (entrance is on the Max-Joseph-Strasse). ℂ **089/5502-9741.** Main courses 21€–26€; fixed-price 2-course lunch 15€. AE, MC, V. Mon–Sat noon–2:30pm; daily 6–10:30pm. U-bahn/S-bahn: Karlsplatz/Stachus.

Mövenpick Restaurant ★ *Kids* INTERNATIONAL/SWISS   This Jugendstil
building (Künstlerhaus) was originally constructed in 1898 as a publicly subsidized community of artists. When Munich's Olympic Games came up, the site was transformed into a network of atmospheric dining rooms, each with a different decorative theme, but similar menus. In the Venezia on the ground floor, turn-of-the-20th-century murals have been refurbished. Other rooms have names like Rosenzimmer, the Pub, the garden-style Pastorale (upstairs), and Longhorn Corner, inspired by the plains of Texas. Service and cuisine are more formal upstairs than on the ground floor, where no one will mind if you ask just for coffee, beer, or a dish of ice cream. Regardless of where you sit, one especially fine choice is Zurich-style veal strips in cream sauce, served with *rösti* (hashed brown) potatoes. Vegetarians might opt for a savory platter of Steinpilze mushrooms served in cream sauce and accompanied by Bavarian dumplings.

Im Künstlerhaus, Lenbachplatz 8. ℂ **089/5-45-94-90.** Main courses in upstairs dining room 12€–25€; main courses in street-level dining room 9€–18€. AE, DC, MC, V. Daily 8:30am–midnight. U-bahn: U4 or U5 to Stachus.

Pfistermühle BAVARIAN   The country comes right into the heart of
Munich at this authentic and old-fashioned place, a series of charmingly decorated dining rooms in a converted old mill. A warm welcome and a refreshing cuisine await you here. Many of the dishes would be familiar to your Bavarian grandmother, and portions are generous and most satisfying. Come here for some of the most perfectly prepared roasts in the city, always served with a selection of fresh vegetables. Instead of these meat courses, you can also opt for a fine array of fresh fish from the lakes and rivers of Bavaria, especially the delectable salmon-trout or brown trout. Most fish dishes come with chive-flecked sour cream and a potato pancake. The fish is also simply prepared, such as pike-perch sautéed in butter. Finish with a pyramid of vanilla custard served with a fresh berry sauce.

In the Platz Hotel, Pfistermühle 4. ℂ **089/2370-3865.** Reservations recommended. Main courses 15€–22€; fixed-price menus 30€–35€. AE, DC, MC, V. Mon–Sat noon–2pm and 6–10pm. U-bahn: Marienplatz.

Ratskeller München BAVARIAN   Throughout Germany, you'll find Ratskellers, traditional cellar restaurants in Rathaus (city hall) basements, serving good inexpensive food and wine. Munich's Ratskeller, one of the best, is typical, with lots of dark wood and carved chairs. The most interesting tables, often staked out by in-the-know locals, are the semiprivate dining nooks in the rear, under the vaulted painted ceilings. Bavarian music adds to the ambience. The menu, generally a showcase of regional fare, includes some international dishes, many of them vegetarian, which is unusual for a Ratskeller. A freshly made soup-of-the-day is featured, and you can help yourself from the salad bar. Some of the dishes are a little heavy and too porky—best left for your overweight Bavarian uncle—but you can find lighter fare too, since, recently, the chef added an array of grilled food that's lighter than the usual heavy fare offered in many German Ratskellers.

Im Altes Rathaus, Marienplatz 8. © **089/2-19-98-90**. Reservations required. Main courses 7.50€–18€. AE, MC, V. Daily 10am–midnight. U-bahn/S-bahn: Marienplatz.

Restaurant Lenbach ★ CONTINENTAL/MEDITERRANEAN   An interesting choice occupies the grandiose premises of a 19th-century palace (the Bernheimerpalais am Lenbachplatz) whose monumental public rooms became a stylish emporium of food, wine, sensuality, and conviviality in 1997, an atmosphere evocative of Berlin.

The elaborate decoration revolves around the traditional moralist theme of the Seven Deadly Sins, with a decidedly stylish and highly permissive twist. Adultery is represented by a provocative large-scale pre-Raphaelite–style painting behind the bar. The theme in the drinking lounge is Sloth, and in a stridently red toilet (accessorized with jailhouse bars and manacles), it's Wrath. The view into the kitchen is, of course, Gluttony, and Vanity is represented by a catwalk, illuminated by tri-colored strobe lights, where you can promenade, fashion-model style, high above other diners. More "sins" await your own discovery.

Food sometimes seems less important here than visual stimuli, but the menu is likely to include a "seven sins" platter that contains foie gras, lobster, carpaccio of beef, and mozzarella tarts; a Lenbach salad with prawns, chicory, and olive-enriched bruschetta; goose liver terrine; lamb loin "Lenbach style," served with a gratin of potatoes and zucchini; salmon-trout *en papillote;* lamb cutlets with tarragon and a cassoulet of morels; and heaping platters of fresh shellfish.

Ottostrasse 6. © **089/5-49-13-00**. Reservations recommended for dinner. In restaurant, main courses 14€–26€; in cafe-bistro, main courses 11€–17€. Set lunch 13.50€. AE, DC, MC, V. Mon–Fri 11:30am–1am, Sat 11am–3am. S-bahn: Karlsplatz.

Spatenhaus BAVARIAN/INTERNATIONAL   At least once during your stay in Munich, you'll want to dine in one of its fabled beer restaurants such as this one. The wide windows of this well-known beer restaurant overlook the opera house on Max-Joseph-Platz. This is an excellent choice if you're attending a performance. Of course, to be loyal, you should accompany your meal with the restaurant's own beer, Spaten-Franziskaner-Bier. You can sit in an intimate, semiprivate dining nook or at a big table. The Spatenhaus has old traditions; it offers typical, but extremely well-prepared Bavarian food, and is known for generous portions and reasonable prices. If you want to know what the fabled Bavarian gluttony is all about, order the "Bavarian plate," which is loaded with pork, sausages, and other meats. (After eating it, you'll have to go to a spa.)

Residenzstrasse 12. *℃* **089/2-90-70-60.** Reservations recommended. Main courses 13€–25€. AE, MC, V. Daily noon–3pm and 5pm–midnight for food (daily 9:30am–2:30am for beer). U-bahn: U3, U4, or U6 to Odeonsplatz or Marienplatz.

Weinhaus Neuner BAVARIAN This is an *Ältestes Weinhaus Münchens*, one of the city's landmark taverns. It dates from the late 15th century and is the only building in Munich that has its original Tirolean vaults. The place brims with warmth and charm. Once young priests were educated here, but after Napoléon brought secularization, it became a wine tavern and a meeting place for artists, writers, and composers, including Richard Wagner. Its rooms have been renovated and its paintings restored.

It's divided into two parts: The less expensive place to dine is the casual Weinstube, with lots of local atmosphere, where you can order typical Bavarian dishes such as home-smoked beef. The restaurant section is elegant, with candles and flowers. The chef happily marries nouvelle cuisine and regional specialties.

Herzogspitalstrasse 8. *℃* **089/2-60-39-54.** Reservations recommended. Main courses 14€–20€; fixed-price lunch 14€; fixed-price dinner 39€. AE, MC, V. Mon–Sat noon–2pm and 6–10pm. U-bahn/S-bahn: Karlsplatz/Stachus.

Zum Alten Markt *Value* BAVARIAN/INTERNATIONAL Snug and cozy, Zum Alten Markt serves beautifully presented fresh cuisine at a good price. Located on a tiny square just off Munich's large outdoor food market, the restaurant has a mellow charm and a welcoming host, Josef Lehner. The interior decor, with its intricately coffered wooden ceiling, came from a 400-year-old Tirolean castle. In summer, tables are set up outside. Fish and fresh vegetables come from the nearby market. You might begin with a tasty homemade soup, such as cream of carrot or black-truffle tortellini in cream sauce with onions and tomatoes. The chef makes a great *Tafelspitz* (boiled beef). You can also order classic dishes such as roast duck with applesauce or a savory roast suckling pig.

Am Viktualienmarkt, Dreifaltigkeitsplatz 3. *℃* **089/29-99-95.** Reservations recommended. Main courses 10.50€–19.50€. No credit cards. Mon–Sat 10am–midnight. U-bahn/S-bahn: Marienplatz. Bus: 52.

INEXPENSIVE

Andechser am Dom GERMAN This restaurant and beer hall is set on two floors of a postwar building adjacent to the back side of the Frauenkirche. It serves large amounts of a beer brewed in a monastery near Munich (Andechser), as well as generous portions of German food. No one will mind if you order a snack, a full meal, or just a beer. Menu items are often accompanied with German-style potato salad and green salad and include such dishes as veal schnitzels, steaks, turkey croquettes, roasted lamb, fish, and several kinds of sausages that taste best with tangy mustard. In good weather, tables are set up both on the building's roof and on the sidewalk in front, both of which overlook the back of one of the city's finest churches.

Weinstrasse 7a. *℃* **089/29-84-81.** Reservations recommended. Main courses 9€–17.50€. AE, DC, MC, V. Daily 10am–1am. U-bahn/S-bahn: Marienplatz.

Café am Beethovenplatz BAVARIAN/INTERNATIONAL/VEGETARIAN This eatery can be patronized either as a cafe or a full-fledged restaurant. It's a bit of a charmer and relatively unnoticed by foreign visitors. A grand piano takes up one section of the spacious dining room in a sort of Art Nouveau styling. At night, the works of many composers—not just Ludwig—are performed here. It's sort of old fashioned and a bit corny, very Middle Europe, and that's why it's so beloved locally. In addition to the classics, you can also hear jazz. Many patrons drop in for breakfast from a large menu. Breakfast here is especially recommended on a Sunday when live classical music is heard. Many in-the-know guests come here for the chef's pork dishes, and roast pig or *Schweinebraten* is the specialty. The restaurant has a deal with a farmer in Bavaria who is said to raise "free range" pigs that are fed an excellent diet. In addition to the pork, an array of international dishes and even some vegetarian specialties are offered as well, so the menu appeals to a wide range of patrons. The freshly made salads are especially delightful.

Goethestrasse 51. ℂ 089/5440-4348. Main courses 6€–17€. AE, MC, V. Daily 9am–1am. U-bahn: Goetheplatz.

Café Dukatz in the Literaturhaus ✦ INTERNATIONAL   Our hangout in

Munich is this cafe/restaurant that pays tribute to the writer Oskar Maria Graf (1894–1967) and is decorated with Graf memorabilia. Jenny Holzer, the New York artist, was called in to carry out the Graf theme. She took sentences from Graf's writings and inscribed them on the cafe's leather benches or on the plates you're served: You have to clean your plate to see what Graf had to say. A typical remark, "It must soon be that I am famous." Munich is the center of publishing in Germany, and writers, editors, and readers drop in throughout the day for coffee and cake. Management invites you to "drink books" and "eat pages." This is no mere coffeehouse, however. The restaurant serves a full-fledged freshly prepared cuisine using some the finest ingredients from the Bavarian countryside. At lunch, try one of the sandwiches such as a baguette with rabbit or the pastrami with sauerkraut. At our most recent dinner, we enjoyed baby roast lamb from Pauillac, which is a delicacy hard to come by even in France. The Blutwurst in pastry, with diced apples, was better than the typical boudin noir in a French bistro. For dessert, we took delight in the pear tart with almond cream. Newsweek recently named this cafe as one of "the world's top gathering places."

Salvatorplatz 1. ℂ 089/291-9600. Main courses 12€–18€. No credit cards. Daily 10am–1am. U-bahn: Odeonsplatz.

Cohen's JEWISH   Long before the Holocaust, a thriving Jewish community

existed in Munich. Cohen's brings back a good pre-war memory of pre-Hitler days. Its wine comes all the way from Israel, and the dishes offered here would make many a transplanted New Yorker feel at home. Portions are large and the food, evocative of its *Mittel Europa* heritage, is authentically heavy. It's a bagel and lox kind of place, with such standard favorites as gefilte fish (in this case doused with Golan wine), along with boiled beef with mushroom gravy and chopped chicken liver. Expect legendary knishes and borscht like your mother made, assuming she was Jewish.

Theresienstrasse 31. ℂ 089/280-9545. Reservations recommended. Main courses 8.80€–13€. AE, MC, V. U-bahn: Odeonplatz.

Deutsche Eiche (German Oak) GERMAN   The building was constructed

in 1864, and there's been a restaurant with a mostly gay, or at least arts-oriented, clientele since its very debut. In the 1970s, Fassbinder, the noteworthy film director, hung out here a lot, usually dressed entirely in chains and leather. Late in the 1990s, the place was renovated into a less evocative, more streamlined-looking beerhall, still with a healthy percentage of gay clients, and with direct access to a 26-room hotel and one of the busiest gay saunas in Munich. Accommodations in the hotel are relatively affordable at 87€ to 98€ for a double.

Each has a TV and telephone and an all-white, efficient-looking collection of furnishings. But we recommend the place as a restaurant and bar hangout. Simple beer-hall-style food includes chili with French bread; vegetarian strudel; roasted pork with potato dumplings; pork schnitzel with french fries; Wiener schnitzels; pork cordon bleu; and grilled turkey steak with fresh mushrooms.

Reichenbachstrasse 13. ℂ **089/231-1660.** Reservations not necessary. Main courses 5€–25€. AE, MC, V. Daily 8am–midnight. U-bahn: Fraunhoferstrasse.

Donisl BAVARIAN/INTERNATIONAL   Donisl is Munich's oldest beer hall, dating from 1715. Readers have praised this Munich-style restaurant as *gemütlich,* with its relaxed and comfortable atmosphere, although the seating capacity is about 550. In summer, you can enjoy the hum and bustle of the Marienplatz by dining in the garden area out front. The restaurant has two levels, the second of which is a gallery. Most of the staff speaks English. The standard menu offers traditional Bavarian food as well as a weekly-changing specials menu. A specialty is *Weisswurst,* the little white sausage that has been a decades-long tradition of this place. The chef also prepares a good duck. Select beers from Munich's own Hacker-Pschorr Brewery to top the evening. A zither player at noon and an accordion player in the evening entertain diners.

Weinstrasse 1. ℂ **089/22-01-84.** Reservations recommended. Main courses 7€–12€. DC, MC, V. Daily 9am–midnight. U-bahn/S-bahn: Marienplatz.

Erstes Münchner Kartoffelhaus BAVARIAN   This "House of Potatoes" elevates the lowly spud to an imperial seat. Regardless of how you like your potatoes, they are likely to be served in your favorite way here. The menu gives you a potato history in Germany. Until the spud started being served on the imperial china of Frederick the Great, the potato was viewed as food for cows, much the way some still look upon the rutabaga in Scotland. Naturally, the potato in time became one of Germany's favorite foods. One diner told us, "I eat potatoes in one form or another at breakfast, lunch, and dinner." His waistline convinced us. Mashed, fried, with brown gravy, whatever, even baked, the potato comes in its simplest form (often served with sour cream, butter, and chopped chives), or else it may be dressed up with smoked salmon or little shrimp.

Hochbrückenstrasse 3. ℂ **089/296-331.** Reservations required. Main courses 3€–12€. AE, MC, V. Mon–Thurs noon–11pm, Fri–Sat noon–midnight, Sun 5:30–11pm. U-bahn: Marienplatz.

Geisel's Vinothek ITALIAN   The Excelsior made a deliberate choice when it decided not to compete with the *grand chic* restaurants of hotels like the Bayerischer Hof with its super-upscale Garden Restaurant. Instead, this government-rated four-star hotel opted for a *gemütlich* (cozy) enclave of rustic charm that evokes an unpretentious trattoria high in the Italian Alps. It's known for its assortment of Italian, French, Austrian, and German wines, dispensed by the glass. You can sit at the bar or, if you want a meal, at one of about a dozen tables. The menu is meant to be a savory foil for the wine: Examples include carpaccio, mozzarella with fresh basil and tomatoes, *vitello tonnato* (veal cooked in tuna sauce), platters of assorted grilled fish, veal, and chicken dishes, and pastas whose composition changes with the season. The fare is well-prepared Italian cuisine, but with the superb wine list as a backup, almost everything tastes good.

In the Hotel Excelsior, Schützenstrasse 11. ℂ **089/55-13-71-40.** Reservations recommended for dining, not necessary for wine tasting. Main courses 12€–20€. Glass of wine 2.50€–10€. AE, DC, MC, V. Restaurant daily noon–12:30am; wine daily noon–1am. U-bahn: Hauptbahnhof.

Graffunder ★★ FRENCH/ITALIAN   Don't expect the grace notes and service rituals of a full-fledged restaurant at this informal place. It wins its stars for
entertainment value alone. At no table in any other Munich restaurant will you
be treated to such a glorious view of the passing parade of the city. It's like
observing the heartbeat of Bavaria. It's a breezy, easygoing spot, specializing in
French and Italian wines, usually sold by the glass. Food, while not actually an
afterthought, is nonetheless considered an accompaniment to the wine. Platters
range from the very simple (tomato, basil, and mozzarella salads or a platter of
carpaccio) to the somewhat more elaborate (pastas, escalopes of veal, chicken
with morels or chanterelles, or Mediterranean ratatouille). In all, it's an excellent
French/Italian alternative to the predictable regime of beer-hall–style suds and
wursts served in so many restaurants in Munich's Altstadt.

Tal 1. ☎ **089/29-24-27.** Snack items and platters 5€–13€; glasses of wine 3€–7€ ($2.70–$6.25).
No credit cards. Mon–Fri 4pm–midnight, Sun 5pm–midnight. U-bahn: Marienplatz.

Hackerhaus BAVARIAN   Back in the 1400s, Bavarian beer drinkers flocked
here to celebrate the opening of yet another brewery, Hacker-Pschorr. It's still
going strong today. We have Bavarian friends who maintain that Pschorr is their
favorite beer even to this day. If Josef Pschorr, who was born in 1770 and was a
famous brewery king of Bavaria, were by some miracle to pay a visit today, he
wouldn't be surprised at the offerings of the kitchen, especially at the specialty,
"Josef Pschorr's own roast beef with remoulade sauce" and fried potatoes.

The list of Bavarian specialties turned out here reads like a classic from
Grandmother Bavarian's kitchen, including the likes of calf's lungs and bread
dumplings or Bavarian ravioli on Sauerkraut with onions. Of course, there is
roast pork with potato dumplings and a cabbage bacon salad or boiled brisket
of beef with horseradish, even crispy roast pork knuckle with potato dumplings.
Strudel filled with sweet cream cheese and raisins, and served with a vanilla
sauce, rounds off most meals. Choose from wood-paneled dining rooms spread
over three floors. In summer, beer drinkers spill into an inner courtyard. In the
Bürgerstube rests what is reportedly the world's largest mug.

Sendlingerstrasse 14. ☎ **089/260-5026.** Main courses 5.60€–19.80€. Fixed-price menus 15.50€–19.90€.
AE, DC, MC, V. Daily 10am–10pm. U-bahn: Marienplatz.

Hundskugel BAVARIAN   The city's oldest tavern dates from 1440 and apparently serves the same food it did back then. Why mess with success? Perhaps half
the residents of Munich at one time or another have made their way to this
alpine-style building, within easy walking distance of the Marienplatz. The
cookery is honest Bavarian with no pretensions. Although the chef makes a
specialty of *Spanferkel* (roast suckling pig with potato noodles), you might
prefer *Tafelspitz* (boiled beef) in dill sauce or roast veal stuffed with goose liver.
To begin, try one of the hearty soups, made fresh daily.

Hotterstrasse 18. ☎ **089/26-42-72.** Reservations required. Main courses 7€–18€. No credit cards. Daily
10:30am–midnight. U-bahn/S-bahn: Marienplatz.

Käfer am Hofgarten FRENCH/ITALIAN   This likable and stylish bistro
and bar is set midway between the imposing bulk of the Residenz and the Bavarian Ministry of Finance. It's a replica of something you might find in Paris or
Lyon. There are outdoor terraces in front and back. Staff members are attentive
and polite. A live pianist bashes out cabaret and jazz tunes every night. Tables
are spaced close to one another, which enhances the sense of intimacy, though
your conversation is likely to be overheard by your immediate neighbors. Menu

items change daily according to the season and the inspiration of the chefs, but might include carpaccio of beef with olive oil and aromatic herbs; pressed filet of duck prepared with braised cabbage, apples, *rösti*, and noodles; pastas with seafood; succulent and very fresh salads; and rabbit braised with a medley of fresh root vegetables.

Odeonsplatz 6–7. ✆ 089/2-90-75-30. Reservations recommended. Main courses 12€–16€. AE, MC, V. Mon–Thurs 10am–1am, Fri 11am–3am, Sat 9:30am–3am, Sun 9:30am–1am. S-bahn: Odeonsplatz.

Nürnberger Bratwurst Glöckl am Dom ★★ (Value) BAVARIAN The homesick Nürnberger comes here just for one dish with those delectable little sausages: Nürnberger Schweinwurst mit Kraut. This old restaurant first opened in 1893. It was rebuilt after World War II and is the coziest and warmest of all the local restaurants. Chairs look almost as if they were hand-carved, and upstairs, reached through a hidden stairway, is a dining room hung with reproductions of Dürer prints. Tables are shared, and food is served on tin plates. Last food orders go in at midnight. A short walk from Marienplatz, the restaurant faces the Frauenkirche.

Frauenplatz 9. ✆ 089/29-52-64. Reservations recommended. Main courses 7.50€–18€. MC, V. Daily 10am–1am. U-bahn: U2 or U3 to Marienplatz.

Palais Keller ★★ (Value) BAVARIAN/GERMAN Massive, with a high turnover and a sense of bustling energy, this richly folkloric restaurant is down a flight of stone steps, deep in the cellar of one of Munich's finest hotels. Despite its elegant associations, its prices are competitive with those of Munich's many beer halls. Waitresses all speak English and wear frilly aprons and genuine smiles. There is a tempting array of such German dishes as veal in sour cream sauce with glazed turnips, cabbage, and carrots; pike balls on buttery leaf spinach with shrimp sauce; and *Tafelspitz* (boiled beef) with horseradish and vinaigrette sauce. Some diners, especially those who make the place a regular stopover, order whatever *Tagesteller* (platter of the day) is being served, along with a foaming mug of beer or one of the restaurant's broad selection of German wines.

In the Hotel Bayerischer Hof (Palais Montgelas), Promenadeplatz 2. ✆ 089/2-12-09-90. Reservations recommended. Main courses 7.50€–21€. AE, DC, MC, V. Daily 10:30am–midnight. Tram 19.

Park-Café Kitchen INTERNATIONAL The darling of a media-hip crowd and sundry celebrities, this late-night eatery and disco is on the see-and-be-seen circuit. The food is not the best in the city, but it's invariably good, prepared with fresh ingredients. Try the *Tafelspitz* (boiled beef with vegetables), the favorite dish of the Emperor Josef Franz of neighboring Austria, as well as an array of other courses inspired by recipes from Asia or the Mediterranean. The vegetable stir-fries here are superb, served with various tomato and curry sauces. The potato gnocchi is another hearty, filling treat. An "all American" barbecue is often served in their Biergarten, and the chef also whips up a mean chile con carne. The lounge up front is in a vaguely minimalist sci-fi style, and the restaurant itself is more traditional with wooden tables and old bistro chairs.

Sophienstrasse 7. ✆ 089/598313. Reservations recommended. Main courses 10€–20€. AE, DC, MC, V. Daily 11am–11pm. U-bahn: Hauptbahnhof.

Pfalzer Weinprobierstube ★ GERMAN/PALATINATE Former Chancellor Kohl used to patronize this place for one dish: *Saumagen*, which is an herb-infused meatloaf baked in a pig's stomach. This time-honored favorite has earned the Stube's culinary reputation—that and other dishes such as original Palatinate -styled grilled sausage and vintner's spicy roast pork(from a region of

Germany bordering France). The chef is big on bellies here (and you'd get one too if you dined here every day), including grilled pork belly. For more modern tastes, there is baked filet of white fish. Every morning the cooks prepare soups Bavarians have eaten for centuries, including liver dumpling soup Palatinate-style and goulash soup. If you'd like an assortment of Palatinate specialties, including liver sausage and baked ham, you can order a farmhouse platter. There is one of the best cheese selections in town here, including many old-fashioned favorites. There is also a large selection of good wines, and service is friendly and efficient.

Residenzstrasse 1. (✆ 089/225-628. Reservations not taken. Main courses 3€–16€. DC, MC, V. Daily 10am–midnight. U-bahn: Odeonplatz.

Prinz Myshkin VEGETARIAN   This popular vegetarian restaurant near the Marienplatz offers freshly made salads, some macrobiotic selections, Indian and Thai vegetarian dishes, as well as vegetarian *involtini* (stuffed roll ups) and casseroles, soups, and zesty pizzas, many of which are excellent. Wine and beer are sold as well. Smaller portions of many items are available for 5€.

Hackenstrasse 2. (✆ 089/26-55-96. Reservations recommended. Main courses 7€–12.50€. AE, MC, V. Daily 11am–2:30am. U-bahn: U2 or U3 to Marienplatz. S-bahn: Marienplatz.

Spöckmeier BAVARIAN   *Weisswurst,* those little white sausages of Munich, are king here. Locals flock here to devour them in the early morning, along with mugs of beer, of course. Both breakfast and beer drinking start early here, as the waitresses bring out fat breakfast sausages. Some diners, mainly men, start their pretzel consumption at breakfast as well. You can drop in any time until late at night, ordering as little or as much as you want. The draft beers, a selection of four, flow throughout the day.

Lunch might be a simple affair, including roast beef with a salad and freshly baked bread. One favorite among residents who live nearby is *Eintopf,* a rich flavored broth of slivers of pork and homemade noodles. We concluded this place is definitely not for the calorie conscious when watching at least two dozen well-fed lady shoppers order fat wedges of an absolutely delicious cheesecake in the afternoon. This is a true Bavarian beer restaurant, with tables placed on three floors. For a true Bavarian atmosphere, retreat to the intimate *Keller* or cellar. Since the menu is changed daily, you get freshness here.

Rosenstrasse 9. (✆ 089/268-088. Main courses 4.10€–20.50€. AE, DC, MC, V. Daily 9am–midnight. U-bahn: Marienplatz.

Straubinger Hof BAVARIAN   This is one of the most recommendable and popular restaurants in the Altstadt, a well-managed, unpretentious, folkloric place sponsored by the brewers of Paulaner beer. Stop in just for a brew during the morning and afternoon, but during peak lunch and dinner hours, it's good form to order at least a small platter of cheese or wurst, if not a steaming platter of *Tafelspitz* (boiled beef with horseradish), Sauerbraten, or roasted knuckle of pork. Nostalgia for the kind of food old-time Bavarians were served as children also appears on the menu—look for the term *Grossmutter Art,* or "in the style of grandmother." A large stein of beer costs from 2.50€ to 3.50€, depending on the type you order. This restaurant's position close to the Viktualienmarkt guarantees—at least in theory—the use of ultrafresh produce. Portions are ample, prices are reasonable, and in summer, seating spills out onto the pavement. Looking for a traditional Bavarian dessert? The specialty of the house is old-fashioned *Apfelschmarrn,* an apple-laced pastry. The restaurant also has all-vegetarian options.

Blumenstrasse 5. ℂ **089/2-60-84-44**. Reservations recommended. Main courses 10€–15€. No credit cards. Mon–Fri 9am–11pm, Sat 8am–4pm. U-bahn/S-bahn: Marienplatz.

Sushi & Soul JAPANESE   Huge windows open onto a quiet residential street. Expect big airy spaces, flickering candles, and a minimalist decor whose main ornamentation derives from a hip and stylish crowd of good-looking singles and couples. The menu is based on sushi, salads, and hot Japanese food. Fresh ingredients go into the tasty fare, which is a refreshing change of pace from the typical Bavarian diet.

Klenzestrasse 71. ℂ **089/20-10-992**. Reservations recommended. Main courses 13€–18€. V. Daily 6pm–1am. U-bahn: Fraunhoferstrasse.

Tattenbach BAVARIAN   Cozy and accommodating, this restaurant offers a dark-paneled, German-traditional decor, and a youthful counterculture clientele that's about 50% gay on weekends, 30% gay the rest of the week. Menu items are Gutburgerlich (traditional) and flavorful, with emphasis on Italian-style pastas, gnocchi, salads, Sauerbraten, and beef filets in pepper sauce. Don't expect grandeur or spit-and-polish formality, as the venue is relatively unpretentious and low-key. In summer, a beer garden opens.

Tattenbachstrasse 6. ℂ **089/22-52-68**. Reservations recommended. Main courses 6.50€–12.50€. AE, MC, V. Mon–Thurs 5pm–1am, Fri–Sat 7pm–2am. U-bahn: Lehel.

Times Square Online Bistro CONTINENTAL   Food is well-prepared here, and its salads are especially humongous—very fresh medleys of exotic-looking greens loaded with vitamins. But the place has a gimmick that many computer-literate travelers especially appreciate: There are banks of online computers lining one side, which you can rent for 2.50€ per quarter hour. The setting is high-ceilinged, sunny, and very large; there's a bar in the middle, and a section for conventional (noncomputerized) dining, where you can order items that include Zürich-style pork cutlets; baked camembert; tagliatelle; and spinach strudel.

Bayerstrasse 10 A (in the Hauptbahnhof). ℂ **089/550-8800**. Reservations not necessary. Breakfasts 4€–10€; snacks 3.25€–7€; main courses 7€–15€ AE, DC, MC, V. Sun–Thurs 6am–1am, Fri–Sat 6am–midnight. U-bahn/S-bahn: Hauptbahnhof.

Weisses Bräuhaus BAVARIAN/RHENISH   Weisses Bräuhaus is big, bustling, and Bavarian. Not for the pretentious, this informal place does what it's been doing for centuries: serving home-brewed beer. At one time, the famous salt-trade route between Salzburg and Augsburg passed by its door, and salt traders were very thirsty. The front room, with smoke-blackened dark-wood paneling and stained glass, is for drinking and informal eating; the back room has white tablecloths and black-outfitted waiters. You can sample typical Bavarian dishes: smoked filet of trout; rich potato soup; roast pork with homemade potato dumplings and cabbage salad; or Viennese veal goulash with mushrooms and cream sauce. You'll have to share your table, but that's part of the fun.

Tal 7. ℂ **089/29-98-75**. Reservations recommended, especially for the back room. Main courses 10€–18€. No credit cards. Daily noon–midnight. U-bahn/S-bahn: Marienplatz.

Zum Burgerhaus GERMAN   Originally built in 1827, this is one of the few restaurants in the Altstadt that escaped relatively unscathed from the devastation of World War II. It's still outfitted with the traditional dark-stained wood paneling and all the *gemütlich* (cozy) accessories you'd expect. Appropriate to its nostalgic charm, it places culinary emphasis on alpine food. Menu choices change with the seasons, but at one time or another might include a Burgerhaus salad (garnished with herbed croutons and bacon), lamb with rosemary sauce, filet of venison with red wine sauce, Zurich-style veal with *rösti* and cream sauce, Viennese-style pork schnitzels; Bavarian duck with orange sauce, Angus steak bordelaise, and a cold-weather favorite, a *Bürgerhaus Pfanne* that combines cutlets of turkey, veal, and pork in one well-seasoned pan. The homemade version of noodles with cream sauce, herbs, and mushrooms may sound a little bland, but it is actually one of the more savory dishes.

Pettenkoferstrasse 5. *C* 089/59-79-09. Reservations recommended. Main courses 15€–20€. AE, MC, V. Mon–Sat 11am–2:30pm and 6–11pm. U-bahn: Sendlinger Tor.

Zum Dürnbräu BAVARIAN   Right in the center of Munich, no place gets more traditional than this long-favored Bavarian tavern, beloved by the locals. If you like lots of people, plenty of ever-flowing suds, a raucous atmosphere, and hearty fare, this is for you. The kitchen tries valiantly, but you should consider this mainly as a place to eat, drink, and be merry, not dine in grand style. Nonetheless, the dishes are quite tasty, especially the freshly roasted pork served with potato dumplings and a cabbage salad. We're also fond of their savory kettle of veal goulash served with potatoes and a green salad. Sliced turkey breast appears in a creamed mushroom sauce. Tables are shared good-naturedly, the largest—almost 2 dozen feet long—placed in the center. Students are fond of this place, and it also attracts a lot of merchants in the area.

Dürnbräu 2. *C* 089/222-195. Main courses 6.60€–21.40€. AE, DC, MC, V. Daily 9am–midnight. U-bahn: Marienplatz.

Zum Hofer BAVARIAN   A restaurant called Weinstadl has stood here longer than anyone remembers. Its origins, in fact, go back to 1551. For some reason, this tavern has recently undergone a name change, although it remains its historic self. At least it didn't become a McDonald's! Right off the Marienplatz, it is a good place to wind down and cool off in summer as you settle into its Biergarten. The fountain depicts a Bavarian burgher enjoying a glass of wine, and is much photographed.

In winter, the place changes, as drinkers and diners retreat inside to a vaulted room, sitting at tables fronted with benches. These tables are freely shared, and there is a convivial, fun-loving atmosphere. On Friday and Saturday nights, the cellar is the place to be if you'd like to listen to live music, often Bavarian favorites. The menu is predictable, but the food is quite good. The Vienna goulash is good and spicy. The boiled beef is another favorite, and is well done, as is the roast chicken salad with potatoes. Every day there are 15 to 20 specials based on the inspiration of the chef.

Burgsstrasse 5. *C* 089/242-10-444. . Main courses 6.50€–14€. AE, DC, MC. Mon–Sat 10am–11:30pm, Sun 10am–1:30pm. U-bahn: Marienplatz.

3 Near the Südbahnhof

VERY EXPENSIVE

Gästhaus Glockenbach ★★★ MODERN CONTINENTAL   There's a good chance you'll be served one of your finest meals in Munich at this restaurant, should you choose to dine here. This unpretentious restaurant is capable of holding its own against more expensive, more *grand bourgeois* establishments, such as Tantris (see below). The setting is a 200-year-old building close to the Glockenbach, a tributary of the nearby Isar. The dignified country-baroque interior is accented with vivid modern paintings and the most elegant table settings in town. Cuisine changes with the season. You'll find imaginative preparations of venison and pheasant in autumn, lamb and veal dishes in spring-time, and shellfish whenever in season. Ultra-fresh vegetables and exotica are imported from local farms and from sophisticated purveyors worldwide. Wines are mostly from Italy, France, and Austria.

Kapuzinerstrasse 29, corner of Maistrasse. ℂ **089/53-40-43.** Reservations recommended. Main courses 23€–28€; fixed-price menus 28€ lunch, 65€–75€ dinner. AE, MC, V. Tues–Sat noon–2pm (last order); Tues–Sat 7–10pm (last order). Closed 1 week at Christmas. U-bahn: U3 or U6 to Goetheplatz.

4 Near the Isar, South of the Center

MODERATE

Asam Schlössel BAVARIAN/INTERNATIONAL   A relaxed, relatively informal hideaway from the congestion of Munich, this restaurant is housed in a building dating from 1724 that was once a private villa belonging to a pair of artists. Some of the original castle-like design remains, though the structure has been expanded and renovated over the years. Several brews, all products of Augustiner (the famous brewery), are offered, including both the pale and dark versions fermented from wheat (*Weissebier*). Menu items include roasted shoulder of pork (*Schweinsschulterbraten*) basted with (what else?) beer and served with braised red cabbage, and potato dumplings; beef braised in red wine (*Böfflamott*) with bread dumplings (*Semmelknödel*); and a dish beloved by Franz Josef, the last of Austria's Habsburg emperors, a savory form of boiled beef with horseradish (*gesottener Tafelspitz mit frischen Kren*).

Maria-Einsiedel-Strasse 45. ℂ **089/7-23-63-73.** Main courses 7€–23€. AE, DC, MC, V. Daily noon–10pm for food, daily 11am–1am for drinks. U-bahn: Thalkirchen.

5 Schwabing

This district, which was called "bohemian" in the 1940s, overflows with restaurants. Many of them are awful, but there are several good ones, some of which attract a youthful clientele. The evening is the best time for a visit.

VERY EXPENSIVE

Tantris ★★★ FRENCH/INTERNATIONAL   Tantris serves Munich's finest cuisine. Chef Hans Haas was voted the top chef in Germany in 1994, and, if anything, he has refined and sharpened his technique since winning that honor. His penchant for exotic nouvelle carries him into ever-greater achievements. No restaurant in Munich comes close to equaling this place, not even Boettner (p. 67) or Gästhaus Glockenbach (p. 83). The setting is unlikely: a drab commercial area, with bare concrete walls and a garish decor. But once inside, you're transported by the fine service, beautiful interior, and excellent food that's a treat for the eye as well as the palate. Leading Munich businesspeople like to entertain here.

The cooking is both subtle and original. Choice of dishes is wisely limited: There's an eight-course menu that changes daily, plus a five-course table d'hôte (fixed-price menu), served at noon. You might begin with one of the interesting soups, or a terrine of smoked fish served with green cucumber sauce, then follow with classic roast duck in mustard-seed sauce, or a delightful concoction of lobster medallions on black noodles. These dishes show a refinement and attention to detail, plus a quest for technical perfection, that is truly rare anywhere.

Johann-Fichte-Strasse 7, Schwabing. © 089/36-19-59-0. Reservations required. Fixed-price 5-course lunch 85€; fixed-price dinner 105€ for 5-courses, 123€ for 8 courses; special 5-course Tues–Thurs (including wine) 130€. AE, DC, MC, V. Tues–Sat noon–3pm and 6:30pm–1am. Closed public holidays and annual holidays in Jan and May. U-bahn: Dietlindenstrasse.

EXPENSIVE

Bistro Terrine *★★* FRENCH   The restaurant looks like an Art Nouveau French bistro, and its nouvelle cuisine is based on traditional recipes as authentic and savory as anything you'd find in Lyon or Paris. There's room for up to 50 diners at a time, but because of the way the dining room is arranged, with banquettes and wood and glass dividers, it seems bigger than it actually is. During clement weather, there's additional seating on an outdoor terrace.

Menu items are innovative, and might include tartar of herring with freshly made potato chips and salad, watercress salad with sweetbreads, cream of paprika soup, an autumn fantasy of nuggets of venison served with hazelnut-flavored gnocchi in port wine sauce, zander baked in an herb-and-potato crust, or an alluring specialty salmon with a chanterelle-studded risotto. After all this novelty, the most satisfying desserts might include a traditional *tarte tatin* (a tart filled with, usually, apples) or even an old-fashioned crème brûlée that's jazzed up with Tahitian-style vanilla sauce.

Amalienstrasse 89. © 089/28-17-80. Reservations recommended. Main courses 16€–25€. Fixed-price lunch 22€; fixed-price dinner 50€. AE, MC, V. Mon–Fri noon–1:45pm and 6:30–10:30pm, Sat 6:30–10:30pm. U-bahn: U3 or U6 to Universität.

MODERATE

Bistro Cézanne *★ Finds* FRENCH   Patrick Geay, both chef and owner here, operates this undiscovered little Parisian bistro, which has glamour, charm, and flair. Before opening his own place, the dream of every chef, he fine-tuned his culinary skills with some of the continent's best chefs. On his blackboard menu, he chalks his specialties of the day, based on his shopping early that morning for market-fresh ingredients. We'd dine here just for his vegetable preparations alone—they're that good. Although his menu is forever changing, some of our favorite dishes here have been a gratin de Sandra (the white fish, zander), along with delightful scallops, cooked just right, and served in a sauce of truffles. His masterpiece is his pigeon served with fresh goat cheese. Geay is also a master at preparing such classic French dishes as coq au vin or chicken in a wine sauce.

Konradstrasse 1. © 089/391-805. Reservations required. Main courses 14€–17€. AE, DC, MC, V. Tues–Sun 6pm–1am. U-bahn: Giselastrasse. Tram: 27.

Der Katzlmacher *★ Finds* ITALIAN   Few Italian restaurants would have had the nerve to adopt as their name a pejorative German term referring to Italians. This one did, however, and its sense of humor has helped make it beloved by loyal local fans. The setting is a postwar building near the university, whose dining rooms are evocative of an elegant and rustic mountain lodge high in the Italian Alps. Stylish and theatrical, and filled with well-dressed, prosperous-looking clients, it contains lavishly carved paneling, masses of artfully arranged flowers, and huge amounts of charm. The cooking is based on the culinary traditions of the Marches, Friuli, and Emilia-Romagna, all known for their fine cuisines and agrarian bounty. The owner is Claudio Zanuttigh, who supervises menu specialties that might include calzone stuffed with spinach and pine nuts, carpaccio of duck breast, a commendable grilled swordfish with red-wine vinaigrette, eel with champagne sauce, and a succulent version of *fritto misto del pesce* (mixed fried fish) based on whatever is in season.

Kaulbachstrasse 48. ✆ **089/348129**. Reservations recommended. Main courses 9€–11€. MC, V. Mon–Fri noon–3pm and 6:30–11pm. U-bahn: Universität.

La Mucca ITALIAN　This is an unpretentious and charming Italian restaurant in the heart of Schwabing, run by Italian expatriates who manage to infuse the ambience here with Mediterranean charm, Mediterranean humor, and—when things get too busy—Mediterranean hysteria. It's small and convivial, with only 55 seats in two dining rooms. Arguably, the most delectable item on the menu is *lotte* (sea bass) baked in a salt crust. The chef shows flair with his carpaccio of lamb with olive oil and white beans, and also prepares that famous dish of Rome, *saltimbocca* (literally "jump-in-your-mouth") with ham and veal. However, you have to be born and bred in Italy, or else a true devotee of Italian cuisine as we are, to opt for a platter of grilled sardines in arugula. Both the antipasti and pasta selections are excellent, especially rigatoni with zucchini strips.

Georgenstrasse 105. ✆ **089/2-71-67-42**. Reservations recommended. Main courses 13€–19€. AE, DC, MC, V. Winter Tues–Sun noon–3pm and 6–11:30pm; summer Tues–Sun 6–11pm. U-bahn: U2 to Josephsplatz.

Locanda Picolit ⋆ ITALIAN　If you come here in the summer and sit on the outdoor terrace with a view over a garden, it's easy to believe that you've suddenly been transported to the Mediterranean world. The interior is full of streamlined furnishings and dramatic, oversize modern paintings. Menu items come from all over Italy, but the favorites are those from the owner's native Friuli, near Venice. There's a lavish use of in-season asparagus, arugula, shellfish, rabbit, wild mushrooms, and venison in such alluring preparations as ravioli stuffed with lobster, tagliatelle, rotini, linguini with braised radicchio and shellfish, and, when available, *saltimbocca* (veal with prosciutto).

Siegfriedstrasse 11. ✆ **089/396447**. Reservations recommended. Main courses 16€–21€; fixed-price menu 34€. AE, DC, V. Tues–Fri noon–2:30pm and daily 6:30–11pm. U-bahn: U3 or U6 to Münchner Freiheit.

Spago ITALIAN　Less self-conscious and self-promotional than its Los Angeles namesake, this amiable multilingual Italian restaurant (with no relation to Wolfgang Puck) still offers lots of Italian pizzazz as well as good, upscale Italian food. Some of the dishes are tagliatelle with porcini mushrooms; braised breast of chicken stuffed with herbs and spinach; ravioli with artichoke hearts or with potatoes and chanterelles; an especially delectable fish baked with herbs in a salt crust and wild mushrooms sautéed with herbs and arugula; a perfectly prepared suckling lamb with mint and balsamic vinegar; and an array of desserts as beautiful as they are tasty.

Neureutherstrasse 15 at Arcisstrasse. ✆ **089/271-2406**. Reservations recommended. Main courses 8.50€–20€; fixed-price lunch 20€; fixed-price dinner 35€. AE, DC, MC, V. Mon–Sat 11:30am–2:30pm and 6–11pm. U-bahn: Josephsplatz or Universität.

INEXPENSIVE

Sausalito's MEXICAN　Imagine a sprawling labyrinth of rooms whose layout and lighting suggests a German beer hall. Then imagine that instead of boozy, middle-aged clients swilling beer, it's loaded with young, nubile students from the nearby university. Add to that a heady blend of tequila-based particolored drinks and tacos, and you'll have the equivalent of Spring Break in Daytona Beach with a German accent. Come here to drink, dialogue, mingle, and to chow down on fajitas, enchiladas, quesadillas, steaks, burritos, and burgers.

Türkenstrasse 50. ✆ **089/28-15-94.** Reservations not necessary. Main courses 8.50€–13.50€. AE, MC, V. Daily 5pm–1am. U-bahn: Universität.

Weinbauer BAVARIAN Just off Leopoldstrasse is this small, relatively untrammeled and affordable restaurant. Despite a complete renovation in 1993, it retains many traditional Bavarian accessories, evoking an unglossy small-town dining room somewhere in the Alps. The food is reliable but hardly spectacular. Menu items include Wiener schnitzel, Nürnberger wurst'l with sauerkraut, sirloin steak with an herb-butter sauce, goulash soup, and *Blutwurst* and *Leberwurst* platters.

Fendstrasse 5. ✆ **089/39-81-55.** Reservations recommended. Main courses 7€–15.50€. No credit cards. Mon–Fri 11am–midnight, Sat 3pm–midnight. U-bahn: Münchner Freiheit.

6 Bogenhausen/Prielhof

MODERATE

Alba ✿ ITALIAN In an upscale neighborhood known as Prielhof, this is one of the town's most glamorous bistros, established in 1998. It was once a sophisticated French-Austrian restaurant, and the decor remains Austrian and urbane, with a green ceramic *Kachelofen* (porcelain stove) dominating one side of the dining room. Menu items are influenced by a lighter Italian cuisine and are based on whatever is good, fresh, and of high quality at the market. Savor the subtle balance of flavors and plan to make an evening of it, as it's a convivial place for food and drink. The *tortellini di patate* (made with potatoes) is a succulent starter or else you may opt for *spaghetti à la diabla* with fiery red peppers. The sea bass with fresh asparagus is delicate and savory. All the meat, poultry, and fish dishes are handled with skill. At the end of the meal, a *gelato à la limon* (ice cream made from fresh lemons) is soothing to the palate.

Oberföhringer Strasse 44. ✆ **089/985353.** Reservations required. Main courses 17.50€–22.50€. Mon–Fri noon–2:30pm and Mon–Sat 6–11pm. No credit cards. U-bahn: U-4 to Arabellapark.

Bogenhauser Hof GERMAN/INTERNATIONAL In the verdant residential suburb of Bogenhausen, 5km (3 miles) east of the Marienplatz, this stylish and sought-after restaurant occupies a stately looking villa that was originally built as a hunting lodge in 1825. With its reputation for well-conceived food and intelligent, sensitive service, the restaurant has flourished here since it was established in the mid-1980s. You'll dine in a high-ceilinged dining room decorated in Jugendstil style, or in good weather, outside in a manicured garden beneath the spreading limbs of massive chestnut trees. The cuisine is as elegantly prepared as the decor; only market-fresh ingredients are used, deftly handled by the skilled chefs. The menu changes with the season, but is likely to include a salad of fresh wild greens garnished with grilled scampi and rock lobster; carpaccio of venison with fresh herbs and olive oil; an excellent saddle of lamb served with thyme sauce, green beans, and gratin of potatoes; filet of veal with morel sauce; glazed sweetbreads with truffle sauce; and a medley of sophisticated desserts.

Ismaninger Strasse 85, Bogenhausen. ✆ **089/985586.** Reservations recommended. Main courses 17€–25€. AE, DC, V. Mon–Sat 11:30am–2:30pm and 6–10:30pm. U-bahn: U5 to Max-Weber-Platz, then tram no. 18 to Essnerplatz.

Käfer-Schänke GERMAN/INTERNATIONAL This is a great spot for casual dining with elegant style, in a setting that evokes a chalet. It's located on the second floor of a famous gourmet shop called Käfer. The cuisine roams the world for inspiration—from Lombardy to Asia. You select your hors d'oeuvres from the most dazzling display in Munich. Often Käfer-Schänke devotes a week to a particular country's cuisine. On one visit, we enjoyed the classic soup of the French Riviera (sea bass with fennel). The salads have what one reviewer called "rococo splendor." From a cold table, you can choose smoked salmon or smoked eel. Venison, quail, and guinea hen are also regularly featured. There's a deluxe gourmet shop on the main floor.

Prinzregentenstrasse 73. ✆ **089/4-16-82-47.** Reservations required. Main courses 16€–26€; fixed-price lunch 28€. AE, DC, MC, V. Mon–Sat 11:30am–midnight. Closed holidays. U-bahn: U4 to Prinzregentenplatz. Bus: 55.

7 Denning

EXPENSIVE

Casale ITALIAN   One of the more restrained, discreet, and formal of Munich's many Italian restaurants, with an upscale decor more self-consciously "expensive" than many of its competitors, this restaurant is north of the city center, near the mega-hotels of the Bogenhausen district. It works hard on such tours de force as a nine-course *menu dégustazione* that requires several hours to consume gracefully. Menu items are savory and stylish and usually served with flair: sea bass prepared with rosemary in a salt crust, filet of beef with Barolo sauce, and an array of pastas that include ravioli stuffed with pulverized veal and spices and an excellent linguine with fresh asparagus or exotic seasonal mushrooms.

Ostpreussenstrasse 42. ✆ **089/936268.** Reservations recommended. Main courses 18€–25€; fixed-price menus 40€. AE, MC, V. Daily noon–2:30pm and 6–10:30pm. U-bahn: U4 to Arabellapark.

8 Grünwald

MODERATE

Grünwalder Einkehr ✿✿ FRENCH   This restaurant, 13km (8 miles) south of the city, was the home of a prosperous landowner around 200 years ago. Its trio of dining rooms is outfitted in an elegantly rustic Bavarian style that is very romantic. The sublime cuisine, however, reflects a different tradition—menu items are conservative and French, featuring such dishes as succulent roast rack of lamb with rosemary sauce, fried trout with almond-butter sauce, filet of beef with green peppercorn sauce, pistou, and a satisfying, old-fashioned version of *tarte tatin*.

Nördlicher Münchner Strasse 2, in Grünwald. ✆ **089/6-49-23-04.** Reservations recommended. Main courses 12€–21€. AE, DC, MC, V. Tues–Sun noon–2:30pm and 6pm–midnight. U-bahn: U2 to Silberhornstrasse, then tram 25.

9 Nymphenburg

MODERATE

Nymphenburger Hof AUSTRIAN   Many Münchners consider an outing to this restaurant's verdant outdoor terrace, about 9.5km (6 miles) west of the Marienplatz and about 5km (3 miles) from Schloss Nymphenburg (p. 103), the next best thing to a week in the country. Although the modern blue-and-white interior is attractive in any season, the place is especially appealing in summer when the terrace, separated from the busy avenue by a screen of trees, is open.

Don't expect even a hint of tradition, as everything here is streamlined and modern. The only nostalgic thing about the place is the courtly but amused service and the cuisine, inspired by what used to be known as the Austro-Hungarian Empire. Examples include Wiener schnitzel, Tafelspitz (boiled beef; the favorite of Austrian Emperor Franz Josef), *Kaiserschmarr* (a sweet dessert made with apples), a variety of Czech pastries made with honey and plums, and the gooey sticky dessert beloved across the border, *Salzburger knockerl* (a light and creamy dessert made from eggs, vanilla, sugar, and butter).

Nymphenburger Strasse 24. ✆ **089/1-23-38-30.** Reservations recommended in summer. Main courses 12€–26€. AE, MC, V. Mon–Sat noon–3pm and 6–11pm. U-bahn: U1 to Steiglmaierplatz.

10 Obermenzing

INEXPENSIVE

Weichandhof BAVARIAN   If you'd like to escape from the hordes in the center of Munich, a traditional favorite among the city residents themselves is this old farmhouse restaurant at the beginning of the Autobahn to Stuttgart. It lies in one of Munich's better suburbs, Obermenzing. Every night seems a festival here; the food is good and affordable, and patrons come here to relax, converse, and drink as much as they do to devour the food.

When the weather turns warm in spring, a terrace covered in vines opens to diners and stays open until there's a bite to the autumn wind. Don't write off a winter visit. With the tiled stoves giving off heat and ambience, it's a mellow and pleasurable choice even in December and January. You are served regional fare here—and plenty of it. Some of the best and most typical dishes are inspired by both the Bavarian and Viennese kitchens. Boiled beef, flavored with herbs, is the eternal favorite and a dish said to have been ordered nightly by Franz-Josef, the Austrian emperor. You're also served large pork knuckles, roast suckling pig, and any number of other dishes including liver. A fish soup, made with zander, is served daily. The chefs are long experienced and are experts at making strudels.

Betzenweg 81. ✆ **089/891-1600.** Reservations recommended. Main courses 6€–16€. MC. Sun–Fri 9am–midnight. S-bahn: Obermenzing.

11 Cafes

Many Münchners take a break during the day to relax over coffee or a beer, read the newspaper, or meet friends. For afternoon coffee and pastry, also see the cafes listed in chapter 9.

INEXPENSIVE
CENTRAL MUNICH

Café Glockenspiel   This is the most frequented cafe in Munich. It's across from the Rathaus, and a crowd gathers here every day at 10:30am to watch the miniature tournament staged by the clock on the Rathaus facade. In addition to the view, the cafe has good coffee costing from 3€ to 4.25€, with pastries beginning at 2.50€. It also makes a fine place to end your day tour of Munich and to fortify yourself for Munich after dark. Arrive around 5pm for a drink and watch the square change its stripes as it goes from daytime to night. It's an ideal place for people watching, too.

Marienplatz 28. ✆ **089/264256.** Daily 10am–1am. U-bahn or S-bahn: Marienplatz.

Café Luitpold   Opened in 1888 and rebuilt in a blandly modern style after the ravages of World War II, this cafe once attracted such notables as Ibsen, Kandinsky, Johann Strauss the Younger, and other musicians, artists, and authors, as well as members of the royal court of Bavaria. What you'll find today, however, is mainstream workaday Munich stopping in for a pastry, a platter of food, coffee, or beer. There's a more formal restaurant associated with the place, but we tend to prefer the cafe section. A large beer costs 3€; coffee starts at 2.50€.

Briennerstrasse 11. ✆ 089/292865. Mon–Fri 9am–8pm, Sat 8am–7pm. U-bahn: Königsplatz or Odeonsplatz.

Guglhopf Though it opened in the 1970s, this cafe's ambience of old-fashioned nostalgia and Bavarian rusticity will make you think it's older than it really is. It's named for the closest thing to a Bavarian "national pastry," the *Guglhopf.* Made with flour, eggs, and sugar, the pastry comes in at least four different variations, including chocolate and/or nuts. Equally nationalistic is the apfelstrudel served with vanilla sauce. If you're craving more than just dessert, try the pan-fried mushrooms with cream and herb sauce, served over a bed of homemade noodles. You can borrow any of a half-dozen newspapers while you eat your pastry and drink your coffee or beer. A slice of the namesake pastry costs 2.50€, beer or Weissbeer is 2.75€, and platters are 5€ to 11€.

Kaufingerstrasse 5. ✆ 089/260-8868. Mon–Fri 7am–8pm, Sat 8am–8pm, Sun 10am–7pm. U-bahn: Marienplatz.

NYMPHENBURG

Schlosscafé im Palmenhaus This cafe is in a historical reconstruction of a 17th-century building that once functioned as a conservatory for palm trees. The original building, older than the Schloss itself, was destroyed in World War II. Here you can have your coffee capped with whipped cream or drink your beer in the garden, weather permitting. Coffee costs from 2€, and beer goes for 3€. Luncheon platters of unpretentious food include rice curries, schnitzels with french fries, and salads, and cost from 3.50€ to 19€.

In the gardens of Schloss Nymphenburg, near entrance 43 and the rose gardens. ✆ 089/175309. Daily 9:30am–6:30pm. Closed on Mon Nov–Mar. Tram: 17.

NEUHAUSEN

Ruffini Münchners head for this turn-of-the-20th-century former residence at the end of U-bahn Line 1 for a respite from the pressures of the inner city. It offers everything you'd expect from a traditional cafe. You can relax over your coffee or beer with the most recent edition of several different newspapers, or view the cafe's current painting exhibition (most are for sale). The cafe maintains its own bakery in the cellar, and a wine shop and delicatessen on a corner nearby. Coffee costs 2€ to 3.50€; snacks such as cheese platters go for 6€. Warm platters are 7€ to 11€. The cafe offers natural food, free from artificial fertilizers, flavors, or coloring.

Orffstrasse 22–24. ✆ 089/161160. Tues–Sat 10am–midnight, Sun 10am–6pm. U-bahn: U1 to Rotkreuzplatz.

12 Beer Gardens

If you're in Munich anytime between the first sunny spring day and the last fading light of a Bavarian-style autumn, you should head for one of the city's celebrated beer gardens (*Biergartens*). Traditionally, beer gardens were simply tables placed under chestnut trees planted above the storage cellars to keep beer cool in summer. People, naturally, started to drink close to the source of their pleasure, and the tradition has remained. (Lids on beer steins, incidentally, were meant to keep out flies.) It's estimated that today Munich has at least 400 beer gardens and cellars. Food, drink, and atmosphere are much the same in all of them.

INEXPENSIVE
CENTRAL MUNICH

Biergarten Chinesischer Turm BAVARIAN   Our favorite beer garden is in the Englischer Garten (p. 111), the park lying between the Isar River and Schwabing. The biggest city-owned park in Europe, it has several beer gardens, of which the Biergarten Chinesischer Turm is the best. The largest and most popular of its kind in Europe, it takes its name from its location at the foot of a pagodalike tower, a landmark that's easy to find. Beer and Bavarian food, and plenty of it, are what you get here. For a large glass or mug of beer (costing 5.50€), ask for *ein mass Bier,* which is enough to bathe in. It will likely be slammed down, still foaming, by a server carrying 12 other tall steins. The food is cheap—a simple meal begins at 7€. Homemade dumplings are a specialty, as are all kinds of tasty sausage. You can get a first-rate *Schweinebraten* (braised loin of pork served with potato dumpling and rich brown gravy), which is Bavaria's answer to the better-known Sauerbraten of the north. Huge baskets of pretzels are passed around, and they're eaten with *radi,* the large, tasty white radishes famous from these parts. Oompah bands often play, adding to the festive atmosphere. It's open May to October until midnight or later, but from November to April, its closing depends on the weather and the number of patrons.

Englischer Garten 3. ℭ 089/3-83-87-30. AE, MC, V. May–Oct daily 11am–1am; Nov–Apr daily but hours vary. U-bahn: U3 or U6 to Giselastrasse.

Gaststätte zum Flaucher BAVARIAN   If you're going to the zoo (p. 111), you might want to stop close by at the nearby **Gaststätte zum Flaucher** for fun and food. The word *Gaststätte* tells you that it's a typical Bavarian inn. This one is mellow and traditional, with tables set in a tree-shaded garden overlooking the river. Here you can order the local specialty, *Leberkäse,* a large sausage loaf eaten with freshly baked pretzels and plenty of mustard, a deli delight. Beer costs from 2.50€ for a half-liter mug. Main courses cost from 5.50€ to 10€.

Isarauen 8. ℭ 089/7-23-26-77. No credit cards. May–Oct, daily 10am–midnight; Nov–Apr Fri–Sun 10am–9pm. Bus: 52 from Marienplatz.

SCHWABING

Bamberger Haus BAVARIAN/INTERNATIONAL   In a century-old house northwest of Schwabing at the edge of Luitpold Park, Bamberger Haus is named after a city noted for mass consumption of beer. Most visitors head for the street-level restaurant. Bavarian and international specialties here include well-seasoned soups, grilled steak, veal, pork, and sausages. If you want only to drink, you might visit the rowdier and less expensive beer hall in the cellar. Main courses in the restaurant range from 10€ to 22€. A large beer costs 2.50€.

Brunnerstrasse 2. ℭ 089/3-08-89-66. AE, MC, V. Restaurant daily 11am–10pm; beer hall daily 10am–1am, restaurant daily 11am–10pm. U-bahn: U3 or U6 to Scheidplatz.

NYMPHENBURG

Hirschgarten BAVARIAN   In the Nymphenburg Park sector (near one of Munich's leading sightseeing attractions, Schloss Nymphenburg; p. 103), west of the heart of town, this beer garden is part of a 200-hectare (500-acre) park with hunting lodges and lakes. The largest open-air restaurant in Munich, it seats some 8,000 beer drinkers and Bavarian merrymakers.

Hirschgartenstrasse 1. ✆ **089/172591**. Meals 6€–13.50€; large beer 2.60€. MC, V. Daily 9am–midnight. S-bahn: Laim. Tram: Romanplatz.

FREIMANN

Zum Aumeister BAVARIAN   If you have a car, and have a nostalgic streak, you'll enjoy dining and drinking beer in the historic and evocative atmosphere of Zum Aumeister. Few places so authentically recapture the life gone by— surely the Bavarian royals, if they could miraculously return, would be delighted to see that their old hunting lodge is still around, and not much changed. It lies off the Frankfurter Ring at München-Freimann, a 20-minute drive north of the center. It offers a daily list of seasonal Bavarian specialties. Especially enjoyable is the cream of cauliflower soup and the rich oxtail soup.

Sondermeierstrasse 1. ✆ **089/325224**. Main courses 7€–19€; large beer 5.80€ . No credit cards. Tues–Sun 9am–11pm. From central Munich, follow the signs for the Autobahn A8, and follow it in the direction of Nürnberg. Exit at the "Freimann" exit, turning left onto the boulevard it funnels into, and then note the signs pointing to Zum Aumeister.

Exploring Munich

Munich is a city of art and culture. It has innumerable monuments, and more museums than any other city in Germany. In quality, its collections even surpass those of Berlin. The Wittelsbachs (the ruling family of Europe from approximately the 13th century to the early 20th century) were great collectors—some might say pillagers—and have left behind a city full of treasures.

Go to Munich to have fun and to enjoy the relaxed lifestyle, the friendly ambience, and the wealth of activities, sightseeing, and cultural events. You'll never be at a loss for something to do or see here. Munich is stocked with so many treasures that any visitor who plans to "do" the city in a day or two will not only miss out on many major sights but will also fail to grasp the city's spirit and absorb its special flavor. That said, below, we've outlined a few itineraries if you absolutely can't spend a good deal of time in this special city.

SUGGESTED ITINERARIES

If You Have 1 Day

Local tourist tradition calls for a morning breakfast of Weisswurst (the traditional little white sausages). Head for Donisl (see chapter 5), which opens at 9am. A true Münchner downs them with a mug of beer. Then walk to Marienplatz (see "Exploring the City Center," below), with its Glockenspiel and Altes Rathaus (Old Town Hall). Later stroll along Maximilianstrasse, one of Europe's great shopping streets.

In the afternoon, visit the Alte Pinakothek and catch at least some exhibits at the Deutsches Museum. Cap the evening with a night of Bavarian food, beer, and music at the Hofbräuhaus am Platzl (see chapter 9).

If You Have 2 Days

Spend the first day as detailed above. In the morning of day 2, visit the Staatsgalerie Moderner Kunst and, if the weather is right, plan a lunch in one of the beer gardens of the Englischer Garten. In the afternoon, explore Nymphenburg Palace, summer residence of the Wittelsbachs.

If You Have 3 Days

Spend days 1 and 2 as outlined above. Occupy your third day exploring the Residenz, the Städtische Galerie im Lenbachhaus, and the Bavarian National Museum. If you have any more time, return to the Deutsches Museum. Have dinner, or at least a drink, at the Olympiapark Tower, enjoying a panoramic view of the Alps.

If You Have 4 or 5 Days

Spend the first three days as outlined above. As fascinating as Munich is, tear yourself away for a side trip on day 4 to one of the Royal Castles built by the "mad king," Ludwig II (see chapter 11). On day 5, visit Dachau, the notorious World War II concentration camp (see chapter 10), or go farther afield to Garmisch-Partenkirchen for a taste of the Bavarian Alps (see chapter 11).

1 Exploring the City Center

Marienplatz ✿, dedicated to the patron of the city, whose golden statue atop a huge column (the Mariensäule) stands in the center of the square, is the heart of the Altstadt, or Old City. On its north side is the **Neues Rathaus (New Town Hall)** built in 19th-century Gothic style. Each day at 11am, and also at noon and 5pm in the summer, the Glockenspiel on the facade stages an elaborate performance, including a miniature tournament, with enameled copper figures moving in and out of the archways. Since you're already at the Rathaus, you may wish to climb the 55 steps to the top of its tower (an elevator is available) for a good overall view of the city center. **Altes Rathaus (Old Town Hall),** with its plain Gothic tower, is to the right. It was reconstructed in the 15th century, after being destroyed by fire.

South of the square you can see the oldest church in Munich, **St. Peter's.** The **Viktualienmarkt,** just off Marienplatz and around the corner from St. Peter's church, has been a gathering place since 1807. Here, people gossip, browse, and snack, as well as buy fresh country produce, wines, meats, and cheese.

To the north lies **Odeonsplatz,** Munich's most beautiful square. The **Residenz (Royal Palace)** is just to the east, and the **Theatinerkirche** is to the south. Adjoining the Residenz is the restored **Nationaltheater,** home of the acclaimed Bavarian State Opera and Bavarian National Ballet.

Running west from Odeonsplatz is the wide shopping avenue, Briennerstrasse, leading to **Königsplatz.** Flanking this large Grecian square are three classical buildings constructed by Ludwig I—the **Propyläen,** the **Glyptothek,** and the **Antikensammlungen.** The busy Ludwigstrasse runs north from Odeonsplatz to the section of Munich known as **Schwabing.** This is the Greenwich Village or Latin Quarter of Munich, proud of its artistic and literary heritage.

Tips **Saving on Sightseeing**

- Visit the Alte Pinakothek, Neue Pinakothek, Glyptothek, Antikensammlung, Bayerisches Nationalmuseum, or Münchner Stadtmuseum on Sunday—when admission to the permanent exhibitions is free (but you'll have to brave the crowds).

- Buy combination tickets wherever possible, such as the combination ticket for the Alte and the Neue Pinakothek, good for 2 consecutive days and cheaper than buying a separate ticket for each.

- Note that some museums and attractions, like the Deutsches Museum, the Münchner Stadtmuseum, and the BMW Museum, offer a family ticket that's cheaper than buying individual tickets for adults and children.

- If you plan on doing a lot of sightseeing using public transportation, buy the 1- or 3-day Munich Welcome Card, allowing unlimited travel and discounts of up to 50% on selected sights.

Ibsen and Rilke lived here, as well as members of the Blue Rider group, which influenced abstract art in the early 20th century. Today, Schwabing's sidewalk tables are filled with young people from all over the world.

Isartor (Isar Gate) is one of the most-photographed Munich landmarks. It's located east of Marienplatz at Isartorplatz. Take the S-bahn to Isartor. This is the only tower left from the wall that once encircled Munich, forming part of the city's fortifications against invaders.

The other major gate of Munich is the **Karlstor,** once known as Neuhauser Tor, lying northeast of Karlsplatz (nicknamed *Stachus;* see explanation on p. 124). Take Tram 18 to Karlsplatz. Karlstor lies at the end of Neuhauser Strasse, which formed part of the town's second circuit of walls, dating from the 1500s. It takes its present name from Elector Charles Theodore in 1791. The Karlstor, built in 1302, lost its main tower in an 1857 explosion.

2 Palaces & Major Museums

Alte Pinakothek ★★★   This is not only Munich's most important art museum, but also one of the most significant collections in Europe. The nearly 900 paintings on display (many thousands more are in storage) in this huge neoclassical building represent the greatest European artists from the 14th to the 18th century. Begun as a small court collection by the royal Wittelsbach family in the early 1500s, the artistic treasure trove grew and grew. There are only two floors with exhibits, but the museum is immense; we do not recommend that you try to cover it all in 1 day.

The following are a few highlights. The landscape painter *par excellence* of the Danube school, Albrecht Altdorfer, is represented by six monumental works. Works of Albrecht Dürer include his final, and greatest, *Self-Portrait* (1500). Here the artist has portrayed himself with almost Christ-like solemnity. Also displayed is Dürer's last great painting, a two-paneled work called *The Four Apostles* (1526). Several galleries are given over to works by Dutch and Flemish masters. The St. Columba Altarpiece (1460–62), by Roger van der Weyden, is the most important of these, in size as well as significance. Measuring nearly 3m (10 ft.) across, it is a triumph of van der Weyden's subtle linear style and one of his last works (he died in 1464).

The numerous works by Rembrandt, Rubens (there are more Rubens here than in any other museum in Europe), and van Dyck include a series of religious panels painted by Rembrandt for Prince Frederick Hendrick of the Netherlands. A variety of French, Spanish, and Italian artists are found in both the larger galleries and the small rooms lining the outer wall. The Italian masters are well represented by Fra Filippo Lippi, Giotto, Botticelli, Raphael (*Holy Family*), and Titian.

You'll also see a *Madonna* by da Vinci, a famous self-portrait by the young Rembrandt (1629), and a number of works by Lucas Cranach, including his *Venus.* In the *Land of Cockaigne,* Pieter Brueghel has satirized a popular subject of European folk literature: the place where no work has to be done and where food simply falls into one's mouth. Note the little egg on legs running up to be eaten and the plucked and cooked chicken laying its neck on a plate. In the background, you'll see a knight lying under a roof with his mouth open, waiting for the pies to slip off the eaves over his head.

Important works are always on display, but exhibits also change. You'd be wise to buy a map of the gallery to guide you through the dozens of rooms.

Central Munich Attractions

Alte Pinakothek **3**
Altes Rathaus
  (Spielzeugmuseum) **26**
Antikensammlungen **8**
Asamkirche **12**
Bayerisches
  Nationalmuseum **31**
Cuvilliés Theater **38**
Deutsches Museum **19**
Deutsches Theater **9**
Deutsches
  Theatermuseum **34**
Feldherrnhalle **37**
Frauenkirche **24**
Gasteig Kulturzentrum **20**
Glyptothek **4**
Haus der Kunst **32**
Hellabrunn Zoo **18**
Hilderbrand Haus **29**
Hofgarten **33**
Isartor **21**
Jüdisches Museum
  München **27**
Jugendstil Museum
  (Stuck-Villa) **29**
Karlstor **10**
Marionetten Theater **14**
Matthäuskirche **13**
Michaelskirche **11**
Münchner Stadtmuseum **15**
Nationaltheater **27**
Neue Pinakothek **1**
Neues Rathaus **25**
Peterskirche **23**
Pinakothek der Moderne **2**
Propyläen **7**
Residenz **39**
Staatliche Museum
  Ägyptische Kunst **36**
Schack-Galerie **30**
Schloss Nymphenburg **6**
Städtische Galerie
  im Lenbachhaus **5**
Staatliches Museum
  für Völkerkunde **28**
Staatsgalerie Moderner
  Kunst **32**
Staatstheater am
  Gärtnerplatz **17**
Theatinerkirche **35**
Viktualienmarkt **16**
ZAM **22**

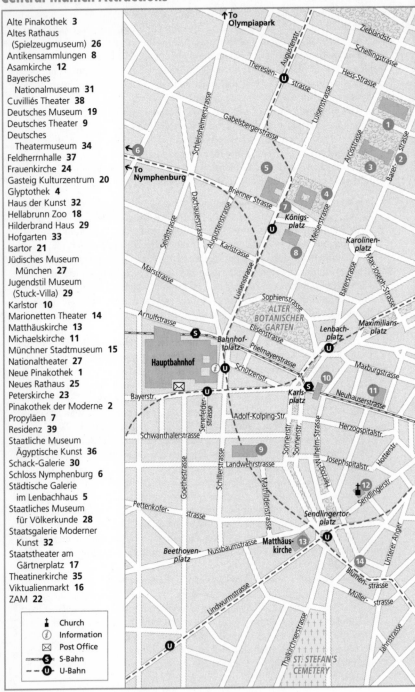

Legend:
- ✝ Church
- ⓘ Information
- ✉ Post Office
- Ⓢ S-Bahn
- Ⓤ U-Bahn

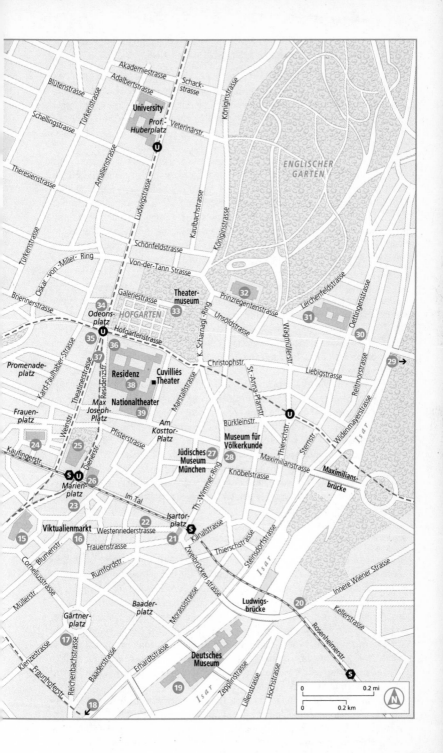

Barerstrasse 27. ⓒ **089/23-80-52-16.** Admission 5€ adults, 3.50€ students, free for children 14 and under. Tues–Sun 10am–5pm (until 10pm Thurs). U-bahn: Königsplatz. Tram: 27. Bus: 53.

Bayerisches Nationalmuseum (Bavarian National Museum) ★★ In 1855, King Maximilian II began an institution to preserve Bavaria's historic and artistic treasures. The collection grew so rapidly that it had to be moved to larger quarters several times over the past 100 years. Its current building, near the Haus der Kunst, contains three vast floors of sculpture, painting, folk art, ceramics, furniture, and textiles, as well as clocks and scientific instruments.

After entering the museum, turn right into the first large gallery, the **Wessobrunn Room,** devoted to early church art from the 5th through the 13th centuries. This room holds some of the museum's oldest and most valuable works. The desk case contains medieval ivories, including the so-called "Munich ivory" from about A.D. 400. The carving shows the women weeping at the tomb of Christ while the resurrected Lord is gingerly stepping up the clouds and into heaven. At the crossing to the adjoining room is the stone figure, the *Virgin with the Rose Bush,* from Straubing (ca. 1300), one of the few old Bavarian pieces of church art influenced by the spirit of mysticism.

The **Riemenschneider Room** is devoted to the works of the great sculptor Tilman Riemenschneider (1460–1531) and his contemporaries. Characteristic of the sculptor's works is the natural, unpainted wood of his carvings and statuary. Note especially the *12 Apostles from the Marienkapelle in Würzburg* (1510), St. Mary Magdalene, the central group from the high altar in the parish church of Münnerstadt (1490–92), and the figure of St. Sebastian (1490).

The second floor contains a fine collection of stained and painted glass—an art in which medieval Germany excelled. Other rooms on this floor include baroque ivory carvings, Meissen porcelain, and ceramics. Also on display are famous collections of 16th- to 18th-century arms and armor, and the collection of antique clocks, some dating from the 16th century.

In the east wing of the basement level are many Christmas cribs (a highly decorated crèche representing the Nativity scene) from Germany, Austria, Italy, and Moravia. The variety of materials competes with the variety of styles—wood, amber, gold, terra cotta, and even wax were used in making these nativity scenes. Also on this level is a display of Bavarian folk art, including many examples of woodcarving.

Prinzregentenstrasse 3. ⓒ **089/21-12-401.** Admission 3€ adults, 2€ students and seniors, free for children under 15; free for all on Sun. Tues–Sun 10am–5pm. U-bahn: U4 or U5 to Lehel. Tram: 17. Bus: 53.

Deutsches Museum (German Museum of Masterpieces of Science and Technology) ★★★ Kids On an island in the Isar River, in the heart of Munich, this is the largest technological museum of its kind in the world. Its huge collection of priceless artifacts and historic originals includes the first electric dynamo (Siemens, 1866), the first automobile (Benz, 1886), the first diesel engine (1897), and the laboratory bench at which the atom was first split (Hahn, Strassmann, 1938). There are hundreds of buttons to push, levers to crank, and gears to turn, as well as a knowledgeable, English-speaking staff to answer questions and demonstrate how steam engines, pumps, or historical musical instruments work.

Among the most popular displays are those on mining, with a series of model coal, salt, and iron mines, as well as the electric power hall, with high-voltage displays that actually produce lightning. There are also exhibits on transportation, printing, photography, textiles, and many activities, including

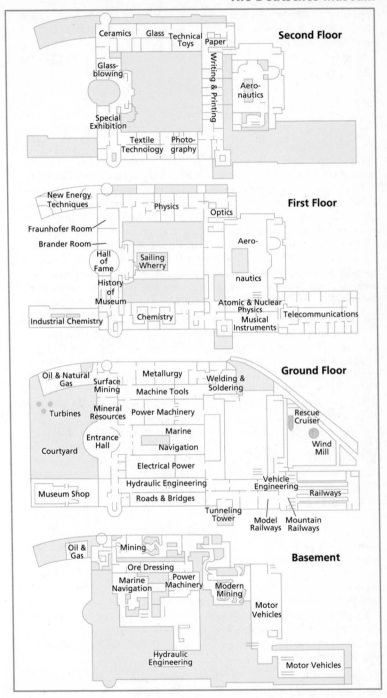

The Deutsches Museum

Second Floor

Ceramics | Glass | Technical Toys | Paper

Glass-blowing

Writing & Printing

Aero-nautics

Special Exhibition

Textile Technology | Photo-graphy

First Floor

New Energy Techniques

Physics

Optics

Fraunhofer Room

Brander Room

Hall of Fame

Sailing Wherry

Aero-nautics

History of Museum

Industrial Chemistry | Chemistry

Atomic & Nuclear Physics

Musical Instruments

Telecommunications

Ground Floor

Oil & Natural Gas | Surface Mining | Metallurgy | Welding & Soldering

Turbines | Mineral Resources | Machine Tools

Power Machinery

Rescue Cruiser

Entrance Hall | Marine

Courtyard | Navigation

Wind Mill

Electrical Power

Museum Shop | Hydraulic Engineering

Roads & Bridges

Vehicle Engineering

Railways

Tunneling Tower | Model Railways | Mountain Railways

Basement

Oil & Gas | Mining

Ore Dressing

Marine Navigation | Power Machinery | Modern Mining

Motor Vehicles

Hydraulic Engineering

Motor Vehicles

glass-blowing and paper-making demonstrations. The air-and-space hall is the largest in the museum. A hall for high-tech exhibits, computer science, automation, microelectronics, and telecommunications is also very intriguing. The museum's astronomy exhibition shows how this science developed from its earliest beginnings to its current status and is the largest permanent astronomy exhibition in Europe. A good restaurant and a museum shop are on the premises.

Museumsinsel 1 (on an island in the Isar River). ℭ 089/21-791. Admission 6€ adults, 4€ seniors, 2.50€ students, and children 6–12, free for children 5 and under. Daily 9am–5pm. Closed major holidays. S-bahn: Isartor. Tram: 18.

Neue Pinakothek ✦   This museum offers a survey of 18th- and 19th-century art, including paintings by Gainsborough, Goya, David, Manet, van Gogh, Monet, and many other works. Among the more popular German artists represented are Wilhelm Leibl and Gustav Klimt; you'll also encounter a host of others whose art is less well known. Note particularly the genre works by Carl Spitzweg, whose paintings poke gentle fun at everyday life in Munich. Across Theresienstrasse from the Alte Pinakothek, the museum was reconstructed after its destruction in World War II; it reopened in 1981.

Barerstrasse 29 (across Theresienstrasse from the Alte Pinakothek). ℭ 089/23-80-51-95. Admission 5€ adults, 3.50€ students and seniors; free for all on Sun. Wed–Mon 10am–5pm (until 10pm on Thurs). U-bahn: U2 to Königsplatz. Tram: 27. Bus: 53.

Pinakothek der Moderne ✦✦   In 2002, one of the world's largest museums devoted to the visual arts of the 19th and 20th centuries opened in Munich, just minutes from the Alte and Neue Pinakothek. This is the most vast display of fine and applied arts in the country as, for the first time, four major collections came together under one roof. This is Munich's version of the Tate Gallery in London or the Pompidou in Paris.

Wander where your interest dictates: the **Staatsgalerie Moderner Kunst (State Gallery of Modern Art)** ✦✦✦ with paintings, sculpture, photography, and video; **Die Neue Sammlung,** which constitutes the national museum of applied art featuring design and craftwork; the **Architekturmuseum der Technischen Universität (University of Architecture museum)** with architectural drawings, photographs, and models; and the **Staatliche Grapische Sammlung,** with its outstanding collection of prints and drawings.

Whenever we visit, we spend most of our time in the modern art collection, lost in a world of our favorite artists such as Picasso, Magritte, Klee, Kandinsky, even Francis Bacon, de Kooning, and Warhol. The museum also owns 400,000 drawings and prints from Leonardo da Vinci to Cézanne up to contemporary artists. They are presented at alternating exhibits.

The architectural galleries hold the largest specialist collection of its kind in Germany, comprising some 350,000 drawings, 100,000 photographs, and 500 models. The applied arts section features more than 50,000 items. You go from the beginnings of the Industrial Revolution up to today's computer culture, with exhibitions of Art Nouveau and Bauhaus along the way.

Barerstrasse 40. ℭ 089/23805-118. Admission: 10€ adults, 6€ students and ages 17 and under. Tues–Sun 10am–5pm. U-bahn: Odeonsplatz.

Residenz ✦   When one of the Bavarian royals said that he was going to the castle, he could have meant any number of places, especially if he was Ludwig II. But if he said that he was going home, he could only be referring to the Residenz. This enormous palace, with a history almost as long as that of

The Residenz

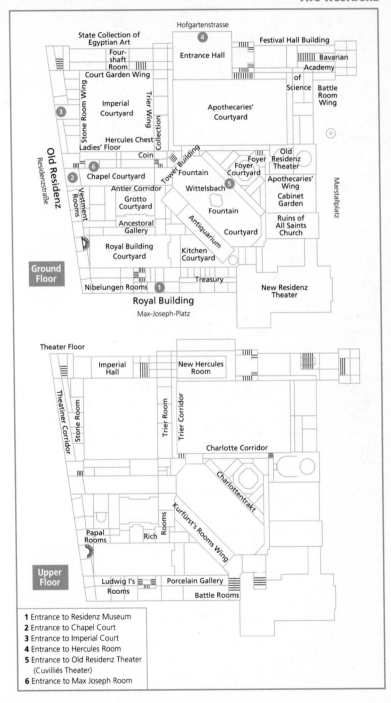

Ground Floor

- Hofgartenstrasse
- State Collection of Egyptian Art
- Four-shaft Room
- Entrance Hall
- Festival Hall Building
- Bavarian Academy of Science
- Court Garden Wing
- Stone Room Wing
- Imperial Courtyard
- Trier Wing
- Collection
- Apothecaries' Courtyard
- Battle Room Wing
- Hercules Chest
- Ladies' Floor
- Coin
- Tower Building
- Fountain
- Foyer
- Foyer Courtyard
- Old Residenz Theater
- Old Residenz
- Residenzstraße
- Chapel Courtyard
- Antler Corridor
- Wittelsbach
- Apothecaries' Wing
- Cabinet Garden
- Vestment Rooms
- Grotto Courtyard
- Fountain
- Ruins of All Saints Church
- Ancestoral Gallery
- Antiquarium
- Courtyard
- Marstallplatz
- Royal Building Courtyard
- Kitchen Courtyard
- Nibelungen Rooms
- Treasury
- New Residenz Theater
- Royal Building
- Max-Joseph-Platz

Upper Floor

- Theater Floor
- Imperial Hall
- New Hercules Room
- Theatiner Corridor
- Stone Room
- Trier Room
- Trier Corridor
- Charlotte Corridor
- Charlottentrakt
- Papal Rooms
- Rich
- Rooms
- Kurfürst's Rooms Wing
- Ludwig I's Rooms
- Porcelain Gallery
- Battle Rooms

1 Entrance to Residenz Museum
2 Entrance to Chapel Court
3 Entrance to Imperial Court
4 Entrance to Hercules Room
5 Entrance to Old Residenz Theater (Cuvilliés Theater)
6 Entrance to Max Joseph Room

An Unlikely Genius: François Cuvilliés

In the 17th and 18th centuries, Bavaria's rulers were determined to rival Rome itself by adorning their city with churches and abbeys and monuments. In the cutthroat competition for commissions that followed, an unexpected candidate emerged to become Munich's most brilliant master of the rococo style.

François Cuvilliés (1695–1768) was a dwarf born in Belgium. There were few roles open to those like him—they were regarded as freaks and collected by the rich as if they were curious objects. Like many of his peers, he became a page and later court jester to Max Emanuele, elector of Bavaria. Ambitious and witty, with a charm that transcended his stature, he won his patron's friendship and support.

When the elector was exiled, François went with him. It was during this exile, at St.-Cloud near Paris, that he first encountered the French baroque style and began to absorb his patron's interest in French aesthetics. When the elector was later recalled to Bavaria and reinstated as ruler with pomp and ceremony, François was allowed to become a draftsman for the court's chief architect.

Cuvilliés proved himself so talented that in 1720 the elector sent him for a four-year apprenticeship to one of the leading architects of Paris, Jacques-François Blondel. When he returned to Munich, his work soon eclipsed that of his master, and by 1745, the former jester had been elevated to the title of chief architect to the Bavarian court.

Commissions he received between 1726 and his death in 1768 include some of southern Germany's most important rococo monuments. His work was noted for a flamboyant sinuousness. His famous masterpiece is, of course, the remarkable **Altes Residenztheater,** familiarly called by his name. He is also responsible for the **Amalienburg Pavilion** in the park at Nymphenburg Palace and the facade of the **Theatinerkirche** (upon which his son, also an architect, put the final touches on after his father's death).

the Wittelsbach family, was the official residence of the rulers of Bavaria from 1385 to 1918. Added to and rebuilt over the centuries, the complex is a conglomerate of various styles. Depending on how you approach the Residenz, you might first see a German Renaissance hall (the western facade), a Palladian palace (on the north), or a Florentine Renaissance palace (on the south facing Max-Joseph-Platz).

The Residenz has been completely restored since its almost total destruction in World War II and now houses the Residenz Museum, a concert hall, the Cuvilliés Theater, and the Residenz Treasury. The **Residenz Museum** (℃ **089/ 29-06-71**) comprises the southwestern section of the palace, some 120 rooms of art and furnishings collected by centuries of Wittelsbachs. To see the entire collection, you'll have to take two tours, one in the morning and one in the afternoon. You may also visit the rooms on your own.

The **Ancestral Gallery** is designed like a hall of mirrors, except that instead of mirrors, there are portraits of the Wittelsbach family, set into gilded, carved paneling. The largest room in the museum section is the **Antiquarium,** possibly the finest example of interior Renaissance secular styling in Germany. Frescoes, painted by dozens of 16th- and 17th-century artists, adorn nearly every inch of space on the walls and ceilings. The room is broken into sections by pilasters and niches, each with its own bust of a Roman emperor or a Greek hero. The central attraction is the two-story chimneypiece of red stucco and marble, completed in 1600. It's adorned with Tuscan pillars and the coat of arms of the dukes of Bavaria.

On the second floor of the palace, directly over the Antiquarium, is an enormous collection of Far Eastern porcelain. Note also the fine assemblage of Oriental rugs in the long, narrow **Porcelain Gallery.**

If you have time to view only one item in the **Schatzkammer** ★★ (or treasury), make it the 16th-century Renaissance statue of *St. George Slaying the Dragon*. This equestrian statue is made of gold, but you can barely see the precious metal for the thousands of diamonds, rubies, emeralds, sapphires, and semiprecious stones embedded in it. Both the Residenz Museum and the Schatzkammer are entered from Max-Joseph-Platz on the south side of the palace.

Both the Residenz Museum and the Schatzkammer are entered from Max-Joseph-Platz on the south side of the palace. From the Brunnenhof, you can visit the Alte Residenztheater, better known as the **Cuvilliés Theater** ★★, whose rococo tiers of boxes are supported by seven bacchants. Directly over the huge center box, where the royal family sat, is a crest in white and gold topped by a jewel-bedecked crown of Bavaria held in place by cherubs in flight. In summer, this theater is the scene of frequent concert and opera performances. Mozart's *Idomeneo* was first performed here in 1781.

The Italianate **Hofgarten,** or Court Garden, is one of the special "green lungs" of Munich. To the north of the Residenz, it's enclosed on two sides by arcades; the garden dates from the time of Duke Maximilian I and was laid out between 1613 and 1617. In the center is the Hofgarten temple, a 12-sided pavilion dating from 1615. Also see the listing for the Staatliche Museum Ägyptischer Kunst (State Museum of Egyptian Art) on p. 109, which is located in the Residenz.

Max-Joseph-Platz 3. ⓒ 089/29-06-71. Museum and Treasury 4€ adults, 3€ students and seniors; Old Residenz Theater 3€ adults, 2€ students, free for children 15 and under. Combined ticket 7€ adults, 5€ students and children. Museum, Treasury, and Theatre daily 9am–6pm. U-bahn: U3, U4, U5, or U6 to Odeonsplatz.

Schloss Nymphenburg ★★   In summer, the Wittelsbachs would pack up their bags and head for their country house, Schloss Nymphenburg. A more complete, more sophisticated palace than the Residenz, it was begun in 1664 by Elector Ferdinand Maria in Italian-villa style and took more than 150 years to complete. The final palace plan was created mainly by Elector Max Emanuel, who in 1702 decided to enlarge the villa by adding four large pavilions connected by arcaded passageways. Gradually the French style took over, and today the facade is a subdued baroque.

The palace interior is less subtle, however. Upon entering the main building, you're in the great hall, decorated in rococo colors and stuccos. The frescoes by Johann Baptist Zimmermann (1756) depict incidents from mythology, especially those dealing with Flora, goddess of spring, and her nymphs, for whom the palace was named. This hall was used for both banquets and concerts during the reign of Max Joseph III, elector during the mid–18th century. Concerts are still presented here in summer.

From the main building, turn left and head for the arcaded gallery connecting the northern pavilions. The first room in the arcade is the Great Gallery of Beauties, painted for Elector Max Emanuel in 1710. More provocative, however, is King Ludwig I's Gallery of Beauties in the south pavilion (the apartments of Queen Caroline). Ludwig commissioned no fewer than 36 portraits of the most beautiful women of his day. The paintings by J. Stieler (created from 1827–50) include the *Schöne Münchenerin* (lovely Munich girl) and a portrait of Lola Montez, the dancer whose "friendship" with Ludwig caused a scandal that factored into the Revolution of 1848.

To the south of the palace buildings, in the rectangular block of low structures that once housed the court stables, is the **Marstallmuseum.** In the first hall, look for the glass coronation coach of Elector Karl Albrecht, built in Paris in 1740. From the same period comes the hunting sleigh of Electress Amalia, with the statue of Diana, goddess of the hunt; even the sleigh's runners are decorated with shellwork and hunting trophies.

The coaches and sleighs of Ludwig II are displayed in the **third hall.** His constant longing for the grandeur of the past is reflected in the ornately designed state coach, meant for his marriage to Duchess Sophie of Bavaria, a royal wedding that never came off. The fairy-tale coach wasn't wasted, however, since Ludwig often used it to ride through the countryside at night, and from castle to castle, creating quite a picture. The coach is completely gilded, inside and out; rococo carvings cover every inch of space except for the panels faced with paintings on copper. In winter, the king would ride in his state sleigh (also on display), nearly as elaborate as the Cinderella coach.

Nymphenburg's park ✿ stretches for 200 hectares (500 acres). A canal runs through it from the pool at the foot of the staircase to the cascade at the far end of the English-style gardens. Within the park are a number of pavilions. The guided tour begins with the **Amalienburg** ✿✿, whose plain exterior belies the rococo decoration inside, designed by Cuvilliés. Built as a hunting lodge for Electress Amalia (in 1734), the pavilion carries the hunting theme through the first few rooms and then bursts into salons of flamboyant colors, rich carvings, and wall paintings. The most impressive room is the Hall of Mirrors, a symphony of silver ornaments on a faint blue background.

The **Badenburg Pavilion** sits at the edge of the large lake of the same name. As its name implies, it was built as a bathing pavilion, although it's difficult to visualize Ludwig dashing in from the water in a dripping swimsuit and across those elegant floors. A trip to the basement, however, will help you appreciate the pavilion's practical side. Here you'll see the unique bath, surrounded by blue-and-white Dutch tiles. The ceiling is painted with frescoes of mythological bathing scenes.

The octagonal **Pagodenburg,** on the smaller lake on the other side of the canal, looks like a Chinese pagoda from the outside. The interior, however, is decorated with pseudo-Chinese motifs, often using Dutch tiles in place of Chinese ones.

Magdalenenklause may look like a ruin, but that was the intention when it was built in 1725. Also called the Hermitage, it was planned as a retreat for prayer and solitude. The four main rooms of the one-story structure are paneled with uncarved stained oak, with simple furnishings and a few religious paintings—a really drastic change from the other buildings.

Nymphenburg

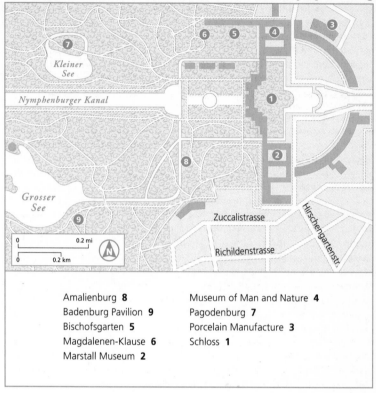

Amalienburg **8**

Badenburg Pavilion **9**

Bischofsgarten **5**

Magdalenen-Klause **6**

Marstall Museum **2**

Museum of Man and Nature **4**

Pagodenburg **7**

Porcelain Manufacture **3**

Schloss **1**

Other attractions include the **Porzellansammlung,** or museum of porcelain, which are above the stables of the Marstallmuseum. Some of the finest pieces of porcelain in the world, executed in the 18th century, are displayed here, along with an absolute gem—miniature copies in porcelain, done in extraordinary detail, of some of the grand masterpieces in the Old Pinakothek. Each was commissioned by Ludwig I.

For places to eat and drink in the area, see the reviews for Schlosscafé im Palmenhaus and Hirschgarten on p. 90 and 91 respectively.

Schloss Nymphenburg 1, 8km (5 miles) northwest of the city center. ✆ **089/17908-0.** Admission to castle 3.50€ free for children under 17. Admission to all attractions 7.50€, free for children under 17. Nov–Mar daily 10am–4pm; Apr–Oct daily 9am–6pm (Thurs until 8pm). Parking beside the Marstallmuseum. U-bahn: Rotkreuzplatz, then tram 17 toward Amalienburgstrasse. Bus: 41.

3 The Great Churches

In addition to the historic churches described below, visitors might also want to visit the **Matthäuskirche,** Nussbaumstrasse 1 (U-bahn: Sendlinger-Tor-Platz), an Evangelical cathedral built between 1953 and 1955.

Asamkirche   St.-Johann-Nepomuk-Kirche, commonly referred to as the *Asamkirche* after its builders, was constructed by the Asam brothers, Cosmas Damian and Egid Quirin. Although modest on the outside, the interior of this small 18th-century church is a baroque fantasy. Above the entrance stands a statue of the church's patron, St. Nepomuk, a 14th-century monk (said to have performed many noble deeds and known for helping the poor), who drowned in the Danube. Upon entering the chapel, visitors are greeted with a burst of frescoes surrounded by rich red stucco and lavishly gilded woodwork, a superb illustration of the Bavarian passion for ornamentation.

Sendlingerstrasse 62. © 089/260-93-57. Free admission. Daily 9am–8pm. U-bahn: Sendlinger Tor.

Frauenkirche (Cathedral of Our Lady) ★   When the smoke cleared from the 1945 bombings, only a fragile shell remained of Munich's largest church, which is affectionately known as Liebfrauenkirche. Workmen and architects who restored the 15th-century Gothic cathedral used whatever remains they could find in the rubble, along with modern innovations. The overall effect of the rebuilt Frauenkirche is strikingly simple, yet dignified.

The twin towers, or Liebfrauendom, which remained intact with their strange early Gothic onion domes, have been the city's landmark since they were added to the church in 1525. Instead of the typical flying buttresses, huge props on the inside support the edifice and separate the side chapels. Twenty-two simple octagonal pillars support the Gothic vaulting over the nave and chancel.

Entering the main doors at the cathedral's west end, you first notice no windows (actually, except for the tall chancel window, they're hidden by the enormous pillars). According to legend, the devil was delighted at the notion of hidden windows and stamped in glee at the stupidity of the architect—you can still see the strange footlike mark called "the devil's step" in the entrance hall.

In the chapel directly behind the high altar is the cathedral's most interesting painting: *The Protecting Cloak,* a 1510 work by Jan Polack, showing the Virgin holding out her majestic robes to shelter all humankind. The collection of tiny figures beneath the cloak includes everyone from the pope to peasants.

Frauenplatz 12. © 089/29-00-82-0. Free admission. Sat–Thurs 7am–7pm, Fri 7am–6pm. U-bahn/S-bahn: Marienplatz.

Michaelskirche   The largest Renaissance church north of the Alps, Michaelskirche was constructed by Duke Wilhelm the Pious in 1583. Seven years into construction, the tower collapsed. The duke took this as divine portent that the church was not large enough. During the second phase of construction, the size of the church was dramatically increased, making it not only the largest north of the Alps, but the possessor of the world's second largest barrel-vaulted roof. Among those who have been laid to rest in the crypt are Duke Wilhelm himself, more than 40 Wittelsbachs, and "Mad" King Ludwig II, perhaps the family's most notorious member.

Neuhauserstrasse 52. © 089/2-31-70-60. Free admission. Guided tour 3€, Wed at 2pm. Church daily 9am–7pm. Crypt Mon–Fri 10am–1pm and 3–4:45pm, Sat 10am–3pm. U-bahn or S-bahn: Karlsplatz, Stachus, or Marienplatz.

Peterskirche (St. Peter's Church)   Munich's oldest church (1180), known locally as Old Peter, has turned over a new leaf, and it's a gold one at that. The white-and-gray interior has been decorated with gilded baroque accents and trompe l'oeil medallions. It contains a series of murals by Johann Baptist Zimmermann, but nothing tops the attraction of the bizarre relic in the second chapel on the left: the gilt-covered and gem-studded skeleton of St. Mundita. From its resting place on a cushion, it stares at you with two false eyes in its skull. Jewels cover the mouth of its rotten teeth, quite a contrast to the fresh roses usually kept in front of the black-and-silver coffin. The church also has a tall steeple, which you can climb. Colored circles on the lower platform tell you whether the climb is worthwhile: If the circle is white, you can see as far as the Alps.

Rindermarkt 1 (near the Rathaus). ℭ **089/2-60-48-28.** Church free; tower 1.50€ adults, 1€ students, .30€ children. Mon–Sat 9am–7pm, Sun 10am–7pm. U-bahn/S-bahn: Marienplatz.

Theatinerkirche   Named for a small group of Roman Catholic clergy (the Theatines), this church, dedicated to Saint Kajetan, is Munich's finest example of Italian baroque. Two Italian architects, Barelli and Zucalli, began building it in 1662. François de Cuvilliés the Elder added the facade a century later, and his son finally completed the structure in 1768. Fluted columns that line the center aisle support the arched ceiling of the nave. Above the transept, dividing the nave from the choir, the ceiling breaks into an open dome, with an ornate gallery decorated with large but graceful statues. Nothing detracts from the whiteness of the interior except the dark wooden pews and the canopied pulpit. Since 1954 the church has been under the care of the Dominican Friars.

Theatinerstrasse 22. ℭ **089/21-06-96-0.** Free admission. Church Mon–Fri 10am–1pm and 1:30–4:30pm, Sat 10am–3pm. U-bahn: Odeonsplatz.

4 More Attractions

MUSEUMS

Antikensammlungen (Museum of Antiquities) ★   After 100 years of floating from one museum to another, the Museum of Antiquities finally found a home in the 19th-century neoclassical hall on the south side of Königsplatz. This collection grew around the vase collection of Ludwig I, who had fantasies of transforming Munich into a second Athens. It was originally called the Museum Antiker Kleinkunst (Museum of Small Works of Ancient Art). Many pieces are small in size but not in value or artistic significance.

Entering the museum, you're in the large central hall. The five main-floor halls house more than 650 Greek vases, collected from all parts of the Mediterranean. The pottery has been restored to near-perfect condition; much of it dates as far back as 500 B.C. The oldest piece here, "the goddess from Aegina," dates from 3000 B.C. This pre-Mycenaean figure, carved from a mussel shell, is on display with the Mycenaean pottery exhibits in Room I. The upper level of the Central Hall is devoted to large Greek vases discovered in Sicily and to Etruscan art.

Returning to the Central Hall, take the stairs down to the lower level to see the collection of Greek, Roman, and Etruscan jewelry. Note the similarities to today's design fashions. Included on this level, as well, are rooms devoted to ancient colored glass, Etruscan bronzes, and Greek terra cottas.

Königsplatz 1. ℭ **089/59-83-59.** Admission 3.50€ adults. Joint ticket to the Museum of Antiquities and the Glyptothek 6€ adults, free for children under 14; free for all on Sun. Tues and Thurs–Sun 10am–5pm, Wed 10am–8pm. U-bahn: U2 to Königsplatz. Tram 18.

Bavarian Film Studio   This is Europe's largest filmmaking center. Production was begun here as early as 1920. In the 1970s, Fassbinder, Wim Wenders, and Herzog worked here; Stanley Kubrick shot his interiors for *Paths of Glory,* and Bob Fosse produced *Cabaret.* Tours take you through the sets of famous films like *Das Boot* and *The Neverending Story,* and you can watch films on the Showscan, a superwide movie screen. Children enjoy the Action Show, a demonstration of movie stunts.

Bavariafilmplatz 7, Geiselgasteig. ⓒ **089/64-99-23-04.** Admission 10€ adults, 9€ students and senior citizens, 7€ children 4–14. Tours Mar–Oct daily 9am–4pm, Nov–Feb daily 10am–3pm; show Mar–Oct daily 11:30am and 1:30pm, additional shows Sat–Sun 2:30pm. Tram: 25.

Deutsches Theatermuseum   Founded in 1910, the German Theater-museum is a haven for theater fans from all over the world. Its collection includes theater plans and stage sets, as well as various props, costumes, and masks used in productions around the world. The archive contains thousands of manuscripts, programs, and revues. The museum's library houses additional manuscripts, scores, and journals. Available here is the *Münchner Spielplan,* a service providing information on all current theatrical performances in the Munich area.

Galeriestrasse 4a. ⓒ **089/2-10-69-10.** Free admission. Tues–Sun 10am–4pm; library Tues 10am–noon and 1:30–4pm. U-bahn: Odeonsplatz.

Glyptothek ⍟   The ideal neighbor for the Museum of Antiquities, the Glyptothek supplements the pottery and smaller pieces of the main museum with the country's largest collection of ancient Greek and Roman sculpture. Included are the famous pediments from the temple of Aegina, two marvelous statues of *kouroi* (youths) from the 6th century B.C., the colossal figure of a *Sleeping Satyr* from the Hellenistic period, and a splendid collection of Roman portraits. In all, the collection is the country's largest assemblage of classical art. King Ludwig I, who had fantasies of transforming Munich into another Athens, ordered it built.

Königsplatz 3. ⓒ **089/28-61-00.** Admission 3€ adults, 2€ seniors, free for children under 14; free for all on Sun. Joint ticket to the Museum of Antiquities and the Glyptothek 6€ adults, free for children under 14. Wed–Sun 10am–5pm, Tues 10am–8pm. U-bahn: U2 to Königsplatz.

Hildebrand Haus   Hildebrand Haus, former home and studio of sculptor Adolf von Hildebrand, now houses the Monacensia Library. Hildebrand, who is best known for designing the Wittelsbach Fountain, created and built the house in 1897. The library's collection is comprised of numerous manuscripts and unpublished works by various Bavarian writers and artists such as Frank Wedekind, Klaus Mann, and Ludwig Ganghofer.

Maria-Theresia Strasse 23. ⓒ **089/4-19-47-20.** Free admission. Mon–Wed 9am–3pm, Thurs 10am–5pm, Fri 9am–1pm. U-bahn: Prinzregentenplatz. Tram: 18.

Jüdisches Museum München   This small, private museum portrays the history of Jews in Nazi Germany through photographs, letters, and exhibits. The horrors suffered during Nazi occupation are startlingly illuminated through powerful portraits of daily life. The yellow stars that Jews were forced to wear continuously are on display, as well as an exhibit that chronicles the hunt for Raoul Wallenburg, the Swedish diplomat who spirited hundreds of Jews to safety during World War II.

Reichenbachstrasse 27. ⓒ **089/20-00-96-93.** Free admission. Tues 2–6pm, Wed 10am–noon and 2–6pm, Thurs 2–8pm. U-bahn: Isartor. Tram: 18.

Münchner Stadtmuseum (Municipal Museum) ⍟   Munich's Municipal Museum is to the city what the Bavarian National Museum is to the whole state. Housed in the former armory building, the museum offers insight into the city's history and the daily lives of its people. Special exhibitions about popular arts and traditions are frequently presented. A wooden model shows Munich in 1572. The extensive furniture collection is changed annually so that visitors have a chance to see various periods from the vast storehouse.

The museum's most important exhibit is its Morris Dancers (*Moriskentanzer*) on the ground floor. These 10 figures, each 60cm (2 ft.) high, carved in wood, and painted in bright colors by Erasmus Grasser in 1480, are among the best examples of secular Gothic art in Germany. In the large Gothic hall on the ground floor you can admire an important collection of armor and weapons from the 14th to the 18th century.

The second-floor photo museum traces the early history of the camera back to 1839. The historical collection of musical instruments on the fourth floor is one of the greatest of its kind in the world. It includes an ethnological collection. Daily at 6 and 9pm, the film museum shows two films from its extensive archives.

St. Jacobs-Platz 1. (C) **089/233-22370**. Admission 2.50€ adults, 1.50€ students and children 6–15, free for children 5 and under; free for all on Sun. Tues–Sun 10am–6pm. U-bahn/S-bahn: Marienplatz.

Schack-Galerie   To appreciate this florid and romantic overdose of sentimental German paintings of the 19th century, you've got to enjoy fauns and elves at play in picturesque, even magical, landscapes. Such art has its devotees. Obviously, if you're a Picasso Cubist, you'd be better off going elsewhere. But this once-private collection adheres to the baroque tastes of Count Adolf Friedrich von Schack of Schwerin (1815–94), who spent a rich life acquiring works by the likes of Spitzweg, Schwind, Fuerbach, and others, many others, some of whom would have been appropriately assigned to the dust bin of art history. Still in all, we find a visit here fun, at least on a rainy, gray day. It's like wandering back to a lost world and getting absorbed in the taste of yesterday.

Prinzregentenstrasse 9. (C) **089/23805-224**. Admission 5€ adults, 3.50€ children. Wed–Mon 10am–5pm. Bus: 53.

Stadtische Galerie im Lenbachhaus ★   This gallery is in the ancient gold-colored villa of portrait painter Franz von Lenbach (1836–1904). It's devoted both to his work and that of other artists. Enter through the gardens. You'll first be greeted by a large collection of early pieces by Paul Klee (1879–1940). There's also an outstanding group of works by Kandinsky, leader of the Blue Rider movement in the early 20th century, and many 19th- and 20th-century paintings throughout the villa. The enclosed patio is pleasant for a coffee break.

Luisenstrasse 33. (C) **089/23-33-20-00**. Admission 5€ adults, 2.50€ students and children 6–12, free for children 5 and under. Tues–Sun 10am–6pm. U-bahn: Königsplatz.

Staatliche Museum Ägyptischer Kunst (State Museum of Egyptian Art)   The Egyptian collection is located in the Residenz (p. 100). The museum evolved from the collections made by Duke Albrecht V and King Ludwig I and contains pieces from every period of Egyptian history, from the predynastic period (4500–3000 B.C.) to the Coptic period (4th–9th centuries A.D.). On exhibit are sculptures, reliefs, jewelry, tools, and weapons, as well as sarcophagi.

Hofgartenstrasse 1. (C) **089/29-85-46**. Admission 3.50€ adults, 2.50€ children. Mon 10am–5pm, Tues 9am–5pm and 7–9pm, Wed–Fri 9am–5pm, Sat–Sun 10am–5pm. U-bahn: Odeonsplatz. S-bahn: Marienplatz.

Stuck-Villa (Jugendstil Museum)   This splendid house was designed by painter Franz von Stuck (1863–1928) for himself and mingles Art Nouveau style with elements of the late neoclassical. The ground-floor living rooms contain frescoes by the artist himself, and many of his paintings are on display. On the first floor is a permanent collection of *Jugendstil* (German Art Nouveau)

Prinzregentenstrasse 60. (C) **089/45-55-51-25**. Free admission. Daily 10am–6pm, Thurs until 9pm. U-bahn: U4 to Prinzregentenplatz.

> ⟨ *Fun Fact* **Looks Like a Soup Tureen But Isn't**
>
> If you think you've seen it all, you haven't until you've visited the Bourdalou (a delicate, glorified "chamber pot") Museum in the ZAM complex. First introduced in the 14th century, Bourdalou's were usually made of glass with a funnel-like mouth and a narrow neck. Often, the user could "do their business" while remaining in bed. It is said that there was a very verbose Jesuit priest named Father Bourdalou. His sermons were unusually long, and proper ladies could answer the calls of nature discreetly in their chamber pots without interrupting the sermon's flow.
>
> By the 18th and 19th centuries, the Bourdalou, named for this long-winded priest, became the rage among ladies of Europe, and their manufacturers lavished costly decorations and intricate details on creating these pots. Today, they are viewed as collector's items. Before people had indoor plumbing, the Bourdalou was to be used in the living or dining room during the day, the chamber pot for the bedroom at night.

Staatliches Museum für Völkerkunde (Ethnology Museum)   This museum, housed in an imposing building completed in 1865, has an extensive collection of art and artifacts from all over the world and is one of the principal museums of its kind in Europe. Particularly interesting is the Peruvian collection; the museum also has exhibitions from other parts of South America, East Asia, and West and Central Africa.

Maximilianstrasse 42. ⟨ **089/2-10-13-60**. Admission 3€, 1€ children 6–10, free for children 5 and under. Tues–Sun 9:30am–4:30pm. Tram: 17 or 19.

ZAM ⟨ *Finds*   It's not the name of a single museum, but an abbreviation for a center of galleries featuring extravagant and extraordinary objects. The most fascinating is the **Bourdalou Museum (Chamber Pot Museum),** the first in the world, where, incredibly, more than 2,000 examples give visitors a fascinating glimpse of two millennia of chamber pot history. This gallery is guaranteed to elicit a smile, if not a giggle, from even the most jaded museum goer.

Down through the centuries all cultures were familiar with some form of the chamber pot and would decorate these very functional items according to their taste. As the centuries went by, the ornamentation grew more baroque and decorative, as if to disguise their real function. Some of these chamber pots—called "faithful companions"—were owned by royalty and other imperial personages.

Another branch of ZAM is the **Pedal-Car Museum,** tracing a century, in miniature, of the automobile. This amazing collection begins in the 19th century and goes on to include sophisticated creations of Bugatti, Mercedes, and Rolls-Royce, all copies for children.

The **Sisi Museum** is the first of its kind to be devoted to the Empress Elisabeth of Austria, the queen of Franz-Josef. Furniture, clothing, paintings, photographs, letters, and several hundreds of the Empress' personal objects recreate her fascinating life, which was ended by an assassin in Switzerland.

The **Padlock Museum** shows us that this was one of the earliest of human inventions for protecting property. Several hundred specimens spanning 2,000 years document what craftsmen concocted to lock up property—everything from medieval instruments of torture to chastity belts.

At the **Easter Bunny Museum,** more than a thousand bunnies illustrate what an important figure the rabbit was in the fantasy world of children.

The **Museum of Scent** displays elaborate perfume flasks, some 5,000 objects, used to bottle scents. These range from the age of Biedermeier to more modern editions, including miniatures. Some of the exclusive limited editions from the houses of Dior, Chanel, Lalique, Baccarat, Mouson, and 4711 are exhibited.

Westenriederstrasse 41. © 089/2904-121. Admission 4€ adults, 3€ children. Daily 10am–6pm. U-bahn: Marienplatz.

5 Parks, Gardens & the Zoo

Munich's city park, the 18th-century **Englischer Garten** ✪, borders Schwabing on the east and extends almost to the Isar River. This is one of the largest and most beautiful city parks in Germany. It was the brainchild of Sir Benjamin Thompson, the English scientist who spent most of his life in the service of the Bavarian government. You can wander for hours along the walks and among the trees, flowers, and sunbathers. Nude sunbathing is permitted in certain areas of the park (some claim these areas are Munich's most popular tourist attraction). For a break, stop for tea on the plaza near the Chinese pagoda, or have a beer at the nearby beer garden. You might also take along a picnic put together at the elegant shop of **Alois Dallmayr,** or less expensive fare from **Hertie,** across from the Hauptbahnhof, from **Kaufhof** at Marienplatz, or from Munich's famous open-air market, the **Viktualienmarkt.**

Bordering Nymphenburg Park to the north is the **Botanischer Garten.** The garden is composed of 20 hectares (49 acres) of land, and has more than 15,000 varieties of flora. Each subdivision is devoted to a particular variety of plants. The highlight is the alpine garden, laid out according to geographic region and altitude. It's at its peak during the summer months. Another favored attraction is the heather garden; visitors to the garden during the late summer months are treated to an explosion of vibrant violets and purples. Other attractions include the rose garden, fern gorge, and the series of hothouses that are home to numerous exotic tropical plants. To reach the Botanischer Garten, located on Menzingerstrasse 67 (© **089/17-86-13-10**), take tram 17. The garden is open November to January, daily from 9am to 4:30pm; February and March, daily from 9am to 5pm; April, September, and October, daily from 8am to 5pm; and May to August, daily from 9am to 7pm. The hothouses close half an hour before the garden does. Admission is 2.50€ for adults and 1€ for children.

In west Munich, between Schloss Nymphenburg and the main railway line, stands the **Hirschgarten.** Designated by Elector Karl Theodor as a deer park in 1791, this 27 hectare (67-acre) tract of land is home to one of Munich's most tranquil stretches of greenery. In the 19th century, Münchners would visit the meadow to view the protected game as they grazed. The head huntsman secured the right to sell beer, which prompted the Hirschgarten to soar in popularity. Eventually a beer garden was established, now the largest in the world, with a capacity for 8,000 thirsty patrons. To reach the park, you can take the S-bahn to Laim; or you can catch bus no. 32 or 83 from Steubenplatz. Although no longer a wildlife preserve, the Hirschgarten still draws the citizens of Munich for picnics, barbecues, or afternoon chess games.

Hellabrunn Zoo stands in Tierpark Hellabrunn, about 6km (4 miles) south of the city center, at Tierparkstrasse 30 (© **089/62-50-80;** U-bahn: Thalkirchen;

bus: 52). It's one of the largest zoos in the world, with hundreds of animals roaming in a natural habitat. A walk through the attractive park is recommended even if you're not a zoo buff. There's a big children's zoo, as well as a large aviary. You can visit the zoo daily 8am to 6pm (in winter, 9am–5pm); admission is 6€ for adults, 4.50€ for students and seniors, 3€ for children ages 4 to 14, and free for children 3 and under. To reach the park, you can take bus no. 52, leaving the Marienplatz, or U-bahn U3 to Thalkirchen.

6 The Olympic Grounds

Olympiapark (② **089/30-67-24-14;** U-bahn: Olympiazentrum), site of the 1972 Olympic Games, occupies 300 hectares (740 acres) at the city's northern edge. More than 15,000 workers from 18 countries transformed the site into a park of nearly 5,000 trees, 43km (27 miles) of roads, 32 bridges, and a lake. Olympiapark is a city in itself: It has its own railway station, U-bahn line, mayor, post office, churches, and elementary school. The planners even broke the city skyline by adding a 293m (960-ft.) television tower in the center of the park.

The area's showpiece is a huge stadium, capable of seating 69,300 spectators, and topped by the largest roof in the world—nearly 67,000 sq. m. (80,000 sq. yds.) of tinted acrylic glass. The roof serves the additional purpose of collecting rainwater and draining it into the nearby Olympic lake.

Olympia Tower, Olympiapark (② **089/30-67-27-50**), is open daily 9am to midnight. A ticket for a ride up the tower (on the speediest elevator on the continent, no less) costs 3€ for adults and 1.50€ for children under 15. An exclusive dining spot in the tower is the **Tower Restaurant** (② **089/30668585**), which features a selection of international and German dishes. Food is served daily 11am to 5:30pm and 6:30pm to midnight. A complete dinner costs 35€ to 50€. The food is good and fresh, but of secondary consideration—most come here for the extraordinary view, which reaches to the Alps. Four observation platforms look out over Olympiapark. The Tower Restaurant revolves around its axis in 60 minutes, giving guests who linger a changing vista of Munich. Diners Club, MasterCard, and Visa are accepted.

Tips **Munich's Soccer Craze**

Like Italy, England, and Brazil, Germany is crazed over soccer. Munich's famous soccer team (and one of Europe's most outstanding) is the **Bayern München.** However, it's a matter of civic pride to many Münchners, especially when they're soaked with beer, to root enthusiastically for a less-well-rated local team, **T.S.V. 1860 München.** This team was around about 40 years before Bayern München was founded, and it still arouses local loyalty—something like the Chicago White Sox as opposed to the much beloved and beleaguered Chicago Cubs. Both teams call the Olympic Stadium in Olympiapark their home.

If you want to attend a soccer match, chances are good there'll be one in Munich's enormous **Olympia stadium** (see above). For more information, call the Soccer League Association at **089/69-93-10.** To get tickets for any sports event, call ② **089/54-81-81-81,** Monday to Friday 9am to 6pm and Saturday 10am to 3:30pm.

Black September for the Olympics

The 1972 Munich Olympics, the largest ever in history, was meant to celebrate peace among nations, and for the first 10 days, they did. However, in the early morning hours of September 5, eight Palestinian terrorists, later claiming to be part of the "Black September" terrorist group, sneaked into the Olympic Village. Within a few minutes of entering the quarters of the sleeping Israeli athletes, they had already killed two Israelis and taken nine of the others hostage.

As the ensuing siege was played out on TV sets around the world, the terrorists demanded the release of 200 Arab guerillas jailed in Israel, and safe passage for themselves and their hostages. Few novelists could have conceived the plot (and mistakes by German law enforcement) that ensued, as negotiations helplessly and hopelessly dragged on between the terrorists and the West German security officials. In Israel, Golda Meir firmly stood by her government's policy of "not dealing with terrorists." The job of dealing with the terrorists fell clearly upon the shoulders of the West Germans.

By 8:30pm on the day of the attack, the first of three helicopters landed at Olympic Village to fly the terrorists and their hostages out of West Germany via a Lufthansa 737 that was waiting at the military air base at Fürstenfeldbruck, 24km (15 miles) away. Blinded and tied close together, the Israeli athletes, along with their heavily armed captors, were placed into the helicopters and flown away, landing at Fürstenfeldbruck at 10:30pm.

The negotiations between the terrorists and West German security officials suddenly collapsed when a West German sharpshooter hidden in the darkness fired unexpectedly at the terrorists. The Palestinians quickly responded by unleashing automatic fire at the tied and bound Israelis; one tossed a hand grenade into a helicopter, killing all of the remaining hostages. In response, the West Germans unleashed their fire power, killing five of the terrorists, and eventually capturing the others.

Mark Spitz, an American Jew and winner of seven gold medals, was flown out of Germany for his own safety as the Olympic Games were suspended for the first time in their history. The world mourned, and in a controversial decision, the Germans continued the games 34 hours later, with mixed reactions from both the world at large and the participating athletes. The presiding officer of the games, Avery Brundage, issued a famous pronouncement, "The Games must go on!" and so they did.

For more on this tragic event, read or watch the book/documentary movie titled *One Day in September.*

At the base of the tower is the **Restaurant Olympiasee,** Spiridon-Louis-Ring 7 (✆ **089/30-67-28-08**), serving genuine Bavarian specialties, with meals costing 8€ and up. Favored items include half a roast chicken and various hearty soups. Food is served daily 9:30am to 7pm (8:30pm in summer). The restaurant is popular in summer because of its terrace. No credit cards are accepted. Take U-bahn U3 or U8 to Olympiazentrum.

Near Olympiapark, you can visit the **BMW Museum,** Petuelring 130 (✆ **089/38-22-33-07**; U-bahn: Petuelring or Olympiazentrum), where the history of the automobile is stunningly displayed in an atmosphere created by Oscar-winner Rolf Zehetbauer, a "film architect." The exhibition "Horizons in Time," housed in a "demisphere" of modern architecture, takes you into the future and back to the past. You can view 24 video films and 10 slide shows (an especially interesting one shows how people of yesterday imagined the future). Many of the exhibits are in English. The museum is open daily 9am to 4pm, charging 3€ for adults and 2€ for children. While here, you might also ask about BMW factory tours. Take U-bahn U3 or U8 to Olympiazentrum.

7 Especially for Kids

From the Deutsches Museum to the Marionetten Theater to the Bavarian Film Studio, kids love Munich.

Take your children to the **Münchner Stadtmuseum,** St. Jakobsplatz 1 (© **089/23-32-23-70;** U-bahn/S-bahn: Marienplatz). On the third floor is an array of puppets from around the world, with star billing going to the puppeteer's art. The comical and grotesque figures include both marionettes and hand puppets. The collection also includes detailed puppet theaters and miniature scenery, a Lilliputian version of the world of the stage. A special department is devoted to fairground art, including carousel animals, shooting galleries, roller-coaster models, and wax and museum figures. The main exhibit contains the oldest-known carousel horses, dating from 1820. For hours and admission fees, see "More Attractions," earlier in this chapter.

If children have a favorite museum in Munich, it's the **Deutsches Museum,** Museumsinsel 1 (© **089/2-17-91**), which has many interactive exhibits. For details, see "Palaces & Major Museums," earlier in this chapter.

Spielzeugmuseum, in the Altes Rathaus, Marienplatz 15 (© **089/29-40-01;** U-bahn/S-bahn: Marienplatz), is a historical toy collection. It's open daily 10am to 5pm. Admission is 3€ for adults, 1€ for children, and 6€ for a family.

At the **Münchner Marionetten Theater,** Blumenstrasse 32A (© **089/26-57-12**), you can attend puppet shows and the *théâtre de marionnettes.* Adults as well as children are delighted with the productions; many are of Mozart operas. Performances are on Wednesday, Thursday, Saturday, and Sunday at 3pm. Admission is 5€ for adults and 3€ for children. Performances on Saturday evening at 8pm cost 8€. Matinees tend to be more animated and crowded than evening performances and are particularly well-suited to younger children age 4 and up. To reach the theater, take the U-bahn to Sendlinger Tor.

At the **Bavarian Film Studio,** Bavariafilmplatz 7, Geiselgasteig (© **089/64-99-23-04;** tram: 25 to Bavariafilmplatz), Europe's largest filmmaking center and Munich's version of Hollywood, children enjoy the film presentations and the Bavaria Action Show, which features a stunt team demonstrating fist fights and fire stunts, tumbling down staircases, and even taking a 28m (92-ft.) high plunge. Guided 1½-hour tours (book 4 weeks in advance for a tour in English) are given March to October, daily 9am to 4pm (off-season 10am–3pm). Admission is 10€ for adults, 9€ for students and senior citizens, 7€ for children ages 4 to 14, and free for children 3 and under. For more information, see p. 107.

The **Hellabrunn Zoo** has a large children's zoo where children can pet the animals. For details, see "Parks, Gardens & the Zoo," earlier in this chapter.

Not to be ignored is the **Circus Krone,** Marstrasse 43 (© **089/55-81-66**). It might be compared to London's Albert Hall, since its productions are so varied. From December 25 to March 31, a circus show is presented. There are matinee circus performances Tuesday to Sunday.

8 Sightseeing Tours

CITY TOURS

Blue buses that give sightseeing tours in both German and English leave from the square in front of the Hauptbahnhof, at Hertie's, year-round. Tickets are sold on the bus; no advance booking is necessary. A 1-hour tour, costing 11€ for adults and 6€ for children 6 to 12, leaves daily every hour from 10am to 4pm.

A 2½-hour tour, including the Olympic Tower, costs 19€ for adults and 10€ for children. Departures are May to October at 10am and 2:30pm and November to April at 2:30pm.

A second 2½-hour tour, costing 21€ for adults and 11€ for children, visits the famous Neue Pinakothek, the cathedral, and the performing clock at Marienplatz. It departs Tuesday to Sunday at 10am.

A third 2½-hour tour, costing 21€ for adults and 10€ for children, visits Nymphenburg Palace and the Schatzkammer. It departs daily at 2:30pm.

These city tours are offered by **Panorama Tours** at Arnulfstrasse 8 (© **089/ 54-90-75-60**).

If you'd like to go farther afield and visit major attractions in the environs (such as Berchtesgaden or Ludwig II's castles), contact **Panorama Tours.** The office is at Arnulfstrasse 8 (© **089/54-90-75-60**), to the north of the Hauptbahnhof. Hours are Monday to Friday 8am to 6pm, Saturday 8am to 2pm, and Sunday and holidays 8am to noon.

DAY TRIPS NEARBY

If you'd like to visit some of the Bavarian attractions outside of Munich, you can sign up with **Panorama Tours,** an affiliate of Gray Line. Their office is at Arnulfstrasse 8 (© **089/54-90-75-60**), to the north of the Hauptbahnhof. Hours are 8am to 6pm Monday to Friday, 8am to 2pm Saturday, and 8am to noon Sunday and holidays. The firm offers about a half-dozen tours of the region around Munich, usually priced at 41€ per adult and 21€ per child.

If you want to visit King Ludwig's famous castles, there's a 10½-hour tour to Neuschwanstein and Linderhof costing 39€. A 10½-hour tour for 41€ takes you to Ludwig's castle at Herremchiemsee. You can also book a tour to Salzburg in Austria that includes a boat ride on the Wolfgangsee and takes about 11½ hours, costing 41€. A tour to the Alpine town of Berchtesgaden and to the site of Hitler's once luxurious retreat at Obersalzburg takes 10½-hours and costs 41€.

On a darker note is a 4½-hour excursion to Dachau, departing every Saturday at 1:30pm. The tour incorporates a visit to the notorious concentration camp and also a tour through the historic town of Dachau itself and the medieval Schloss Dachau. During the visit to the death camp, participants are requested to respect the dignity of the site by wearing appropriate attire. It is priced at 21€.

BIKE TOURS

Pedal pushers will want to try Mike Lasher's popular **Mike's Bike Tour,** Hochbrückenstrasse (© **089/255-43-987**). His bike-rental services include maps and locks, child and infant seats, and helmets at no extra charge. English and bilingual tours of central Munich run from March to November at 11:30am and 4pm daily (call to confirm). Customers love Mike's charm. Participants meet under the tower of the old town hall, a gray building on the east end of

Marienplatz. Mike, the consummate guide, will be here—whistle in mouth—letting everyone know who he is. The tour veers from the bike paths only long enough for a lunch stop at a beer garden. Fear not, fainthearted: the bikes are new and the rides are easy, with plenty of time for historical explanations, photo opportunities, and question-and-answer sessions. Bike rentals for tours without a guide (Mike will supply a map) are 15€ for the day; full-day guided tours begin at 33€.

Since 1988, **Radius Tours & Bikes,** Arnulfstrasse 3 (© 089/596113), offers bike rentals at a little shop in the main train station opposite tracks 30 to 36. You're offered a choice of more than 200 bikes ranging from 3-gear bikes to 21-gear mountain bikes. Prices are 3€ per hour or 14€ per day. The outfit is open daily from May 1 to mid-October from 10am to 6pm.

Some of the best bike and walking tours in Munich are offered by the appropriately named **Bike & Walk Company,** Tal 22 (© 089/589-589-33). In addition to the standard bike and walking tours, which, of course, include visits to Munich-style beer gardens, the company also arranges hiking through the Bavarian Alps and white-water rafting and canyon tours. Its most unusual walk is a historic Third Reich Tour through the heart of Munich, focusing on the Nazi period that led to Hitler's rise to power. The meeting point for all the walking tours, costing 7.65€ per person, is the main entrance to the Rathaus (Town Hall) directly under the Glockenspiel on Marienplatz. Just show up—no reservations are necessary. Bike rentals are also available, and the staff here will outline their favorite routes for visitors.

9 Activities & Outdoor Pursuits

BEACHES, POOLS & WATER SPORTS

On hot weekends, Münchners travel to nearby lakes, the **Ammersee** and the **Starnbergersee,** where bathing facilities are clearly marked. Both are a short drive from the city, and are favorites for sailing, windsurfing, and other water sports (see chapter 10 for more information). Visitors can also go for a dip at **Maria-Einsiedel,** in the frigid, snow-fed waters of the Isar River.

The city has several public swimming pools. The largest of these is the giant competition-size pool in the Olympiapark, the **Olympia-Schwimmhalle** (© 089/30-67-22-90; U-bahn: Olympiazentrum). Admission is 7€ for adults and 2.50€ for children. Information on both sailing and windsurfing is available from the **Bayerischer Landes-Sportverbund,** Georg-Brauchle-Ring 93 (© 089/15-70-23-66).

BIKING

The city is full of bike paths. Most major streets have bike lanes, and the many parks and gardens scattered throughout Munich offer hours of riding. The tourist office provides suggested tours in its *Radi Touren.* Although printed in German, the excellent maps are easily followed. You can rent bikes at **City Hopper Tours,** Hohenzollern Strasse 95 (© 089/2-72-11-31); **Mike's Bike Tour** (© 089/255-43-987; see above); and **Radius Tours & Bikes,** Arnulfstrasse 3 (© 089/596113). Many S-bahn stations also rent bikes and allow them to be returned at other S-bahn stations.

BOATING

Rowboats add to the charm of the lakes in the **Englischer Garten.** (There's also a kiosk located at the edge of the Kleinhesselcher See for rentals during clement weather.) There are rowboat rentals on the southern bank of the **Olympiasee,** in the Olympiapark.

Raft trips on the Isar River, between the town of Wolfrathausen and Munich, begin in early May and last until late September. A raft may contain up to 60 other passengers, but if the idea appeals to you, contact **Franz and Sebastian Seitner,** Heideweg 9, D-82515 Wolfrathausen (℡ **089/15-70-23-66**).

GOLF

One of the best courses is **Golf Club Feldafing,** Tutzingerstrasse 15, D-82340 Feldafing (℡ **08157/9-33-40**), situated beside a clear Bavarian lake, the Starnbergersee. It's open from April to mid-November every day from 8am to 7pm (closed in winter.) Depending on the day of the week you arrive, greens fees cost 60€ for 18 holes. Be warned in advance that although you can play without a reservation every Monday to Friday (if you have a handicap of 34 or less), on Saturday and Sunday, you'll need to be accompanied by a club member.

Golfclub Strasslach (also known as the Munich Golf Club), Grünwald (℡ **08170/450**), requires visitors to reserve their tee-times in advance. The course charges greens fees of 60€. From April to October only, this course is open to the general public Monday to Friday 8am to 7pm; otherwise weekends are reserved for members only. Both of the above-mentioned clubs lie within a 45-minute drive south of Munich's center.

HIKING & HILL-CLIMBING

See chapter 11, "The Bavarian Alps."

JOGGING

Regardless of the season, the most lushly landscaped place in Munich is the **Englischer Garten** (U-bahn: Münchner Freiheit), which has a 11km (7-mile)

Moments Moon Over Munich

German health guru Gaby Just operates **Just Pure Day Spa,** 13 Siegesstrasse (℡ **089/3835-6999**), offering treatments and therapies from ancient times that correspond to lunar phases. A "waxing" or full moon, according to Just, is a time when "the body breathes in." This is when spa devotees are pampered from head to foot, with skin and hair vitamins, body and face treatments, and nutrition programs.

A "waning" or new moon is, again according to Just, when "the body breathes out." This is when the body releases, eliminating water, detoxifying and purifying itself. Deep-cleansing measures for the body are emphasized, including salt and alga baths along with peelings. Rejuvenating "bio body packs" are good enough to eat. Just believes that everything that supplies the body with nutrients from the inside is also good as an external wrapper. She applies, for example, fresh fruit as a moisturizer to the skin combined with cream and yogurt. Avocados, cucumbers, or carrots provide the vitamins. The almond and coconut oil or the honey and aloe vera might wean one from cold cream forever. Baths such as a "blossom" bath or an herbal bath range from 35€ to 45€, with body massages priced from 65€ to 90€.

circumference and an array of dirt and asphalt tracks. Also appropriate are the grounds of the **Olympiapark** (U-bahn: Olympiazentrum) or the park surrounding **Schloss Nymphenburg** (U-bahn: Rotkreuzplatz, then tram 17 toward Amalienburgstrasse; Bus: 41.). More convenient to the center of the city's commercial district is a jog along the embankments of the Isar River.

SKIING

Downhill skiers will want to make an excursion to the Zugspitze, the highest mountain peak in Germany. Ski slopes begin at an elevation of 2,610m (8,700 ft.). For information on ski resorts and other snow-related activities in the Munich area, contact **Bayerischer Landes-Sportverbund,** Georg-Brauchle-Ring 93 (② **089/15-70-23-66**).

TENNIS

At least 200 indoor and outdoor tennis courts are scattered around greater Munich. Many can be booked in advance by calling ② **089/54-81-81-81.** For information on Munich's many tennis tournaments and competitions, contact the **Bayerischer Tennis Verbund,** Georg-Brauchle-Ring 93, 80992 München (② **089/15-70-23-66**).

7

Munich Strolls

A walk through Munich is the only true way to get to know it. The Altstadt (Old Town/historic center) is the traditional walking tour for most visitors, but travelers with more time may enjoy visiting some of the lesser known but equally interesting sights near this historic city center. And a walk through Schwabing is a must for those who want to have a more offbeat experience.

| WALKING TOUR 1 | THE HISTORIC CENTER |

Start:	Frauenkirche.
Finish:	Königsplatz.
Time:	2½ hours, not counting shopping or any visits inside places mentioned here.
Best Times:	Daylight hours during clement weather.
Worst Times:	Monday to Friday from 7:30 to 9am and 4:30 to 6pm, because of heavy traffic.

With a history spanning centuries of building and rebuilding, Munich is one of Europe's most architecturally interesting cities. Postwar developments have marred Munich's once homogeneous look, but in rebuilding their city after the war, Münchners tried to respect tradition as much as possible. If you, like the average visitor, have time for only one walking tour, make it the historic center. This tour will take you through the monumental center of Munich, the point where the city began before it branched out in all directions. And even though all of Munich covers 311 sq. km (120 sq. miles), the section covered on this tour is the best for walking around.

To launch your tour on foot, you can first take public transportation, either the U-bahn or S-bahn to Marienplatz, the very heart of Munich—comparable to what Times Square is to New York City. After leaving the subway stop, the tour of the historic center begins to the immediate west where you'll see a dignified cathedral with impressive brickwork.

❶ Frauenkirche

This cathedral was begun in 1468 on the site of a much older church and was completed after 20 years. The majestically somber building is capped with twin towers. In spite of massive bombings, these towers escaped Allied bombardments during World War II and now serve as landmarks on Munich's skyline and are used so much so that they've also become a symbol of the city.

After admiring the towers' design, walk southeast along any of the pedestrian alleyways radiating away from the rear of the church. In a couple of minutes, you'll find yourself in the most famous medieval square of Munich.

❷ Marienplatz

In the center of this square, a golden statue of the Virgin Mary (the **Mariensäule**) rises above pavement that was first laid in the 1300s when the rest of the city's streets were a morass of mud and sewage. On the square's northern boundary sits the richly ornamented neo-Gothic Neues Rathaus (New City Hall), built between 1867 and 1908 as a symbol of Munich's power. On its facade is the famous Glockenspiel, the mechanical clock that performs a miniature tournament several times a day. At the square's eastern border, beyond a stream of traffic, is the simpler and smaller Altes Rathaus (Old City Hall), which was rebuilt in its present form in 1470 after fire destroyed an even earlier version.

From the square, walk south along Rindermarkt, encircling the masonry bulk of the:

❸ Peterskirche

This church's interior is a sun-flooded fantasy of baroque stucco and gilt. Completed in 1180, the church was built on the foundations of a Romanesque basilica erected around A.D. 1000. St. Peter's is the oldest parish church in Munich, and for many years, it was the only one. If you have time, you can explore the richly decorated interior. Otherwise, on a walking tour, you might settle for a view of the impressive Gothic facade, which was constructed between 1379 and 1386 when a fire destroyed the church in 1327.

Walk around the outside of the church to the back, where you'll find the sprawling premises of one of the best-stocked food emporiums in Europe, the:

❹ Viktualienmarkt

Known as "Munich's stomach," this is where you can snack, have a beer, pick up the makings of a picnic, or just observe the ritual of European grocery shopping.

At the northern end, at the corner where streets Rosen Tal and Im Tal meet, rises the richly ornate baroque walls of the:

❺ Heiliggeist (Holy Ghost) Church

Originally belonging to the 14th century Hospice of the Holy Ghost, a medieval order flourishing in the 1300s, this is called a Gothic "Hall Church." It was built on foundations laid by another structure in the 12th century, and the church was completed in 1730. Except for the church, the other hospice buildings were demolished in 1885. Architects at that time added three bays on the western facade of the church, giving it a neo-baroque facade. World War II bombs brought much destruction, and only the original choir, buttresses, and the north wall of the nave remain intact. The rest of the building is a reconstruction.

From here, cross the busy boulevard identified as Im Tal and walk north along Maderbraustrasse (within a block it will change its name to Orlandostrasse and then to Am Platzl). Here, look for the entrance to the most famous beer hall in Europe, the state-owned:

❻ Hofbräuhaus

For a description, see p. 149. For the moment, note its location for an eventual return.

Now, walk northwest along Pfisterstrasse. To your left are the walls of the:

❼ Alter Hof

This palace was originally built in 1255, and once served as the palace of the Wittelsbachs, although it was later eclipsed by even grander palaces. Since 1816, it has housed the rather colorless offices of Munich's financial bureaucracies. On the opposite (northern) edge of Pfisterstrasse rise the walls of the:

❽ Münzhof

Built between 1563 and 1567, this building has, during its lifetime, housed, in turn, the imperial stables, the first museum north of the Alps, and (between 1809 and 1986) a branch of the government mint. Today, it's headquarters for Munich's Landmark Preservation office (Landesamt für Denkmalschutz). If it's open, the double tiers and massive stone columns of the building's Bavarian

Book your air, hotel, and transportation all in one place.

Hotel or hostel? Cruise or canoe? Car? Plane? Camel? Wherever you're going, visit Yahoo! Travel and get total control over your arrangements. Even choose your seat assignment. So. One hump or two? travel.yahoo.com

YAHOO!
Travel

Walking Tour 1: The Historic Center

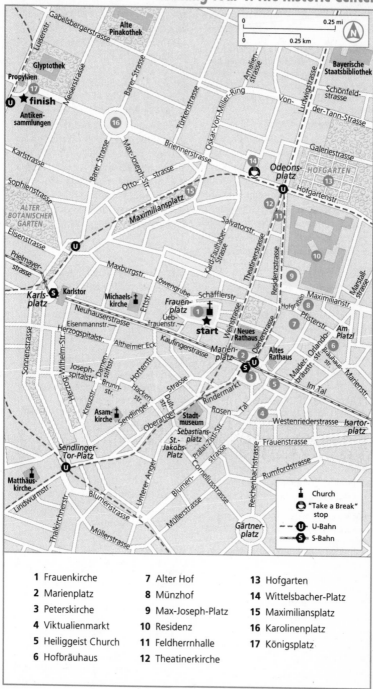

1 Frauenkirche
2 Marienplatz
3 Peterskirche
4 Viktualienmarkt
5 Heiliggeist Church
6 Hofbräuhaus
7 Alter Hof
8 Münzhof
9 Max-Joseph-Platz
10 Residenz
11 Feldherrnhalle
12 Theatinerkirche
13 Hofgarten
14 Wittelsbacher-Platz
15 Maximiliansplatz
16 Karolinenplatz
17 Königsplatz

Renaissance courtyard are worth a visit.

Pfisterstrasse funnels into a broader street, Hofgraben. Walk west for 1 block, then turn right (north) along Residenzstrasse. The first building on your right will be the city's main post office (Hauptpost), and a few paces father on you'll reach:

⑨ Max-Joseph-Platz

Designed as a focal point for the monumental avenue (Maximilianstrasse) that radiates eastward, the plaza was built during the 19th century on the site of a Franciscan convent in honor of Bavaria's first king. At the north edge of the plaza lie the vast exhibition space and labyrinthine corridors of one of Munich's finest museums, the:

⑩ Residenz

Constructed in different stages and styles from 1500 to 1850, the Residenz served as the official home of the rulers of Bavaria until 1918. Restored and rebuilt in its original form after the bombings of World War II, its complicated plan contains seven semiconcealed courtyards, lavish apartments that have housed foreign visitors like Elizabeth II and Charles de Gaulle, and museums that include the Residenz Museum, the Treasure House of the Residenz, the richly gilded rococo Cuvilliés Theater (1753), and the Herkulessaal, a concert hall noted for its baroque decorations.

Walk from Max-Joseph-Platz north along Residenzstrasse. Make the first left and walk west along Salvatorstrasse; then, within another block, turn right (north) along Theatinerstrasse. On your right you'll immediately notice an important Munich landmark, the:

⑪ Feldherrnhalle

This open-air loggia was designed and constructed by Friedrich von Gärtner between 1841 and 1844. Von Gärtner chose as his model the famous Loggia dei Lanzi in Florence. King Ludwig I commissioned the construction of the loggia as a tribute to the Bavarian

army. The bronze figures honoring Bavarian generals Tilly (1559–1632) and Wrede (1767–1838) were based on drawings by Ludwig Schwanthaler.

The two lions on the steps were the work of a sculptor, Ruemann, in 1906. Although Hitler's attempted putsch in Munich failed, along with the subsequent march to the Feldherrnhalle, the loggia later became a Nazi rallying point. Today, the Brown Shirts are replaced by street singers and musicians who hold out their hats, hoping for coins.

On the western (opposite) side of the same street (Theatinerstrasse) is the:

⑫ Theatinerkirche (Church of St. Kajetan)

Completed in 1690, this church's triple-domed, Italian-baroque facade was added about a century later by the Cuvilliés team of father and son. Its crypt contains the tombs of many of the Wittelsbachs.

Now, continue walking north, passing through Odeonsplatz, below which several subway lines converge. On the northeastern side of this square lie the flowers, fountains, and cafes of one of Munich's most pleasant small parks, the:

⑬ Hofgarten

Originally laid out for members of the royal court in 1613, this garden was opened to the public in 1780. Along the edges of the Hofgarten, as well as along the avenues radiating away from it, lie many opportunities for you to:

TAKE A BREAK
Do as the Münchners do and enjoy the panorama of Odeonsplatz and the nearby Hofgarten. One particularly attractive choice is **Café Luitpold**, Briennerstrasse 11 (☏ **089/29-28-65**). Rebuilt in a streamlined design after the bombings of World War II, it has, in the past, welcomed such cafe-loving habitués as Ibsen, Johann Strauss the Younger, and Kandinsky.

Now, walk westward along Briennerstrasse, through a neighborhood lined with impressive buildings. On your right, notice the heroic statue of Maximilian I, the Great Elector (1597–1651), rising from the center of:

⑭ Wittelsbacher-Platz

One of the most famous squares of Munich, Wittelsbacher-Platz evokes, for some, a grand hall. It's enveloped by palaces, most of which were designed by Leo von Klenze, including the 1820 Palais Arco-Zinneberg on the western side of the square. The 1825 Wittelsbacher-Palais, where von Klenze lived for a quarter of a century, rises on the north side of the square. Today, it is the head office of the Siemens Corporation. A monument in the center, an impressive neoclassical equestrian statue depicting Elector Maximilian I, is much photographed. Bertel Thorvaldsen, (1770–1844), one of Denmark's leading sculptors, created this statue in 1830. Also in the center of the square is Wittelsbacher-Brunnen or Wittelsbach Fountain, the most celebrated in the city. It is another neoclassical work, this one by Adolf von Hildebrandt (1893–95), the noted sculptor. The most intriguing part of the fountain depicts a nude youth on a "water-horse" hurling a boulder.

Continue along Briennerstrasse until you see the gentle fork to your left, Sonnen Strasse. This leads into the verdant and stylish perimeter of:

⑮ Maximiliansplatz

This leafy square stands at the heart of one of Germany's most prestigious shopping streets, Maximilianstrasse. The street itself begins at Max-Joseph-Platz and runs to the east. Maximilian II wanted to create a platz and a street more loosely defined than the more rigidly designed Ludwigstrasse. Maximiliansplatz and Maximilianstrasse were conceived and designed so that shops, hotels, gardens, restaurants, offices, and public buildings could coexist side by side. Thus, the "Maximilianic style" was created, which is a medley of various styles with many elements from past architectural movements, such as Gothic. Shop at your leisure or plan to return later for a more in-depth sampling of this prestigious neighborhood.

For the moment, return to Briennerstrasse, turn left (west), and head toward the 85-foot obelisk (erected in 1833) that soars above:

⑯ Karolinenplatz

This was the city's first star-shaped open space. Based on his model for the Place de l'Etoile in Paris, Karl von Fisher mapped out this square from 1809 to 1812. Although it doesn't match the radiance of its inspiration in Paris, it is nonetheless a landmark and an impressive square. But don't judge von Fischer too harshly when you see the square today. His uniform neoclassical look has been regrettably altered in the postwar era by buildings no longer in harmony with his original design. In the center of the square, Leo Von Klenze placed an obelisk commemorating the 30,000 (or more) Bavarian soldiers who were lost in the ill-fated Russian campaign of 1812.

Karolinenplatz in the east is linked to Königsplatz in the west by a wide boulevard, Brienner Strasse. After taking in the view of Karolinenplatz, continue slightly northwest and you'll come upon:

⑰ Königsplatz

In the early 19th century, Crown Prince Ludwig (later Ludwig I) selected this formal neoclassical design from an architectural competition. Its perimeter is ringed with some of Germany's most impressive museum buildings, the Doric-inspired Propyläen monument (west side), the Antikensammlungen (south side), and the Ionic-fronted Glyptothek (north side).

Once at Königsplatz, you will be at one of the major subway stops of Munich, a 5-minute ride south to the Hauptbahnhof where you can catch subways to most of the major sightseeing attractions of Munich, or even to attractions in Bavaria or in the suburbs of Munich.

WALKING TOUR 2	EXPLORING WEST OF MARIENPLATZ

Start: Marienplatz.
Finish: Münchner Stadtmuseum.
Time: 2 hours, not counting shopping or any visits inside places mentioned here.
Best Times: Daylight hours during clement weather.
Worst Times: Monday to Friday from 7:30 to 9am and 4:30 to 6pm, because of heavy traffic.

Those walkers with more time, who would like a more penetrating look at the Altstadt (Old Town) can take yet a second tour, this one lying west of the heart of Munich, the Marienplatz. Among other attractions, such as monuments and fountains, this tour passes by some of Munich's best known churches.

To reach the starting point of this walking tour from the Marienplatz, walk west down the shop-lined Koffingerstrasse to Liebfrauenstrasse and past the Frauenkirche (visited on the previous tour) and continue west to:

❶ St. Michael's

This is the largest Renaissance church north of the Alps. The ruler, Duke William "the Pious" (1583–97), made the church the spiritual center of the Counter-Reformation. Resting under a barrel-vaulted roof, which is the second largest in the world after St. Peter's in Rome, the church, completed in 1597 (architect unknown), houses the tomb of King Ludwig II and other Wittelsbach rulers. The facade is graced with a large sculpture of the Archangel Michael, a splendid bronze figure made by Hubert Gerhard in 1588.

Continue west on Neuhauserstrasse to the:

❷ Richard Strauss Fountain

The fountain's central column has scenes from Strauss's *Salome* (1905) interpreted, with flair, in bas-relief.

Then, continue west on Neuhauserstrasse to the:

❸ Bürgersaal

Dating from 1710, this "Citizens' Hall" was the meeting place and house of worship for the Marian Congregation, a branch under the Jesuits. Designed by the architect Giovanni Antonio Viscardi, the hall became a fully consecrated church in 1778 but was mostly destroyed by Allied air raids in World War II. Immediately rebuilt in 1945 and 1946, it looks like it used to, and many visitors assume it is much older. The facade, with its double pilasters, is the original, as is the figure of Madonna and Child on a crescent moon seen in the double staircase. The Bürgersaal also has a lower floor, containing the tomb of Rupert Mayer (1876–1945), a Jesuit who bravely resisted the Nazi regime. Many Jews from all over the world come here to pay their respects to this famous Jesuit.

Continue to the end of the pedestrian mall, where you'll see the fountain of the little boy at the medieval Karlstor. You've come to the:

❹ Stachus (Karlsplatz)

This is a busy intersection that was designed and constructed when the old town walls of Munich were demolished in 1791. The official name of the new square was to be Karlsplatz, named in honor of the Elector Karl Theodor. Because he was viewed as an

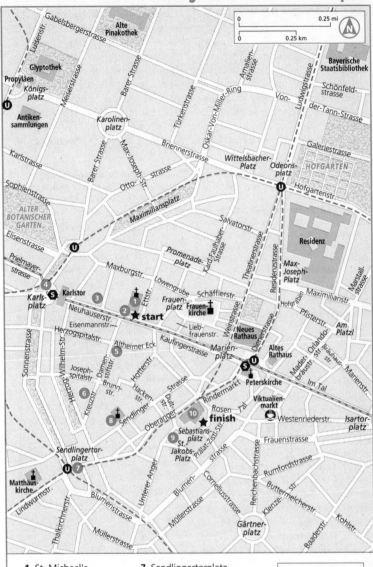

1 St. Michael's
2 Richard Strauss Fountain
3 Bürgersaal
4 Stachus (Karlsplatz)
5 St.-Anna-Damenstift
6 Allerheiligenkirche am Kreuz
7 Sendlingertorplatz
8 Asam Kirche and Haus
9 Ignaz-Günther-Haus
10 Münchner Stadtmuseum

† Church
🔵 "Take a Break" stop
–Ⓤ– U-Bahn
–Ⓢ– S-Bahn

unfair ruler, however, the townspeople defiantly refused to call the square Karlsplatz. Instead, they came up with the nickname "Stachus." The exact meaning has never been officially established, and no one seems to agree. Stachus might have referred to either a local eatery that stood on this square in the 18th century, or the word could even refer to a marksman who practiced nearby.

Diagonally and to the right is the 19th-century Palace of Justice. Directly in front of you, at a distance, is the main train station. Now turn 180 degrees and walk back to the Richard Strauss fountain. You will enjoy one of the finest views in Munich as the silhouette and facade of St. Michael's Church appears before you on the skyline. Turn right at Eisenmannstrasse and head for:

⑤ St.-Anna-Damenstift
This beautiful late-baroque church on the corner was once attached to a convent and is today a secondary school for girls. The architect, Johann Baptist Gunetzhainer, constructed the church between 1732 and 1735, and the brothers Egid Quirin and Cosmas Damian Asam did notable stucco and fresco work inside. Destroyed in part by World War II bombs, the church was reconstructed in its original style in the early 1950s. Miraculously, the facade you see today escaped the bombing unscathed, although most of the rest of the building was demolished. From the debris of war, many statues and figures were discovered which were incorporated into the reconstructed altars, giving them an antique look.

The street name changes to Damenstift-strasse as you go south for the duration of the block as you pass number 4, a pretty old house, and the 18th-century Palais Lerchenfeld. Although we've not made a turn, the street is now named Kreuzstrasse, home of the:

⑥ Allerheiligenkirche am Kreuz
Jorg von Halspach, popularly known as Ganghofer, not only designed the more famous Frauenkirche, but also created this parish church in 1478. Today, its parishioners are primarily Ukrainian Catholics. In 1620, the church received a heavy baroque overlay, and many major artists from the 17th century contributed to its present look, including Johan Rotten-hammer who painted "The Madonna Appearing Before St. Augustine" on the High Altar.

Continue directly south along Kreuzstrasse until you come to the junction with Herzog-Wilhelm-Strasse. Across this street lies:

⑦ Sendlingertorplatz
The Sendlinger Tor, once a medieval fortification, was built in 1318, about the same time as the Karlstor (one of the town gates to the Altstadt, or Old Town). The two side towers of the gates are the only visible remains.

Sendlinger Strasse, a lengthy, brightly-colored avenue of small commercial outlets, leads back into the center. However, before you get there (walking northeast), stand back on the right side of the street admiring the facadeof the:

⑧ Asamkirche and Haus
The Asam brothers created this church building in 1746 as a sort of monument to themselves. Be sure to step inside to see the extravagant Bavarian rococo interior, courtesy of Egid Quirin, along with frescoes and paintings by brother Cosmas Damian Asam. A figure of St. John of Nepo-muk, to whom the building is dedicated, is above the door. Next door to the church is the Asam brothers' private house; note the graceful facade with its many allusions to art and poetry.

After viewing Asamkirche, continue north-east along Sendlinger Strasse, taking the second right southeast along Dultstrasse, cross the Oberanger Rinder, and head into St.-Jakobs-Platz, where you'll see the:

⑨ Ignaz-Günther-Haus
This memorial house is a tribute to the 18th-century Bavarian rococo

artist who lived and worked out of the edifice during his lifetime. Restoration was completed in 1977 and the house is now maintained by the Münchner Stadtmuseum (see below). The Madonna out front is a Günther replica, and an exhibit inside displays some of his other works.

On the same block is the:
⑩ Münchner Stadtmuseum

Housed in the old, 15th-century city arsenal, this museum is turreted in front. Exhibits vary seasonally, often featuring one of the countless local artists in Munich's cultural history. Several displays, however, are permanent and are reviewed on p. 108.

WINDING DOWN
You've finished! If you want to take a break, continue down the street veering left into Sebastiansplatz and admire the old houses lining the street. Exit the Sebastiansplatz from its eastern edge and walk for 3 blocks along the meandering length of the Prälat-Zistl-Strasse until you reach the Viktualienmarkt. The **Münchner Suppenküche** (no phone) is a Munich legend, a true "soup kitchen" at what is called "the stomach of the city." On the coldest days, join the Münchners devouring hearty soups such as Gulaschsuppe, sausage and sauerkraut, and Krustis (sandwiches). Or buy some bread and fruit at one of the many stands, sit back, and enjoy the fountains and statues that surround you.

WALKING TOUR 3   SCHWABING

Start:	Wedekindplatz.
Finish:	Englischer Garten.
Time:	2½ hours with minimal stopovers.
Best Times:	Morning to mid-afternoon while students bustle to and from class.
Worst Times:	Monday to Friday from 7:30 to 9am and 4:30 to 6pm.

Schwabing was incorporated into the city in 1890. Its golden era as an artists' center was from 1890 to 1914. Novelists Thomas Mann and Herman Hesse, the poet Rainer Maria Rilke, satirist Karl Kraus, and playwright Franz Wedekind were some of the better-known authors who lived in the area. For a short period after World War II, it became legendary as Germany's hip center. But now the days of vie de bohème are long gone, and Schwabing has lost most of its distinctive character. In many ways, its situation is comparable to New York's Greenwich Village, which is hardly the haven for artists, writers, and poets that it once was. Since rents have soared to ridiculous highs, the artists is Schwabing have long ago retreated to cheaper climes. A more monied crowd occupies Schwabing today, as it's become the "in" place to live in Munich.

The tour begins in the section of Schwabing behind the Münchner Freiheit station known as Old Schwabing. Movie theaters, music clubs, and even a handful of cabarets give it the markings of cosmopolitanism.
❶ Wedekindplatz
Once the community market, the Wedekindplatz is named for Franz Wedekind, whose "Lulu" plays about a *femme fatale* provided the basis for

the 1929 Louise Brooks film, *Pandora's Box,* and for Alban Berg's opera, *Lulu.* The platz is the focal point of the neighborhood.

Head west down Fellitzschstrasse past the Freiheit rail station, and cross the:
❷ Leopoldstrasse
The most famous street in Schwabing is also the most fun to walk down and

to take in scenes of local life. It is a favorite promenade both for visitors and the local residents themselves. Cafes line both sides of the street, and there are many restaurants and bars to enjoy. In winter, life calms down considerably here, but on a summer evening, Leopoldstrasse is the place to be. Students, struggling artists, whatever, fill the streets hawking their wares, usually arts and crafts—often trash. Leopoldstrasse becomes like an outdoor souk, with vendors selling everything from carvings to leather items, some of dubious quality.

A block farther on, take a left on Wilhelmstrasse, travel south for 2 blocks, then take a right on:

❸ Hohenzollernstrasse

Here you can further study Jugendstil. The facades that adorn the buildings lining this street are fine examples of the bright and geometric decoration that typify that style. Look also for the little, quirky fashion boutiques that give the street its fame.

To take in the full view of the street, continue west to the junction with Römerstrasse. Once here, head south along Römerstrasse until you come to Ainmillerstrasse, at which point you walk east.

❹ Ainmillerstrasse

The artistic unshackling of the Jugendstil movement laid the foundation for a further development of an artistic consciousness that was the basis for many of the eager manifestos set forth by the *Blaue Reiter* (Blue Rider) school. Appropriately, Wassily Kandinsky, the premiere artist associated with the Blue Rider movement, once lived down the street. You will find many of the finest examples of Jugendstil on the east end of the street—including the facade at No. 22 that sports Adam and Eve lying at the base of the tree of knowledge.

TAKE A BREAK
The cafe-bar, **Café Roxy**, Leopoldstrasse 48 (© 089/ 34-92-92), is owned by Iris Berben, star of German TV. She presides over the neo-Deco interior, the Italian cuisine, and an affectedly urbane crowd. It's chic, it's hip, and it's the best place to relax in the neighborhood.

Once on Ainmillerstrasse, continue walking east until you come once again to Leopoldstrasse. Kandinsky once lived on this street in a building long gone. Head south down Leopoldstrasse until you approach the:

❺ Akademie der Shönen (Academy of Fine Arts)

This building, erected at the end of the 19th century, enthusiastically recalls the Italian Renaissance. The academy is best known for the "Secession" movement that was spearheaded by its students in the 1890s. This protest against "traditional aesthetics" and a call for a new creativity in the arts led quickly to the growth of Jugendstil and helped define Munich as a centerpiece of the Art Nouveau movement.

Continue south on Leopoldstrasse and you will enter the:

❻ Ludwig-Maximilian Universität (University of Munich) campus

Frederich von Gärtner engineered the construction of the edifice, one of the most aesthetically fine in all of Munich. Gärtner relieved Leo von Klenze (who designed the Alte Pinakothek) as Bavaria's court architect, and the relative flamboyance of this structure is compared favorably to Klenze's more staid approach. It was here that the student society, the White Rose, made a last effort to resist Hitler in 1942 to 1943. Its leaders, Sophie and Hans Scholl, were brutally

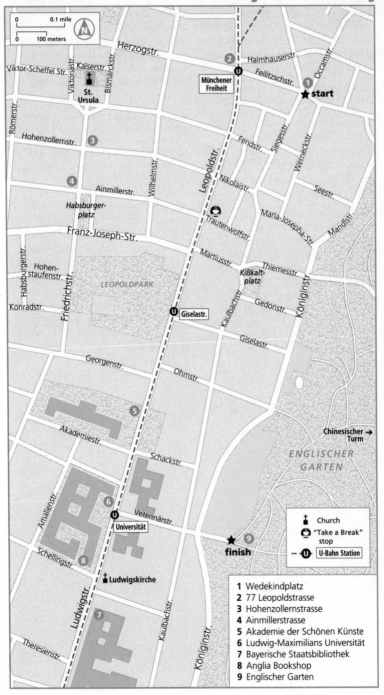

0   0.1 mile
0   100 meters

Herzogstr.
Haimhauserstr.
Occamstr.
Viktor-Scheffel Str.
Kaiserstr.
Viktoriastr.
Bismarckstr.
St. Ursula
Feilitzschstr.
Münchener Freiheit
2
1 ★ start
Römerstr.
Hohenzollernstr.
3
Fendstr.
Siegesstr.
Wernerckstr.
Leopoldstr.
4
Ainmillerstr.
Wilhelmstr.
Nikolaistr.
Seestr.
Habsburger-platz
Franz-Joseph-Str.
Trautenwolfstr.
Maria-Josepha-Str.
Mandlstr.
Habsburgerstr.
Hohen-staufenstr.
Friedrichstr.
LEOPOLDPARK
Martiusstr.
Kißkalt-platz
Thiemesstr.
Königinstr.
Konradstr.
U   Giselastr.
Kaulbachstr.
Gedonstr.
Giselastr.
Georgenstr.
Ohmstr.
Akademiestr.
5
Chinesischer →
Turm
Schackstr.
ENGLISCHER GARTEN
Amalienstr.
6
U
Veterinärstr.
Universität
★ 9
finish
Schellingstr.
8
Ludwigstr.
Ludwigskirche
Kaulbachstr.
Königinstr.
7
Theresienstr.

† Church
"Take a Break" stop
U U-Bahn Station

1 Wedekindplatz
2 77 Leopoldstrasse
3 Hohenzollernstrasse
4 Ainmillerstrasse
5 Akademie der Schönen Künste
6 Ludwig-Maximilians Universität
7 Bayerische Staatsbibliothek
8 Anglia Bookshop
9 Englischer Garten

129

executed for "civil disobedience." (A memorial to the movement is located in the lower mezzanine at Geschwister-Scholl-Platz 1; open weekdays from 10am–4pm.)

A 2-minute walk south is the twin-spired university church of St. Ludwig's and the:

❼ Bayerische Staatsbibliothek (Bavarian State Library)

This mammoth library is one of the largest in all of Europe. It stands where the Schwabing Gate of medieval Munich once cast its shadow.

Before leaving campus, duck down Schellingstrasse and drop in at:

❽ Anglia English Bookshop

Schellingstrasse 3. The student district's liveliest street is south of the university in a suburb of Schwabing known as Maxvorstadt. Munich is Germany's publishing center, and the bookstores throughout Schwabing will satisfy the most avid reader. Our favorite bookstore along this street, and, as its name indicates, the one with the most English-language titles, is Anglia English Bookshop, which is a hangout for visiting Americans and English-speaking expatriates living in Munich.

Head back north up Leopoldstrasse, returning to the university's center. Take a right on Veterinärstrasse, directly across the street from Gärtner's famed building. Those without inhibition may want to begin disrobing. You're being routed to the:

❾ Englischer Garten

Munich's most famous park is full of nude sunbathers. The Chinese Tower is the most recognizable landmark of the gardens. The wooden tower, trimmed with gold leaf, was destroyed during World War II but re-emerged in the 1950s to the delight of its beer-garden devotees—a Munich tradition revered even by upstart Schwabingers, and a good place to take a break and end your walk.

Shopping

Visitors to Munich usually come for the fun, the beer gardens, the cultural scene, or the nightlife—not for the shopping. However, Munich is full of beautiful and elegant (and expensive) shops and has a number of really intriguing retailers.

1 The Shopping Scene

In the historic city center, you'll find an extensive pedestrian-only shopping area. **Kaufingerstrasse** and **Neuhauserstrasse,** the principal shopping streets, extend from the Hauptbahnhof to Marienplatz, then north to Odeonsplatz. For even more upscale shopping, head to **Maximilianstrasse,** where you'll discover numerous chic boutiques and fashion houses that rival any on Fifth Avenue. For funkier wares, head to Schwabing, the former bohemian quarter. **Schellingstrasse** and **Hohenzollernstrasse** are home to many unusual galleries and hip boutiques.

Shops in the downtown area are generally open from 9am to 6pm during the week. Stores may stay open until 8:30pm on Thursday. On Saturday the shops generally close around 2pm. The smaller neighborhood stores usually open their doors from 8:30am to 12:30pm and then reopen from 3 to 6pm. On the first Saturday of the month, *Langer Samstag,* the downtown stores are open until 4pm from April to September and until 6pm from October to March.

2 Shopping A to Z

ANTIQUES

Munich is not a center for antiques buyers, since relatively little remained after the World War II bombings, and anything really valuable is snapped up instantaneously by the prosperous bourgeoisie. There is some estate-sale stuff "from Grandmother's cupboard" but little of major consequence. In fact, many older pieces come from England, France, or elsewhere.

If you enjoy random wanderings and window-shopping for collectibles, the streets that are particularly rich in antique shops radiate outward from the Viktualienmarkt. One of the most important of these is the Westenriederstrasse. Also, check out Carl Jagemann's, reviewed below.

Antike Uhren Eder   Here you'll find antique clocks from the 19th and early 20th centuries. Antike Uhren Eder can supply you with timepieces that have told many, many other people exactly what time it is for a very long time. Both stores are adjacent to the Hotel Bayerischer Hof, and attract a glamorous clientele from virtually everywhere. They're open Monday to Friday from 11am to 6pm and Saturday from 11am to 2pm. Prannerstrasse 4. ℂ 089/22-03-05. U-bahn: Marienplatz.

Carl Jagemann Ancestors of the present owner established this store more than a century ago, and today, you're likely to see the grandchildren of former clients coming in for appraisals of objects their forebears might have received as long-ago wedding presents. The specialty here is estate and antique jewelry, plus reproductions of baroque clocks. It's open Monday to Friday from 10am to 6pm and Saturday from 10am to 2pm. Residenzstrasse 3. ✆ **089/22-54-93**. U-bahn: Marienplatz.

Philographikon Galerie Rauhut This important gallery is one of the great successes of Munich's art world—it was established in 1978 by a television producer, Rainer Rauhut, who transformed his hobby of collecting rare engravings, prints, and manuscripts into a career. It's on two floors of a century-old building near the Marienplatz. Merchandise ranges from 19th-century steel engravings priced from 30€, to pre-Gutenberg illuminated manuscripts (sometimes sold as individual sheets) worth hundreds of thousands. Other curiosities include antique maps; botanical prints from English, French, and German sources; and a series of rare prints by a Swiss-born engraver, Karl Bodmer, whose depictions in the 1820s of Native Americans are increasingly valuable on both sides of the Atlantic. It's open Monday to Friday from 10am to 6pm and Saturday from 10am to 2pm. Maximilianstrasse 15. ✆ **089/22-50-82**. U-bahn or S-bahn: Marienplatz.

Squirrel This unusual shop was established 21 years ago by its charming owner, Urban Geissel and his wife Gisela. A delightful alternative for dedicated collectibles buyers, it carries a collection of luggage made by English and French purveyors to the aristocrats and millionaires of the Jazz Age. There are suitcases and steamer trunks from Louis Vuitton, whose *LV* logo was inaugurated about 20 years after the company's establishment in 1878; some antique pieces by Hermès; and examples from English makers such as Finnegan's and Harrods. Although they tend to be heavy, they're still serviceable and richly imbued with the nostalgia of the great days of oceangoing travel. The place is open Monday to Friday from 11am to 6pm and Saturday from 11am to 2pm. Schellingstrasse 54. ✆ **089/2-72-09-29**. U-bahn: U3 or U6 to Universität.

ART

Galerie für Angewandte Künst München This is the largest, most visible, and most historic art gallery of its type in Germany, established by the Bavarian government in the 1840s as a showcase for local artists. One of its two interconnected buildings is a Jugendstil monument, the other "of no artistic importance." Works by more than 400 artists are displayed and sold in the art gallery, where merchandise begins at 900€. In a sales outlet, the Ladengeschäft, crafts in all kinds of media, textiles, and woven objects are sold at prices that begin at 25€. It's open Monday to Friday from 9:30am to 6pm and Saturday from 9:30am to 2pm. Pacellistrasse 6-8. ✆ **089/2-90-14-70**. U-bahn: Karlsplatz.

BOOKS

Anglia English Bookshop This shop has the best collection of English language titles in Bavaria, both fiction and nonfiction. You can also purchase postcards here as well as travel maps and aids. Also see the review, below, for Words'Worth. Open Monday to Friday 9am to 6:30pm, Saturday 10am to 1pm. Schellingstrasse 3. ✆ **089/28-36-42**. U-bahn: Universität.

Hugendubel Not only is this Munich's biggest bookstore, but it also enjoys a central location. It sells a number of English-language titles, both fiction and nonfiction, and also offers travel books and helpful maps. Open Monday to Friday from 9am to 6:30pm and Saturday from 9am to 2pm. Marienplatz 22. ℂ **089/48-44-84.** U-bahn or S-bahn: Marienplatz.

Words'Worth   Few competitors in Munich cooperate with each other as gracefully as these two independent bookstores (Words'Worth and Anglia English Bookshop; see above) that deal exclusively in English-language periodicals and books. Their stock runs the gamut from 19th-century English and American classics to the most recent releases, with art books and offbeat modern literature thrown in as well. Words'Worth is a bit larger than Anglia. One corner is devoted to a display of English tea caddies and marmalades, profits from which go directly to Britain's National Trust. Both stores will cheerfully refer you to the other if they don't have what you're looking for. Words'Worth is open Monday, Tuesday, and Friday from 9am to 6:30pm, Wednesday and Thursday 9am to 8pm, and Saturday 10am to 2pm. Schellingstrasse 21. ℂ **089/2-80-91-41.** U-bahn: U3 or U6 to Universität.

CHINA, SILVER & GLASS

Kunstring Meissen   This establishment's close links to the porcelain factories of Meissen and Dresden in what was then East Germany stretch back to the coldest days of the Cold War. It was then Munich's exclusive distributor of Meissen and Dresden (Germany's most famous styles of porcelain). Though exclusive access is now a thing of the past, Kunstring's still carries one of Munich's largest selections of elegant porcelain. *Note:* With two of Europe's most impeccable pedigrees in porcelain, neither Meissen nor Dresden have adopted the assembly-line methods used by many of their more industrialized modern-day competitors. Anything you buy can be shipped, although if you're looking for the more esoteric objects, there might be a delay if Kunstring doesn't have the object in stock. Kunstring is open Monday to Friday from 9:30am to 5pm and Saturday from 9:30am to 2pm. Briennerstrasse 4. ℂ **089/28-15-32.** U-bahn: Odeonsplatz.

Nymphenburger Porzellanmanufaktur   About 8km (5 miles) northwest of the heart of Munich, you'll find one of Germany's most famous porcelain factories on the grounds of Schloss Nymphenburg. You can visit its exhibition and sales rooms Monday to Friday from 8:30am to 6:30pm and Saturday 10am to 6pm. Shipments can be arranged if you make purchases. (This is a bit of a trek, but you'll probably be taking a sightseeing trip to Schloss Nymphenburg anyway.) There's also a more central branch in Munich's center at Odeonsplatz 1 (ℂ **089/282428;** U-bahn: U6 to Odeonsplatz. Nördliches Schlossrondell 8. ℂ **089/1-79-19-70.** Bus: 41.

Rosenthal-Studio-Haus   Established in 1879 in the Bavarian town of Selb near the Czech border, Rosenthal is one of the most prestigious names in German porcelain. Although traditional patterns are still made, most of the line now focuses on contemporary designs. Prices for Rosenthal designs are preestablished by the manufacturer, and there are no price breaks at this factory outlet. The outlet is owned and operated by Rosenthal itself, so you will find the widest selection of Rosenthal patterns available in Germany here. In addition to porcelain, the line includes furniture, glass, and cutlery, all scattered over two floors of spotlessly maintained showrooms. It's open Monday to Friday from 9:30am to 8:30pm and Saturday from 9:30am to 2pm. Dienerstrasse 17. ℂ **089/22-26-17.** U-bahn or S-bahn: Marienplatz.

CHOCOLATE & PASTRIES

Confiserie Kreutzkann   This is one of Munich's most famous purveyors of elaborate chocolates, pastry, and the artistically shaped and colored almond paste, marzipan. It dates back to 1861. If you want to consume your high-calorie treats on the spot, there's a cafe on the premises where you can order coffee or tea to go with whatever appeals to you. It's open Monday to Friday 8am to 7pm and Saturday 8am to 6pm. Maffeistrasse 4. © **089/29-32-77.** U-bahn/S-bahn: Marienplatz.

Kaffe Hause Reber   Pralines, chocolates, and marzipan are the products of this famous and nostalgia-laden store. It has been here since 1876, and many locals remember coming here on childhood outings with their grandparents. About eight bite-size morsels (100 g/3½ oz.) cost 4€. There's a cafe on its street-level premises that has a reputation for its chocolate-slathered cakes filled with Cointreau-flavored whipped cream. Slices of this sell for 2.50€ and can be consumed with coffee, or for chocoholics, with hot chocolate. Herzogspitalstrasse 9. © **089/26-52-31.** U-bahn: Karlsplatz.

CRAFTS & FOLKLORE

Bayerischer Kunstgewerbeverein (Bavarian Association of Artisans) At this showcase for Bavarian artisans, you'll find excellent handcrafts: ceramics, glass, jewelry, woodcarvings, pewter, and Christmas decorations. It's open Monday to Friday from 9:30am to 6pm and on Saturday from 9:30am to 2pm. Pacellistrasse 6-8. © **089/2-90-14-70.** U-bahn: Karlsplatz.

Ludwig Mory   This is a famous place to buy traditional Bavarian beer steins. It's near the cathedral, its one-room setting is folkloric, and it basks in a reputation that has been building since the 1830s. After seeing this place, you'll never want to drink Budweiser from a can again. Fashioned from pewter, and to a lesser degree, ceramic, sometimes lidded, sometimes not, the steins range from the honest but unpretentious to richly decorative works of art that might round off a private collection. For your souvenir of Munich you can pay anywhere from 25€ to 600€. It's open Monday to Friday from 9am to 6pm and Saturday from 9am to 1pm. Marienplatz 8. © **089/22-45-42.** U-bahn or S-bahn: Marienplatz.

Otto Kellnberger Holzhandlung   Established just after World War II, this is a small but choice emporium of traditional woodcarvings. In the Altstadt near the Marienplatz, it evokes the bucolic charms of remote alpine Bavaria. The inventory has all the folkloric charm and some of the folkloric kitsch you might have found if you had made the trek to remote Oberammergau, but with a lot less time, trouble, and expense. It's open Monday to Friday from 9am to 6pm and Saturday from 10am to 1pm. Heiliggeiststrasse 8. © **089/22-64-79.** U-bahn or S-bahn: Marienplatz.

Prinoth   Most of the woodcarvings sold here are produced in small workshops in South Tirol, that folklore-rich part of Austria that was annexed to Italy after World War I. The selection is wide-ranging and broad, and since the setting lies 5.5km (3½ miles) west of Munich's tourist zones, prices are reasonable compared to shops closer to the Marienplatz. It's open Monday to Friday from 9am to 6pm. Guido Schneblestrasse 9A. © **089/56-03-78.** U-bahn: U4 or U5 to Laimerplatz.

Wallach   Established more than a century ago, Wallach is the largest emporium in Munich for Bavarian handcrafts, both new and antique, as well as the evocative, sometimes kitschy folk art. You'll find antique butter churns, hand-painted wooden boxes and trays, painted porcelain clocks, wooden wall or mantelpiece clocks, and doilies whose use faded along with antimacassars (the cloth covers, sometimes embroidered, used to protect the back or arms of upholstered furniture), but which are charming nonetheless. Most of the store's street level is devoted to handcrafted folk art. One floor above street level, you'll find dirndls, lederhosen, loden coats, and other traditional Bavarian garments for men, women, and children. Look also for fabrics (sold by the meter), and housewares like sheets and towels, many patterned in Bavarian themes. The store is open Monday to Friday from 10:30am to 6pm (Thurs until 8:30pm) and Saturday from 10:30am to 4pm. Residenzstrasse 3. ℂ 089/22-08-71. U-bahn or S-bahn: Marienplatz.

DEPARTMENT STORES

Hertie   This is our favorite Munich department store, a sprawling four-story-plus-basement emporium of all aspects of the good life as interpreted by Teutonic tastes. A fixture near the main railway station since the turn of the 20th century, it has survived wars and revolutions with predictable mercantile style. It's open Monday to Friday from 9am to 6:30pm (Thurs until 8:30pm) and Saturday from 9am to 4:30pm. Bahnhofplatz 7. ℂ 089/5-51-20. U-bahn: Hauptbahnhof.

Karstadt   This department store can sell you just about everything you'd need to maintain a well-accessorized home, to dress yourself for virtually any occasion, or to pursue almost any activity. Temporary visitors to Munich especially value the collection of Bavarian handcrafts on the third floor, and many of the pieces become traveler's souvenirs. It's open Monday to Friday from 9am to 8pm and Saturday from 9:30am to 8pm. Neuhauserstrasse 18. ℂ 089/29-02-30. U-bahn: Karlsplatz-Stachus.

Kaufhof   This is the Munich branch of the upscale department store chain that was originally established in Cologne during the late 19th century. It came to Munich in 1972 and is one of the largest stores in town, on five floors in a building on the city's historic square. Wander freely among displays that are art forms in their own right. You'll find men's, women's, and children's clothing, housewares, groceries, and virtually everything else you might think of. It's open Monday to Friday from 9am to 6:30pm (Thurs until 8:30pm) and Saturday from 8:30am to 2pm. There's a smaller branch of this emporium at Karlsplatz 2 (ℂ 089/5-12-50; U-bahn: Karlsplatz) that maintains the same hours. Marienplatz. ℂ 089/23-18-51. U-bahn or S-bahn: Marienplatz.

Ludwig Beck am Rathauseck   This is Munich's major department store. Most merchandise is intended for local residents; however, visitors will also be interested in this four-floor shopping bazaar, which sells handmade crafts from all over Germany, both old and new. Items include decorative pottery and dishes, etched glass beer steins and vases, painted wall plaques depicting rural scenes, and decorative flower arrangements. There's unusual kitchenware, colored flatware, calico hot pads and towels, and a collection of casually chic leather-trimmed canvas purses. The shop also offers fashions, textiles, and even jazz recordings. Within the same block, the store has opened two more outlets: Wäsche-Beck, selling lingerie, linens, and curtains, and Strumpf-Beck, featuring the town's largest selection of stockings and hosiery. All three locations are open Monday to Friday from 10am to 8pm and Saturday from 9:30am to 4pm. Marienplatz 11. ℂ 089/23-69-10. U-bahn or S-bahn: Marienplatz.

ELECTRONICS

Saturn Electro Technocenter Anyone interested in electronics will enjoy comparing what's available at home to what's widespread and selling like gangbusters in Germany. For insight into design, speed, capabilities, and accessories, head for Munich's two superstores that deal exclusively in computers, cameras, VCRs, sound systems, and all kinds of electronics. If it's sold anywhere in Europe, you'll almost certainly find it here. Open Monday to Friday 9am to 7pm and Saturday 9am to 4pm. Schwanenthaler Strasse 115. ✆ **089/51-08-50.** U-bahn: Theresienwiese.

ENGRAVINGS & POSTCARDS

Philatelie und Ansichtskarten It doesn't really look like a shop, but rather like a dusty storeroom at a museum. It's the rendezvous for academics and collectors throughout Germany, who phone in special requests for antique engravings and postcards that depict specific settings, personalities, and places. Merchandise, each piece carefully filed and stored in cardboard boxes that are arranged by subject, ranges from the sober to the schmaltzy. Open Monday to Friday 9am to 5pm, Saturday 9am to 1pm. Bahnhofplatz 2. ✆ **089/59-67-57.** U-bahn: Bahnhofplatz.

FASHION
MEN & WOMEN

Bogner Haus Founded by Willy Bogner, former Olympic champion downhill racer, this store stocks well-made women's clothing upstairs, men's clothing on the street level, and clothing suited for whatever sport happens to be seasonal at the time of your visit in the cellar. Somewhere in the store, you'll find whatever you need to be appropriately clad for any occasion. One of its best is the Fire & Ice Department in the cellar, where garments for young men and women have the kind of flair that might please some of the most demanding people in your life—your teenage children. The store is open Monday to Wednesday and Friday from 9:30am to 6:30pm, Thursday from 9:30am to 7:30pm, and Saturday from 9:30am to 2pm. Residenzstrasse 15. ✆ **089/2-90-70-40.** U-bahn or S-bahn: Marienplatz.

Dirndl-Ecke One block up from the famed Hofbräuhaus, this shop gets our unreserved recommendation as a stylish place specializing in high-grade dirndls, feathered alpine hats, and all clothing associated with the alpine regions. Everything sold is of fine quality—there's no tourist junk. Other merchandise includes needlework hats, beaded belts, and pleated shirts for men. You may want to buy the stylish capes, the silver jewelry in old Bavarian style, the leather shoes, or the linen and cotton combinations, such as skirts with blouses and jackets. Bavarian clothing for children is also available. The store is open Monday to Friday from 9am to 6pm and Saturday from 9am to 1pm. Am Platzl 1/Sparkassenstrasse 10. ✆ **089/22-01-63.** U-bahn or S-bahn: Marienplatz or Isartor.

Frankonia This store carries Munich's most prestigious collection of traditional Bavarian dress (called *Tracht*). If you see yourself dressed in a hunter style, this place can outfit you well. There's a fine collection of wool cardigan jackets with silvery buttons. It's open Monday to Friday from 9am to 6:30pm and Saturday from 9am to 2pm. Maximiliansplatz 10. ✆ **089/2-90-00-20.** U-bahn: Odeonsplatz.

Loden-Frey The twin domes of the Frauenkirche are visible above the soaring glass-enclosed atrium of this shop's showroom. Go here for the world's largest selection of Loden (folkloric) clothing and traditional costumes, as well as for international fashions from top European designers such as Armani, Valentino, and Ungaro. It's open Monday to Friday from 9am to 6pm, except on Thursday when hours extend to 8:30pm, and on Saturday from 9am to 2pm. Maffeistrasse 7–9. ✆ 089/21-03-90. U-bahn or S-bahn: Marienplatz.

Red/Green of Scandinavia   This shop, near the Marienplatz, will sell you everything you need for appearing relaxed, casual, and at home on someone's private yacht or on the local golf links. Most of the inventory comes from Denmark, and since it was all designed to withstand the blustery winds or the clear sunlight of the Baltic, everything is ready to outfit you appropriately for whatever outdoor activity (or *après-sport* fireside chitchat) you're planning. Garments for men, women, and children are all available. It's open Monday to Friday from 10am to 6pm and Saturday from 10am to 2pm. Kaufingerstrasse 9. ✆ 089/2-60-64-89. U-bahn or S-bahn: Marienplatz.

MEN

Hirmer   In the pedestrian zone, this menswear shop has the best collection in town of German-made men's clothing. The staff here is especially helpful in outfitting you with something that looks good on you, the selection coming from such brand names as Boss, Barbour, Rene Lezard, and van Laak. Both business and leisure suits are sold at middle to upper-bracket prices. They even cater to "big beer bellies." Open Monday to Friday 9am to 6pm, Saturday 9am to 2pm. Kaufingerstrasse 28. ✆ 089/2368-3210. Tube: Marienplatz.

Moshammer Rudolph's   This store could be your first resource in a search for appropriate menswear. Merchandise is continental, and the staff seems aware of their own prestige and the glamour of their address. In other words, although a visit won't necessarily leave you with a warm and fuzzy feeling (*Gemütlichkeit*), you might at least learn how high some of the prices can be in an upscale Münchner menswear store. It's open Monday to Friday from 10:30am to 6pm and Saturday from 11am to 4pm. Maximilianstrasse 14. ✆ 089/22-69-24. U-bahn: Isartor.

Uli Knecht   This is the men's division of the same retailer recommended below, the kind of place where a business executive could clothe himself for the office, the golf course, a hunting lodge, or an amorous weekend getaway. Designers represented on the two floors of the showroom include Ralph Lauren, Armani, Italian designer Antonio Fusco, and such German outfitters as Closed and Strenesse. It's open Monday to Friday from 10am to 7pm and Saturday 10am to 4pm. Residenzstrasse 19–20. ✆ 089/29-16-04-06. U-bahn: Odeonsplatz.

WOMEN

Furore   This elegant store offers fashionable lingerie (brassieres, bustiers, slips, etc.) with tasteful designs, in some cases filmy, feminine, and subtly erotic, in silk, cotton, and a few synthetics by Spain-born André Sard. It also has a home-wear collection: nightgowns, pajamas, sheets, towels, and decorative accessories from New York design superstar Donna Karan. Furore was the first store in Germany to distribute her designs. The store is open Monday to Friday from 10am to 6:30pm and Saturday from 10am to 2pm. Franz-Joseph Strasse 41. ✆ 089/34-39-71. U-bahn: U3 or U6 to Giselastrasse.

Maendler   This store caters to the well-dressed woman with a series of bou-tiques scattered over two floors. You may prefer to just wander around the store, appreciating the creative vision of Joop, Claude Montana, New York New York, and Jil Sander, but a quick consultation with any of the staff poised near the store's entrance can point you in the right direction. Looking for that special something for your dinner with the city's mayor or the president of Germany? Ask to see the formal eveningwear of English designer David Fielden. Looking for something more daring and avant-garde? Head for this outfit's other branch, **Rosy Maendler,** Maximiliansplatz 12 (same phone). Here you'll find a youthful version of the same store and garments by Madonna's favorite designer, Jean-Paul Gaultier, whose exhibitionistic and/or erotic leather and rubber clothing will cause a stir on either side of the Atlantic. Both shops are open Monday to Friday from 9:30am to 6:30pm and Saturday from 9:30am to 2pm. Theatinerstrasse 7. ☎ **089/24-22-88-50.** U-bahn: Odeonsplatz or Marienplatz.

Uli Knecht   This store's employees are quick to tell you that Uli Knecht is not a designer, but rather, a clever and successful retailer with a gift for distributing the creations of some of the best-known clothiers in the world. This branch for women, two doors down from the Uli Knecht store for men, covers two floors. It's laden with garments that include sportswear and some formalwear, but the emphasis is on upscale, elegant, and highly wearable clothing—everything from business suits to cocktail dresses. It is open Monday to Wednesday 10am to 7pm, Thursday and Friday 10am to 8pm, and Saturday 10am to 4pm. Residenzstrasse 15. ☎ **089/22-15-10.** U-bahn: Odeonsplatz.

FOOD

Dallmayr   What Fauchon is to Paris, and Fortnum & Mason is to London, the venerable firm of Dallmayr is to Munich. Gastronomes as far away as Hamburg and Berlin sometimes telephone orders for exotica not readily available anywhere else, and its list of prestigious clients reads like a Who's Who of German industry and letters. Wander freely among racks of foodstuffs, some of which are too delicate to survive shipment abroad, others that can be shipped anywhere. The shop is open Monday to Friday from 9am to 6:30pm and Saturday from 9am to 1pm. The restaurant associated with this store is reviewed separately on p. 71. Dienerstrasse 14–15. ☎ **089/2-13-50.** Tram: 19. U-bahn/S-bahn: Marienplatz.

JEWELRY & WATCHES

Andreas Huber   This store sells all the big names in Swiss and other European wristwatches, as well as clocks. It offers some jewelry, but the specialty is timepieces. It's open Monday to Friday 10am to 9pm and on Saturday 10am to 4pm. They have two other locations, one at Residenzstrasse 11 (☎ **089/29-82-78**) and another at Neuhauserstrasse 2 (☎ **089/29-82-83**). Weinstrasse 8. ☎ **089/29-82-95.** U-bahn or S-bahn: Marienplatz.

Carl Jagemann's   Jagemann's reputation for quality and honesty goes back to 1864, as does some (but not all) of the merchandise it sells. It's one of the Altstadt's largest purveyors of new and antique timepieces of all types, ranging from wristwatches to grandfather clocks, from the severely rectilinear to rococo kitsch. There's also a collection of new and antique jewelry. It's open Monday to Friday from 10am to 6pm and Saturday from 10am to 2pm. Residenzstrasse 3. ☎ **089/22-54-93.** U-bahn: Marienplatz.

Hemmerle   This is *the* place in Munich for jewelry. The original founders of this stylish shop made their fortune creating bejeweled fantasies for the Royal Bavarian Court of Ludwig II. Today, in a setting of southern baroque-style pastel-painted paneling, you can buy some of the most exciting jewelry in the area. All pieces are limited editions, designed and made in-house by Bavarian craftspeople. The company also designs its own wristwatch, the Hemmerle, and distributes what is said to be one of the world's finest watches, the Breguet. The store is open Monday to Friday from 9:30am to 6pm and Saturday from 9:30am to 1pm. Maximilianstrasse 14. 📞 **089/2-42-26-00.** U-bahn: Odeonsplatz or Max-Weber Platz.

KITCHENWARE

Biebl   In the central pedestrian zone, this reputable and fairly-priced emporium sells razor-sharp German steel. Your first impression of the premises may make you think you're in a warehouse for surgical implements, but the choice is so overwhelming and the prices so fair that you'll soon see why it's one of the best-recommended stopovers in this survey. Many excellent knives can be had for 10€ and up. Even the best rarely exceed 50€ each. The outlet is open Monday to Friday 9:30am to 7pm and Saturday from 9:30am to 4pm. Karlsplatz 25. 📞 **089/59-79-36.** U-bahn: Karlsplatz.

MARKETS

In addition to those listed below, a traditional market, **Auer Dult,** is held three times a year in the Mariahilfplatz. Dates vary but the months are April, July, and October (see also the "Munich Calendar of Events," in chapter 2). Antiques dealers, food, and Bavarian bands are present; it's a great place to find bargains. Take tram 7, 15, 25, or 27.

Christkindlmarkt   One of the most visible and traditional in Munich, this December Christmas market attracts visitors from all over Germany and Europe—only the Christmas market in Nürnberg is more famous. Hundreds of stalls offer Christmas ornaments, handmade children's toys, carved figures, and nativity scenes. The square is full of local color; the stallkeepers are picturesque in their woolen coats, hats, and gloves; and the scene is enhanced by frequent snowfalls. Opening hours vary with the enthusiasm of the merchants. In most cases, stalls are open 10am to 8pm on Monday to Saturday, although as Christmas approaches, many open on Sunday as well, until 7pm. Marienplatz. U-bahn: Marienplatz.

Elisabethmarkt   This is Schwabing's smaller and less dramatic version of Munich's premier outdoor market, the Viktualienmarkt (see below). It's held every Monday to Saturday from 7am to about 11am, although some die-hard merchants manage to hold out until 1:30pm. Completely decentralized, each individual vendor operates exclusively on his or her own account. Stalls tend to be more laden with bounty in spring, summer, and fall, but a few hardy souls maintain a presence here even in the depths of winter. Elisabethplatz. Tram: 18.

Grossmarkthalle   This is Munich's equivalent of Paris's Rungis (formerly Les Halles). Buyers from virtually every restaurant in Munich make an early morning pilgrimage to this industrial-looking complex in the city's southern suburbs. Purveyors arrive with lorries from as far away as Italy; buyers congregate from throughout Bavaria and beyond. Be warned, though, that there's an entrance fee of 3€ that allows you only to browse and admire the way business is conducted; buying is wholesale only—homemakers who do show up usually bring bushel baskets or wheeled carts to haul away impressive quantities of peaches, apples, or whatever. It's open Monday to Saturday from 5am to 10:30am. Thalkirchen. U-bahn: U3 to Fürstenried West.

Viktualienmarkt   Unless you happen to be staying in a place where you have access to a kitchen, it's doubtful that you'll want to be hauling groceries back to your hotel room during your stay in Munich. That doesn't detract, however,

from the allure of wandering through the open-air stalls of the city's most prominent food market, a few minutes' walk south of the Marienplatz (there is no
specific address, but the market sprawls over a wide area and can't be missed).
It's composed of hundreds of independently operated merchants who maintain
whatever hours they want, often closing up their cramped premises whenever
the day's inventory is sold out. Most economy-minded shoppers, however, show
up, shopping basket in hand, around 8am, to stock their larders before noon. By
5pm, only the hardiest of merchants remain in place, and by early evening, the
kiosks are locked up tight. On the premises are a worthy collection of wine,
meats, cheeses, and all the other bounty of the Bavarian agrarian world. U-bahn
or S-bahn: Marienplatz.

PEWTER

Sebastian Wesely   This is one of the best sites in Munich for the acquisition
of everybody's favorite utilitarian metal, pewter. Favored throughout the 16th
and 17th centuries because of the ease with which it can be crafted into baroque
forms, it burnishes to a low luster that's still prized today. This shop carries an
impressive array of reproductions, any of which would make a valuable addition
to your home. It's open Monday to Friday 8:30am to 6:30pm and Saturday
8:30am to 4pm. Petersplatz 1. 📞 089/26-45-19. U-bahn: Marienplatz.

TOYS

Münchner Poupenstuben und Zinnfiguren Kabinette   This is the kind
of store you either thrill to or find impossibly claustrophobic. Here is a miniature world where houses, furniture, birdcages, and people are cunningly crafted
from pewter or carved wood. Many of the items look deceptively realistic.
Famous throughout Germany, the shop has been managed for 150 years by
women of the same family, and some of the figures are still made from the original 150-year-old molds that are collectors' items in their own right. Anything
in this place would make a great gift not only for a child but also for an adult
with a nostalgic bent. It's open Monday to Friday from 10am to 6pm and
Saturday from 10am to 1pm. Maxburgstrasse 4. 📞 089/29-37-97. U-bahn: Karlsplatz.

Obletter's   Established in the 1880s, this is one of the largest emporiums
of children's toys in Munich, with five floors that contain everything from folkloric dolls to computer games. Some of the most charming toys are replicas of
middle European antique dolls and toys; they often look suspiciously capable of
coming alive beneath someone's Christmas tree, á la the *Nutcracker* ballet. It's
open Monday to Friday from 9am to 7:30pm and Saturday from 9am to
4pm. Karlsplatz 11–12. 📞 089/55-08-95-10. U-bahn: Karlsplatz.

WINE

Geisel's Vinothek   Other than Dallmayr, which does this kind of thing on a
much bigger scale, this is the most sophisticated wine shop in Munich. It's next
to the Excelsior Hotel, with displays that celebrate grapes and winemaking in
one way or another. (It doubles as a restaurant, recommended separately on
p. 78.) Its inventory includes wines from Germany, Austria, Italy, and France,
with bottles starting at 8€. Because the chef here is a passionate advocate of
wines from western France, there's an especially strong selection of Bordeaux.
Most of the selections offered by the glass at the restaurant's bar are sold by the
bottle in the wine shop, allowing you to taste before you buy the whole bottle.
The shop is open daily 10am to 1am. Schützenstrasse 11. 📞 089/55-13-71-40. U-bahn:
Hauptbahnhof.

9

Munich After Dark

Munich is a major performing arts center and has a lively nightlife as well. The city is home to no fewer than four major orchestras plus a world-class opera company and a ballet company. Many theaters are scattered throughout the city, offering everything from classic to modern German drama.

Munich's nightlife varies with the weather. When the weather is fair and the night air balmy, the Biergartens and Biersteins are brimming with cheer. During the winter months, patrons of the beer gardens turn to Munich's beer halls, such as the illustrious Hofbräuhaus (p. 149), to quaff beer and share in the typical Bavarian singsong. Beer gardens and beer halls usually empty around midnight; then the club scene cranks up. Munich's club scene is quite eclectic. It is possible to find almost any type of club, from country-western bars to ultratechno dance halls. Many clubs rave until the wee hours of the morning. Haidhausen and Schwabing vie with each other as the place to go, with the trendiest clubs and nightlife.

To find out what's happening in the Bavarian capital, go to the tourist office at platform 12 in the Hauptbahnhof and request a copy of *Monatsprogramm* (a monthly program guide), costing 1.50€. It contains a complete cultural guide, telling you not only what's being presented—from concerts to opera, from special exhibits to museum hours—but also how to purchase tickets. (The *Monatsprogramm* is in German, but it's a simple German, with lots of emphasis on addresses, dates, and listings, and as such, even people without a firm grasp of German can get a lot of information from it.)

1 The Performing Arts

Nowhere else in Europe, other than London and Paris, will you find so many musical and theatrical performances. And the good news is the low cost of seats—so count on indulging yourself and going to several concerts. You'll get good tickets if you're willing to pay anywhere from 10€ to 45€. Pick up a *Monatsprogramm* (see above) for information and schedules.

For events that sell out and popular events where the number of available tickets is reduced by season tickets and long-term subscriptions (such as soccer games or the opera's summer festival performances), you'll have to make a trip to the box office—organizers of these events tend not to cooperate with outside ticket agencies. But for virtually everything else in Munich, you'd be well advised to head for **WOM (World of Music)**, Kaufingerstrasse 15 (© **089/26-01-91-00**), whose employees can obtain tickets to virtually every cultural venue, concert, or sporting event in Bavaria. Be warned in advance that use of a credit card for payment, both at WOM and at its competitors, carries a surcharge of at least 10€ per order. WOM's leading competitors include **München Tickets** (© **089/54-81-81-81**) and **Hieber am Dom** (© **089/29-00-80-14**), both of which deal basically in the same tickets, with access to the same computer database.

OPERA & CLASSICAL MUSIC

Besides the organizations listed below, Munich is home to the **Bavarian State Radio Orchestra (Bayerischer Rundfunk Münchner Rundfunkorchestra)**, the **Bavarian Radio Orchestra (Bayerischer Rundfunk Symphonieorchester)**, and the **Graunke Symphony Orchestra.**

Bayerische Staatsoper   The **Bavarian State Opera** is one of the world's great companies. The Bavarians give their hearts and souls to opera. Productions here are beautifully mounted and presented, and the company's roster includes some of the world's greatest singers. Hard-to-get tickets may be purchased at the box office Monday to Friday 10am to 6pm and Saturday 10am to 1pm, plus 1 hour before each performance. The Nationaltheater is also the home of the **Bavarian State Ballet.** Performing in the Nationaltheater, Max-Joseph-Platz 2. ✆ 089/2185-1920. Tickets 8€–145€, including standing room. U-bahn/S-bahn: Marienplatz.

Münchner Philharmoniker (Munich Philharmonic)   This famous orchestra was founded in 1893. James Levine is its music director. Its home is the Gasteig Cultural Center, where it performs in Philharmonic Hall. The center also shelters the Richard Strauss Conservatory and the Munich Municipal Library, and has five performance halls. You can purchase tickets at the ground-level Glashalle, Monday to Friday from 9am to 8pm and on Saturday from 9am to 4pm, though these hours frequently change, so you should call before making a special trip there. The Philharmonic season begins in mid-September and runs to July. Performing in the **Gasteig Kulturzentrum,** in the Haidhausen district, at Rosenheimerstrasse 5. ✆ 089/54-81-8-181. Tickets, 12€–60€. S-bahn: Rosenheimer Platz. Tram: 18 to Gasteig. Bus: 51.

MAJOR THEATERS & CONCERT HALLS

There are theaters and performance halls all over town. Concerts are given in the **Herkulessaal** (in the Residenz, Hofgarten; ✆ 089/29-06-71). The **Staatstheater am Gärtnerplatz** (✆ 089/2-01-67-67) offers a varied program of opera, operetta, ballet, and musicals.

Altes Residenztheater (Cuvilliés Theater)   A part of the Residenz (p. 100), this theater is a sightseeing attraction in its own right. The Bavarian State Opera and the State Theater perform small-scale works here in keeping with the tiny theater's intimate character (it seats 550). It was designed by court architect François Cuvilliés in the mid–18th century, and is celebrated as Germany's most outstanding example of a rococo tier-boxed theater. During World War II, the interior was dismantled and stored. After the war, it was reassembled in the reconstructed building. For an admission of 3€, visitors can view the theater daily 9am to 6pm. Box-office hours are Monday through Friday from 10am to 6pm, Saturday from 10am to 1pm, and 1 hour before the beginning of every performance. Residenzstrasse 1. ✆ 089/2185-1940, or 089/21-85-19-20 for ticket information. Opera tickets 15€–150€; play tickets 13€–55€. U-bahn: U3, U4, U5, or U6 to Odeonplatz.

Bayerisches Staatsschauspiel (State Theater)   This repertory company is known for its performances of the classics: Shakespeare as well as Goethe and Schiller, and others. The box office, around the corner on Maximilianstrasse, is open Monday to Friday 10am to 6pm, Saturday 10am to 1pm, and 1 hour before performances. Max-Joseph-Platz. ✆ 089/21-85-19-40. Tickets 12.50€–40€. U-bahn/S-bahn: Marienplatz.

Deutsches Theater   The regular season of the Deutsches Theater lasts throughout the year. Musicals are popular, but operettas, ballets, and international shows are performed as well. It's the only theater in Germany that's both a theater and a ballroom. During Carnival in January and February, the seats are removed and stored, replaced by tables and chairs for more than 2,000 guests. Handmade decorations by artists combined with lighting effects create an enchanting ambience. Waiters serve wine, champagne, and food. The costume balls and official black-tie festivities here are famous throughout Europe. Schwanthalerstrasse 13. ℂ **089/55-23-44-44.** Tickets 15.50€–85€; higher for special events. U-bahn/ S-bahn: Karlsplatz/Stachus or Hauptbahnhof.

Kulturzentrum Gasteig   This huge brick-and-glass complex stands on the bluffs of the Isar River in the Haidhausen District. The center, which opened in 1985, has five performance halls, including the Philharmonic Hall. It also shelters the Richard Strauss Conservatory and the Munich Municipal Library. Two other concert halls of interest to most visitors are the Kleiner Konzertsaal and the Richard Strauss Musikschule. Rosenheimerstrasse 5. ℂ **089/54-81-81-81.** S-bahn: Rosenheimer Platz. Tram: 18 to Gasteig. Bus: 51.

Münchner Kammerspiele   Contemporary plays as well as classics from German or international playwrights, ranging from Goethe to Brecht and Shakespeare to Goldoni, are performed by the company here. The season lasts from early October to the end of July. You can reserve tickets by phone Monday to Friday from 10am to 6pm, but must pick them up at least 2 days before the performance. The box office is open Monday to Friday from 10am to 6pm and on Saturday from 10am to 1pm, plus 1 hour before performances.

The theater also has a second smaller venue called **Werkraum,** where new productions—mainly by younger authors and directors—are presented. The location is at Hildegardstrasse 1 (call the number below for more information). Maximilianstrasse 26–28. ℂ **089/233-3700.** Tickets 8€–35€. U-bahn: Marienplatz. S-bahn: Isartorplatz. Tram: 19 to Maximilianstrasse.

2 The Club & Music Scene

NIGHTCLUBS

Bayerischer Hof Night Club   This sophisticated club is in a large room in the extensive cellars of the Bayerischer Hof (p. 44). Between 7 and 10pm every night, the club is a piano bar. Behind a partition that disappears after 10pm is a bandstand for live orchestras, which play to a crowd of dancing patrons every night from 10pm to 3 or 4am, depending on business. Entrance to the piano bar is free, but there's a cover charge to the nightclub on Friday and Saturday nights. Drinks begin at 7.50€. The club and bar are open daily 7pm to 3 or 4am. Daily happy hour is 7pm to 8:30pm, with drinks starting at 5€. In the Hotel Bayerischer Hof, Promenadeplatz 2–6. ℂ **089/2-12-09-94.** Cover 10€ Fri–Sat after 10pm; higher for special events. No cover for hotel guests. Tram: 19.

Night Flight *Finds*   This nightclub is designed to highlight the visual effect of airplane departures and arrivals. To get here, you'll have to drive 40km (25 miles) north of the city or take a 30-minute ride on the S-bahn. The site is on the periphery of the Munich Airport, in an industrial-looking building midway between three enormous hangars. You can drink at three different bars, dance, and listen to the loud music that changes according to the night of the week. There's even a restaurant. In summer, there's an outside terrace where virtually everything at the airport can be seen with eerie clarity. Friday nights, with techno-rap as the theme, draw the youngest audience. Other nights, the crowd ranges from 25 to a youthful 40. It's open Tuesday to Thursday from 9pm to at least 2am, and in some cases, until 8am the following morning. Franz Josef Strauss Airport, Wartungsallee 9. ✆ 089/97-59-79-99. Cover 4€ Tues–Thurs, 5€–8€ Fri–Sat. S-bahn: S8 to Flughafen.

JAZZ

Jazzclub Unterfahrt This is Munich's leading jazz club, attracting artists from throughout Europe and North America. It is not only the city's best, but one of Europe's ten best jazz clubs, according to *Wire*, a leading music magazine in Europe. Reaching it requires wandering down a labyrinth of underground cement-sided corridors that might remind you of a bomb shelter during the Cold War. Once inside, the space opens to reveal flickering candles, a convivial bar, high ceilings, and clusters of smallish tables facing a stage and whatever singers and musicians happen to be emoting at the time. Off to one corner is an art gallery. The bar here opens daily at 7:30pm; live music is Monday to Thursday from 9pm until midnight; Friday through Saturday 7:30pm to 3am. Einsteinstrasse 42. ✆ 089/448-2794. Cover 8€–12€. U-bahn: Max-Weber-Platz

Mister B's Small, dark, and popular with blues and jazz aficionados, this club hosts a slightly older, mellower crowd than the rock and dance clubs. Blues, jazz, and rhythm-and-blues combos take the stage Thursday to Saturday. Hours are Tuesday to Sunday from 8pm to 3am. Herzog-Heinrichstrasse 38. ✆ 089/53-49-01. Cover 4.50€–6€. U-bahn: Goetheplatz.

COUNTRY

Oklahoma File under surreal. German and European bands decked out in cowboy hats and boots struggle with the nuances of an extremely foreign musical form. Even when the results are dead-on mimicry, there's something strange about watching German "cowboys" line dance or lean on the bar while guzzling Spaten. Cover is usually at the low end of the scale, rising when English and American acts hit the stage. Depending on your mood, this place can be a lot of fun. Pull on your jeans and come on in Tuesday to Saturday 7pm to 1am. Schäftlarnstrasse 156. ✆ 089/7-23-43-27. Cover 7.50€–10€. U-bahn: Thalkirchen.

Rattlesnake Saloon One of Munich's two country-western saloons, this is a down-home homage to the redneck charms of hound dogs, battered pickup trucks, and cowboy hats and boots. Rib-sticking platters (rib-eye steaks, barbecued pork, and chili) can be ordered to wash down with the steins of Spaten beer that go so well with the live country music. Performers come from Munich, England, Canada, and, in some cases, even Nashville, Tennessee. Regardless of how authentic the twang in the music might be, you'll have a fun evening here, and someone will invariably rise to the challenge of conducting a rodeo-style line dance lesson for anyone who's interested in learning. Rattlesnake is open Wednesday to Sunday from 7pm to 1am. The location is 5km (3 miles) north of the Marienplatz. Schneeglöckchenstrasse 91. ✆ 089/1-50-40-35. Cover 5€–8€. S-bahn: S1 to Fasanerie.

DANCE CLUBS & DISCOS

Alabama In a former military base in Schwabing, this is an offbeat center for nightlife that houses three different clubs in one complex. The night begins at 8pm in a beer garden when the place starts filling up, attracting a crowd mainly in their 20s and 30s. After a few mugs, you can choose your favorite club. Featuring the beat of pop music, **Temple Club** operates on Saturday from 10pm to 5am. International jams are the feature at **Schwabinger Ballhouse,** open Friday and Saturday 10pm to 5am. For Teutonic oldies, head for another of the three clubs, **Alabama,** on Friday from 9pm to 4am, where you can also hear hits from the 60s to the 90s on Saturday 10am to 5pm. The cover charge to enter the dance clubs ranges from 5€ to 7€ at each club, depending on the night of the week (you must pay separately for each club). Domagkstrasse 33. ℭ **089/450-800-75.** U-bahn: U6 to Alte Heide, where a free shuttle bus runs to the complex.

Backstage Club & Biergarten   This seems to be some sort of Munich hybrid: a beer garden, a dance hall, and a concert hall for music ranging from Jamaican reggae to hip-hop and funk. You'll also hear blues, jazz, and techno here. A wide array of young Münchners, from the very poor to the very rich, show up here and mingle in a democratic atmosphere. The dress code? The more outrageous the better. On our last visit, one male/female couple showed up dressed like chartreuse cats. The spacious outdoor beer garden overflows on weekends, and there's never a cover. Open Sunday to Thursday 7pm to 3am, Friday and Saturday 7pm to 5am. Helmholtzstrasse 18. ℭ **089/183330.** No cover. S-bahn: Donnersberger Brücke.

Feierwerk   Alterna-scene central. If it's independent theater or rock and roll, the multiple stages inside this complex have hosted it. Entertainment ranges from the commercially viable to the truly underground. In the summer, this already-roomy complex expands outside into circus tents. It's open daily from 9pm to 4am. Hansastrasse 39–41. ℭ **089/743-1340.** Cover 5.50€–10€. U-bahn: Heimeranplatz.

Kunstpark Ost   Set within the sprawling premises of what used to be a factory, this is Munich's newest complex (23 in total) of bars, restaurants, and dance clubs. People tend to move randomly from venue to venue, without any particular loyalty to one or the other. Your best bet is to show up sometime after 8pm, when all the bars will be functioning. The discos don't get going until at least 10:30pm. Entrance charges to each of the discos usually costs from 5€ to 7€ per disco, depending on the night of the week (restaurants and bars are entered for free). Grafingerstrasse 6. ℭ **089/49-00-29-28.** Cover 5€–7€. S-bahn: Ostbahnhof.

Max Emanuel Brauerei   Beer hasn't been brewed here since the 1920s, when the place was transformed into a showcase/beer hall for Löwenbräu beer. It still serves steins of beer and platters of filling German grub every day from 11am to 1am. Three nights a week, the cavernous floor above street level reverberates with salsa music (Wed and Fri from 9pm) or 1950s-style rock and roll (Sun beginning at 8pm). During salsa nights, most of Munich's Latino population, from the Dominican Republic to southern Chile, make it a point of honor to show up to show off their merengue steps. Sunday nights the site can also be fun in a convertible-Chevy and saddle-shoes kind of way. There is a cover of 7€ if you want to be in one of the rooms offering special live music such as salsa, swing, or rock and roll. Adalbertstrasse 33. ℭ **089/2-71-51-58.** U-bahn: U3 or U6 to Universität.

Nachtwerk   This dance club in a huge factory warehouse also books bands. It's a festive place, not nearly as pretentious as other, more "exclusive" discos. Patrons even dance to rock music. The club is open Friday 10:30pm to 2:30am and Saturday 10:30pm to 5am. Landesbergerstrasse 185. ℭ **089/5-78-38-00.** Cover 5€–12€. S-bahn: Donnersbergerbrücke.

Moments Wenches, Knaves & Medieval Delicacies

Welser Kuche, Residenzstrasse 27 (© **089/29-65-65**), recreates a hearty medieval feast every night, beginning at 8pm. Guests must be prepared to stick around for 3 hours. In many ways, this is a takeoff on the Tudor banquets that are so popular with tourists in London. Food is served in hand-thrown pottery by *Magde* and *Knechte* (wenches and knaves) wearing 16th-century costumes, and guests eat the medieval delicacies with their fingers, aided only by a stilettolike dagger. Many recipes are authentic, based on a 16th-century cookbook discovered in 1970. You can order a 6-course or 10-course menu called a *Welser Feast;* they cost 40€ and 50€, respectively. On Tuesday only, a 5-course *Bürgermahl* (gourmand menu) costs 35€. The place can be good fun if you're in the mood; but it's likely to be overflowing with tourists, so reservations are recommended. It's open daily from 7pm to 1am. To get there, take the U3 U-bahn to Odeonsplatz.

Parkcafé   Who'd ever guess this home to chic freaks was a Nazi hangout in the 1930s? The place contains five lively bars, two of them outfitted like the inside of a ship plus a strident color scheme using oranges and reds, among other colors. Many nights are themed, ranging from "Black Beat" music on Wednesdays to "gay Sundays." It's open Wednesday to Sunday 10pm to 4am. It's also open the first Tuesday of every month 11pm to 4am. Sophienstrasse 7. © **089/59-83-13.** Cover 5€–15€. U-bahn: Königsplatz or Lenbachplatz.

Schwabinger Podium   Loud, urban, underground, smoky, crowded, and often raucous—this place's fans wouldn't change it even if they could. There's some kind of live music every night, and a crowd that is up on the musical scenes in London and Los Angeles. It's open Sunday to Thursday from 8pm to 1am and Friday and Saturday from 8pm to 3am. Wagnerstrasse 1. © **089/39-94-82.** Sun–Mon no cover charge; Fri–Sat nights, 4€ cover. U-bahn: Münchner Freiheit.

3 The Bar & Cafe Scene

Alter Simpl   Once a literary cafe, Alter Simpl takes its name from a satirical review of 1903. There's no one around anymore who remembers that revue, but Alter Simpl is still on the scene, made famous by its legendary owner, Kathi Kobus. Lale Andersen, who popularized the song "Lili Marlene," frequented this cafe/bar when she was in Munich. (She also maintained, as she pointed out repeatedly in her autobiography, that the correct spelling of the song was "Lili Marleen.") Today it attracts locals, including young people, counterculturists, and *Gastarbeiter* (foreign workers). The real fun occurs after 11pm, when the artistic ferment becomes more reminiscent of iconoclastic Berlin than Bavaria. Light meals cost 8€ to 15€. It's open daily 10am to 4am. Türkenstrasse 57. © **089/2-72-30-83.** Tram: 18. Bus: 53.

Café Extrablatt   Owned by a prominent Munich newspaper columnist, Michael Grater, this cafe epitomizes the nocturnal essence of Schwabing. The sprawling, sometimes smoky room is adorned with photographs of celebrities and features a spacious well-designed bar, but the sidewalk tables are preferable during warm weather. The cafe attracts many of Munich's writers, artists, and counterculture fans. Regulars convene here to converse and keep tabs on who's doing what, where. A simple *Tagesmenu* (menu of the day) will fend off starvation for around 10€, while a large beer costs around 2.50€. It's open Monday to Thursday from 8am to midnight, Friday and Saturday from 9am to 1am, and Sunday from 9am to midnight. Leopoldstrasse 7, Schwabing. (*C*) 089/33-33-33. U-bahn: U3 or U6 to Universität.

Cafe Puck   This is a convivial, dark-paneled combination of cafe, restaurant, and bar—depending on what time of day or night you happen to drop in. You'll find a hip scene, from locals who come to dine to students who use it as a beer- and wine-drinking hangout. Menu items change daily, and dishes can be German, North American, Mexican, or Chinese. Platters range in price from 8€ to 13€, and full-fledged American breakfasts—which can even include pancakes with maple syrup—are served every day between 9am and 6pm (these are sometimes requested late in the afternoon as a kind of status symbol by those recovering from too many drinks consumed the night before). One particular favorite is a pork steak *teller* (platter) that's actually a meal in itself. The atmosphere is convivial and infectious, encouraged by the foam and suds of Spaten and Franziskaner, but if you get bored, you'll find a selection of German- and English-language newspapers to read. It's open daily from 9am to 1am. Türkenstrasse 33. (*C*) 089/2-80-22-80. U-bahn: U3 or U6 to Universität.

Croccodrillo   In a cellar setting from around 1890, this bar is suddenly chic, drawing a hip crowd in their 20s to their early 40s who crowd in here nightly. It offers one of the longest bars in town, with modern lighting and excellent cocktails. A DJ plays disco and house on weekends, and live bands such as funk and rock often perform here during the week. Hours are daily from 7pm to 2am. Hohenzollernstrasse 11. (*C*) 089/33-66-39. U-bahn: Münchnerfreiheit.

Haus der 111 Biere   This unassuming corner bar is the type of small dark place that adds character to any urban neighborhood. Among the beer selections is the strongest brew in the world—EKU Doppelbock Kulminator, a 22-proof treat. It's open Sunday to Thursday from 8pm to 1am and Friday and Saturday from 8pm to 3am. Franzstrasse 3. (*C*) 089/33-12-48. U-bahn: Münchnerfreiheit.

Havana Club   This is not the spicy Cuban club you might expect from its name—it's actually named after a brand of rum. Employees may tell you about the bar's brush with fame, when Gloria Estefan made an appearance here during a sojourn in Munich; but its day-to-day function is as a lively singles bar fueled by rum-based cocktails, ranging in price from 7€ to 12€ each, which help lubricate the rolling good times. The only food served is salty, snacklike fare, usually peanuts. It's open Sunday to Wednesday from 6pm to 1am and Thursday to Saturday from 6pm to 2am. Herrnstrasse 30. (*C*) 089/29-18-84. S-bahn: Isartor.

Master's Home   This is one of the historic core's most animated and convivial bars. It seems to attract a wider range of clients than most other watering holes in Munich. The setting is the ground floor of an imposing, 19th-century building close to the Marienplatz. The large room, outfitted with antiques and warm colors, is in the style of an Edwardian-era club in London, suggests a living room in a comfortably battered but upscale private home. There's also a restaurant offering Italian-inspired cuisine, serving fixed-price seven-course meals that cost 40€. The bar is open nightly from 6:30pm till 3am, with the last order accepted in the kitchen at 1am. Frauenstrasse 11. (*C*) 089/22-99-09. S-bahn: Marienplatz or Isartor.

Nachtcafé   It hums, it thrives, and it captures everyone's nocturnal imagination. No other nightspot in Munich attracts such an array of soccer stars, film celebrities, literary figures, and, as one employee put it, "ordinary people, but only the most sympathetically crazy ones." Waves of patrons appear at different times of the evening: at 11pm, when live shows here begin; at 2am, when the restaurants close; and at 4am, when die-hard revelers seek a final drink in the predawn hours. There are no fewer than four indoor bars (and an additional 3 on an outdoor terrace in summertime) and lots of tiny tables. The decor is updated 1950s; the music jazz, blues, and soul. Beer costs 3€, drinks run from 6€, and meals go for 12€ to 21€. It's open daily from 9pm to 6am. Maximiliansplatz 5. ℂ 089/59-59-00. No cover. Tram: 19. S-bahn: Karlsplatz.

O'Reilly's Irish Pub   The all-Irish staff lends an air of authenticity to this pub, located in a historic vaulted cellar close to the Hotel Vier Jahreszeiten. Besides the obligatory Irish and German beers, you can also find good brews from England and the Czech Republic, as well as decent Irish stew, steaks, burgers, and mixed grills. Live Gaelic music is performed at irregular intervals throughout the month. Beer costs from 2.50€ to 3.50€, main courses from 9€ to 18.50€. Hours are Monday to Thursday from 4pm to 1am, and Friday to Sunday from noon to 3am. Maximilianstrasse 29. ℂ 089/29-33-11. U-bahn/S-bahn: Marienplatz.

Pusser's New York Bar   This themed bar/restaurant is about British navy nostalgia and the grog that helped keep it afloat throughout the 18th and 19th centuries. (This is the only European franchise of a small, well-run chain of restaurant-bars based in Tortola, British Virgin Islands.) It's on two levels of a prewar building near the Marienplatz; look for the fishing boat from Tortola (British Virgin Islands) suspended from the ceiling. The most popular drink is a rum-based Painkiller in a special mug that holds a whopping 16 ounces of Caribbean kick. Menu items are international but with a Caribbean flair (black bean soup, grilled fish in Mexican salsa). Main courses range from 10€ to 15€. Despite its international outlook, Pusser's is a local hangout, with a clientele from around the Altstadt. In the cellar bar, a pianist performs every day from 9pm until closing. It's open daily from 5pm to 3am. Falkenturmstrasse 9. ℂ 089/22-05-00. U-bahn/S-bahn: Marienplatz.

Schultz   Schultz is a New York–style bar in Schwabing. It's popular with theater people, who crowd in as they do at Schumann's (see below) for smoke-filled chatter. The food is uncomplicated, and the decor, as they say here, is "unobvious and understated." Beer starts at 2.50€; drinks run from 8€ and up. It's open daily from 5pm to 1am. Barerstrasse 47. ℂ 089/2-71-47-11. U-bahn: U3 or U6 to Universität.

Schumann's   Located on Munich's most desirable shopping street, Schumann's is known as a "thinking man's bar." Charles Schumann, author of three bar books, wanted a bar that would be the artistic, literary, and social focus of the metropolis, and his bar is said to have contributed to a remarkable renaissance of bar culture in the city. Schumann's doesn't waste any money on decor: Popular with the film, advertising, and publishing worlds, it doesn't have to—it can depend on its clientele to keep it fashionable. In cold weather, guests retreat inside, but in summer, they prefer the terrace that spills out onto the street. The drinks run 4.50€ to 12€. Beer is 3.50€. It's open Monday to Friday 5pm to 3am and Sunday 6pm to 3am. Oddly enough, it's closed on Saturdays. Maximilianstrasse 36. ℂ 089/22-90-60. U-bahn/S-bahn: Marienplatz. Tram: 19.

Shamrock At this beer-lover's bar, you can compare the great brews of Germany with the best of the Irish exports. It features the brews of both countries, including Kilkenny and Guinness, which usually sell for between 3.50€ and 4€ per mug. A modest assortment of food is served (nothing to write home about), such as baguette-style sandwiches and stuffed pita pockets, but most clients come here to drink. There's free entertainment every night between 9pm and midnight, when a mixed bag of Irish, rock, country, folk, funk, or blues musicians take to the stage. Located near the university, Shamrock gets a fair share of the student crowd. It's open Monday to Thursday from 5pm to 1am, Friday from 5pm to 3am, and Saturday and Sunday from 2pm to 3am. Trautenwolfstrasse 4–6. ✆ 089/33-10-81. U-bahn: Giselastrasse.

Stadtcafé This place considers itself the communications center of young Munich—an intellectual beacon that attracts creative people. By Munich nightlife standards, it closes relatively early, so when they're finished here, night owls then drift on to other late-night venues. Expect lots of chitchat from table to table and to find at least one person scribbling away at his or her unfinished novel. It's open Monday to Thursday 11am to midnight; Friday to Saturday 11am to 1am; Sunday 10:30am to midnight. St. Jakobsplatz 1. ✆ 089/26-69-49. No cover. U-bahn or S-bahn: Marienplatz.

Tomate Sports Why is this bar named after a fruit? That's the only mystery about the place, which, upon entrance, is immediately recognizable as a traditional sports bar, with a big-screen television broadcasting an overdose of athletics throughout the evening. Besides the soccer and rugby you might expect, the regulars also watch U.S. events, so stop in if you're a homesick American sports fan. Despite its name, there are almost no references inside to the tomato. Owned and operated by the Paulaner brewery, whose beer is showcased, the place is open Wednesday to Friday from 7:30pm to 3am, Saturday 5:30pm to 3am, and Sunday to Tuesday 7:30pm to 1am. Beer costs 3.50€. Siegesstrasse 19. ✆ 089/34-83-93. U-bahn: U3 or U6 to Münchner Freiheit.

4 Beer Halls

The *Bierhalle* is a traditional Munich institution, offering food, entertainment, and, of course, beer.

Augustinerbrau On the principal pedestrian-only street of Munich, this beer hall offers generous helpings of food, good beer, and a mellow atmosphere. Dark-wood panels and ceilings in carved plaster make the place look even older than it is. It's been around for less than a century, but beer was first brewed on this spot in 1328, as the literature about the establishment claims. The long menu changes daily, and the cuisine is not for dieters: It's hearty, heavy, and starchy, but that's what customers want. Half a liter of beer begins at 3.50€; meals cost from 12€ to 20€. It's open daily from 9am to midnight. Neuhauserstrasse 27. ✆ 089/23-18-32-57. U-bahn or S-bahn: Karlsplatz. Tram: 19.

Hofbräuhaus am Platzl ✮ The state-owned Hofbräuhaus is the world's most famous beer hall. Visitors with only 1 night in Munich usually come here. The present Hofbräuhaus was built in 1897, but the tradition of a beer house on this spot dates from 1589. In the 19th century, it attracted artists, students, and civil servants, and it was called the Blue Hall because of its dim lights and smoky atmosphere. When it grew too small to contain all the patrons who wanted to come here, architects designed another, in 1897.

The Bavarian Brew

Few cities in the world cling to a beverage the way Munich clings to beer. Münchners—with a little help from their visitors—consume a world's record of the stuff: 280 liters a year, per capita (as opposed to a wimpy 150 liters in other parts of Germany). This kind of "heroism" usually prompts a cynical comment from the wine drinkers of Berlin and the Rhineland—they say that Bavarians never open their mouths except to pour in more beer! The Münchner response is that settling questions of politics, art, music, commerce, finance, as well as the affairs of the human heart, requires plenty of beer and lots of good, unfussy food.

Some of Munich's most notable events have floated on the suds. There was Hitler's Beer Hall Putsch (Hofbräuhaus, 1923); a bungled attempt to assassinate Hitler (in the Bürgerbräukeller, 1939); and most recently, the Beer Garden Revolution, a 1995 event, when the proposed closing of a neighborhood beer garden at 9:30pm was seen as a threat to the civil liberties of all the city's beer drinkers, and prompted mass rallies by infuriated Münchners. These, along with dozens of smaller but still sudsy tempests, have trained Munich's politicians to view the effects of the brew on their constituents with considerable respect.

Statistics regarding Oktoberfest are daunting indeed—7 million visitors flood into the city for 2 drink-sodden weeks, surging into every beer hall in town and filling the sprawling network of tents set up in the Theresienwiese for the event. But while the festival promotes the consumption of millions of liters of beer, beer drinking continues on (almost as heartily) year-round. Under the trees of the Biergarten in summer and in the noisy Bierhalle and cellars, solid citizens in feathered hats, Schicki-Mickies, grandmothers, students, and tourists rub shoulders as they down their hefty liter mugs of beer. And as you drink, it's a tradition to complain about anything and everything—linguists have even coined a word for the local habit of mumbling into a stein of beer—*guanteln*. And why not? It's a therapeutic, relatively inexpensive way to let off steam.

The perfect accompaniment for beer (especially if it happens to be consumed before noon), as everyone knows, is *Weisswurst,* those little white sausages. And every year, the anniversary of their invention, in 1857, is celebrated as something of a national holiday. *Prost!*

Today, 4,500 beer drinkers can crowd in here on any given night. Several rooms, including a top-floor room for dancing, are spread over three floors. With its brass band (which starts playing at 11am), the ground-floor Schwemme is most typical of what you probably expected—here it's eternal Oktoberfest. In the second-floor restaurant, strolling musicians entertain, and dirndl-clad servers offer mugs of beer between sing-alongs. Every night the Hofbräuhaus presents a typical Bavarian show in its Fest-Hall, starting at 8pm and lasting until midnight. (This was also the 1920 setting for the notorious meeting of Hitler's newly launched German Workers Party, when a brawl erupted between the Nazis and their Bavarian enemies.) The entrance fee is 5€, and the food is the same as that served in other parts of the beer palace. A liter of beer costs 5.50€ here; meals run 6.50€ to 15€. The hall is open daily 9am to midnight. Am Platzl 9. ✆ 089/22-16-76. U-bahn/S-bahn: Marienplatz.

Türkenhof   With its 150-year-old setting, this big and fun place looks, at first glance, like a traditional beer hall. But you'll quickly realize from the animated dialogue and the youthful energy of many of the (mostly) student patrons that it's more than a venue for conventional Bavarian schmaltz. One of the owners is Greek, a fact that accounts for the relatively cosmopolitan food. Within an over-size room where lively and intelligent conversations hum and reverberate against the walls, you can hoist a stein of five kinds of Augustiner beer, the only brand sold in this brewery-sponsored place. Salads and platters of food are relatively inexpensive, priced from 6€ to 12€. They are open Sunday to Thursday 11am to 1am; Friday and Saturday 11am to 3am. Türkenstrasse 78. ℂ 089/2-80-02-35. U-bahn: Universität.

Waldwirtschaft Grosshesselohe   This popular summertime rendezvous, located above the Isar River near the zoo, has seats for some 2,000 drinkers. In clement weather, the gardens are open daily from 11am to 11pm (they have to close early because neighborhood residents complain). They are closed alto-gether in winter, when it's too cold to sit outside. Music, from Dixieland to English jazz to Polish band music, is played throughout the week. Entrance is free and you bring your own food. A liter of beer costs 5.50€. George-Kalb-Strasse 3. ℂ 089/7-49-99-40-30. S-bahn: Isartal Bahnhof. Tram: 7.

5 Gay & Lesbian Clubs

Much of Munich's gay and lesbian scene takes place in the blocks between the Viktualienmarkt and Gärtnerplatz, particularly on Hans-Sachs-Strasse.

Bau   Macho and swaggering, this gay bar encourages leather, denim, and as many uniforms as can be crammed onto the bodies that surround its street-level bar. Dimly lit and international, it's not as scary as it might look at first. Don't be surprised if you spot several New York City cop uniforms on either level—they appear to be the most popular costumes at this place. It's open nightly from 8pm to 3am. Müllerstrasse 41. ℂ 089/311-88-009. U-bahn: Sendlinger Tor.

Bei Carla *Finds*   Although little known among foreign visitors, this is one of the best women's bars in Munich, attracting a crowd mainly in their late 20s to early 40s. Women come here to meet other women, to enjoy the friendly ambi-ence, to make conversation, or perhaps toss off a round or two of darts. Open Monday to Saturday 4pm to 1am, Sunday 6pm to 1am. Buttermelcherstrasse 9. ℂ 089/227901. S-bahn: Isartor.

Morizz   One of Munich's most stylish gay bars, Morizz sprawls over mirror-ringed premises outfitted with red leather armchairs and marble-topped tables. Full meals, including Thai dishes, cost from 25€ and are served until midnight. Despite a clientele that tends to be 70% gay and male, the place prides itself on a convivial welcome for straight clients as well. Hours are Sunday to Thursday 7pm to 2am and Friday and Saturday 7pm to 3am. Klenzestrasse 43. ℂ 089/2-01-67-76. No cover. U-bahn: U2 to Frauenhoferstrasse.

New York   The strident rhythms and electronic sounds might just have been imported from New York, Los Angeles, or Paris. This is Munich's premier gay (male) disco. Most clients, ranging in age from 20 to 35, wear jeans. The sound system is accompanied by laser light shows. It's open daily 11pm to 4am. There is no cover from Monday to Thursday. However, from Friday through Sunday, the cover is 6€, which includes the first drink. Sonnenstrasse 25. ℂ 089/59-10-56. U-bahn: U1, U2, U3, or U6 to Sendlingertorplatz.

Nil   It's fun, it's convivial, and it has a clientele that's somewhat younger than the one at Teddy-Bar, just across the street (see below). In addition to fit and youthful German men hanging with one another at the octagon-shaped bar, you're likely to see faded stars (including Barbara Valentine, hailed during the 1960s as Germany's answer to Brigitte Bardot) from German stage and screen, sipping drinks with their men friends, reflecting on the glory days of their youth. Most of the clients come here to drink and mingle, but if you're hungry, platters of food are well-prepared and relatively inexpensive at 7€ to 12€. Open daily 3pm to 3am. Hans-Sach-Strasse 2. ℂ 089/26-55-45. U-bahn: Sendlinger Tor. or Frunhofer Strasse.

Ochsen Garten   Although it's a lot smaller and more cramped than most of its competitors, this is the leading leather bar in Munich, site of most of the city's leather S&M conventions and a hangout for regular guys who appreciate their sense of machismo. It's at its most crowded Thursday, Friday, and Saturday nights; on other nights it's likely to be virtually empty. It's open nightly 10pm to 3am. Müllerstrasse 47. ℂ 089/26-64-46. U-bahn: Sendlinger Tor.

Soul City   This is the most popular and animated gay disco in Munich. There are enough nooks and crannies for quiet dialogue and a sound system that's among the best in the city. Lesbians make up a respectable proportion of the clients, although gay men comprise the majority. Don't even try to phone this place—whenever staff members are there, they're usually so busy monitoring the crowd that there's barely time to answer the phone. It's open Thursday to Saturday from 10pm to 5am. Maximiliansplatz 5. ℂ 089/59-52-72. Cover 5€. U-bahn: Karlsplatz.

Teddy-Bar   Gay and neighborly, and ringed with varnished pine and a collection of teddy bears, this is a congenial bar patronized by gay men over 30. It's relatively easy to strike up a dialogue here, and if you're hungry, there are platters of Bavarian and German food, including an excellent version of Gulaschsuppe (goulash soup). It's open nightly 6pm to 3am. There's a Sunday brunch from October to April at 11am. Hans-Sachs-Strasse 1. ℂ 089/260-33-59. U-bahn: Sendlinger Tor.

10

Side Trips from Munich

Mountains, lakes, spas, and medieval towns lie within an hour of Munich, and the landscape is dotted with castles, as well as villas and alpine resorts (see chapter 11).

A short drive from Munich delivers visitors to the heart of Starnberg's "Five Lakes Region." The **Starnberger See** and **Ammersee** are weekend destinations that afford an enormous assortment of sports. The **Tegernsee** region is also a popular destination. The spa town of **Bad Tölz** is known

for its healing waters and clear mountain air.

The environs of Munich are as rich in culture and history as in natural beauty. However, in the midst of all this serenity, the former concentration camp at **Dachau** sounds an ominous note. Before Hitler and the Holocaust, it was a little artists' community, but it's now visited almost solely as a symbol of the great horror of the Nazi regime.

1 Dachau Concentration Camp

16km (10 miles) NW of Munich

In 1933, what had once been a quiet little artists' community just 16km (10 miles) from Munich became a tragic symbol of the Nazi era. Shortly after Hitler became chancellor, Himmler and the SS set up the first German concentration camp on the grounds of a former ammunition factory here. The list of prisoners at the camp included enemies of the Third Reich, including everyone from communists and Social Democrats to Jews, homosexuals, gypsies, Jehovah's Witnesses, clergymen, political opponents, some trade union members, and others.

During its notorious history, between 1933 and 1945, more than 206,000 prisoners from 30 countries were imprisoned at Dachau, perhaps a lot more. Some were forced into slave labor, manufacturing Nazi armaments for the war and helping to build roads, etc. Others fell victim to SS doctors, who conducted grotesque medical experiments on them. And still others were killed after Dachau became a center for mass murder: Starvation, illness, beatings, and torture killed thousands who were not otherwise hanged, shot by firing squads, or lethally injected. The death toll was then compounded in December of 1944 when a typhus epidemic took thousands of lives within and around the camp, and forced marches in and out of the camp claimed thousands of others as well. At least 30,000 people were registered as dead while in Dachau between 1933 and 1945. However, there are many other thousands who were also murdered there, even if they weren't registered as dead.

The SS abandoned the camp on April 28, 1945, and the liberating U.S. Army moved in to take charge the following day. In all, a total of 67,000 living prisoners—all of them on the verge of death—were discovered at Dachau and its subsidiary camps.

ESSENTIALS
GETTING THERE
BY TRAIN   The frequent suburban train (S-bahn S2) to Dachau is a 20-minute ride from Marienplatz or Hauptbahnhof in the heart of Munich (direction: Petershausen). From the station, take bus no. 724 or 726 to the camp.

BY CAR   The best road for motorists is a country road, B12. Motorists can also take the Stuttgart Autobahn, exiting at the signposted Dachau turnoff.

TOURING THE CAMP 🞋
Upon entering the camp, **KZ-Gedenkstätte Dachau,** Alte-Roemar-Strasse 75 (🕿 **08131/17-41;** www.kz-gedenkstaette-dachau.de/english/index.html), you are faced by three memorial chapels—Catholic, Protestant, and Jewish—built in the early 1960s. Immediately behind the Catholic chapel is the "Lagerstrasse," the main camp road lined with poplar trees, once flanked by 32 barracks, each housing 208 prisoners. Two barracks have been rebuilt to give visitors insight into the horrible conditions endured by the prisoners here.

The museum is housed in the large building that once contained the kitchen, laundry, and shower bathrooms, where the SS often brought prisoners for torture. Photographs and documents show the rise of the Nazi regime and the SS. There are also exhibits depicting the persecution of Jews and other prisoners. Every effort has been made to present the facts. The tour of Dachau is a truly moving experience.

The camp is open Tuesday to Sunday from 9am to 5pm; admission is free. The English version of a 22-minute documentary film, *KZ-Dachau,* is shown at 11:30am and 3:30pm. All documents are translated in the catalog, which is available at the museum entrance. Visitors are requested to wear appropriate attire (walking shorts and a T-shirt are acceptable).

2 Starnbergersee

27km (17 miles) SW of Munich

This large lake, southwest of Munich, is a favorite with Münchners on holiday. If you take a cruise on the lake, you can observe how the terrain changes from low-lying marshlands on the north to alpine ranges towering above the lake to the south. The town of Starnberg is the best-equipped holiday resort on the lake, with beaches, pools, and lakefront promenades.

ESSENTIALS
GETTING THERE
BY TRAIN   The suburban train (S6) is a 40-minute ride from Marienplatz in the heart of Munich to the town of Starnberg, at the top of Starnbergersee.

BY CAR   From Munich, motorists can follow Autobahn 95 toward Garmisch to the Starnberg exit.

VISITOR INFORMATION
For information, contact the **tourist office** (🕿 **08151/9-06-00**) at Kirchplatz 3, in the city of Berg, open year-round, Monday to Friday from 8am to 6pm; from May to October only the office also has hours on Saturdays from 9am to 1pm.

made them public. Since Ludwig had practically bankrupted the Bavarian treasury and was a disgrace and a "menace to the throne," Prince Luitpold, who took over from the king as regent, may have wanted the insane former king removed from the picture so he could have all the power and the glory of the kingdom.

Lying on the eastern shore of Lake Starnberg, the small town of **Berg** is 4km (2½ miles) south of the larger town of Starnberg. **Schloss Berg,** Wittelsbacher Strasse 27-29, in Berg, has been owned by the ruling house of Wittelsbach since 1669. Its fame stems from the fact that it was the final residence of King Ludwig II of Bavaria. All the Gothic details added to the castle by King Ludwig in the mid–19th century have been removed, the Schloss returned to its appearance as it would have looked in the 17th and 18th centuries. The castle is still privately owned and not open to the public, and a gatehouse blocks a view of its facade. From the lake, summer foliage also blocks the view, though it can be seen from the lake in winter. Even though you can't go inside, you can wander through the former grounds of the castle, which have been turned into a public park.

The town of **Possenhofen** lies on the western shore of Lake Starnberg. This was the summer retreat for Ludwig's favorite cousin, the Empress Elisabeth, nicknamed "Sisi." She was married to Franz Joseph I, the emperor of Austria and the king of Hungary. Sisi spent about 20 summers at this retreat, sending affectionate notes by boatmen across the lake to her cousin, Ludwig. Schloss Possenhofen is still standing at Karl-Theodor-Strasse 14 in Possenhofen. Although once owned by royalty, such as Duke Max of Bavaria in 1834, by 1920, the castle had become derelict, having had many uses, ranging from a military hospital to a motorcycle repair workshop. In the early 1980s, it was converted into privately owned condos. Although the castle itself is not open to the public, there is a wooden park surrounding the Schloss. It can be visited at any time.

CRUISES & OUTDOOR PURSUITS   The main attractions here are sunshine and water sports. Speedboats, paddleboats, and Windsurfers crowd the lake. All of these can be rented from **Surf Tools** (© **08151/8-93-33**).

Two of the most appealing beaches on the lake include **Possenhofer Strand,** at the lakefront in the village of Possenhofen, and **Perchen Strand** at the village of Perchen. Access to the beaches is free, but parking costs 3€. Lifeguards are on duty between May and September from 9:30am to 5:30pm.

For information on cruises around the lake, contact the **Staatliche Schiffahrt,** (© **08151/80-61**) at Dampfschiffstrasse 5, in Starnberg. Cruises are frequent in the summer months.

WHERE TO STAY & DINE

Hotel Leoni ℱ   Comfortable and low-slung, this hotel rises three stories between the edge of the lake and a rolling Bavarian hillside. Built in the early 1970s, it has a cozy, country-cousin decor, and the public rooms offer big-windowed views of the lake with its swimmers and sailboats. The midsize bedrooms are outfitted in a tasteful Bavarian manor house style. A swimming pier owned by the hotel juts out into the lake. In summer, a *Biergarten* serves frothy mugs of beer in a setting a few feet from the edge of the water.

Ortsteil Leoni, Assenbucher Strasse 44, D-82335 Berg. © **08151/50-60.** Fax 08151/50-61-40. www.see hotel-leoni.de. 70 units. 126€–167€ double; 282€–410€ suite. Rates include breakfast. AE, DC, MC, V. Parking 8€. **Amenities:** Restaurant; bar; lounge; pool; sauna; solarium; steam room; room service; babysitting. *In room:* TV, minibar, hair dryer.

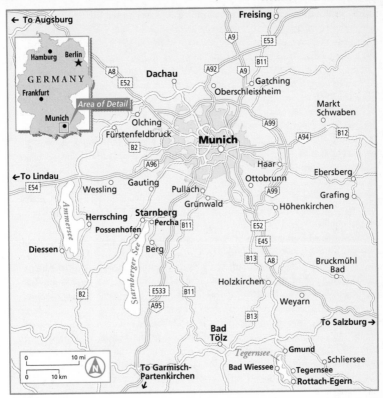

EXPLORING THE LAKE

Around the 64km (40-mile) shoreline, you can see no fewer than six castles, including the Schloss Berg, where Ludwig II was sent after he was certified as insane in 1886. Across the lake from Berg, the unofficial capital of the lake, stands the castle of Possenhofen, the home of Ludwig's favorite cousin, Sisi. It was in this lake that the king drowned under mysterious circumstances—local legend asserts that he was trying to swim to Possenhofen to ask his cousin's help in making an escape from Schloss Berg, since he was under house arrest. Many historians suggest he was murdered. A cross on the water marks the spot where his body was found. A *Votivkapelle* (memorial chapel) dedicated to Ludwig is on the shore above the cross. It is reached by walking up the hill from the village of Berg, into the Hofgarten, and along the wall of Schloss Berg (no connection with the hotel of the same name recommended below), which lies 5km (3 miles) southeast of Starnberg (the schloss is not open to the public).

What, exactly, happened to King Ludwig the day his body and that of his doctor (attending physician Doctor Gudden) were found floating on the waters of Lake Starnberg may never be known. It is believed that relevant documents could shed some light on Ludwig's fate, but they are held privately in the Archives of the Bavarian State and by the Wittelsbach family who have never

Hotel Schloss Berg   This hotel is within about 450m (500 yds.) of the town's famous Schloss (privately owned) and is the most luxurious and comfortable hotel in town. It occupies two buildings, one a 1994 remake of an older building, the other an all-new chalet-style structure. They are separated from one another by a parking lot and copses of trees.

Rooms on the upper end of the price scale are in the older building, whose windows overlook the lake. Bedrooms are comfortable, conservatively decorated, and eminently appropriate for weekend getaways from Munich. All units have well-kept bathrooms with shower-tub combinations. Our favorite hangout here is the bar, an atmospheric prelude to a Bavarian-style restaurant.

Seestrasse 17, D-82335 Berg. ✆ **08151/96-30.** Fax 08151/9-63-52. www.hotelschlossberg.de. 50 units. 89€–139€ double; 129€–189€ suite. Rates include breakfast. AE, MC, V. Free parking. **Amenities:** Restaurant; bar; Jacuzzi; sauna. *In room:* TV, minibar, hair dryer, safe.

3 Tegernsee ✮

48km (30 miles) SE of Munich

This alpine lake and the resort town on its eastern shore have the same name. Although small, this is one of the loveliest of the Bavarian lakes, with huge peaks reaching to 1,890m (6,300 ft.), seemingly rising right out of the water, and a circumference of 22km (13¾ miles). The lake has four major towns around its edges: Tegernsee (on the east side), Rottach-Egern (ritziest of all of the four, loaded with the private second homes of wealthy Münchners, on the south side), Gmund (a small village composed only of houses, on the north side, marking the entrance up the valley of the Tegernseetal), and Bad Wiessee (on the west side). For more on Bad Wiessee, see p. 186.

ESSENTIALS
GETTING THERE
BY TRAIN   The station of Tegernsee is a 1-hour and 20-minute ride from Munich's Hauptbahnhof. To reach the hotels in Rottach-Egern, you must take a taxi from the station. The trains make stops only in the town of Tegernsee and (less frequently) in the village of Gmund. The distance from the town of Tegernsee to the hamlet of Rottach-Egern is only about 2km (1¼ miles). The two towns are separated only by a small stream. Taxis make runs all the time between them, charging 4.50€–5.50€ per trip.

BY CAR   From Munich, take the A8/A9 Autobahn toward Salzburg. At exit 97 (Holzkirchen) veer south and follow the signs to Tegernsee.

VISITOR INFORMATION
For information, contact the **tourist office** (✆ **08022/18-01-40**) at Haus de Gastes, Hauptstrasse 2, Tegernsee, open May to October, Monday to Friday from 8am to 6pm and Saturday and Sunday from 10am to noon and 3 to 5pm; November to March, Monday to Friday from 8am to noon and 1 to 5pm and Saturday and Sunday from 10am to noon and 3 to 5pm.

EXPLORING THE LAKE
One of the most scenic routes in Bavaria is around the tiny Tegernsee, an easy morning drive. Surrounding the lake is a string of resort towns, including the elegant Rottach-Egern with its ritzy health clinics. Bad Wiessee (see chapter 11) is a year-round resort with curative springs, used in the treatment of rheumatism and heart and respiratory conditions.

In the town of Tegernsee, the major sights span some 12 centuries. The oldest of these is the former Benedictine monastery of Sankt Quirinus. Built in the 8th century, it was turned into a secular castle and village church in the 19th century by Bavarian king Maximilian I when he bought it for a summer retreat. The monastery is closed for a radical renovation at press time, and won't be open till late in 2003 or the middle of 2004.

Another attraction is a contemporary church, a fine example of modern German church architecture, designed by Olaf Gulbransson of Munich. There's also an Olaf Gulbransson Museum, im Kurgarten, Tegernsee (✆ **08022/3338**). Open Tuesday through Sunday from 11am to 5pm it charges 2€ for adults and 1€ for students and persons under 18, free for children under 6. It's loaded with the cartoons and political satires of Norwegian-born caricaturist Olaf Gulbransson (1873–1958), who lived in Tegernsee and satirized many of Bavaria's and Germany's leaders. He was also influential as editor of a satirical newspaper covering arts and politics, *Simplicissimus*.

There is a beer hall known and celebrated throughout the region, the Braüstüberl (Schlossplatz 1; ✆ **08022/4141**). Open daily from 9am to 11pm, it's the oldest beer hall in the region, serving only the beer brewed in the nearby brewery, a small-brand, small-production called Tegernsee beer. *Gemütlich* (friendly) and historic, with all the folkloric charm you'd expect, it's owned by Her Royal Highness Elizabeth im Bavaria, a direct descendant of King Ludwig and a member of the Wittelsbach family.

There is one minor museum, the Kutschen-Wagen-Schlitten Museum (Postal Carriage Museum), Nordliche Hauptstrasse 9 (✆ **08022/671341**), which celebrates the horses, wagons, carriages, conveyances, and sorting techniques that got mail and cargo hauled through the mountainous regions of Bavaria during the 19th century. It's open year-round Tuesday through Sunday from 2 to 5pm. Entrance costs 2€ adults; students and children under 14 can enter for free.

CRUISES & OUTDOOR PURSUITS   Sailing and windsurfing are the most popular sports here. Both can be arranged (June–Sept) at **Steck Segel-und-Surf Schule** (no phone) near the town of Gmund, 9.5km (6 miles) north of Rottach-Egern. Windsurfers cost from 18€ to 25€ for a half-day rental.

You can take a 1-hour cruise around the lake on one of the ferryboats operated by **Bayerischer Zehnschiffart GmbH** (✆ **08022/9-33-11**). Boats operate about every 1½ hours from 8am to 8pm, and a circular tour from Tegernsee costs 10.80€.

In summer, you can walk and hike along the lakeshore. In winter, because of its small size, the lake freezes over, making it an attraction for skaters.

WHERE TO STAY IN ROTTACH-EGERN
VERY EXPENSIVE

Bachmair Hotel am See 🏵🏵   This posh resort is the most elegant beside the Tegernsee and is set in the heart of town. Today, eight additional buildings supplement the original, generously proportioned *Gartenhaus*, which was constructed in 1827 as a farmhouse. It is almost like a village of minihotels, ringed with terraced gardens. Bedrooms are outfitted with lots of varnished pine and country-baroque pieces. Each has well-kept bathrooms with shower-tub combinations.

On-site restaurants include two folkloric bistros, a main dining room, and the upscale Gourmet Restaurant. Virtually everyone who has ever checked in here does so on the half-board plan, including former clients Helmut Kohl, Tom

Jones, Engelbert Humperdinck, and many of Munich's influential movers and shakers.

Seestrasse 47, D-83700 Rottach-Egern. ✆ **08022/27-20.** Fax 08022/27-27-90. www.bachmair.de/. 288 units. 210€–260€ double; 515€–1,025€ suite. Rates include half board. AE, DC, MC. Free parking. **Amenities:** 9 restaurants; 2 bars; nightclub; pool; health club; spa; sauna; Jacuzzi; boutiques; salon; room service; babysitting; laundry/dry cleaning. *In room:* TV, minibar, hair dryer, safe.

EXPENSIVE

Bachmair-Alpina   This is the government-rated three-star sibling of the more glamorous, better located Bachmair Hotel am See (see above). It's in a pleasant but uninspired modern Swiss chalet style and is inland from the lake, in a quiet residential neighborhood. Bedrooms are simple but comfortable and contain well-maintained bathrooms with shower-tub combinations. The Alpina serves breakfast daily. However, if guests want dinner, they must arrange for it in advance.

Valepper Strasse 24, D-83700 Rottach-Egern. ✆ **08022/20-41.** Fax 08022/27-27-90. www.bachmair-alpina.de. 20 units. 115€–145€ double, 240€–280€ suite. AE, DC, MC. **Amenities:** Breakfast room; bar; pool; sauna; room service; babysitting; laundry/dry cleaning. *In room:* TV, minibar, hair dryer, safe (in most).

Parkhotel Egerner Hof ✪   This hotel's detractors suggest that this modern hotel maintains a constant struggle to become a more up-to-date version of the town's government-rated five-star aristocrat, the Bachmair am See (see above). Despite that, many urbanites from Munich actually prefer the Parkhotel's four-star comfort and alert staff, although there's no lake view—the hotel is surrounded by meadows and trees—and the establishment is a 20-minute walk south of the town center. Bedrooms are traditionally cozy and warm and come equipped with tidily kept bathrooms with shower-tub combinations.

   There are three charming restaurants on site. The hotel's main dining room, the Sankt-Florian, accommodates guests on half board. Most nonresidents, however, opt for a meal in the Dichterstube (dinner only), or the Hubertus-Stüberl (lunch and dinner), see below for both. The hotel also has a cozy bar.

Aribostrasse 19–25, D-83700 Rottach-Egern. ✆ **08022/66-60.** Fax 08022/66-62-00. www.egernerhof.de. 93 units. 166€–244€ double; 235€–358€ suite. Half board 28€ supplement per person per day. AE, DC, MC, V. Free parking. **Amenities:** 3 restaurants; bar; pool; fitness center; sauna; beauty salon; room service; babysitting. *In room:* TV, minibar, hair dryer, safe.

MODERATE

Haltmair am See   Unpretentious, this hotel was expanded in the mid-1970s from a 100-year-old architectural core. The decoration is almost obsessively Bavarian, with lots of alpine accessories and dark wood paneling in the bedrooms. Suites are equipped with kitchenettes. All units contain well-kept bathrooms with shower units. It's near the center of the town, across the street from the edge of the lake. Other than a worthy buffet breakfast, no meals are served here.

Seestrasse 33–35. D-83700 Rottach-Egern. ✆ **08022/27-50.** Fax 08022/2-75-64. www.haltmair.de. 50 units. 100€–120€ double; 130€ suite. Rates include breakfast. No credit cards. Free parking. **Amenities:** Breakfast room; lounge; sauna; room service; babysitting. *In room:* TV, minibar, hair dryer, safe.

INEXPENSIVE

Gästhaus Maier-Kirschner ✪ *(Finds*   This is one of the best bets in town for comfortable, reasonably priced accommodations with a personal touch. A farmhouse is recorded to have been here as early as 1350. Some of the antique architectural details remaining date from 1870 when the site was a local farmer's homestead. Bedrooms contain simplified reproductions of antique baroque furniture, comfortable armchairs, and well-maintained bathrooms mostly with shower-tub combinations. No meals, other than breakfast and mid-afternoon coffee and snacks, are served. Only the street separates this hotel from the edge of the lake.

Seestrasse 23, D-83700 Rottach-Egern. © 08022/6-71-10. Fax 08022/67-11-37. 41 units. 80€–95€ double. Rates include breakfast. No credit cards. Free parking. **Amenities:** Restaurant; bar; spa; sauna; beauty salon. *In room:* TV, minibar, hair dryer, safe.

WHERE TO DINE

Dichterstube/Hubertus-Stüberl *(K)* *(Finds)* CONTINENTAL (in Dichterstube)/BAVARIAN (in Hubertus-Stüberl) Reaching these two restaurants requires a 20-minute trek on foot or a very brief drive south of the town center; however, it's worth the effort, considering the quality of the food. The less expensive of the two, Hubertus-Stüberl, is outfitted like the interior of a hunting lodge, with all the requisite references to "the hunt." Here, menu items include cream of garlic soup with croutons, goulash soup, carpaccio of bonito with a paprika-flavored vinaigrette, smoked filet of trout with horseradish sauce, and such main courses as ragout of venison with chive-flavored polenta, and veal schnitzel "in the style of the Tegernsee" with roasted potatoes.

Meals are more formal, more ambitious, and more expensive in the Dichterstube, site of the best cuisine in town. The seven-course, set-price menu is a veritable banquet that requires serious gastronomic attention. Ordering a la carte might be wise for those with less hearty appetites. Depending on the season, menu items might include a galette of wild rice with tartare of salmon and caviar, braised zander with a ragout of crabs, glazed John Dory with chicory sauce, lobster salad with avocados and orange-pepper marmalade, and such desserts as stuffed chocolate cake with champagne-flavored mousse and lemon-flavored sorbet.

In the Parkhotel Egerner Hof, Aribostrasse 19. © 08022/66-60. Reservations recommended. In the Dichterstube, main courses 30€–40€; fixed-price dinner 75€–88€. In the Hubertus-Stüberl, main courses 15€–20€. AE, DC, MC, V. Daily noon–2pm (Hubertus-Stüberl only) and 6–10pm (both restaurants).

ROTTACH-EGERN AFTER DARK

The most convivial tavern in town is the **Weinhaus Moschner,** Kisslinger Strasse 2 (© 08022/55-22), at the edge of this resort, an old, time-mellowed tavern where not only regional wine but a hearty dark brew made by a monastery in Tegernsee is served. This is a place for a real Bavarian hoedown, and many of the local men do show up in lederhosen, dancing in the disco on the second floor. An older crowd stays downstairs sampling Franconian wine or else orders hearty Bavarian fare, especially a wide variety of thick sausages with sauerkraut.

4 Ammersee *(★)*

39km (24 miles) SW of Munich

Smaller and less popular than Starnbergersee, Ammersee is a bit more rustic and wild than its cousin. In the past, Ammersee was thought too far from the city for excursions. For that reason, it was never overdeveloped and retains much of its natural splendor. Although it does have its share of summer homes and hotels, its shores are not quite so saturated or overcrowded as are those at Starnbergersee.

ESSENTIALS
GETTING THERE
BY TRAIN   The suburban train (S-bahn 5) is a 40-minute ride from Marien-platz in the heart of Munich to Herrsching.

BY CAR   Take the A96 Autobahn west toward Lindau. Get off at the Herrsching/Wessling exit (Highway 2068) and follow signs to Herrsching.

EXPLORING THE LAKE
The village of **Herrsching,** with a population of 10,000, is home to an enor-mous villa with fabulous turrets, facades, and pagoda roofing, the **Kurpark Schlösschen** (✆ **08152/42-50**). It was constructed in the late 19th century as a summer getaway for the artist Ludwig Scheuermann. It is now home to the municipal cultural center and is the venue for occasional summer concerts.

The small fishing village of **Diessen,** popular for its pottery and its church, the Marienmünster, is a short ferry ride from Herrsching. Ferries depart about nine times a day from the Seepromenade; the ride takes 20 minutes, and the fare to Diessen is 3€ each way. Call ✆ **08143/9-40-21** for information.

Also a short journey from Herrsching, and well worth the time, is the ancient monastery of **Andechs.** Set high on a mountain, the Heiliger Berg, this Bene-dictine monastery (open daily from 7am–7pm) draws multitudes of pilgrims and beer aficionados. The pilgrims visit to venerate the religious relics from the Holy Land; the less devout make the journey for the stupendous beers and cheeses produced by the monks. Buses depart from the front of Herrshing's railway station every hour year-round. Contact Omnibusverhehr Rauner (✆ **08152/34-57**) for information. You can also hike the 5km (3 miles) uphill to the monastery—head east along the trails marked from the center of town.

CRUISES & OUTDOOR PURSUITS   For a magnificent tour of the lake, take a steamship cruise. Boats depart hourly from 9am to 6pm. For information on various trips, contact **Staatliche Schiffahrt** (✆ **08143/9-40-21**) at Lands-berger Strasse 81 in Ammersee. You can also circumnavigate the lake by taking one of the ferryboats (see above) that departs seven times a day, making stops at seven lakefront towns. For 13€, you can get on and off all day, boarding the next boat to continue the tour (visitors average 2 or 3 stops throughout the day).

You can rent a Windsurfer, paddleboat, or rowboat at **Stummbaum** (✆ **08152/13-75**) at Summerstrasse 22, in Herrsching.

WHERE TO STAY
Ammersee-Hotel   This well-maintained and unpretentious government-rated three-star hotel sits behind a turn-of-the-20th-century facade in the heart of town. It has three floors of conservatively modern guest rooms, all renovated and upgraded in the late 1990s. Most have views over the lake. All units have well-kept bathrooms with shower-tub combinations. On the premises is a simple, Weinstube-style restaurant, plus a bar.

Summerstrasse 32, D-82211 Herrsching. ✆ 08152/96-870. Fax 08152/53-74. www.ammersee-hotel.de. 40 units. 100€–120€ double. Rates include breakfast. Free parking. **Amenities:** Restaurant; bar; health spa; sauna; room service. *In room:* TV, minibar, hair dryer.

Hotel Promenade   This is a small, businesslike hotel, which occupies a site directly in the center of town. Built in 1988, and with fewer than a dozen guest rooms, it has a blandly modern decor, a bar, and a restaurant that serves Croatian and international food (see below). Each bathroom is well managed and contains a shower unit. Its position directly beside the lake permits sweep-ing views from the balconies of some rooms, and there's also a lakeside terrace.

Summerstrasse 6, D-82211 Herrsching. © **08152/10-88.** Fax 08152/59-81. 11 units. 91€–113€ double. Rates include breakfast. DC, MC, V. Parking 6€. Closed Dec 20–Jan 10. **Amenities:** Restaurant; bar; lounge. *In room:* TV, minibar, hair dryer.

WHERE TO DINE

Andechser Hof BAVARIAN   This popular dining spot is the kind of place that offers beer and snacks throughout the afternoon and substantial platters of Bavarian food at dinner. The setting is a 1905 building with a decor full of references to the Bavarian experience and style. A Biergarten adjacent to the hotel offers such specialties as ragout of beef or pork schnitzel with fresh vegetables.

Don't overlook the possibility of an overnight stopover here. There's a total of 25 clean units, full of nostalgic charm, all with private baths, phones, and TVs, renting for 90€ to 115€ for a double.

Zum Landungssteg 1, D-82211 Herrsching. © **08152/85-79.** Main courses 8€–18€. AE, DC, MC, V. Daily 11am–10pm.

Restaurant Promenade CROATIAN/GERMAN   If you've never had Croatian food before, this is your chance to try it. This 80-seat dining room has a view over the lake. Croatian food places lots of emphasis on grilled meats and fish, seasoned with herbs, which emerge crisp and seared on the outside, tender on the inside, in the form of grilled lakefish, calf's liver, lamb and pork cutlets, and all kind of steaks, invariably served with vegetables braised in butter. Also tempting is the marinated rumpsteak, usually a tough cut of meat that, thanks to long marinades and slow cooking, comes up tender and steaming.

In the Hotel Promenade, Summerstrasse 6. © **08152/10-88.** Main courses 10€–20€. AE, DC, MC, V. Thurs–Tues noon–3pm and 6.30–10pm. July–Aug open daily noon–3pm and 6:30–10pm.

5 Bad Tölz ⋆

50km (31 miles) S of Munich

The historic spa town of Bad Tölz offers something for every traveler. Situated where the rolling foothills become the mountains of the Alps, the town flanks both sides of the Isar River, which divides it into two distinct sectors. On the eastern side of the river stands the historic medieval town, complete with chapels, turrets, and walls. Older than Munich, this section offers fine examples of medieval and baroque art and architecture. The major attraction here is **Stadtpfarrkirche,** a church built in 1466—it's an exquisite example of German late-Gothic architecture.

On the western bank of the Isar lies the *Kurverwaltung,* or modern spa, whose iodine-rich waters are known for their soothing and healing powers.

ESSENTIALS
GETTING THERE
BY TRAIN   The train ride takes an hour from Munich's Hauptbahnhof.

BY CAR   From Munich, motorists can take the Autobahn A8 or A9 toward Salzburg. Exit at Holzkirchen and follow signs southward toward Bad Tölz.

VISITOR INFORMATION
For information, contact the **Kurverwaltung** (© **08041/7-86-70**), at Ludwigstrasse 11 in Bad Tölz, Monday to Friday from 9am to noon and 2 to 5:30pm and Saturday from 9am to noon and 4 to 6:30pm.

SPORTS & OUTDOOR PURSUITS

Anyone interested in sports will never be bored in Bad Tölz. Golfers have access to two 9-hole courses. **Golf Club Isarwinkel** (𝄐 **08041/7-78-78**), on the town's northern tier, was built for U.S. military officers when there was a local military base here. On the western tier, **Golfplatz am Buchberg**, Strasse 124 (𝄐 **08041/99-94**) is a challenging but less prestigious course. Both charge greens fees of 35€ and are open April to October, daily from 9am to 6:30pm. Advance reservations are a good idea.

Alpamare, Ludwigstrasse 14 (𝄐 **08041/50-99-99**), is one of the most up-to-date swimming pools in the region, complete with water slides, waterfalls, kiddie pools, and saunas. Admission is 15€ to 35€, and it's open Monday to Friday from 9am to 9pm and Saturday and Sunday from 9am to 10pm. For more information on their attractions, visit www.alpamare.com. You can also swim in the Isar, but at your own risk. There are no official sites for swimming, and the river is both cold and swift moving.

The clear, swift waters of the Isar are perfect, however, for white-water canoeing, kayaking, or rafting. Contact **Kajakschule Oberland,** Ganghoferstrasse 7, D-83661 Lenggries/Fall (𝄐 **08045/916-916**), run by Gunther Carmelli, one of Bavaria's most experienced white-water guides, and his family. A 4-hour excursion in a rubber-sided raft costs 34€. Lessons in kayaking and canoeing cost 199€ per person for a four-day course, with discounts for the second and third participant in a party.

The nearest skiing slopes are on the Brauneck mountain. For information, contact **Ski-Centrum,** Berg Brauneck (𝄐 **08042/89-10**), in the nearby hamlet of Lenggries, a 20-minute drive east of Bad Tölz. A day pass on any of the 30 lifts is 28€.

WHERE TO STAY
MODERATE

Jodquellenhof-Alpamare ⚹   This is Bad Tölz's equivalent of a "grand hotel," with a longer history than any other hotel in town. Originally built in 1860, and modernized inside and out many times since then, it helped launch Bad Tölz into the full-fledged resort you see today. If you opt to stay here, however, don't expect 19th-century authenticity: The hotel has, both commercially and architecturally, kept up with the times. Unlike some spa hotels that appeal to older, more staid clients, Jodquellenhof attracts a family clientele on yearly vacations. That's not surprising, for the hotel shares a verdant park with Alpamare (see above) Entrance to Alpamare, open Monday to Friday from 9am to 9pm and Saturday and Sunday from 9am to 10pm, is free for residents of this hotel but costs between 15€ and 35€ per person for nonresidents. Also on the premises is an array of spa facilities. There's a pleasant hotel bar, and a dining room whose main function is feeding hotel guests on meal plans. Bedrooms are outfitted in a neutral, rather bland style and all have bathrooms with shower-tub combinations and balconies.

Ludwigstrasse 13–15, D-83646 Bad Tölz. 𝄐 **08041/50-90.** Fax 08041/50-95-55. www.jodquellenhof.com. 71 units. 150€–270€ double. Half board 28€ extra per person per day. AE, DC, MC, V. Free parking. **Amenities:** Restaurant; bar; pool; health spa; room service; massage; babysitting; laundry/dry cleaning. *In room:* TV, hair dryer, safe.

Kurhotel Eberl ⭐ Set in a meadow about a quarter-mile west of the resort's center, this is a white-fronted, timber-studded replica of the kind of modern chalet you're likely to see a lot in Switzerland. Public rooms are lavishly finished with rough-textured beams and timbers for a look that, at least from the inside, might make you think that the hotel is older than it is. Guest rooms are conservatively and comfortably outfitted with pale colors and exposed wood, and many have balconies. All units come equipped with well-kept bathrooms with shower-tub combinations. This is the kind of hotel where guests (mostly German) expect to eat all their evening meals on-site. Only residents are allowed in the *Stübe* (beer hall–like) dining room and the hotel's lounges (the hotel is closed to nonguests). Although the town's more superior public spa facilities are nearby, the hotel has its own all-inclusive health-and-rest regime package.

Buchenerstrasse 17, D-83646 Bad Tölz. ⓒ **08041/78-720.** Fax 08041/78-72-78. www.kurhotel-eberl.de. 34 units. 96€–120€ double; 124€–140€ suite. Rates include breakfast. No credit cards. Closed Nov 21– Dec 16. **Amenities:** Restaurant; bar; pool; health spa; fitness center; sauna; massage; salon. *In room:* TV, hair dryer, safe.

INEXPENSIVE

Alexandra This modern hotel has a facade of traditional dark-stained wood, lavishly accented with flower boxes. It's near the town center, on the opposite side of the riverfront promenade from the banks of the Isar. Rooms are unpretentious and outfitted with reproductions of Bavarian furniture. Most units have bathrooms with shower-tub combinations. Other than breakfast, no meals are served. Overall, it's a worthwhile and reasonably-priced hotel choice.

Kyreinstrasse 33, D-83646 Bad Tölz. ⓒ **08041/7-84-30.** Fax 08041/78-43-99. www.alexandrahotel.de. 23 units. 72€–100€ double. Rates include breakfast. MC, V. Free parking. **Amenities:** Breakfast room; bar; fitness center; health spa; sauna; room service; massage; laundry/dry cleaning. *In room:* TV, hair dryer, safe.

Kolbergarten ⭐⭐ The finest and most lavish in Bad Tölz, this hotel is set in a historic zone on the east bank of the Isar that's sometimes used for outdoor concerts and parades. It was built in 1905 by the famous Jugendstil architect, Gabriel von Seidel, who added many more folkloric touches, including lavishly ornate eaves, than are usual in his work. The interior has a turn-of-the-20th-century dignity, always with a noteworthy emphasis on humanity, warmth, and charm. Guest rooms are as authentic and antique-laden as anything you'll find in the area. All units come with well-managed bathrooms with shower-tub combinations.

The hotel's restaurant, Kolbergarten, is an upscale oasis of well-prepared cuisine dedicated to the traditions of South Tirol, a German-speaking alpine region annexed by Italy from Austria after World War I. Lunch and dinner are served every day except Tuesday.

Because of its limited number of bedrooms, management funnels the overflow to the larger and slightly less expensive sibling hotel, the Posthotel Kolberbräu, which is separately recommended below.

Fröhlichgasse 5, D-83646 Bad Tölz. ⓒ **08041/90-67.** Fax 08041/90-69. www.hotel-kolbergarten.de. 15 units. 82€–128€ double. AE, DC, MC, V. Free parking. **Amenities:** Restaurant; lounge; room service; babysitting; laundry/dry cleaning. *In room:* TV, hair dryer, safe.

Posthotel Kolberbräu This is a cozy, old-fashioned, urban hotel that belongs to the same owner as the Kolbergarten (see above) but is in a less congested setting. It has an imposing neoclassical facade whose foundations date from the 1600s. Its popular bistro is recommended below. Guest rooms are more prosaic than those at the more aristocratic Kolbergarten and have the kind of cozy, traditional decor that nobody dislikes, but nobody thrills to either. All units contain bathrooms with shower-tub combinations and 10 have private balconies.

Marktstrasse 29, D-83646 Bad Tölz. © 08041/7-68-80. Fax 08041/7-68-82-00. 45 units. 75€ double. Rates include breakfast. Half board 14€ supplement per person per day. AE, DC, MC, V. Free parking. **Amenities:** Babysitting; laundry/dry cleaning. *In room:* TV, hair dryer.

WHERE TO DINE
MODERATE
Altes Fahrhaus ⊛ CONTINENTAL This is a *restaurant avec chambres* where the pleasant overnight accommodations are less significant than the restaurant. Three kilometers (2 miles) south of the resort's center, adjacent to the right bank of the Isar River, it's in a .75 hectare (185-acre) compound.

The owner is Ely Reiser, who closely supervises (or prepares herself) everything coming out of her kitchens. The food is the best in the region, and Munich-based gastronomes often come here just to have a meal. Menu items change with the seasons but might include a salad of green asparagus with strips of braised goose liver; bouillon of venison with ravioli or a filet of venison baked in herbs with a pepper-flavored cream sauce; filet of turbot in champagne sauce; or filet of veal with red wine sauce, noodles, and exotic mushrooms. Because the menu changes almost every day, even the owner is reluctant to name a particular house specialty, although one superb dish that's usually available is a well-seasoned rack of lamb served with eggplant, gratin of potatoes, and zucchini in a mustard sauce. Dessert might be a Grand Marnier soufflé with rhubarb.

On the premises are five bedrooms, each with its own terrace overlooking the river. With breakfast included, doubles cost 95€.

An der Isarlust 1, D-83646 Bad Tölz. © 08041/60-30. Reservations recommended. Main courses 18€–25€. No credit cards. Wed–Sun noon–2pm and 6–10pm. Closed 1 week in Nov and 1 week in Feb (dates vary).

INEXPENSIVE
Restaurant Posthotel Kolberbräu GERMAN/BAVARIAN This is the kind of no-nonsense, high-volume restaurant that virtually everyone in town has visited at least once in his or her lifetime. A labyrinth of small dining areas, it's a civic rendezvous point. The place is always crowded during the lunch and dinner hours, but throughout the afternoon, it remains open for coffee, pastries, beer, wine, and an abbreviated roster of warm food and platters.

Marktstrasse 29. © 08041/76880. Main courses 9€–15€; fixed-price menus 18€–28€. AE, DC, MC, V. Daily 11am–2pm and 5–9pm.

A SIDE TRIP TO BENEDIKTBEUREN
This 8th-century monastery (a flourishing cultural center in the Middle Ages) is the oldest Benedictine site north of the Alps. The frescoes in the monastery's baroque church were painted by the father of the famous Asam brothers. It was here, in this ecclesiastical enclave, that the 12th-century secular musical work, the *Carmina Burana* (the Goliardic songs) first appeared, later to become a popular 20th-century work by Bavarian composer Carl Orff.

Benediktbeuren is 14.5km (9 miles) southeast of Bad Tölz. Admission is free, but a guided tour costs 3€. The church is open daily 8am to 6pm. Guided tours of the monastery are offered July to September, daily at 2:30pm; October to mid-May, Saturday and Sunday only at 2:30pm; mid-May to June, Saturday and Wednesday at 2:30pm and Sunday at 10:30am and 2:30pm. For information about the monastery and concerts, call © 08857/8-80.

6 Freising

32km (20 miles) N of Munich

Freising, one of Bavaria's oldest towns, grew up around a bishopric founded in the 8th century. By the 12th century, under Bishop Otto von Freising, the area had begun a spiritual and cultural boom. Freising, however, was caught in a bitter rivalry with Munich that had repercussions lasting from the 12th century until the beginning of the 19th century. Bishop Otto owned a profitable toll bridge (which was not good for other areas) over the Isar until 1156 when Henry the Lion destroyed it and built his own bridge, wresting control of the lucrative salt route from the bishop and founding his settlement, München. It was Freising that went into decline then as Munich prospered. As a result of the quarrel, up until 1803, Munich was forced to pay compensation to Freising for Henry's action. We do list one restaurant below. However, if you're looking for a place to stay, we recommend going to Munich, instead (see chapter 4).

ESSENTIALS

GETTING THERE

BY TRAIN   Take line 1 of the S-bahn to Freising, a 25-minute ride.

BY CAR   Freising is northeast of Munich on the B11.

VISITOR INFORMATION

The **tourist information office** is at Marienplatz 7 (© **08161/5-41-22**). Hours are Monday to Friday 10am to 4pm.

SEEING THE SIGHTS

All the main sights are within walking distance of the Bahnhof. The Altstadt contains a number of restored canons' houses (the house occupied by a canon, which is a clergyman belonging to the chapter or the staff or a cathedral or collegiate church) with fine baroque facades along the Hauptstrasse and in the Marienplatz-Rindermarkt area. The Gothic **St. George's Parish Church** with its lovely baroque tower was built by the same architect who designed Munich's Frauenkirche. Opposite, in the former Lyceum of the prince-bishops, is the **Asamsaal,** a room decorated by the father of the famous Asam brothers, with a fine stucco and fresco ceiling. Tours are offered occasionally; check the tourist office for information.

Southwest of the Altstadt on a gentle hill is the **Staatsbrauerei Weihenstephan,** the world's oldest brewery. The monks of the Benedictine monastery of Weihenstephan were granted the privilege of brewing and serving their own beer in 1040, a tradition that still continues. Guided tours, including beer tasting, are conducted on the hour from 9am to 2pm, except at noon, from Monday to Thursday, costing 3€.

Located on the Domberg, a low hill above the Altstadt, **Mariendom** is a twin-towered Romanesque basilica, constructed between 1160 and 1205. The building is rather plain on the outside, but the interior was lavishly ornamented in the baroque style by the Asam brothers in 1723–24. Egid Quirin Asam designed the interior, and Cosmas Damian Asam created the ceiling fresco of the *Second Coming,* with its floating figures and swirling clouds. A notable early medieval sculpture is the famous *Bestiensäule* (Beast Column), an entwined mass of men and monsters. The church's principal feature is the large Romanesque crypt, one of the oldest in Germany, which has survived in its original form.

The 15th-century **cloister** on the east side of the cathedral was decorated with frescoes and stuccowork by Johann Baptist Zimmerman. To the west of the church is the **Dombibliothek,** a library that dates from the 8th century. In the 18th century, the library acquired a lively ceiling fresco designed by François Cuvilliés.

The **Diözesanmuseum** (Domberg 1; © **08161/4879-0**) is the largest diocesan museum in Germany and contains a comprehensive collection of religious art, including the famous *Lukasbild,* an exceptional Byzantine icon. The museum's exhibits document the history of the Catholic Church over 9 centuries. It's open Tuesday to Sunday from 10am to 5pm; admission is 1€.

WHERE TO DINE

Gästhaus Landbrecht BAVARIAN   Small-scale and family run, this is an 1860s inn where food is prepared in the old-fashioned Bavarian style. In a country-rustic dining room, you can begin with the "filet of beef" soup, one of the richest we've ever tasted or a delicate cream of celery soup with fresh herbs. Main courses include roast suckling pig, roast rack of venison with red-wine sauce, a main dish of mushrooms, and fresh pike-perch in butter and parsley sauce.

Freisinger Strasse 1, Freising-Handlfinig. © 08157/89-26. Reservations recommended. Main courses 10€–18€. No credit cards. Sat–Sun 12:30–3pm, Wed–Sun 6–10:30pm. 5km (3 miles) NW of the town center; follow signs to Freising-Handlfinig.

11

The Bavarian Alps

If you walk into a rustic alpine inn along the German-Austrian border and ask the innkeeper if he or she is German, you'll most likely get the indignant response, "Of course not! I'm Bavarian." Some older inhabitants of the region can still remember when Bavaria was a kingdom with its own prerogatives, even while a part of the German Reich (1871–1918).

The huge province of Bavaria includes not only the Alps but also Franconia, Lake Constance, and the capital city of Munich. However, we'll take this opportunity to explore separately the mountains along the Austrian frontier, a world unto itself. The area's hospitality is famous, and

the picture of the plump, rosy-cheeked innkeeper who has a constant smile on his or her face is no myth. Many travelers think of the Alps as a winter vacationland, but you'll find that nearly all the Bavarian resorts and villages boast year-round attractions.

Munich is the gateway to the region for those arriving by plane. From Munich, Autobahns lead directly to the Bavarian Alps. Frequent trains also connect the region to Munich. If you're beginning your tour in Garmisch-Partenkirchen in the west, you should fly to Munich. However, if you'd like to begin your tour in the east, at Berchtesgaden, then Salzburg, in Austria, has better plane connections.

OUTDOORS IN THE BAVARIAN ALPS

The Bavarian Alps are both a winter wonderland and a summer playground.

In summer, **alpine hiking** is a major attraction that includes climbing mountains, enjoying nature, and watching animals in the forest. Hikers are able, at times, to observe endangered species firsthand. One of the best areas for hiking is the 1,218m (4,060-ft.) **Eckbauer,** lying on the southern fringe of Partenkirchen (the tourist office at Garmisch-Partenkirchen will supply maps and details).

From Garmisch-Partenkirchen, serious hikers can embark on full-day or overnight alpine treks, following clearly marked footpaths and staying in mountain huts. Some huts are staffed and serve meals; others are remote and unsupervised. For information, inquire at the local tourist office or write to the government-subsidized **German Alpine Association,** Von-Kaahr-Strasse 2–4, 80997 München (© **089/14-00-30;** fax 089/1-40-03-11).

If you're a true outdoorsperson, you'll briefly savor the somewhat touristy facilities of Garmisch-Partenkirchen, and then use it as a base for explorations of the rugged **Berchtesgaden National Park,** an easy commute from Garmisch. Many visitors come to the Alps in summer just to hike through the national park, which borders the Austrian province of Salzburg. The 2,427m (8,091 ft.) Watzmann Mountain, clear alpine lakes like the Königssee, and parts of the Jenner are within the park's boundaries, and well-mapped trails cut through protected areas that lead the hiker through spectacular natural beauty. For information about hiking in the park, contact **Nationalparkhaus,** Franziskan-erplatz 7, 83471 Berchtesgaden (© **08652/6-43-43**).

You can also stay at one of the inns in Mittenwald or Oberammergau and take advantage of a wide roster of outdoor diversions there. Any of the outfitters below will provide directions and link-ups with their sports programs from wherever you decide to stay. Street maps of Berchtesgaden and its environs are usually available for free from the **Kurdirektion** (the local tourist office), Königsseer Strasse at Berchtesgaden (© **08652/96-70**), and more intricately detailed maps of the surrounding alpine topography are available for a fee.

Anglers will find plenty of **fishing** opportunities (especially salmon, pike-perch, and trout) at Lake Hintersee and the rivers Ramsauer Ache and Königsseer Ache. To acquire a fishing permit, contact the **Kurdirektion** (tourist office; see above) at Berchtesgaden, which will direct you to any of four differ-ent authorities, based on where you want to fish. For fishing specifically within the Hintersee, contact tourist officials or hotel Gamsboch in Ramsau (© **08657/ 9-88-00**).

Another summer activity is **ballooning,** which, weather permitting, can be arranged through **Outdoor Club Berchtesgaden,** Ludwig-Ganghofer-Strasse 20½ (© **08652/50-01**). And despite the obvious dangers, **hang gliding** or **paragliding** from the vertiginous slopes of Mount Jenner can be thrilling. To arrange it, contact **Full Stall** (Maximilianstrasse 16; © **08652/94-84-50**).

You can also practice your **kayaking** or **white-water rafting** techniques on one of the area's many rivers (water level permitting), such as the Ramsauer, Königsseer, Bischofswiesener, and Berchtesgadener Aches. For information and options, contact the above-mentioned **Outdoor Club Berchtesgaden.**

If you would like to go **swimming** in an alpine lake—which is not to every-one's body temperature—there are many lidos found in the Bavarian Forest.

In winter, you'll find some of the greatest **alpine** and **cross-country skiing** in all of Europe. The **skiing** here is Germany's best. A regular winter snowfall in January and February usually measures from 12 to 20 inches. This leaves about 2m (6 ft.) of snow in the areas served by ski lifts. The great **Zugspitzplatt** snow-field can be reached in spring or autumn by a rack railway. The Zugspitze, at 2,916km (9,720 ft.) above sea level, is the tallest mountain peak in Germany. Ski slopes begin at a height of 2,610km (8,700 ft.).

The second great ski district in the Alps is **Berchtesgadener Land,** with alpine skiing centered on Jenner, Rossfeld, Götschen, and Hochschwarzeck. Snow conditions are consistently good until March. Call the local "Snow-Telefon" at © **08652/967-297** for current snow conditions.

Visitors will also find a cross-country skiing center with many miles of tracks kept in first-class condition, natural toboggan runs, an artificial ice run for toboggan and skibob runs, and artificial ice-skating and curling rinks. There's skating between October and February at the world-class ice-skating rink in Berchtesgaden. Less reliable, but more picturesque, is skating on the surface of the Hintersee Lake, once it's sufficiently frozen.

1 Exploring the Region by Car

One of Europe's most scenic drives is the **Deutsche Alpenstrasse** (German Alpine Road), which stretches for some 480km (300 miles) between Berchtes-gaden in the east, all the way to Lindau on Lake Constance in the west. The road goes through mountains, lakes, "black" forests, and "castles in the sky." Where commercial reality hasn't intruded, it's a true fantasy. In winter, driving can be perilous, and mountain passes are often shut down. We always prefer to take the drive in early spring or early autumn.

DAY 1

From Munich, head south along Autobahn A8 (and drive in the right lane if you want to avoid the hysterical speeders on the left). Turn south on Route B20 for **Berchtesgaden,** 158km (98 miles) southeast of Munich. After settling in and having lunch, take an afternoon excursion to Obersalzberg and Kehlstein (you can go by bus). The Kehlstein road was blasted from bedrock, and an elevator ascends to the summit, once Hitler's famed Eagles Nest. The panorama is quite spectacular.

DAY 2

While still based in Berchtesgaden, take the 2-hour boat ride on the **Königssee,** 5km (3 miles) to the south. This long, narrow lake, famed for its steep banks and dark waters, is one of Europe's most dramatic and romantic sights. In the afternoon, drive west along the alpine road and then north on Route B20 some 19km (12 miles) to **Bad Reichenhall.** This is one of Germany's most famous spas on the Saalach River. The town was built around its Kurpark (spa center), and it's filled with both luxury and moderately priced hotels.

Right outside town, in a tasteful baroque style, **Kirchberg-Schlössel** on Thumseestrasse (© **08651/27-60**), is the best spot to dine in the area. Try its pike in beer sauce served with the inevitable sauerkraut, or filet of zander. A three-course lunch is 20€, offered from 11am to 3pm. A four-course dinner is served from 6pm to midnight for 35€ to 50€. Main courses begin at 15€. Return to Berchtesgaden for the night.

DAY 3

Get back on Autobahn A8 toward Munich but turn off at Prien am Chiemsee, 85km (53 miles) southeast of Munich. The premier attraction here is the **Neues Schloss,** a fantastic castle begun by Ludwig II in 1878 on the island of Herrenchiemsee. You can find food and lodging at Prien.

DAY 4

Get back on the Autobahn to Munich, but take a cross-country route (472) to **Bad Tölz,** one of Bavaria's leading spas. Its spa quarter (Kurverwaltung) makes a good place to take a break. **Hotel Am Wald,** Austrasse 39 in Bad Tölz (© **08041/78830**), is a reasonable place to dine, with meals beginning at 12€. It serves good Bavarian fare—nothing fancy, but fit fortification for this breezy part of the country. Standing on its own grounds, the hotel lies about a 10-minute walk from the Altstadt (Old Town).

Leave Bad Tölz and go along Highway 472 for another 8km (5 miles) to **Bad Heilbrunn,** another typical Bavarian spa. There's not much to see, but in another 6.5km (4 miles) you reach **Benediktbeuren,** Upper Bavaria's oldest Benedictine monastery. Records trace it back to the year 739. After a look, continue along for 6.5km (4 miles) to Kochel am See, with its alpine vistas, and from here take B20 for 32km (20 miles) to **Mittenwald** on the Austrian frontier. Plan an overnight stay.

DAY 5

You'll want to spend as much time as possible in Mittenwald—Goethe called it a "living picture book." It is also a major center for violin making. At least give

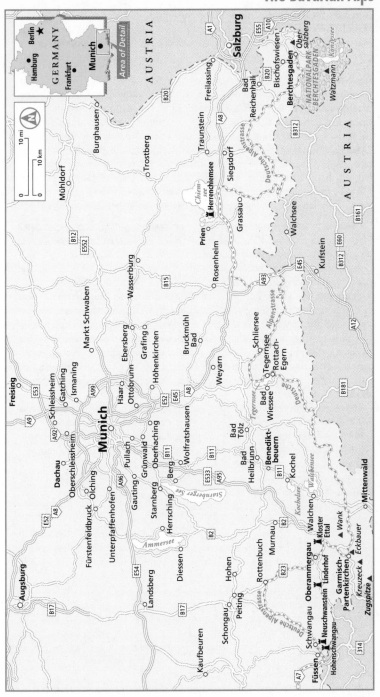

Area of Detail

GERMANY
Berlin ★
Hamburg
Frankfurt
Munich

AUSTRIA

10 mi
10 km

Salzburg
Freilassing
Bad Reichenhall
Berchtesgaden
Bischofswiesen
Obersalzberg
Watzmann
NATIONALPARK BERCHTESGADEN
Königssee

A1
E55
A10
B20
B312
A8

Burghausen
Trostberg
Traunstein
Siegsdorf
Grassau
Walchsee
Kufstein

Mühldorf
Herrenchiemsee
Prien
Rosenheim
Schliersee
Rottach-Egern
Bad Wiessee
Tegernsee
Bad

AUSTRIA

B20
B12
E552
B15
A99
A93
A45
A12
B161
E60
B312
B181

Wasserburg
Markt Schwaben
Ebersberg
Grafing
Höhenkirchen
Bruckmühl
Weyarn

Freising
Schleissheim
Gatching
Ismaning
Haar
Ottobrunn

Munich
Dachau
Oberschleissheim
Olching
Pullach
Grünwald
Oberhaching
Wolfratshausen
Bad Tölz
Benedikt-beuern
Bad Heilbrunn
Kochel

A9
E53
A99
A92
A96
B11
B11
E52
A45
A8
E533
A95
B2
B11

Fürstenfeldbruck
Unterpfaffenhofen
Gauting
Starnberg
Herrsching
Berg
Starnberger See
Ammersee
Kochelsee
Walchensee
Walchen
Kloster Ettal
Wank
Mittenwald

Augsburg
Landsberg
Diessen
Hohen
Murnau
Oberammergau
Linderhof
Garmisch-Partenkirchen
Kreuzeck
Eckbauer
Zugspitze

Schongau
Peiting
Rottenbuch
Schwangau
Neuschwanstein
Hohenschwangau
Füssen
Kaufbeuren

E54
B23
A52
A8
B17
B17
314
A7

Deutsche Alpenstrasse

it a morning before driving northwest for 19km (12 miles) on Route 2 to **Garmisch-Partenkirchen,** two towns combined. After checking in, head for the major attraction, the **Zugspitze,** the highest peak in Germany (more about this on p. 197). Wear warm clothing.

DAY 6

Leaving Garmisch-Partenkirchen, head north for 19km (12 miles) to Oberammergau. Along the way you'll pass **Kloster Ettal,** founded by Ludwig the Bavarian in 1330. Its original 10-sided church is a stunning example of the Bavarian rococo style. Some 9.5km (6 miles) to the west is **Schloss Linderhof,** one of "Mad King" Ludwig's royal residences, built on the grounds of his hunting lodge between 1874 and 1878. These two attractions will take up most of your day, but you'll still arrive in the little old woodcarver's village of **Oberammergau,** 11km (7 miles) northeast of Linderhof, in time to wander about. Later, enjoy a hearty Bavarian dinner before turning in to your alpine bed.

2 National Park Berchtesgaden ★★★

This national park occupies the southeast corner of Germany, comprising a large portion of the state of Bavaria and bordering Austria's province of Salzburg. The park was established in 1978 by a decree from the Bavarian government. It is a lush expanse of 218 sq. km (84 sq. miles), with altitudes ranging from 540m (1,800 ft.) at lowland Königssee to the towering Watzmann Mountain.

The 2,670m (8,900-ft.) Watzmann, the Königssee, and parts of the Jenner— the pride of Berchtesgaden's four ski areas—are within the boundaries of the national park, which has well-mapped trails cut through protected areas. Conservation goals and preservation of the natural ecosystems take precedence in the park. An effort is made to keep visitor impact low and to make visitors aware of the ecosystem's fragility.

Limestone dominates most of the rock bed, suggesting that this was once a highly aquatic region. Formed by sediment deposited on the ocean floor 200 million years ago, the rock folded and lifted. Although most of the accompanying sandstone has eroded away, the limestone remains. The steep mountain valleys and moraines suggest recent glacial recession was responsible for many of the grand landscapes found in the park. Of the several alpine lakes that dot the landscape, the most significant is the Königssee, Germany's cleanest, clearest lake (see "Day Trips from Berchtesgaden," later in this chapter, for information about boat trips on the lake).

Atlantic and continental influences characterize the climate. A substantial annual rainfall fosters the heavy forestation of the region. The valleys receive approximately 60 inches of rainfall a year; the mountains are doused by approximately 110 inches annually.

Vegetation is affected by altitudinal gradient. Nearly half of the vegetation is remnants of deciduous forests, interspersed with spruce, pines, and beeches. Nearly a third of the vegetation sprouts on rock debris and in crevices. The mixed mountain forest thrives below 1,350m (4,500 ft.); the coniferous forest above it reaches up to 1,650m (5,500 ft.), and above that, wind-dwarfed bushes and alpine meadows predominate. Once the forest was exploited for salt mines; it's now overpopulated and overgrazed by game.

In spring, summer, and autumn, many different rare species of plants flower. (They are protected, and don't live long once picked, so they should be left for the next person to enjoy.) Alpine animals such as the chamois, ibex (reintroduced in 1930), the marmot, snow hare, alpine salamander, golden eagle, ptarmigan, black grouse, capercaillie, alpine chough, black woodpecker, and the three-toed woodpecker still inhabit the area, but other animals—the wolf, lynx, bear, and golden vulture—once thriving inhabitants, have not survived. See "The Natural World of the Alps," later in this chapter, for more specifics on vegetation and wildlife.

Information about hiking in the park is provided by the **Nationalparkhaus,** Franziskanerplatz 7, D-83471 Berchtesgaden (© **08652/64343**).

3 Berchtesgaden ★★

158km (98 miles) SE of Munich, 18km (11 miles) SE of Bad Reichenhall, 23km (14 miles) S of Salzburg

Ever since Ludwig I of Bavaria chose this resort as a favorite hideaway, the tourist business in Berchtesgaden has been booming. According to legend, the many summits of Watzmann Mountain that tower over the village were once a king and his family who were so evil that God punished them by turning them into rocks. The evil king has evidently not been completely silenced, however, because the Watzmann has been responsible for the deaths of a number of mountain climbers on the mile-high cliff on its eastern wall.

Berchtesgaden is an old alpine village with ancient winding streets and a medieval marketplace and castle square. Since the name of the village has often been linked with Hitler and the Nazi hierarchy, many visitors mistakenly believe they are seeing one of the Führer's favorite haunts. This impression is erroneous. Hitler's playground was actually at Obersalzberg, on a wooded plateau about .5km (½ mile) up the mountain. Berchtesgaden is very much a quiet Bavarian town.

ESSENTIALS
GETTING THERE
BY TRAIN The Berchtesgaden Bahnhof lies on the Munich-Freilassing rail line. Twelve trains a day arrive from Munich (trip time: 1½ hr.). For rail information and schedules, call © **011805/99-66-33.** Berchtesgaden has three mountain rail lines—the Obersalzbergbahn, Jennerbahn, and Hirscheckbahn—that connect the mountain plateaus around the resorts. For more information, contact **Berchtesgadener Bergbahn AG** (© **08652/9-58-10**) and **Obersalzbergbahn AG** (© **08652/25-61**).

BY BUS Long-distance bus service from Passau as well as from Bad Reichenhall is provided by **RBO Regionalbus Ostbayern GmbH in Passau** (© **0851/75-63-70**). Regional bus service to alpine villages and towns around Berchtesgaden is offered by **Regionalverkehr Oberbayern RVO at Berchtesgaden** (© **08652/54-73**).

BY CAR Access by car is via the A8 Autobahn from Munich in the north or Route 20 from the south. The drive from Munich takes about 2 hours.

VISITOR INFORMATION
For tourist information, contact the **Kurdirektion,** Königssee Strasse 2 (© **08652/96-70**), open Monday to Friday from 8am to 5pm and Saturday from 9am to noon.

SEEING THE SIGHTS
The **Schlossplatz** ★, partially enclosed by the castle and Stiftskirche, is the most attractive plaza in town. On the opposite side of the square from the church is

Impressions

My memories of winter days in Berchtesgaden are ones of glorious sun-shine, crisp air and a ring of sparkling mountains: a deep drink of blue fire from a chalice of ice.

—Hugo von Hofmannstal (1874–1929)

a 16th-century arcade that leads to Marktplatz, with typical alpine houses and a wooden fountain from 1677 (restored by Ludwig I in 1860). Some of Berchtesgaden's oldest inns and houses border this square. Extending from Marktplatz is the Nonntal, lined with more old houses, some built into the rocks of the Lockstein Mountain that towers above.

The Stiftskirche (Abbey Church), dating from 1122, is adjacent to the Königliches Schloss Berchtesgaden (see below). The church is mainly Romanesque, with Gothic additions. One of its ancient twin steeples was destroyed by lightning and rebuilt in 1866. The interior contains many fine works of art; the high altar has a painting by Zott dating from 1669. In the vestry is a small silver altar donated by Empress Maria Theresa of Austria.

A minor but interesting museum, the **Heimatmuseum,** Schloss Aldelsheim, Schroffenbergallee 6 (℃ **08652/44-10**), is devoted to alpine woodcarving. Woodcarving as a craft here predates the more fabled woodcarving at Oberammergau, and some of the best examples in Germany are on display in the museum. Entry is allowed only as part of a guided tour, offered Monday to Friday at 10am and again at 4pm for a charge of 2€.

Königliches Schloss Berchtesgaden   Berchtesgaden grew up around a powerful Augustinian monastery whose monks introduced the art of woodcarving, for which the town is noted to this day. When the town became part of Bavaria in 1809, the abbey was secularized and eventually converted to a palace for the royal family of Wittelsbach. Now it is a museum, mostly devoted to the royal collection of sacred art, including wood sculptures by the famed artists Veit Stoss and Tilman Riemenschneider. You can also explore a gallery of 19th-century art. There's a collection of Italian Renaissance furniture from the 16th century and three armoires displaying many pistols and guns of the 17th and 18th centuries, plus swords and armor. Precious porcelain and hunting trophies are also shown.

Schlossplatz 2. (℃ **08652/20-85**. Admission 4€ adults, 2€ children 6–16, free for children 5 and under. Easter–Sept, Sun–Fri 10am–noon and 2–4pm; Oct–Easter, Mon–Fri 10am–noon and 2–5pm. Bus: 9539.

Salzbergwerk Berchtesgaden   At the eastern edge of town are the salt mines once owned by the Augustinian monastery. Operations began here in 1517. The mines contain two types of salt, one suitable only for salt licks for cattle and other animals. The deposits are more than 990 feet thick and are still processed today from four galleries or "hills." Older children will especially enjoy the guided tours that begin with a ride into the mine on a small wagon-like train after donning protective miner's clothing. After nearly a .5km (½-mile) ride, visitors leave the train and explore the rest of the mine on foot, sliding down a miner's slide and riding on the salt lake in a ferry. The highlight of the tour is the "chapel," a grotto containing unusually shaped salt formations illuminated for an eerie effect. The 1½-hour tour can be taken any time of the year, in any weather.

Bergwerkstrasse 83. © **08652/6-00-20.** Admission 10.50€ adults, 5.50€ children. May–Oct 15, daily 9am–5pm; Oct 16–Apr, Mon–Sat 12:30–3:30pm. Bus: 9539.

ORGANIZED TOURS

Guided tours in English are offered by the American-run **Berchtesgaden Mini Bus Tours,** Königsseerstrasse 2 (© **08652/6-49-71**). Tours, including Obersalzberg, the Eagles Nest, and the Bunker System, as an afternoon history package, are conducted daily from mid-May to mid-October, starting at the Berchtesgaden tourist office. The service also takes visitors to sights such as the Salt Mines and the Königssee. A 3½-hour tour costs 35€ adults, 28€ for those under 12, and is free for children 11 and under. There's a tour information and ticket booth at the Berchtesgaden tourist office, across the street from the train station. One of the most popular tours offered is the "Sound of Music" tour to nearby Salzburg.

OUTDOORS IN THE AREA

Berchtesgaden has a world-class **ice-skating** rink, the **Eisstadion,** An der Schiessstätte (© **08652/6-14-05**). A local variation of **curling (Eisstock)** that makes use of wooden, rather than stone instruments is also played there. It's open from October through February.

   Mountain bike rentals are available through **Full Stall,** Maximilianstrasse 16 (© **08652/94-84-50**). They will also arrange **hang gliding** or **paragliding,** which can be thrilling, if dangerous, from the vertiginous slopes of Mount Jenner.

WHERE TO STAY
MODERATE

Hotel Fischer ★   A short uphill walk from the Berchtesgaden railway station, in a spot overlooking the town, this hotel was built in Bavarian style in the late 1970s. Fronted with dark-stained wooden balconies against a cream-colored facade, it rambles pleasantly along the hillside. The bedrooms are cozy and traditional, each with a regional theme and a bathroom with a shower unit.

Königsseer Strasse 51, 83471 Berchtesgaden. © **08652/9550.** Fax 08652/6-48-73. www.hotel-fischer.de. 40 units. 88€–126€ double. Rates include buffet breakfast. V. Closed Nov to mid-Dec and mid-Mar to Apr 10. Parking 3€. **Amenities:** Restaurant; bar; pool; sauna; solarium; room service. *In room:* TV, hair dryer.

Vier Jahreszeiten   An old inn with modern extensions, Vier Jahreszeiten has been in the hands of the Miller family since 1876. It's in the heart of the village and has a colorful and distinguished restaurant. The inn has been remodeled and improved over the years and now offers a good level of comfort, making it a formidable rival of the Fischer. Some of the newer guest rooms, with tiny sitting rooms and balconies, resemble suites. All of the accommodations have well-kept bathrooms with shower units. In addition to the main dining room, there's a terrace for summer dining and viewing.

Maximilianstrasse 20, D-83471 Berchtesgaden. © **08652/95-20.** Fax 08652/50-29. www.berchtesgaden. com/vier-jahreszeiten. 59 units. 87€–138€ double. Rates include buffet breakfast. AE, MC, V. Free parking outside, 5€ in the garage. **Amenities:** Restaurant; bar; lounge; pool; sauna; solarium. *In room:* TV, minibar, hair dryer.

Wittelsbach   The Wittelsbach, a hotel that dates from the 1890s, has been stylishly modernized and now offers well-furnished rooms in the heart of Berchtesgaden. The rooms are quiet and sunny; most have balconies with fine views of the mountains. Breakfast is the only meal served. All units have bathrooms with shower units.

Maximilianstrasse 16, D-83471 Berchtesgaden. © **08652/9-63-80.** Fax 08652/6-63-04. 32 units. 65€–87€ double; 90€–110€ suite. Rates include buffet breakfast. AE, DC, MC, V. Closed Nov–Dec 15. Free parking. Bus: 9539. **Amenities:** Breakfast room; bar; lounge; solarium. *In room:* TV, minibar, hair dryer.

INEXPENSIVE

Hotel Krone *Value*   One of the most appealing bargains in Berchtesgaden is this well-built chalet-inspired hotel. Operated by live-in managers, the Grafe family, and permeated with a sense of alpine thrift and good cheer, it offers cozy bedrooms sheathed with lots of varnished pine. Each has a balcony or terrace of its own, and a compact bathroom containing a shower. The dining room and its adjacent bar, charges only 10€ per person extra for half board, a price so low that it virtually guarantees that most guests will take at least one of their daily meals here.

AM Rad 5, 83471 Berchtesgaden. © **08652/9-46-00.** Fax 08652/94-60-10. 21 units. 55€–80€ double; from 100€ suite. Closed: Nov 1–Dec 20. **Amenities:** Dining room; bar; lounge; room service. *In room:* TV, hair dryer.

Watzmann *Value*   Built as part of a brewery 300 years ago, the Watzmann is your best budget bet in town, although it doesn't have the style or amenities of the properties previously described. Set opposite the church on the main square, it has a large outdoor terrace, a cozy Bavarian-inspired decor, and dozens of turn-of-the-20th-century artifacts. Everyone in town seems to stop by sometime during the day or night for a beer, coffee, or lunch. Inside, you'll find huge carved wooden pillars, oak ceilings, wrought-iron chandeliers, and hunting trophies. The doors of the simply furnished guest rooms are painted with floral murals. Rooms are small but well maintained. Those with bathrooms have shower stalls; for those without, corridor bathrooms are adequate.

Franziskanerplatz 1, D-83471 Berchtesgaden. © **08652/20-55.** Fax 08652/51-74. 38 units, 30 with shower. 37€ double without shower, 40€ double with shower. AE, DC, MC, V. Closed Nov 1–Dec 25. Free parking. **Amenities:** Restaurant. *In room:* No phone.

WHERE TO DINE

Demming-Restaurant Le Gourmet BAVARIAN/INTERNATIONAL The Demming Hotel contains one of the town's best restaurants. Formerly a wealthy private house, it looks over a panoramic view of mountains and forests. Many locals regard dining here as something of an event. Only fresh ingredients are used in the well-prepared dishes, including hearty mountain fare, such as roast beef with chive sauce and an array of veal and fish dishes. Sometimes we wish the chef could be less timid in his cookery, but what you get isn't bad unless you're seeking zesty flavors.

The hotel rents plainly furnished but comfortable bedrooms, costing around 85€ for a double, including breakfast.

Sunklergässchen 2, D-83471 Berchtesgaden. © **08652/96-10.** Reservations required. Main courses 12€–20€. AE, DC, MC, V accepted for hotel guests only. Daily 11:30am–2pm and 5:30–8:30pm. Closed Oct 26–Dec 10. Bus: 9539.

Hubertusstube GERMAN You'll get an undeniable sense of Bavarian *gemütlichkeit* (coziness) in this richly-paneled restaurant; where a trio of old-fashioned dining rooms, each with a century-old history of hospitality, offers well-prepared food and a view of the Alps. Menu items include rich servings of such game dishes as roasted venison with red wine sauce as well as perfectly prepared peppersteaks, roasted pork shank, and salmon-trout. Service is traditional and very polite.

In the Hotel Vier Jahreszeiten, Maximilianstrasse 20. (C) **08652/95-20.** Reservations recommended. Main courses 12€–21€. AE, DC, MC, V. Daily 11am–2pm and 6pm–midnight.

Panorama Restaurant GERMAN/INTERNATIONAL The decor includes lots of blond birchwood paneling and touches of pale blue, but virtually no one notices it because of the windows that encompass a sweeping view of Obersalzburg and the nearby mountains. Good-tasting menu items within the pair of dining rooms include braised trout with almonds; pepper steak; goulash or *leberknödelsuppe* (liver dumpling and noodle soup—it sounds better in German!); veal or pork schnitzels; and a savory version of the traditional rib-sticker, *Schweinshaxen* (pork shank).

In the Alpenhotel Kronprinz, Am Brandholz. (C) **08652/60-70.** Reservations recommended. Lunch main courses 9€–18€; dinner main courses 9€–21€. AE, DC, MC, V. Daily noon–3pm and 6–11pm.

DAY TRIPS FROM BERCHTESGADEN
KÖNIGSSEE ★★
This "jewel in the necklace" of Berchtesgaden is one of Europe's most scenic bodies of water. Its waters appear to be dark green because of the steep mountains that jut upward from its shores. On the low-lying land at the northern edge of the lake are a few charming inns and bathing facilities and also a parking lot, but the rest of the lake is enclosed by mountains, making it impossible to walk along the shoreline. The only way to explore the waters (unless you're like one of the mountain goats you may catch sight of on the mountains) is by boat.

Electric motorboats (no noisy power launches allowed) carry passengers on tours around the lake in summer, and occasionally even in winter. The favorite spot on Königssee is the tiny flat peninsula on the western bank. It was the site of a basilica as early as the 12th century. Today the Catholic Chapel of St. Bartholomew is still used for services (except in winter). The clergy must arrive by boat since there's no other way to approach the peninsula. The adjacent buildings include a fisher's house and a restaurant; which was once a favored hunting lodge of the Bavarian kings. Here you can sample trout and salmon caught in the crisp, clean waters. At the southern end of the lake you come to the Salet-Alm, where the tour boat makes a short stop near a thundering waterfall. If you follow the footpath up the hillside, you'll reach the summer pastures used by the cattle of Berchtesgaden Land.

Just over the hill is Lake Obersee, part of Königssee until an avalanche separated them 8 centuries ago. If you prefer a shorter trip, you can take the boat as far as St. Batholomä and back. To reach the lake from Berchtesgaden by car, follow the signs south from the town only 5km (3 miles). It's also a pleasant hour's walk or a short ride by electric train or bus from the center of town.

For information about excursions, call **Schiffahrt Königssee** at (C) **08652/96-36-13.** An entire tour of Königssee requires about 2 hours. There are boats in summer every 15 minutes, so getting off one boat and climbing aboard another is easy if you want to break up the tour. During the summer, the first boat departs every morning at 7:15am and the last boat leaves at 5:30pm. In winter, boats leave about every 45 minutes. The important stops are at Salet and St. Batholomä. A round-trip fare for a lake tour is 15€ for adults and half-fare for children.

OBERSALZBERG
The drive from Berchtesgaden to Obersalzberg at 990m (3,300 ft.) is along one of Bavaria's scenic routes. Here Hitler settled down in a rented cottage while he completed *Mein Kampf.* After he came to power in 1933, he bought Haus

Springtime for Hitler

The big news blowing through the windswept Alps is that a luxury hotel is being built in Obersalzberg, the former site of Hitler's alpine command center. Over protests that the site would become a magnet for neo-Nazis, the Bavarian State Bank is moving ahead to create this alpine retreat, a project that is expected to take 3 years and one which will include a golf course on the site of the former holiday mansion of *Luftwaffe* commander Herman Göring.

Hitler's Berghof, where he lived with his mistress, Eva Braun, was destroyed in 1945, but this "Eagles Nest" mountaintop retreat and bunker still exists. Once occupied by the U.S. Army, it was handed over to Bavaria in 1997. The American-based Intercontinental chain, which will operate the hotel, has committed itself to "not allowing any neo-Nazi tourism in the area." Definitely, vendors won't be allowed to sell Third Reich souvenirs.

Jewish leaders weren't particularly enthusiastic about the plans, but their concerns have been eased somewhat since a Documentation Center was opened nearby in 1999. The center documents how the Nazi top brass commanded their forces from this mountain eyrie, and planned the destruction of the Jews and other minorities within Europe.

Wachenfeld and had it remodeled into his residence, the Berghof. Obersalzberg became the center of holiday living for Nazis such as Martin Bormann and Hermann Göring.

At Obersalzberg, you can walk around the ruins of Hitler's **Berghof.** Here the 1938 meeting between Hitler and British Prime Minister Neville Chamberlain resulted in the Munich Agreement. Chamberlain came away hailing "peace in our time," but the Nazi dictator felt he had merely given the prime minister his "autograph" and continued preparations for World War II. The Berghof was destroyed in 1952 by Bavarian government authorities at the request of the U.S. Army—the Americans did not want a monument to Hitler. One of the only remaining structures from the Nazi compound is a guesthouse, the General Walker Hotel, used by U.S. troops stationed in Europe. Wear good walking shoes and be prepared to run into some VERBOTEN! signs in use during Hitler's heyday.

Hitler built the **bunkers** and air-raid shelter in 1943. Three thousand laborers completed the work in 9 months, connecting all the major buildings of the Obersalzberg area to the underground rooms. Many readers have expressed their disappointment when reaching this site, apparently thinking they would tour Hitler's sumptuously decorated private apartments. Instead, all they can see today are spooky, macabre-looking bunkers stripped of all their former trappings, which are a barren reminder of a tawdry dream about what was supposed to have been "A Thousand-Year Reich." A bunker, part of Hitler's air-raid-shelter system, is open for a visit. Newly opened are prison cells used by the *Reichssicherheitsdienst* (State Security Police). They were to be a last refuge for Hitler and other high officials of the Third Reich. Entrance to the bunker and prison cells is 2.50€; they're open Tuesday to Sunday from 9am to 5pm. Guided tours in English are conducted daily from mid-May through mid-October, starting at the Berchtesgaden tourist office and offered by **Berchtesgaden Mini Bus Tours** (✆ **08652/6-49-71;** see "Organized Tours," earlier in this section).

A major point of interest to visitors is the **Kehlstein** ★★, or Eagles Nest, which can be reached only by a thrilling bus ride up a 7km (4½-mile) long mountain road, blasted out of solid rock and considered an outstanding feat of construction and engineering when begun in 1937 under the leadership of Bormann, who intended it as a 50th birthday gift for Hitler. The Eagles Nest was not, as the name may suggest, a military installation. It was a site for relaxation (complete with a teahouse) and was not popular with Hitler, who rarely visited it. To reach the spot, you must enter a tunnel and take a 120m (400-ft.) elevator ride through a shaft in the Kehlstein Mountain. The building, with solid granite walls and huge picture windows, now houses a mountain restaurant. Called the **Kehlsteinhaus,** the restaurant is open from the end of May to the end of October.

You can also explore the rooms of the original teahouse, which include Eva Braun's living room. Below, you can see the Obersalzberg area where Hitler's Berghof once stood, and nearby, the site of Martin Bormann's house and the SS barracks. To the north, you can see as far as Salzburg in Austria, and just below the mountain to the west, is the village of Berchtesgaden, with its rivers dwindling off into threads in the distance.

For information about trips to Kehlstein, call ✆ **08652/54-73.** RVO buses (local buses based in Berchtesgaden) run from the Berchtesgaden Post Office to Obersalzberg-Hintereck. Buses from the Hintereck parking lot run to the Kehlstein parking lot about every half-hour. The ticket price includes the elevator ride to the Eagles Nest at the top. By local bus, the round-trip journey from Berchtesgaden to Obersalzberg costs 3€. From Obersalzberg (Hintereck), the special mountain bus and elevator ride through the rock costs 10€. If you're hardy, instead of taking the elevator, you can walk up the final stretch to the Eagles Nest from the summit parking lot in about 30 minutes. The Kehlstein line operates daily from mid-May to mid-October, when there are full catering services offered at Kehlsteinhaus. The Kehlstein road is closed to private vehicles.

Obersalzberg is becoming an important health resort; the ruins of Bormann's Gusthof Farm are now the location of Skytop Lodge, a popular golfing center in summer and a ski site in winter.

Where to Stay

Hotel Zum Türken   In Obersalzberg, the alpine-style Hotel zum Türken is legendary. On its facade is a large painted sign showing "the Turk," and the foundation is stone, with the windows framed in shutters. A large handmade sign across the hillside, labeled THE BUNKER, chillingly reminds us that this was Hitler's vacation retreat in the heyday of Nazi power.

The story goes that a veteran from the Turkish war erected the original building here. At the turn of the century, it was acquired by Karl Schuster, who turned it into a well-known restaurant that drew many celebrities of the day, including Brahms and Crown Prince Wilhelm of Prussia. However, anti-Nazi remarks he made in the 1930s led to trouble. Herr Schuster was arrested. Bormann took over the building as a Gestapo headquarters, and air raids and looting in April 1945 nearly destroyed the Türken. (Many tourists erroneously think that the Türken was Hitler's famed Berghof.)

Herr Schuster's daughter, Therese Partner, was able to buy the ruin from the German government for a high price in 1949. She opened a cafe and rooms for overnight visitors. Today, the Türken is run by Frau Ingrid Scharfenberg, granddaughter of Karl Schuster. Pleasantly furnished rooms are rented, and a self-service bar is on the ground floor. The rooms have no private phones, but there is an international pay phone in the main hallway. All units are well kept, including the bathrooms with shower units. Note that its terraces and views are for hotel guests only.

D-83471 Berchtesgaden-Obersalzberg. ✆ **08652/24-28.** Fax 08652/47-10. 17 units, 13 with bathroom. 70€ double without bathroom, 110€ double with bathroom. Rates include continental breakfast. AE, DC, MC, V. Free parking. Closed Tues. Obersalzburg bus from Berchtesgaden. **Amenities:** Breakfast room; bar; lounge. *In room:* No phone.

4 Bad Reichenhall ✶

135km (84 miles) SE of Munich, 19km (12 miles) SE of Salzburg

The best German spas can call themselves *Staatsbad,* and Bad Reichenhall bears that title with pride. This old salt town is the most important curative spa in the Bavarian Alps. Mountain chains surround it, protecting it from the winds. Its brine springs, with a salt content as high as 24%, are the most powerful saline springs in Europe, and the town has been a source of salt for more than 2,400 years. The combination of the waters and the pure air has made Bad Reichenhall an important spa for centuries.

In 1848, King Maximilian of Bavaria stayed here, popularizing Bad Reichenhall as a fashionable resort. Today, visitors come from all over the world to take the waters. Bad Reichenhall is especially recommended for the treatment of respiratory disorders such as asthma, chronic bronchitis, and sinus infection as well as skin diseases. It is known for its holistic approach: Types of spa treatments include inhalation, brine drinking cures, mud baths, breathing exercises, and other types of physical therapy. Although Bad Reichenhall takes the medical side of the cure seriously, a number of beauty and fitness programs are also featured.

ESSENTIALS
GETTING THERE
BY TRAIN   Bad Reichenhall is connected to the airport at Munich by frequent train service through Rosenheim. The trip takes about 2½ hours. For information and schedules, call ✆ **01805/99-66-33.**

BY BUS   Regional bus service to and from Bad Reichenhall is provided by **Regionalverkehr Oberbayers Betrieb** (✆ **08652/54-73** for information). From the spa, you can take a bus to various beautiful spots in the Bavarian Alps, including Berchtesgaden.

BY CAR   Access is by the A8 Autobahn, from Munich in the north and Salzburg in the south. Exit on Federal Highway 21 into Bad Reichenhall.

VISITOR INFORMATION
For tourist information, go to the **Kur und Verkehrsverein im Kurgastzentrum,** Wittelsbacherstrasse 15 (✆ **08651/60-63-03**). It's open Monday to Friday 9am to 5pm and Saturday 9am to 2pm.

SIGHTS & ACTIVITIES
The ideal climate permits a complete spectrum of outdoor events, from excursions into the mountains for skiing or hiking to tennis tournaments. Gardeners

and botanists will enjoy the spa gardens: The sheltered location of the town amid the lofty Alps permits the growth of several varieties of tropical plants, giving the gardens a lush, exotic appearance. There's also a wide choice of indoor activities, from symphony concerts to folklore presentations to gambling in the casino.

The great fire of 1834 destroyed much of the town, but many of the impressive churches survived. An outstanding example is **St. Zeno,** a 12th-century Gothic church showing a later baroque influence. Its most remarkable feature is its painted interior, centering on the carved altarpiece, the *Coronation of the Virgin.*

The **Bad Reichenhaller Saltmuseum,** Alte Saline Reichenhall (© **08651/ 70-02-51**), just a short walk from the Kurgarten, is the home of the ancient industry responsible for the growth and prosperity of Bad Reichenhall from Celtic times to the present. Parts of the old plant still stand today, but most of it was reconstructed in the mid–19th century by Ludwig I of Bavaria. The large pumps and huge marble caverns are impressive. Tours are offered April to October 31, daily from 10am to noon, and 2 to 4pm; November to March, Tuesday and Thursday from 2 to 4pm. Admission is 4.50€ for adults and 2.50€ for children; 12.50€ adults and 6€ children if the ticket combines the Saltmuseum with the Salzbergwerk Berchtesgaden.

SHOPPING   Shops here are predictably upscale, rather limited in scope, and conservative. The town's only department store, **Kaufhaus Huhasz,** Ludwigstrasse 23 (© **08651/9-73-80**), stocks some traditional items. About 90% of the resort's shops are in a pedestrian-only zone, which is centered on the Ludwigstrasse and the Salzburgerstrasse. Since 1856, **Josef Mack Co.,** Ludwigstrasse 36 (© **08651/7-82-80**), has been the region's best place for medicinal herbs, many of which are grown in the Bavarian Alps.

WHERE TO STAY
VERY EXPENSIVE
Steigenberger Axelmannstein ✦✦✦   This first-class hotel, set in its own 3 hectare (7½-acre) garden, is the best in town for traditional charm and spa conveniences, far superior to its closest rival, the Parkhotel Luisenbad (see below). Public rooms are traditionally furnished with antiques and reproductions. Many of the well-furnished bedrooms have views of the encircling Bavarian Alps. Rooms are generally spacious. Bathrooms are medium in size, and come with shower-tub combinations and deluxe toiletries.

The Parkrestaurant, opening onto a garden, attracts many nonresidents, as does the cozy Axel-Stüberl, with regional dishes. The wood-paneled Axel-Bar features live entertainment daily.

Salzburger Strasse 2–6, 83435 Bad Reichenhall. © 800/223-5652 in the U.S. and Canada, or 08651/77-70. Fax 08651/59-32. www.bad-reichenhall.steigenberger.de. 159 units. 220€–300€ double; 290€–505€ suite. Rates include buffet breakfast. AE, DC, MC, V. Parking 5€. **Amenities:** 2 restaurants; bar; pool; tennis court; fitness center; spa; sauna; solarium; salon; room service; laundry/dry cleaning. *In room:* TV, minibar, hair dryer.

EXPENSIVE
Parkhotel Luisenbad ✦✦   A world unto itself, Parkhotel Luisenbad is an 1860s hotel with a new guest-room wing in a garden setting. It's a good second choice to the Steigenberger, especially if you like traditional hotels. Its best feature is the indoor pool with a glass wall, bringing the outdoors inside. The more modern rooms are handsome, with bold colors and tasteful furnishings, but many guests prefer the older, more traditional rooms. All rooms range in size

from medium to spacious. The bathrooms are well maintained, with shower-tub combinations and deluxe toiletries.

The lobby and the Restaurant die Holzstube (see "Where to Dine," below) have been renovated in a classic provincial style and decorated in warm colors, making the hotel more attractive than ever.

Ludwigstrasse 33, 83435 Bad Reichenhall. © **08651/60-40.** Fax 08651/6-29-28. www.parkhotel.de. 89 units. 135€–195€ double; 315€ suite. Rates include continental breakfast. DC, MC, V. Parking 1.50€–5€. **Amenities:** Restaurant; lounge; pool; sauna; room service; massage; mud baths; laundry/dry cleaning. *In room:* TV, minibar, hair dryer.

MODERATE

Hotel Bayerischer Hof *(Value)* This modern and inviting hotel is in the center of the spa on Main Street. It has a surprising number of facilities for a small place, although it's hardly in the same league as the Steigenberger or the Parkhotel Luisenbad (see above). The well-maintained guest rooms are furnished in a functional modern style. All units have well-maintained bathrooms with shower-tub combinations. The staff is well trained. In addition to the main restaurant; there's a cafe with live music and a nightclub with international acts. The reception desk is helpful in arranging excursions to Obersalzburg, Berchtesgadener Land, and Salzburg. Guests can also rent bikes. If you visit in winter, the staff can arrange cross-country and downhill skiing.

Bahnhofplatz 14, 83426 Bad Reichenhall. © **08651/60-90.** Fax 08651/60-91-11. www.bay-hof.de. 64 units. 75€–110€ double. Rates include buffet breakfast. AE, DC, MC, V. Parking 5€. **Amenities:** Restaurant; bar; pool; sauna; solarium; bowling alley; salon; room service; massage. *In room:* TV, minibar, hair dryer.

INEXPENSIVE

Salzburger Hof *(Value)* This three-story hotel is one of the best buys in town. Its public rooms are filled with old-Bavarian charm. Best of all are the compact guest rooms, most of which contain streamlined sofas, window desks, beds with built-in headboards, and armchairs around a breakfast table and well-kept bathrooms with shower-tub combinations; all open onto tiny balconies. The room prices depend on the view.

Mozartstrasse 7, 83435 Bad Reichenhall. © **08651/9-76-90.** Fax 08651/97-69-99. www.salzburgerhof.de. 25 units. 70€–95€ double. Rates include continental breakfast. AE, MC, V. Free parking. **Amenities:** Breakfast room; lounge; room service. *In room:* TV, hair dryer.

WHERE TO DINE

Restaurant die Holzstube GERMAN/INTERNATIONAL/ITALIAN The old-fashioned tradition and service here attract many regular patrons. This is a place where you can watch the flowers bloom and enjoy a world-class cuisine (with many diet-conscious selections). You might try one of the kitchen's own original recipes: for example, marinated and roasted medallions of venison *Königin Luise,* served with bacon, chanterelles, and whortleberries.

In the Parkhotel Luisenbad, Ludwigstrasse 33. © **08651/60-40.** Reservations recommended. Main courses 12€–18€. AE, DC, MC, V. Daily noon–2pm and 6:30–9pm.

Schweizer Stuben ✦ INTERNATIONAL No restaurant, even those in the luxury hotels, can hold a candle to this place for cuisine. It's located southwest of town in the center of the suburb of Kirchberg. The kitchen prepares light international dishes, along with specialties from Bavaria and the Berchtesgaden region. The decor is appropriately rustic. The chef seems to have a bent for updating contemporary classics. The fixed-price menu at lunch is an especially good value.

Kirchberg Schlössl, Thumseestrasse 11, Kirchberg. © 08651/27-60. Reservations required. Main courses 12€–22€; fixed-price meals 20€ at lunch, 30€–45€ at dinner. AE, DC, MC, V. Tues–Sun 11am–3pm and 6–11pm.

BAD REICHENHALL AFTER DARK

Most guests on the nighttime circuit head for the **Bad Reichenhall Casino,** Wittelsbacherstrasse 17 (© **08651/40-91**), which offers roulette, American roulette, blackjack, and 50 types of slot machines. You must show your passport if you plan to do any gaming. It's open daily from 3pm to 3am; admission is 2.50€. Men must wear jackets and ties. A **theater** is also located here at the Kurgastzentrum, site of the casino. This is a setting for concerts, operas, operettas and musicals, plays, ballets, and folkloric evenings. The tourism office (see "Visitor Information," above) keeps a complete list of events and ticket prices. When weather permits, performances are staged in an open-air pavilion. Tickets cost from 20€ to 35€.

If you want to hang out with the locals, go to the **Axel Bar,** a woodsy bar in the Steigenberger Axelmannstein Hotel, Salzburgerstrasse 2–6 (© **08651/ 77-70**). Here you can dance to rather sedate disco music interspersed with folk tunes. There's also the **Tiffany Bar** at the Hotel Bayerischer Hof, Bahnhofplatz 14 (© **08651/24-80**), where folks sometimes dance to live music but mostly just drink. The Bayerischer Hof's nightclub hosts international acts. Good old-fashioned Bavarian suds is the order of the evening at everybody's favorite beer hall, **Burgerbräu,** Rathausplatz (© **08651/60-89**).

5 Chiemsee ⓐ

Prien am Chiemsee: 85km (53 miles) SE of Munich, 23km (14 miles) E of Rosenheim, 64km (40 miles) W of Salzburg

Known as the "Bavarian Sea," Chiemsee is one of the most beautiful lakes in the Bavarian Alps, set in a serene landscape. In the south, the mountains reach almost to the water. Many resorts line the shores of the large lake, but the Chiemsee's main attractions are on its two islands, Frauenchiemsee, with its interesting local customs, and Herrenchiemsee, site of the palace built by Ludwig II with the intent of recreating Versailles.

ESSENTIALS
GETTING THERE
BY TRAIN The Prien Bahnhof is on the major Munich-Rosenheim-Freilassing-Salzburg rail line, with frequent connections in all directions. Ten daily trains arrive from Munich (trip time: 1 hr.). For information, call © **08051/99-66-33.**

BY BUS Regional bus service in the area is offered by **RVO Regionalverkehr Oberbayern, Betrieb Rosenheim** (© **08031/6-20-06** for schedules and information).

BY CAR Access by car is via the A8 Autobahn from Munich.

VISITOR INFORMATION
For tourist information, contact the **Chiemsee Tourismus,** Rottauerstrasse 6, in Bernau am Chiemsee (© **08051/22-80**), open Monday to Friday from 8:30am to 6pm and Saturday from 9am to noon.

GETTING AROUND
BY STEAMER From the liveliest resort, Prien, on the west shore, you can reach either Frauenchiemsee or Herrenchiemsee via lake steamers that make regular trips

throughout the year. The round-trip fare to Herrenchiemsee is 5.50€, 6.50€ to Fraueninsel. The steamers, operated by **Chiemsee-Schiffahrt Ludwig Fessler** (© **08051/60-90**), make round-trips covering the entire lake. Connections are made from Gstadt, Seebruck, Chieming, Übersee/Feldwies, and Bernau/Felden. Large boats leave Prien/Stock for Herrenchiemsee at the island of Herreninsel from May to September, daily about every 20 minutes between 8am and 6pm.

BY BUS There is also bus service from the harbor to the DB station in Prien (Chiemsee-Schiffahrt) and around the lake by RVO.

EXPLORING THE ISLANDS
FRAUENCHIEMSEE

Frauenchiemsee, also called Fraueninsel, is the smaller of the lake's two major islands. Along its sandy shore stands a fishing village whose boats fish the lake for pike and salmon. At the festival of Corpus Christi, these boats are covered with flowers and streamers, the fishers are outfitted in Bavarian garb, and the young women of the village dress as brides. As the boats circle the island, they stop at each corner for the singing of the Gospels.

The island is also the home of a Benedictine nunnery, founded in 782. The convent is known for a liqueur called *Kloster Likör*. Sold by nuns in black cowls with white-winged head garb, it's supposed to be an "agreeable stomach elixir."

HERRENCHIEMSEE ✿✿

Herrenchiemsee, also called Herreninsel, has the most popular visitor attraction on the lake, one of King Ludwig's fantastic castles.

Neues Schloss Begun by Ludwig II in 1878, this castle was never completed. It was meant to be a replica of the grand palace of Versailles that Ludwig so admired. A German journalist once called it "a monument to uncreative megalomania." However, the creation of the castle gave impetus to a revival of arts and crafts. One of the architects of Herrenchiemsee was Julius Hofmann, whom the king had also employed for the construction of his famous alpine castle, Neuschwanstein. When money ran out and work was halted in 1886, only the center of the enormous palace had been completed. The palace and its formal gardens, surrounded by woodlands of beech and fir, remain one of the most fascinating of Ludwig's adventures, in spite of their unfinished state.

The palace entrance is lit by a huge skylight above the sumptuously decorated state staircase. Frescoes depicting the four states of existence alternate with Greek and Roman statues set in niches on the staircase and in the gallery above. The vestibule is adorned with a pair of enameled peacocks, Louis XIV's favorite bird.

The Great Hall of Mirrors ✿✿ is unquestionably the most splendid hall in the palace and the most authentic replica of Versailles. The 17 door panels contain enormous mirrors reflecting the 33 crystal chandeliers and the 44 gilded candelabras. The vaulted ceiling is covered with 25 paintings depicting the life of Louis XIV.

The dining room is a popular attraction for visitors because of the table nicknamed "the little table that lays itself." A mechanism in the floor permitted the table to go down to the room below to be cleared and relaid between courses. Over the table hangs an exquisite chandelier of Meissen porcelain, the largest in the world and the single most valuable item in the palace.

The state bedroom ✿ is brilliant to the point of gaudiness, as practically every inch of the room has been gilded. On the dais, instead of a throne stands the richly decorated state bed, its purple-velvet draperies weighing more than 300 pounds. Separating the dais from the rest of the room is a carved wooden balustrade covered with gold leaf. On the ceiling a huge fresco depicts the descent of Apollo, surrounded by the other gods of Olympus. The sun god's features bear a strong resemblance to Louis XIV.

Herrenchiemsee 3. ℂ 08051/68-87-0. Admission (in addition to the round-trip boat fare) 5.50€ adults, 4.50€ students, free for children under 16. Apr–Sept 30, tours daily 9am–5pm; off-season, daily 10am–4pm.

WHERE TO STAY

Bayerischer Hof The Estermann family will welcome you to the Bayerischer Hof. The rustic aspects of the decor create the illusion that this relatively severe modern hotel is indeed older and more mellow than it really is. Of particular note is the painted ceiling in the dining room, where regional meals are served. The rest of the hotel is more streamlined—modern, efficient, but quite appealing. Rooms are all well maintained including the bathrooms, which contain shower units.

Bernauerstrasse 3, D-83209 Prien am Chiemsee. ℂ 08051/60-30. Fax 08051/6-29-17. www.bayerischer hof-prien.de. 46 units. 84€ double. Rates include buffet breakfast. AE, MC, V. Closed Nov and last week of Jan. Parking 5€. **Amenities:** Breakfast rooms; lounge; room service. *In room:* TV, hair dryer.

Yachthotel Chiemsee ✦ The best place to stay on the lake is the Yachthotel Chiemsee, on the western shore of the "Bavarian Sea." This modern hotel offers attractively furnished rooms, all with king-size beds, well-kept bathrooms with shower-tub combinations, and balconies or terraces opening onto the water. Lakeside rooms are equipped with two double beds and a pull-out sofa for groups of four or more.

There's a choice of restaurants, complete with a lakeside terrace and a marina, although you can order from the same menu in all three. The most elegant room, patronized for its view if not its food, is the Seepavillion. The Seerestaurant is slightly more rustic but with an elegant flair, and the Zirbelstüberl goes alpine-Bavarian all the way.

Harrasser Strasse 49, 83209 Prien am Chiemsee. ℂ 08051/69-60. Fax 08051/51-71. www.yachthotel.de. 135€–170€ double; 180€–270€ suite. Rates include buffet breakfast. AE, DC, MC, V. Free parking. **Amenities:** Restaurant; bar; pool; squash court; fitness center; spa; sauna; solarium; yacht rental; room service; babysitting; laundry/dry cleaning. *In room:* TV, minibar, hair dryer.

WHERE TO DINE

Restaurant Mühlberger ✦✦ CONTINENTAL Set within a 2-minute drive (or a 5-min. walk) from the center of Prien, this is a cozy, relatively modern building whose exposed pine and coziness makes you think it might be older. The thoughtful and hospitable staff will present menu items that reflect the diversity of local culinary traditions, and although lots of imagination is shown in the kitchens, some of the recipes evoke strong memories of their childhoods in many of the patrons. Examples include *saibling* (a local freshwater whitefish) served in herb sauce with new potatoes; filet of veal with exotic wild mushrooms and a sauce made from a local white wine, a tender form of veal-based *tafelspitz* (the boiled-beef dish that's always associated with Vienna and its last emperor, Franz-Josef); many well-flavored versions of chicken; and such saltwater fish dishes as tuna steak with a curried tomato sauce; or turbot with béarnaise sauce. You might begin a meal here with a terrine of guinea-fowl with pearl onions; and end it with a house-made strudel that's layered with wild cherries, vanilla ice cream, and chocolate sauce.

Bernauerstrasse 40 Prien. ℂ 08051/966-888. Reservations recommended. Main courses 19€–24€; lunch set menus 24€–61€; dinner set menus 52€–61€. MC, V. Thurs–Mon 12:30–2pm and Wed–Mon 6–10pm. Closed: 1 week in Feb and 1 week in Nov.

The Fairy-Tale King

Often called "Mad" King Ludwig (although Bavarians hate that label), Ludwig II, son of Maximilian II, was only 18 years old when he was crowned king of Bavaria. Handsome Ludwig initially took an interest in affairs of state, but he soon grew bored and turned to the pursuit of his romantic visions. He transformed his dreams into some of the region's most elaborate castles, nearly bankrupting Bavaria in the process.

Linderhof, the first and smallest of Ludwig's architectural fantasies, was his favorite castle, and the only one completed at the time of his death. His most elaborate effort was his attempt to construct his own Versailles on the island of Herrenchiemsee, but best known is the multi-turreted Disneyland-like Neuschwanstein. From a distance, the castle appears more illusory than real. It's the most photographed castle in Germany, and one of Germany's greatest tourist attractions.

The "dream king" was born in 1845 at Nymphenburg, the summer residence of the Bavarian rulers. A bisexual loner who never married, Ludwig's most intense relationship was his friendship with the composer Richard Wagner. An admirer of Wagner when that composer's music was considered crude, loud, and even demonic by almost everyone, it was Ludwig's enthusiastic and generous support that gave Wagner the opportunity to develop his art. It is probable that Ludwig, who was not musical, was captivated less by the music than by the opera's world of fantasy. The king sometimes had Wagner's operas mounted for his own pleasure and watched them in royal and solitary splendor. In the magical grotto at Linderhof, he recreated the Venus grotto from the Munich opera stage design for *Tannhäuser*. Although the money he

6 Bad Wiessee ⚔

53km (33 miles) S of Munich, 18km (11 miles) SE of Bad Tölz

If you've always believed that the best medicine is the worst tasting, you should feel right at home in Bad Wiessee—the mineral springs of this popular spa on the Tegernsee are saturated with iodine and sulfur. However, the other attractions of this small town more than make up for this healthful discomfort. The spa, with a huge lake at its feet and towering Alps rising behind it, is a year-round resort. In summer, swimming and boating are popular; in winter, you can ski on the slopes or skate on the lake.

The springs are used for the treatment of many diseases, including rheumatism and heart and respiratory conditions. In spite of its tiny size, Bad Wiessee is advanced in its medical facilities, as well as in its accommodations and restaurants.

The main season begins in May and ends in October. During these busy times, you should definitely make a reservation. Many hotels close in winter, so be warned if you're an off-season visitor. In recent years, the town has become increasingly popular with vacationers from Munich.

From Bad Wiessee, any number of tours are possible, including visits to Munich, Chiemsee, and the castles of Neuschwanstein, Herrenchiemsee, and

lavished upon Wagner came from his own fortune, Ludwig's ministers became alarmed and Wagner was persuaded to leave Munich, although the friendship continued at a distance.

Ludwig had few close friends. He was devoted to his cousin Sisi—Elisabeth, the empress of Austria—but estranged from the rest of his family. He led a solitary life, slept most of the day, and spent his nights going for long, lonely rides through the countryside, often dressed in full kingly regalia. More and more, he withdrew into his dream world; he ran up huge debts and refused all advice to curb his extravagant building projects.

Finally, the cabinet decided he had to go—his excesses were too much. He was declared insane in 1886 when he was 41 years old, and his uncle Luitpold was made regent. Three days later, he was found drowned in Lake Starnberg on the outskirts of Munich—he may have committed suicide, or he may have been murdered. His death remains a mystery. On the bank of the lake is a memorial chapel dedicated to him. He is buried with other royals in the crypt beneath the choir of St. Michael's Church.

Today, Ludwig enjoys something of a cult status in Munich. Was he really insane? His theatricality, self-absorbed lifestyle, morbid shyness, and outbursts of temper certainly made him a very strange person, but there is not much evidence of real insanity. He seems mainly to have been an eccentric who had the means and power to try to turn his fantasies into reality.

Linderhof (see chapter 6). You can also visit Salzburg and Innsbruck in Austria. The tourism office (see below) will supply details.

ESSENTIALS
GETTING THERE
BY TRAIN   Travelers arriving by train disembark at Gmund, 3km (2 miles) away. At the railway station there, a flotilla of buses (between 9 and 11 per day, depending on the day of the week) meet every major train, with easy connections on to Bad Wiessee. For rail information, call ✆ **01805/99-66-33.**

BY BUS   Between 3 and 5 buses depart every day for Bad Wiessee from Munich's Hauptbahnhof, with additional stops along the Zweibrückestrasse, adjacent to Munich's Deutsches Museum. Travel time is about 90 minutes. Round-trip transport costs 11€ per person. For bus information, call ✆ **08022/86-03-20.**

BY CAR   Access from either Munich or Salzburg (Austria) is via the A8 Autobahn. Take the Holzkirchen exit heading toward Bad Wiessee and follow the signs.

VISITOR INFORMATION
For information, go to the **Kuramt,** Adrian-Stoop-Strasse 20 (✆ **08022/ 8-60-30**). From May to October, the tourism office's hours are Monday to

Friday 8am to 6pm and Saturday 9am to noon. In the off-season, hours are Monday to Friday 8am to 5pm.

SIGHTS & ACTIVITIES

Bad Wiessee offers plenty of activities, apart from its health treatments. In summer, visitors can go sailing or windsurfing on the lake, or head to the mountains for mountain biking and hiking. A drive up the **Wallberg Road** winds through the Moorsalm pasture to an altitude of 990m (3,300 ft.). There's also plenty of golf and tennis. In winter, experienced alpine skiers are drawn to the Wallberg, and there are many cross-country trails as well. Wintertime hiking is also a possibility, as about 97km (60 miles) of paths are cleared of snow. The less adventurous or athletic can enjoy horse-drawn sleigh rides. Finally, you can also take a **mountain cable car,** which travels up 1,530m (5,100 ft.).

The town of Bad Wiessee has an old-world charm. It's best explored via the old-fashioned steam train or by taking a carriage ride. During the annual lake festivals in summer, locals don traditional clothing and parade through the town. Worth the trip is the nearby **Tegernsee Ducal Palace,** which contains the former monastery of St. Quinn, founded in A.D. 746.

SHOPPING   You'll find traditional Bavarian souvenirs, loden coats, and lederhosen here. For a full selection of traditional Bavarian clothes, go to **Friedl Mandel,** Lindenplatz (② **08022/8-14-58**). If you want to acquire one-of-a-kind woodcarvings, either religious or secular, head for the studio of **Franz Trinkl,** Dr. Scheid Strasse 9A (② **08022/87-49**), where you'll find a charming and idiosyncratic collection of artfully carved figurines.

WHERE TO STAY
EXPENSIVE

Hotel Lederer ⭐   This spa and holiday hotel is clearly the most distinguished choice in town. From the balcony of your room, you'll look out onto the Tegernsee and the Lower Bavarian Alps. The atmosphere is pleasant, with good service and attractive, well-maintained rooms, ranging in size from medium to spacious. All units have well-kept bathrooms with shower-tub combinations. The hotel stands in a large park, and there's a dock and an indoor pool for swimming, as well as a meadow for sunbathing.

The hotel restaurant turns out an international cuisine of good standard. Sometimes there's a barbecue on the terrace facing the lake, followed by entertainment or dancing in the nightclub.

Am See Bodenschneidstrasse 9–11, 83707 Bad Wiessee. ② **08022/82-90.** Fax 08022/82-92-61. www. lederer.com. 114 units. 90€–200€ double. AE, DC, MC, V. Closed Oct–Feb. Free parking. **Amenities:** Restaurant; lounge; pool; ; tennis courts; sauna; solarium; salonroom service; laundry/dry cleaning. *In room:* TV, hair dryer.

MODERATE

Hotel Rex   A modern hotel with much charm and character, Hotel Rex is set against a backdrop of the Lower Bavarian Alps. It's an ideal choice for a vacation by the lake. The decorator tried to make the place as warm and inviting as possible. The well-maintained guest rooms are furnished in Bavarian style and contain neatly kept bathrooms with shower-tub combinations. The hotel has good food and caters to special dieters, and its Bierstuberl is a lively gathering place.

Münchnerstrasse 25, 83707 Bad Wiessee. ② **08022/8-62-00.** Fax 08022/862-01-00. www.hotel-rex.de. 58 units. 100€–120€ double; 135€ suite. No credit cards. Closed Nov 1–Apr 5. Free parking. **Amenities:** Restaurant; bar; lounge; room service; laundry. *In room:* TV, hair dryer.

Landhaus Am Stein   This typical Bavarian inn, with geranium-filled balconies and a roof overhang, is a real alpine resort, where people come to have a good time. It attracts scenery lovers in summer, and skiers in winter. The guest rooms are completely modern; each has a balcony, a well-kept bathroom with shower-tub combination, and they range from small to medium in size. The hotel has a sauna where, as is usual for Germany, men and women are segregated.

Im Sapplfeld 8, 83707 Bad Wiessee. ℭ 08022/9-84-70. Fax 08022/8-35-60. www.landhausamstein.de. 16 units. 100€–150€ double, 145€–160€ suite. Rates include buffet breakfast. MC, V. Free parking. Garage 10€. **Amenities:** Breakfast room; lounge; sauna; room service; laundry/dry cleaning. *In room:* TV, hair dryer.

Park Hotel Resi von der Post *Value*   This enduring favorite has been around much longer than many of its fast-rising competitors. It has been considerably modernized, and now has well-furnished, traditional guest rooms. Bathrooms (containing showers) are a bit cramped. The atmosphere in the hotel's restaurant is often bustling, as diners who live nearby fill up the place; many show up in Bavarian dress. Ask for the special cheese of the Tegernsee district, *Miesbacher.* Make reservations early for this hotel; it's usually booked up for the year by summer.

Zilcherstrasse 14, 83707 Bad Wiessee. ℭ 08022/9-86-50. Fax 08022/98-65-65. 30 units. 100€ double; from 115€ suite. Rates include buffet breakfast. AE, DC, MC, V. Free parking. **Amenities:** Restaurant; lounge; room service. *In room:* TV, hair dryer.

INEXPENSIVE

Kurhotel Edelweiss   This chalet/guesthouse is ornamented with wooden balconies and painted detailing around its doors and windows. Rooms are functionally but comfortably furnished and all come with well-kept bathrooms with shower-tub combinations. Additional, but less desirable, rooms are available in the motel-like outbuildings beside the main structure. The modern public rooms are suffused with a certain German kitsch. The Bavarian-style restaurant is open for hotel guests only.

Münchnerstrasse 21 (.5km/¹/₄-mile north of Bad Weissee's center), 83707 Bad Wiessee. ℭ 08022/8-60-90. Fax 08022/8-38-83. www.bad-wiessee.de/edelweiss. 40 units. 80€ double. Rates include continental breakfast. No credit cards. Free parking. **Amenities:** Restaurant; lounge; room service. *In room:* TV, hair dryer.

Wiesseer Hof   This modern, but still traditional, hotel looks like an overgrown chalet, with four floors of rooms, many with views over a lawn dotted with greenery. The guest rooms are snug and cozy in the alpine tradition, with tidily kept bathrooms containing showers. Most have balconies, festooned in summer with boxes of geraniums. The stuccoed wooden walls of the public rooms create a *gemütlich* (cozy) warmth. The kitchen features many good Bavarian specialties.

Sanktjohanserstrasse 46, 83707 Bad Wiessee. ℭ 08022/86-70. Fax 08022/86-71-65. www.wiesseerhof. com. 60 units. 82€–130€ double. Rates include buffet breakfast. MC, V. Free parking. **Amenities:** Restaurant; lounge; room service. *In room:* TV, hair dryer, safe.

WHERE TO DINE

Freihaus Brenner ℛ CONTINENTAL   Its setting is a cozy, steep-roofed farmhouse whose intricate murals and weathered balconies evoke the old-fashioned Teutonic world. The original version of this place was built in the early 1800s. Burned to the ground around 1900, it was rebuilt nearby a few years later about 18m (20 yards) from the main location, as a series of photos and architectural drawings in the dining rooms will reveal. Today, young and energetic proprietors keep the recipes fresh and international, and the service zippy, for clients who enjoy the *gemütlich* (cozy) setting and the woodsy location overlooking the lake, about a 5-minute drive west from the center of Bad Wiessee. Menu items include selections from every country that borders Germany, including Italy, Switzerland, France, and Austria. The best examples of the local fare this place prepares with zestiness include roasted duckling with red cabbage and potato salad; and several different forms of wurst, sometimes served with braised celery and new potatoes.

Freihaushöhe. ℂ **08022/82004.** Reservations recommended. Main courses 9€–29€. MC, V. Daily 9am–10pm. Restaurant daily 11:30am–2pm and 6:30–10pm, though you can visit anytime during the day for coffee and drinks.

7 Garmisch-Partenkirchen

89km (55 miles) SW of Munich, 118km (73 miles) SE of Augsburg, 60km (37 miles) NW of Innsbruck

In spite of its urban flair, Garmisch-Partenkirchen, Germany's top alpine resort, has kept some of the charm of an ancient village. It's actually made up of two towns, the older Partenkirchen and the more modern Garmisch. Even today you occasionally see country folk in traditional costumes, and you may be held up in traffic while the cattle are led from their mountain-grazing grounds down through the streets of town.

Increasingly, this ski center is also promoting itself as a climatic health resort. Although it is hardly the equal of such fabled German spas as Baden-Baden, it offers a number of holiday packages for those seeking an array of programs that include walks in the hills, massages, river rafting, mountain bike tours, water treatments (Kneipp), beauty treatments, water gymnastics, bubble baths with ethereal oil, steam baths, and so much more. Information about these activities is available from the Garmisch-Partenkirchen Tourist Board (see below).

ESSENTIALS
GETTING THERE
BY TRAIN   The Garmisch-Partenkirchen Bahnhof is on the Munich-Weilheim-Garmisch-Mittenwald-Innsbruck rail line with frequent connections in all directions. Twenty trains per day arrive from Munich (trip time: 1 hr., 22 min.). For rail information and schedules, call ℂ **01805/99-66-33.** Mountain rail service to several mountain plateaus and the Zugspitze is offered by the **Bayerische Zugspitzenbahn** at Garmisch (ℂ **08821/79-70**).

BY BUS   Both long-distance and regional buses through the Bavarian Alps are provided by **RVO Regionalverkehr Oberbayern** (ℂ **08821/94-82-74**).

BY CAR   Access is via the A95 Autobahn from Munich; exit at Eschenlohe.

VISITOR INFORMATION
For tourist information, contact the **Verkehrsamt der Kurverwaltung,** on Dr. Richard-Strauss-Platz 1A (ℂ **08821/18-07-00**), open Monday to Saturday from 8am to 6pm and Sunday from 10am to noon.

GETTING AROUND
An unnumbered municipal bus services the town, depositing passengers at Marienplatz or the Bahnhof, from which it is possible to walk to all centrally located hotels. This free bus runs every 15 minutes.

EXPLORING THE AREA
The symbol of the city's growth and modernity is the **Olympic Ice Stadium,** built for the 1936 Winter Olympics and capable of holding nearly 12,000

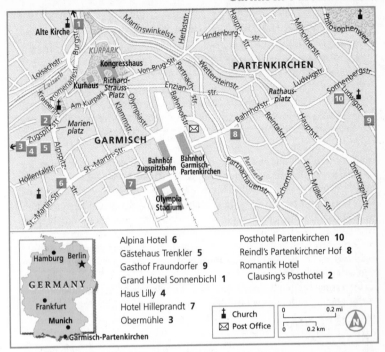

Alte Kirche 1
KURPARK
Kongresshaus
Kurhaus
Richard-
Strauss-
Platz
Am Kurpark
Marien-
platz
GARMISCH
Martinswinkelstr. Herbststr. Hindenburg- str.
Von-Brug-Str. Partnach-str. Wettersteinstr.
Enzian- str.
Olympiastr. Bahnhofstr.
Klammstr.
St.-Martin-Str.
Bahnhof
Zugspitzbahn
Bahnhof
Garmisch-
Partenkirchen
Partnachauenstr.
Olympia
Stadium
PARTENKIRCHEN
Rathaus-
platz 10
Bahnhofstr. Reintalstr.
Hauptstr.
Philosophenweg
Münchnerstr.
Ludwigstr.
Sonnenbergstr.
Ludwigstr. 9
Fritz- Müller- Str.
Dreitorspitzstr.
8

GERMANY
Hamburg · Berlin ★
Frankfurt
Munich
Garmisch-Partenkirchen

Alpina Hotel **6**
Gästehaus Trenkler **5**
Gasthof Fraundorfer **9**
Grand Hotel Sonnenbichl **1**
Haus Lilly **4**
Hotel Hilleprandt **7**
Obermühle **3**

Posthotel Partenkirchen **10**
Reindl's Partenkirchner Hof **8**
Romantik Hotel
Clausing's Posthotel **2**

✝ Church
✉ Post Office

0   0.2 mi
0   0.2 km

people. On the slopes at the edge of town is the much larger **Ski Stadium,** with two ski jumps and a slalom course. In 1936, more than 100,000 people watched the events in this stadium. Today, it's still an integral part of winter life in Garmisch—the World Cup Ski Jump is held here every New Year.

Garmisch-Partenkirchen is a center for winter sports, summer hiking, and mountain climbing. In addition, the town environs offer panoramic views and colorful buildings. The pilgrimage **Chapel of St. Anton,** on a pinewood path at the edge of Partenkirchen, is all pink and silver, inside and out. Its graceful lines are characteristic of 18th-century style. The **Philosopher's Walk,** in the park surrounding the chapel, is a delightful spot to wander, just to enjoy the views of the mountains around the low-lying town. Along Frülingstrasse in Garmisch are some beautiful examples of **Bavarian houses,** and the villa of composer Richard Strauss is at the end of Zöppritzstrasse. The **church of St. Martin,** off the Marienplatz, is worth a look for its stucco work.

This area of Germany has always attracted the German romantics, including the "dream king," Ludwig II. Perhaps with Wagner's music sounding in his ears, the king ordered the construction of a hunting lodge in the style of a Swiss chalet, but commanded that the interior look like something out of *The Arabian Nights.* The **Jadschloss Schachen** can only be reached by an arduous climb. The tourist office will supply details. Tours are offered at 11am and 2pm daily and often leave from the Olympic Ski Stadium heading for the lodge—but check this first.

SHOPPING Your best bets are in the traffic-reduced Ludwigstrasse in Partenkirchen and in the almost traffic-free zone from Dr. Richard-Strauss-Platz to Marienplatz in Garmisch. There's a vast array of stores here selling everything

---

Moments The Romantic, Historic Way to Go

The town's historic horse-drawn mail coach is operating once again from May to September. More than 60 years old, the coach takes guests for a romantic ride between the Olympic site and the town center under the Zugspitze. Daily departures are at 1:50pm in front of the railway station. The coach returns to town at 6:20pm, a one-way ride costing 10€ per person. Tickets are sold at the tourist office (© **08821/180-700**; see above).

---

from boots to boutique items, from clothing to jewelry, from art to antiques. An unusual store is **Kaufmann,** Am Kurkpark 27 (© **08821/5-52-48**), lithograph-meister to visitors to Garmisch. This shop not only sells a wide collection of artful lithographs depicting the glories of the Bavarian Alps but also offers tinsmith work, glass, ceramics, gold and silver jewelry, and various souvenirs of your visit. If you like traditional Bavarian folkloric dress but were scared off by the extremely high prices, head for **Loisachtaler,** Burgstrasse 20 (© **08821/5-23-90**). Here, Petra Ostler has assembled the area's finest collection of secondhand clothing, which for the most part is in such good shape it looks new. Take your pick amongst choices such as a jaegermeister loden coat, an alpine hat with pheasant feathers, or a cast-off dirndl to name a few.

WHERE TO STAY
EXPENSIVE

Alpina Hotel   In this Bavarian hostelry only 3 minutes from the Hausberg ski lifts, guests have all sorts of luxury facilities, including a garden with wide lawns and trees and an open patio. But even so, this is not the town's leading hotel, an honor going to such classics as the Grand Hotel Sonnenbichl or the more traditional Posthotel Partenkirchen. Alpina nonetheless has many winning features. Its facade is graced with a wide overhanging roof and Tirolean-style entranceway and windows. Each of the guest rooms sports a personalized decor: Yours may have a snow-white sofa, chairs, walls, lamps, and carpet, with original paintings as accents; or it might feature sloped pine ceilings, a Spanish bedspread, and matching armchairs. All rooms have well-maintained bathrooms with shower-tub combinations.

The open tavern dining room has two levels, and there's an extensive brick wine cellar offering a wide choice. Bavarian and international dishes are served in a beamed rustic dining room and on the sun terrace.

Alpspitzstrasse 12, D-82467 Garmisch-Partenkirchen. © **08821/78-30.** Fax 08821/7-13-74. www.alpina-gap.de. 70 units. 96€–188€ double. Rates include buffet breakfast. AE, DC, MC, V. Parking 5€. **Amenities:** 2 restaurants; bar; pool; fitness center; sauna; solarium; room service; laundry/dry cleaning. *In room:* TV, minibar, hair dryer.

Grand Hotel Sonnenbichl ✦✦   The finest hotel in the area, but not the most atmospheric, is on the hillside overlooking Garmisch-Partenkirchen, 1.5km (1 mile) from the city center and 3km (2 miles) from the Bahnhof, with views of the Wetterstein mountain range and the Zugspitze from its front rooms (those in the rear open onto a rock wall). The hotel was built in 1898 by the family of Georg Bader. After World War II, it was used as a military hospital. Some of the bedrooms are showing wear and tear, and, although usually spacious, some only have a shower (no tub), so you should ask for what you need or prefer. The decor is more or less Art Nouveau.

The hotel serves excellent food. You can have light, modern cuisine in the elegant gourmet restaurant; the Blauer Salon, or Bavarian specialties in the Zirbelstube. Afternoon coffee and fresh homemade cake are served in the lobby or on the sunny terrace. Drinks are available in the Peacock Bar.

Burgstrasse 97, 82467 Garmisch-Partenkirchen. (C) 08821/70-20. Fax 08821/70-21-31. www.sonnenbichl. de. 93 units. 115€–166€ double; 217€–409€ suite. Rates include buffet breakfast. AE, DC, MC, V. Free parking. Take Route 23 toward Oberammergau. **Amenities:** 2 restaurants; bar; pool; fitness center; sauna; solarium; room service; massage; laundry/dry cleaning. *In room:* TV, minibar, hair dryer.

Obermühle ⚐   This hotel is a 5- to 10-minute walk from Garmisch's center, in a quiet, isolated spot much favored by repeat guests. The Wolf family, the owners, have operated a hotel on this spot since 1634, although the present building was constructed in 1969. They still maintain the traditional hospitality that has characterized their family for so long. Although a bit more sterile than either the Posthotel Partenkirchen or Alpina, the mountain panoramas from its beer garden and terrace are compensating factors. All units are well maintained and have bathrooms with shower-tub combinations. Most rooms have balconies with views of the Alps. Nearby are miles of woodland trails criss-crossing the nearby foothills. The rooms often have style and comfort, some with traditional Bavarian character.

Bavarian and international dishes are featured in the excellent restaurant. The Weinstube is cozy and the garden a pleasant place to wander.

Mühlstrasse 22, D-82467 Garmisch-Partenkirchen. (C) **800/528-1234** in the U.S., or 08821/7040. Fax 08821/ 704112. www.garmisch-partenkirchen.com/obermuehle. 95 units. 133€–185€ double; 200€–250€ suite. Rates include buffet breakfast. AE, DC, MC, V. Free parking. Take Route 24 (Zugspitzstrasse) toward Griesen. **Amenities:** Restaurant; lounge; pool; sauna; solarium; room service; babysitting; laundry/dry cleaning. *In room:* TV, minibar, hair dryer.

Posthotel Partenkirchen ⚐⚐   Once a posting inn, Posthotel Partenkirchen is now one of the town's most prestigious hotels and has the added asset of an unusually fine restaurant (see "Where to Dine," below). The traditional facade has decorative murals around the front entrance and window boxes planted with red geraniums. The U-shaped rooms are stylish, with hand-decorated or elaborately carved furnishings. Each comes with a well-kept bathroom equipped with a shower-tub combination. The balconies are sun traps, overlooking a garden and parking for your car, and offer a view of the Alps. Here you'll experience old-world living, with personalized service offered by the owners.

Of the two dining rooms, the larger is known for its decor: a wooden-beamed ceiling, wrought-iron chandeliers, and huge arches that divide the room, making it more intimate. In the rustic Weinlokal Barbarossa, there are nooks for quiet before- or after-dinner drinks. Musicians provide background music.

Ludwigstrasse 49, 82467 Garmisch-Partenkirchen. (C) **08821/9-36-30.** Fax 08821/93-63-22-22. 59 units. 120€–140€ double; 160€–250€ suite. Rates include continental breakfast. AE, DC, MC, V. Free parking. **Amenities:** Restaurant; lounge; golf course; tennis courts; skiing; mountain climbing; room service; laundry. *In room:* TV, minibar, hair dryer.

MODERATE

Reindl's Partenkirchner Hof ⚐   Reindl's opened in 1911, and from the beginning it attracted a devoted following. Owners Bruni and Karl Reindl maintain a high level of luxury and hospitality in this special Bavarian retreat. The annexes, the Wetterstein and the House Alpspitz, have balconies, and the main four-story building has wraparound verandas, giving each room an unobstructed view of the mountains and town. The accommodations are among the most attractive in town, often furnished with Bavarian objects, making for a cozy charm. The best rooms are the suites opening onto panoramic views of mountains or the garden. Tasteful pastel fabrics, fine wool carpeting, and rustic pine furniture add to the allure. All units have well-kept bathrooms with shower-tub combinations. The Reindl's restaurant is well respected (see "Where to Dine," below).

Bahnhofstrasse 15, 82467 Garmisch-Partenkirchen. © 08821/94-38-70. Fax 08821/7-34-01. www. garmisch-partenkirchen.com/Reindl. 88 units. 94€–160€ double; 132€–300€ suite. AE, DC, MC, V. Closed Nov 9–Dec 15. Parking 8€. **Amenities:** Restaurant; lounge; pool; health club; sauna; room service; laundry. *In room:* TV, minibar, hair dryer.

Romantik Hotel Clausing's Posthotel ⭐ This historic hotel with its florid pink facade has seen a series of events that are a part of Garmisch's very identity. It was originally built in 1512 in the heart of town as a tavern. During the Thirty Years War, it became a haven for refugees when nearby Munich was ravaged and besieged. In 1891, it was sold to a prosperous beer baron from Berlin, whose claim to fame came from his invention of a new brand of beer, *Berliner Weissen*, with hints of yeast and raspberry flavoring, which quickly became one of the most popular brands in Garmisch.

In the early 1990s, the interior was radically upgraded without losing the establishment's historic ambience. Guest rooms successfully mingle antique charm with modern, well-insulated comforts. Unused space beneath the eaves has been transformed into what are now the inn's best accommodations. All rooms have beautifully kept bathrooms, which for the most part contain shower-tub combinations.

The most glamorous restaurant here is the Stüberl, a paneled enclave of warmth and carefully presented cuisine. The Verandah offers simple platters, drinks, and glassed-in comfort in winter, and open-air access to the bustling Marienplatz in summer. Bavarian schmaltz is the venue at the Post-Hörnd'l, where live music is presented every evening.

Marienplatz 12, 82467 Garmisch-Partenkirchen. © 08821/70-90. Fax 08821/70-92-05. www.clausings-posthotel.de. 45 units. 104€–132€ double; from 205€ suite. AE, DC, MC, V. **Amenities:** 2 restaurants; bar; room service. *In room:* TV, minibar, hair dryer.

INEXPENSIVE

Gästhaus Trenkler For a number of years, Frau Trenkler has made travelers feel well cared for in her guesthouse, which enjoys a quiet central location. She rents five doubles with showers and toilets and five doubles with hot and cold running water. The rooms are simple but comfortably furnished.

Kreuzstrasse 20, 82467 Garmisch-Partenkirchen. © 08821/34-39. Fax 08821/15-67. 10 units (5 w/shower). 43€–48€ double without shower; 50€–55€ double with shower. Rates include continental breakfast. No credit cards. Free parking. **Amenities:** Breakfast room; lounge. *In room:* No phone.

Gasthof Fraundorfer ⭐ *Finds* The family-owned Gasthof Fraundorfer is directly on the main street of town, just a 5-minute walk from the old church. Its original style has not been updated, so it retains the character of another day. There are three floors under a sloping roof, with a facade brightly adorned with window boxes of geraniums and decorative murals depicting a family feast. You'll be in the midst of village-centered activities here, near interesting shops and restaurants. The guest rooms are furnished in traditional alpine style, some with four-poster beds. Some larger units are virtual apartments, suitable for up to five guests. All units have neatly kept bathrooms with shower units. Owners Josef and Barbel Fraundorfer are proud of their country-style meals. There's

Bavarian yodeling and dancing every night except Tuesday. Dinner reservations are advisable.

In addition, the owners operate the Gästhaus Barbara in back, with 20 more beds. A typical Bavarian decor includes a *Himmelbett* (a high four-poster bed with curtains). A double in this more recent house costs 75€.

Ludwigstrasse 24, 82467 Garmisch-Partenkirchen. ℭ 08821/92-70. Fax 08821/9-27-99. www.gasthof-fraundorfer.de. 30 units. 70€–90€ double; 100€–160€ family room for 2–5 people. Rates include buffet breakfast. AE, MC, V. Free parking. **Amenities:** Dining room; lounge; room service. *In room:* TV, hair dryer.

Haus Lilly   This spotlessly clean guesthouse, a 15-minute walk from the Bahnhof, wins prizes for its copious breakfasts and the personality of its smiling owner, Maria Lechner, whose English is limited but whose hospitality is universal. Each cozy room includes free access to a kitchen, so in-house meal preparation is an option for guests wanting to save money. Bathrooms in each room are compact with shower stalls. Breakfast offers a combination of cold cuts, rolls, cheese, eggs, pastries, and coffee, tea, or chocolate.

Zugspitzstrasse 20a (a 15-min. walk from the Bahnhof), 82467 Garmisch-Partenkirchen. ℭ 08821/5-26-00. 8 units. 52€ double; 78€ triple or quad. Rates include buffet breakfast. No credit cards. Free parking. **Amenities:** Breakfast room; lounge; room service. *In room:* TV.

Hotel Hilleprandt   This cozy, tranquil chalet is a good budget choice. Its wooden balconies, attractive garden, and backdrop of forest-covered mountains give the impression of an old-time alpine building. However, a complete renovation has brought streamlined modern comfort. Guests enjoy a pleasant breakfast room. Rooms are small but comfortable. Each has a private balcony and a tiled, shower-only bathroom.

Riffelstrasse 17 (near the Zugspitze Bahnhof and the Olympic Ice Stadium), 82467 Garmisch-Partenkirchen. ℭ 08821/28-61. Fax 08821/7-45-48. www.hotel-hilleprandt.de. 18 units. 74€–96€ double; 102€ suite. Rates include buffet breakfast. MC, V. Free parking. **Amenities:** Breakfast room; lounge; fitness center; sauna. *In room:* TV, hair dryer.

WHERE TO DINE
EXPENSIVE

Posthotel Partenkirchen ★★ CONTINENTAL   Posthotel Partenkirchen is renowned for its distinguished Continental cuisine—in fact, its reputation is known throughout Bavaria. The interior dining rooms are rustic, with lots of mellow, old-fashioned atmosphere. Everything seems comfortably subdued, including the guests. Perhaps the best way to dine here is to order one of the fixed-price menus, which change daily depending on the availability of seasonal produce. The a la carte menu is extensive, featuring game in autumn. You can order fresh cauliflower soup followed by main dishes such as schnitzel cordon bleu or mixed grill St. James. The Wiener schnitzel served with a large salad is the best we've had in the resort.

Ludwigstrasse 49, Partenkirchen. ℭ 08821/9-36-30. Reservations required. Main courses 13€–21€; AE, DC, MC, V. Daily noon–2pm and 6–9:30pm.

Reindl's Restaurant ★ CONTINENTAL   One of the best places to dine in Partenkirchen is Reindl's, a first-class restaurant in every sense of the word. It is the only hotel in town that competes successfully with Posthotel Partenkirchen. The seasonal menu comprises cuisine moderne as well as regional Bavarian dishes. Some famous French wines and champagnes—Romanée Conti, Château Lafite Rothschild, and Château Petrus—are offered. The chef de cuisine is Marianne Holzinger, daughter of founding father Karl Reindl. She has worked in the kitchens of The Breakers in Palm Beach and Aubergine in Munich. The restaurant is known for honoring each "food season." For example, if you're here in asparagus season in spring, a special menu samples the dish in all the best-known varieties.

As a good opening to a fine repast, we suggest the scampi salad Walterspiel with fresh peaches, lemon, and tarragon; or homemade goose-liver paté with Riesling jelly. Among main dishes, we recommend *coq au Riesling* (chicken in wine) with noodles; or veal roasted with *Steinpilze,* a special mushroom from the Bavarian mountains. Among the fish dishes, try wild salmon with white and red wine and butter sauce. For dessert, you can select Grand Marnier sabayon with strawberry and vanilla ice cream or something more spectacular—a Salzburger Nockerl for two.

In the Partenkirchner Hof, Bahnhofstrasse 15. ✆ **08821/5-80-25.** Reservations required. Main courses 15€–25€. AE, DC, MC, V. Daily noon–2:30pm and 6:30–11pm. Closed Nov 10–Dec 15.

MODERATE

Alpenhof ✦ BAVARIAN Alpenhof is probably the best restaurant in Garmisch outside the hotel dining rooms (see above). The cuisine here is neatly grounded in tradition, with a flavorful use of ingredients. In summer, try for an outside table; in winter, retreat to the cozy interior, which is flooded with sunlight from a greenhouse extension. Renate and Josef Huber offer a variety of Bavarian specialties, as well as trout "any way you want," salmon grilled with mousseline sauce, and ragout of venison. For dessert, try a soufflé with exotic fruits. An exceptional set meal for 15€—the best for value at the resort—is presented daily.

Am Kurpark 10. ✆ **08821/5-90-55.** Reservations recommended. Main courses 12€–22€. DC, MC, V. Daily 11:30am–2pm and 5:30–9:30pm. Closed 3 weeks in Nov.

INEXPENSIVE

Flösserstuben GREEK/BAVARIAN/INTERNATIONAL Regardless of season, a bit of the Bavarian Alps always seems to be in flower amid the wood-trimmed nostalgia of this intimate restaurant near the town center. The weathered beams are likely to reverberate with laughter and good times. You can select a seat at a colorful wooden table or on an ox yoke–inspired stool in front of the spliced saplings that decorate the bar. Moussaka and souvlaki, as well as sauerbraten and all kinds of Bavarian dishes, are abundantly available.

Schmiedstrasse 2. ✆ **08821/28-88.** Reservations recommended. Main courses 8€–18€. AE, MC. Daily 11am–2:30pm and 5–10pm (or as late as 1:30am, depending on business).

Riessersee ✦ *Finds* BAVARIAN On the shores of a small lake with emerald-green water, this restaurant can only be reached after a lovely 2-mile stroll from the center of town. A cafe-restaurant; it is the ideal place for a leisurely lunch, an afternoon tea or coffee and cake, ice cream, or chocolates. It makes a particularly good place to stop over after your exploration of the Zugspitze. The zither music played on Saturday and Sunday will soothe your nerves after such an adventure. You may like the place so much you'll stick around for one of the good-tasting dishes that feature Bavarian fish or game specialties. Caviar and lobster are available on occasion, and you can order some of the best-tasting veal dishes here at all times.

Reiss 6. (3km/2 miles from the center of town). ✆ **08821/9-54-40.** Main courses 7€–18€. Daily 8am–9pm. AE, MC, V.

GARMISCH-PARTENKIRCHEN AFTER DARK

You can test your luck at the town's casino, **Spielbank Garmisch-Partenkirchen,** Am Kurpark 10 (© **08821/9-59-90**). Admission costs 2.50€ per person, and presentation of a passport is required. It's open daily from 3pm to 2am. Between 3 and 7pm, only roulette and the slot machines are available, and men must wear jackets. Beginning at 8pm, men must wear jackets and ties, and to the noise of the roulette tables and slot machines is added the sound of the blackjack tables. Baccarat, because of lack of interest, is no longer offered at the casino, but every Friday and Saturday, games of seven-card stud poker are arranged.

Many hotels have dance floors that keep the music pumping into the wee hours, but for earlier dancing of a different sort, check out the summer program of Bavarian folk music and dancing, held every Saturday night from mid-May to September in the **Bayernhalle,** Brauhausstrasse 19. During the same weeks from Saturday to Thursday, classical and pop concerts are sponsored at the **Garmisch Park bandstand.** On Friday, these live shows move to the **Partenkirchen bandstand.** Check with the local tourist office (see above) for details about these programs as well as a 5-day **Wagner Festival** held in the dual resort during June.

If you'd like to join the locals at night, head for one of the taverns for a beer. All major hotels serve up a brew, but for a change of pace go to the **Irish Pub,** Rathausplatz 8 (© **08821/7-87-98**), and order a Guinness. This pub, exactly in the center, attracts one of the most convivial crowds in town.

A particularly cozy way to spend about an hour on a winter's night involves being huddled with a companion in the back of a **horse-drawn sled.** For a fee of around 50€ per hour, this can be arranged through Brandtner, GmbH, at the **Café Waldstein,** Königsseer Fussweg 17 (© **08652/24-27**).

8 Exploring the Alps

THE ZUGSPITZE 🏵🏵🏵

From Garmisch-Partenkirchen, you can see the tallest mountain peak in Germany, the **Zugspitze** 🏵, at the frontier between Austria and Germany. Its summit towers 2,916m (9,720 ft.) above sea level, and you can ski all summer in the great Zugspitzplatt snowfield. Ski slopes begin at a height of 2,610m (8,700 ft.). For a panoramic view of both the Bavarian and the Tirolean (Austrian) Alps, go all the way to the peak.

There are two ways to reach the Zugspitze peak from the center of Garmisch. We usually recommend that you ascend and descend via different trajectories, a plan that will allow maximum exposure to the panoramas that sweep outward en route. Both originate from the back side of Garmisch's main railway station. A cog railway, the **Zugspitzbahn,** departs daily every hour between 8:35am and 2:35pm. The train will meander uphill, past lichen-covered boulders and coursing streams, to a high-altitude alpine plateau, the **Zugspitzplatt,** where views sweep out over Bavaria. At the Zugspitzplatt, you'll transfer onto a cable car, the **Gletscher Seilbahn,** for a 4-minute uphill ride to the top of the Zugspitze. Here, far-reaching panoramas, a cafe and restaurant; gift shop, and the terminus of many alpine trails provide options for diversions. Total travel time, including transfers at the Zugspitzplatt, is about 55 minutes.

An alternative means of reaching the summit of the Zugspitze involves taking the above-mentioned cog railway, the Zugspitzbahn, for a short distance, disembarking 14.5km (9 miles) southwest of Garmisch at the lower end of the **Eibsee Seilbahn (Eibsee Cable car).** The station for the Eibsee Cable car lies next to the edge of a clear alpine lake, the Eibsee. The cable car will carry you directly to the summit of the Zugspitze. Total transit time is about 38 minutes. The Seilbahn makes the summit run at least every half-hour from 8:30am to 4:30pm (until 5:30pm during July and Aug).

Regardless of which method you choose to ascend and descend the Zugspitze, the round-trip fare between April and October costs 42€ for adults, 25€ for travelers age 5 to 15, and 29€ for travelers age 16 to 17. In winter, between November and March, round-trip fares are reduced to 33€ adults, 20€ ages 5 to 15, and 23€ ages 16 to 17. For more information, contact the **Bayerische Zugspitzbahn,** Olympiastrasse 27, in Garmisch-Partenkirchen (© **08821/79-70**).

From Garmisch-Partenkirchen, many other peaks of the Wetterstein range are accessible as well, via the 10 funiculars ascending from the borders of the town. From the top of the **Wank** (1,755m/5,850 ft.) to the east, you get the best view of the plateau on which the twin villages of Garmisch and Partenkirchen sit. This summit is also a favorite with patrons of Garmisch's spa facilities because the plentiful sunshine makes it ideal for the *Liegekur* (deck-chair cure).

HIKING IN THE BAVARIAN ALPS

Hiking is a national pastime in Bavaria. When winter snows melt, everybody seems to hit the trails, from preschoolers to seniors living on pensions. The tourist office in Garmisch-Partenkirchen will help you find trails of varying degrees of difficulty. After that, you just follow the signs. The Zugspitzbahn, the rail line between Garmisch-Partenkirchen and Eibsee, at the base of the Zugspitze, offers a brochure outlining seven trails most favored by hikers. You don't have to be an Olympic athlete to try them. Some hikes will take 4 to 5 hours, and a few are suitable for the entire family.

An easily accessible destination is the 1,218m (4,060-ft.) **Eckbauer** peak that lies on the southern fringe of Partenkirchen. The easy trails on its lower slopes

---

Moments   A Dramatic Alpine Fantasy

Another interesting hike is through the **Partnachklamm Gorge,** a canyon with a roaring stream at the bottom and sheer cliff walls rising on either side of the hiking trail. Take the Graseck Seilbahn from its departure point at the bottom of the gorge, less than a half-mile south of Garmisch's ski stadium, and get off at the first station, which is adjacent to a cozy hotel, the **Forsthaus Graseck** (© **08821/5-40-06**). You might want to get a meal or drink at the Forsthaus first. Afterward, descend on foot along narrow paths by the sides of the stream, as it cascades downhill. The path crosses the gorge and returns you to the point where you entered. Many readers have found this one of their most memorable adventures in Bavaria. The experience of walking along a rocky ledge just above a rushing river and behind small waterfalls while looking up at 360m (1,200 ft.) of rocky cliffs, is truly awesome (and sometimes wet).

From its departure point to the Forsthaus, the 3-minute cable car ride costs 2.50€ per person each way. For information about the Seilbahn, contact Forsthaus Graseck (© **08821/5-40-06**). The cable car operates at 20-minute intervals between 8am and 8pm.

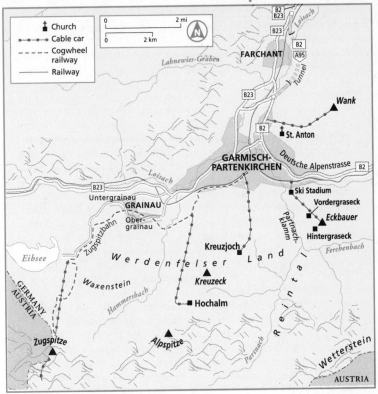

are recommended for first-time alpine hikers. You can even take a chairlift to the top, where in real Bavarian style, the Bergasthof will serve you a glass of buttermilk. In less than an hour you can descend on relatively easy trails through a forest. The cable car stretching from Garmisch to the top of the Eckbauer departs year-round from a facility (the Eckbauerbahn) that sits adjacent to the ski stadium in Garmisch. The round-trip costs 10€ for adults, 6€ for children. For information on the Eckbauerbahn, call ☎ **08821/79-70.**

The **Alpspitz** region is a paradise for hikers and nature lovers in general. From early spring until late fall, its meadows and flowers are a delight and its rocks evoke a prehistoric world. At altitudes of 1,380m to 1,890m (4,600–6,300 ft.), the Alps present themselves in a storybook fantasy. The highest trails are between Osterfelderkopf at 2, 016m (6,720 ft.) and the final point of the Alpspitzbahn, which ends in Austria at 2,786m (9,285 ft.). Those who want to explore the northern foot of the Alpspitz can take the Alpspitz round-trip by going up on the Alpspitz cable car, over the Hochalm, and back down on the Kreuzeck or Hausberg cable car, allowing time in between for hikes lasting from ½ hour to 1½ hours. Snacks are served at the Alpspitz cable car's top station or at the more rustic Hochalm Chalet.

The **Alpspitz cable car** to Osterfelderkopf, at a height of 1,890m (6,300 ft.), makes its 9-minute run at least every hour from 8am to 5pm. The round-trip cost is 20€ for adults and 12€ for children 5 to 14.

The Natural World of the Alps

Many alpine animals such as the lynx, otter, and alpine ibex have all but disappeared from the Bavarian Alps during this century. Other endangered animals include wildcats, susliks, certain nesting birds, toads, and fish.

Efforts to reintroduce species eradicated from their habitats by hunters and farmers have been an unqualified success. Brown bears have been sighted in increased numbers over recent years, along with migrating elk. Wolves, however, have not re-emerged since their final annihilation in the 1950s (attempts in the United States to reintroduce wolves in the American Rocky Mountains have been controversial). Without any check on their numbers by their natural enemies, the deer and stag population has enjoyed such exponential growth that hunting in some regions has become necessary to keep the population in check and preserve the natural balance.

Other species continue to thrive in the alpine environment. Unobtrusive hikers will find the Alps teeming with creatures—the chamois gracefully bounding up alpine heights, golden eagles circling in flight, the griffon vulture floating with its intimidating 9-foot wing spread. A hiker might even be befriended by a marmot or an alpine chough basking in a sunny meadow. (Never threaten the gentle marmot or you might learn why it's nicknamed the whistle pig.) The hill country and lower mountain ranges are often home to badgers, martens, and hares. Hedgehogs are rare, one of the endangered species of rodents.

Ornithologists literally have a field day in the Bavarian Alps. The range of birds is immense. Great white herons guide you on a teasing trail—they pause for respite along the Danube's banks long enough for you to catch up to them, only to depart in flight to another sanctuary 20m (66 ft.) downstream. Storks, marsh warblers, gray geese, spoonbills, and terns can also be sighted. The streak of blue you see may be a blue kingfisher, diving for insects in the rippling streams and rivers. The distinctive red and black wings of the gray alpine wall creeper distinguish it from the gray cliff faces it ascends. The spotted woodpecker,

---

The **Hochalm cable car** from the Hochalm to Osterfelderkopf makes its 4-minute run at least every hour during the operating hours of the Alpspitz cable car. A single ride costs 4€ for adults and 2.50€ for children.

These fares and times of departure can fluctuate from season to season. For the latest details, check with the tourist office, the **Verkehrsamt der Kurverwaltung,** on Dr. Richard-Strauss-Platz (© **08821/18-06**), open Monday to Saturday from 8am to 6pm and on Sunday from 10am to noon only.

Serious hikers can embark on overnight alpine treks from Garmisch-Partenkirchen, following clearly marked footpaths and staying in mountain huts maintained by the German Alpine Association. Some huts are staffed and serve meals. For the truly remote unsupervised huts, you'll be provided with information on how to gain access and your responsibility in leaving them tidy after your visit. For information, inquire at the local tourist office or write to the

goldfinch, redstart, thrush, and bluelit barter sing all winter, but the finch, lark, and song thrush save their voices for spring. Only keen eyes will spot falcons, buzzards, and other birds of prey. Don't forget to watch for nocturnal birds like the tawny owl if you're hiking at night.

Of course, if you spend the entire time with your head in the clouds, you'll miss what's underfoot. Edelweiss are the harbingers of spring. They blossom ahead of most wildflowers, often cropping up amid a blanket of snow, enjoying a short and fragile life. The season for mountain wildflowers varies depending on spring temperatures and snowpack. Most wildflowers blossom by the end of July or early August. Many are protected; it is against the law to pick them or take the plants. More than 40,000 plant species are threatened by extinction worldwide, and the alpine species are no exception. In any case, the snowdrop, the pink meadow saffron, and the gorgeous colors of the mountain rose and gentian are finest in their natural setting in flowering alpine meadows. You can, however, pick the bluebells, pinks, cornflowers, buttercups, daisies, and primroses that blossom in abundance.

You might even find a snack along your trail—wild raspberries, strawberries, blueberries, blackberries, cranberries, flap mushrooms, chanterelles, and parasol mushrooms are often found. However, edible varieties can be easily confused with inedible or poisonous varieties, so know what you're picking and be careful. Autumn in the mountains brings an array of colors and splendor with the turning of the leaves. Those interested in finding out more about the flora of Bavaria can visit an alpine garden or an instructional guided path.

An ongoing effort is being made to conserve the area's valuable biotopes: high-altitude forests, water marshes, and the specialized plant life of steep cliffs and mountain banks. Nature reserves buffer the detrimental impact of agriculture and forestry, and outside their domains, farmland has been reallocated to include low-yield cultivation and extended pastures. But it's also important that hikers be sensitive to their ecological impact as they enjoy nature in the Alps.

government-subsidized **German Alpine Association** (Deutscher Alpenverein/DAV), Von-Kaahr-Strasse 2-4, 80997 München (© **089/14-00-30**). At the same address and phone number, you'll also be routed to staff members of a privately owned tour operator, the **Summit Club,** an outfit devoted to the organization of high-altitude expeditions throughout Europe and the world.

9 Oberammergau ⊛

95km (59 miles) SW of Munich, 19km (12 miles) N of Garmisch-Partenkirchen

In this alpine village, the world-famous Passion Play is generally performed every 10 years. It's the world's longest-running show (in more ways than one—it lasts about 8 hr.). It began in 1634 when the town's citizens took a vow to present the play in gratitude for being spared from the devastating plague of 1633. The actors in the play are still the townspeople of Oberammergau. For the most recent presentation in the summer of the year 2000, a professional director and producer were used for the first time.

Oberammergau stands in a wide valley surrounded by forests and mountains, sunny slopes, and green meadows. It has long been known for the skill of its woodcarvers. Here in this village right under the Kofel peak, farms are still intact, as well as first-class hotels, cozy inns, and family boarding houses.

Numerous hiking trails lead through the mountains around Oberammergau to hikers' inns such as the Kolbenalm and the Romanshohe. You can, however, simply go up to the mountaintops on the Laber cable railway or the Kolben chairlift. Oberammergau also offers opportunities for tennis buffs, minigolf players, cyclists, swimmers, hang-gliding enthusiasts, and canoeists. The recreation center, **Wellenberg,** with its large alpine swimming complex with open-air pools, hot water and fountains, sauna, solarium, and restaurant; is one of the most beautiful recreation centers in the Alps. The Ammer Valley, with Oberammergau in the (almost) center, is a treasure trove to explorers, who use it as a base for visiting Linderhof Castle, the Benedictine monastery at Ettal, or the fairy-tale Neuschwanstein and Hohenschwangau castles (see section 11, "Neuschwanstein & Hohenschwangau," later in this chapter).

ESSENTIALS
GETTING THERE
BY TRAIN   The Oberammergau Bahnhof is on the Murnau-Bad Kohlgrum-Oberammergau rail line, with frequent connections in all directions. Through Murnau all major German cities can be reached. Daily trains arrive from Munich (trip time: 2 hr.) and from Frankfurt (trip time: 7 hr.). For rail information and schedules, call © **01805/99-66-33.**

BY BUS   Regional bus service to nearby towns is offered by **RVO Regionalverkehr Oberbayern** in Garmisch-Partenkirchen (© **08821/94-82-74**). An unnumbered bus goes back and forth between Oberammergau and Garmisch-Partenkirchen.

BY CAR   Oberammergau is 1½ hours from Munich and 5½ hours from Frankfurt. Take the A95 Munich–Garmisch–Partenkirchen Autobahn and exit at Eschenlohe.

VISITOR INFORMATION
For tourist information, contact the **Verkehrsbüro,** Eugen-Papst-Strasse 9A (© **08822/9-23-10**), open Monday to Friday from 8:30am to 6pm and Saturday from 8:30am to noon.

EXPLORING THE TOWN
Oberammergau has much to offer besides the play. Consider taking an excursion to either the **Berg Laber (Mt. Laber),** which rises to the east of the town, or **Berg Kolber (Mt. Kolber),** to the west. Berg Laber, which is slightly more dramatic, is accessible year-round via a cable-gondola (© **08822/47-70**) that operates from 9am to 11:30am and from 1 to either 4:30 or 5pm. The 10-minute ascent costs 11€ per person. The top of Berg Kolber is accessible via a two-passenger chairlift (© **08822/47-60**) that operates year-round from 9 to 4:30 or 4:45pm. The cost is 5€ round-trip.

If you visit Oberammergau in an "off" year, you can still visit the **Passionspielhaus,** Passionmiese (© **08822/3-22-78**), the modern theater at the edge of town where the Passion Play is performed. The roofed auditorium holds 4,700 spectators, and the open-air stage is a wonder of engineering, with a curtained center stage flanked by gates opening onto the so-called streets of Jerusalem. While today's theater and production methods are contemporary, the spirit of the play is still marked by medieval tradition. The play is divided into episodes, each introduced by an Old Testament tableau connecting predictions of the great prophets to incidents of Jesus's suffering. The entire community is involved—those without speaking parts are included in the crowd scenes. The impressive auditorium is open daily from 9:30am to noon and 1 to 4pm; admission is 2.50€ for adults and 1.50€ for children and students.

Aside from the actors, Oberammergau's most respected citizens include another unusual group, the woodcarvers, many of whom have been trained in the village woodcarver's school. In the **Pilatushaus,** Ludwigthomstrasse (℡ **08822/16-82**), you can watch local artists at work, including woodcarvers, painters, sculptors, and potters. Hours are Tuesday to Friday from 1:30 to 6pm. You'll see many examples of these art forms throughout the town, on the painted cottages and inns and in the churchyard. Also, when strolling through the village, watch for the houses with frescoes by Franz Zwink (18th c.), named after fairy-tale characters, such as "Hansel and Gretel House" and the "Little Red Riding Hood House."

Heimatmuseum, Dorfstrasse (℡ **08822/9-41-36**), has a notable collection of Christmas crèches, all hand-carved and hand-painted, from the 18th to the 20th century. It's open May 15 to October 15, Tuesday to Saturday from 2 to 6pm; off-season, only on Saturday from 2 to 6pm. Admission is 2€ for adults and 1€ for children and students.

SHOPPING FOR WOODCARVINGS

Oberammergau's woodcarvings are among the most sought-after in the Germanic world, and many an example has graced the mantelpieces and shelves of homes around the globe. Most subjects are religious, deriving directly from 14th-century originals; however, to cater to the demands of modern visitors, there's been an increased emphasis lately on secular subjects, such as drinking or hunting scenes. Competition is fierce for sales of these woodcarvings, many of which are made in hamlets and farmhouses throughout the region. Know before you buy that even some of the most expensive "handmade" pieces might have been roughed in by machine prior to being finished off by hand.

The **Holzschittschule (Woodcarving School)** has conditions of study that might remind you of the severity of the medieval guilds. Students who labor over a particular sculpture are required to turn it in to the school, where it's either placed on permanent exhibition or sold during the school's once-a-year sell-off, usually over a 2-day period in July.

Josef Albl, Devrientweg 1 (℡ **08822/64-33**), a taciturn but prestigious woodcarver, specializes in bas-reliefs, some of which are complicated and highly detailed. His subjects are both religious and secular, including hunting scenes. Some of the simple pieces sell for as little as 5€, but commissioned pieces can stretch into the tens of thousands of dollars.

Tony Baur, Dorfstrasse 27 (℡ **08822/8-21**), has the most sophisticated inventory of woodcarvings. The shop employs a small cadre of carvers who usually work from their homes to create works inspired by medieval originals. The outgoing and personable sales staff is quick to admit that the forms of many of the pieces are roughed in by machine, but most of the intricate work is completed by hand. Pieces are crafted from maple, pine, or linden (basswood). Prices start at 10€ and go up to 5,100€. Carvings are in their natural grain, stained, or poly-chromed (some of the most charming), and in some instances, partially gilded.

Peter Zwink, Schnitzlergasse 4 ((C) **08822/8-57**), is the place to go for clocks. If you have your heart set on buying a cuckoo clock, you'll probably find one to your liking here, even though, as the staff will point out, the cuckoo clock belongs to the Schwarzwald region. The more simply-carved, handmade clocks are battery-run and cost 75€. More sophisticated clocks with mechanical movement and sound start at 310€. Look for mantel clocks and floor clocks carved in baroque designs. Some need to be wound only once a year, a tradition that some families carry out as part of their New Year's Day rituals.

NEARBY ATTRACTIONS
SCHLOSS LINDERHOF ★★

Until the late 19th century, a modest hunting lodge stood on a large piece of land, 13km (8 miles) west of the village, owned by the Bavarian royal family. In 1869, "Mad Ludwig" struck again, this time creating a French rococo palace in the Ammergau Mountains. Unlike Ludwig's palace at Chiemsee, Schloss Linderhof was not meant to copy any other structure. And unlike his castle at Neuschwanstein, its concentration of fanciful projects and designs was not limited to the palace interior. In fact, the gardens and smaller buildings at Linderhof are, if anything, more elaborate than the two-story main structure. It is his most successful venture, and the only one that was completed.

The most interesting palace rooms are on the second floor, where ceilings are much higher because of the unusual roof plan. Ascending the winged staircase of Carrara marble, you'll find yourself at the music room, known as the West Gobelin (tapestry) Room, with carved and gilded paneling and richly-colored tapestries. This leads directly into the Hall of Mirrors. The mirrors are set in white and gold panels, decorated with gilded woodcarvings. The ceiling of this room is festooned with frescoes depicting mythological scenes, including *The Birth of Venus* and *The Judgment of Paris.*

The king's bedchamber is the largest room in the palace and is placed in the back, overlooking the Fountain of Neptune and the cascades in the gardens. In the tradition of Louis XIV, who often received visitors in his bedchamber, the king's bed is closed off by a carved and gilded balustrade.

In the popular style of the previous century, Ludwig laid out the gardens in formal parterres with geometric shapes, baroque sculptures, and elegant fountains. The front of the palace opens onto a large pool with a piece of gilded statuary in its center, from which a jet of water sprays 32m (105 ft.) into the air.

The park also contains several other small but exotic buildings, including the Moorish Kiosk, where Ludwig often spent hours smoking chibouk and dreaming of himself as an oriental prince. The magic grotto is unique, built of artificial rock, with stalagmites and stalactites dividing the cavelike room into three chambers. One wall of the grotto is painted with a scene of the Venus Mountain from *Tannhäuser.* The main chamber is occupied by an artificial lake illuminated from below; in Ludwig's time it had an artificial current produced by 24 dynamo engines. A shell-shaped boat, completely gilded, is tied to a platform called the Lorelei Rock.

The fantasy and grandeur of Schloss Linderhof, D-82488 Ettal-Linderhof ((C) **08822/35-12**), is open to the public throughout the year and makes a day trip from Munich, as well as from Oberammergau. It's open April to September daily from 9am to 6pm; from October to March, the grotto and Moorish Kiosk are closed, but the castle is open daily from 10am to 4pm. Admission is 6€ for adults, 5€ for students 16 to 24, and free for children 15 and under.

Buses run between Oberammergau and Schloss Linderhof seven times per day beginning at 9am; the last bus leaves Linderhof at 5:35pm. A round-trip passage costs 5€.

KLOSTER ETTAL ⭐

In a lovely valley sheltered by the steep hills of the Ammergau, Kloster Ettal, on Kaiser-Ludwig-Platz at Ettal (© 08822/7-40), was founded by Ludwig the Bavarian in 1330. Monks, knights, and their ladies shared the honor of guarding the statue of the Virgin, attributed to Giovanni Pisano. In the 18th century, the golden age of the abbey, there were about 70,000 pilgrims every year. The Minster of Our Lady in Ettal is one of the finest examples of Bavarian rococo architecture in existence. Around the polygonal core of the church is a two-story gallery. An impressive baroque facade was built from a plan based on the designs of Enrico Zuccali. Inside, visitors stand under a vast dome to admire the fresco painted by John Jacob Zeiller in the summers of 1751 and 1752.

The abbey is 3km (2 miles) south of Oberammergau, along the road to Garmisch-Partenkirchen and Oberammergau. Admission is free, and it's open daily from 8am to 6:30pm (closes at 4:30pm in winter). Buses from Oberammergau leave from the Rathaus and the Bahnhof once an hour during the day, with round-trip passage costing 2.50€. Call © 08821/94-82-74 for information.

WHERE TO STAY & DINE
MODERATE

Hotel Restaurant Böld ⭐   This inn has steadily improved in quality and is now among the town's premier choices. Only a stone's throw from the river, the well-designed chalet hotel offers comfortable public rooms in its central building and well-furnished guest rooms in its contemporary annex. All rooms have well-kept bathrooms with showers and private baths. Most units open onto balconies. The restaurant features both international and regional cuisine. In the bar, you'll find a tranquil atmosphere, plus attentive service. Raimund Hans and family are the hosts.

König-Ludwig-Strasse 10, 82487 Oberammergau. © 08822/91-20. Fax 08822/7102. www.hotel-boeld.de. 57 units. 85€–125€ double, 156€–180€ suite. Rates include continental breakfast. AE, DC, MC, V. Free outdoor parking; 5€ in the garage. **Amenities:** Restaurant; bar; whirlpool; sauna; room service; solarium. *In room:* TV, minibar, hair dryer.

Parkhotel Sonnenhof ⭐   Short on charm and alpine rusticity, this modern hotel still has a lot going for it. First, it's far enough away from the crowds that descend in summer—often in tour buses. It offers peace and tranquility but is within walking distance of the center. The hotel overlooks the Ammer River and a beautiful *Pfarrkirche* (parish church). Every room has a balcony with an alpine vista, often of Oberammergau's mountain, the Kobel. Although devoid of old-fashioned charm, guest rooms are well maintained and filled with first-class comforts. All units are equipped with well-kept bathrooms containing a shower-tub combination. The hotel has more luxuries than most in the area—an indoor pool, sauna, and such extra features as a bowling alley. It's also a family favorite, with a children's playroom. Two restaurants serve many international dishes, although the Bavarian specialties are what are really good here.

König-Ludwig-Strasse 12, 82487 Oberammergau. ✆ **08822/9130.** Fax 08822/3047. www.sonnenhof-oberammergau.de. 65 units. 100€–115€ double; 115€–130€ suite. Rates include buffet breakfast. AE, DC, MC, V. **Amenities:** 2 restaurants; bar; pool; sauna; bowling alley; room service; babysitting. *In room:* TV, hair dryer.

INEXPENSIVE

Alte Post ⭐ A provincial inn in the village center, Alte Post is built in chalet style—wide overhanging roof, green-shuttered windows painted with decorative trim, a large crucifix on the facade, and tables along a sidewalk under a long awning. It's the village social hub. The interior has storybook charm, with a ceiling-high green ceramic stove, alpine chairs, and shelves of pewter plates. The rustic guest rooms have wood-beamed ceilings and wide beds with giant posts; most open onto views. All units have neatly kept bathrooms with shower units. The main dining room is equally rustic (with a collection of hunting memorabilia) and serves excellent Bavarian dishes.

Dorfstrasse 19, 82487 Oberammergau. ✆ **08822/91-00.** Fax 08822/91-01-00. www.altepost.ogau.de. 32 units. 62€–81€ double. Rates include continental breakfast. AE, DC, MC, V. Closed Oct 25–Dec 19. Free parking. **Amenities:** Restaurant; lounge; room service. *In room:* TV.

Hotel Café-Restaurant Friedenshöhe (Value) The hotel name means "peaceful height." Built in 1906, the villa enjoys a beautiful location and is one of the better inns in town, although not in the same league as Böld or Parkhotel Sonnenhof. It was reconstructed into a pension and cafe in 1913. It hosted Thomas Mann, who stayed and wrote here. The guest rooms, furnished in tasteful modern style, are well maintained. Bathrooms are a bit small but do contain showers. The hotel offers a choice of four dining rooms, including an indoor terrace with a panoramic view and an outdoor terrace. The Bavarian and international cuisine is known for its taste and the quality of its ingredients.

König-Ludwig-Strasse 31, 82487 Oberammergau. ✆ **08822/35-98.** Fax 08822/43-45. www.friedenshoehe.de. 17 units. 62€–92€ double. Rates include buffet breakfast. AE, DC, MC, V. Closed Nov–Dec 14. **Amenities:** Restaurant; 4 dining rooms; lounge. *In room:* TV.

Hotel der Schilcherhof An enlarged chalet with surrounding gardens, the Schilcherhof has a modern wing with good-value rooms. Each unit is well kept and comes with a shower-only bathroom. In summer, the terrace overflows with beer and festivities. Five minutes away lies the Passion Play theater; also nearby is the Ammer River. In summer, you need to reserve well in advance to get a room. Although the house is built in the old style, with wooden front balconies and tiers of flower boxes, it has a fresh look.

Bahnhofstrasse 17, 82487 Oberammergau. ✆ **08822/47-40.** Fax 08822/37-93. 26 units. 55€–85€ double. Rates include buffet breakfast. AE, V. Closed Nov 20–Christmas. Free parking. **Amenities:** Breakfast room; lounge; room service. *In room:* No phone.

Schlosshotel Linderhof ⭐ (Finds) This hotel originally was constructed about a century ago as one of the outbuildings of the famous palace. Designed with gables, shutters, and half-timbering in the style of a Bavarian chalet, it has been tastefully enlarged and renovated by members of the Maier family. Bedrooms are dignified and high-ceilinged, tasteful and comfortable, in a style that suggests 19th-century gentility. Each unit comes with a well-kept bathroom with a shower.

Much of its business derives from its cozy restaurant; which extends onto a stone terrace accented with parasols and potted flowers. An array of fixed-price menus focuses on such hearty regional food as pork schnitzels with mixed salad and cream of tomato soup.

Linderhof 14 (near the palace), 82488 Ettal. ☏ **08822/7-90.** Fax 08822/43-47. www.schlosshotel-linderhof. com. 29 units. 86€–98€ double. Rates include breakfast. AE, DC, MC, V. **Amenities:** Restaurant; lounge; room service. *In room:* TV, minibar, hair dryer.

Turmwirt   A cozy Bavarian-style hotel, the Turmwirt offers rooms with well-kept bathrooms containing showers and private balconies opening onto mountain views. It's an intricately painted, green-shuttered country house with a well-maintained homelike interior. A lodging house stood on this spot in 1742, and the present building was constructed in 1889. It has been altered and renovated many times over the past few decades. The owners are three generations of the Glas family, who often present Bavarian folk evenings. The town center is an invigorating 5-minute walk from the hotel.

Ettalerstrasse 2 (5 min. from the town center), 82487 Oberammergau. ☏ **08822/9-26-00.** Fax 08822/14-37. www.minotel.com. 22 units. 112€ double. Rates include buffet breakfast. AE, DC, MC, V. Free parking. **Amenities:** Breakfast room; lounge; room service. *In room:* TV, minibar.

Wolf Restaurant-Hotel *(Value)*   An overgrown Bavarian chalet, the Wolf Restaurant-Hotel is at the heart of village life. Its facade is much like others in the area: an encircling balcony, heavy timbering, and window boxes spilling cascades of red and pink geraniums. Inside it retains some local flavor, although certain concessions have been made: an elevator, conservative room furnishings, a dining hall with zigzag paneled ceiling, and spoke chairs. Five singles are available. All units have well-maintained tiled bathrooms with showers.

The Hafner Stub'n is a rustic place for beer drinking as well as light meals. Dining here can be both economical and gracious. There's always a freshly made soup of the day, followed by a generous main course, such as Wiener schnitzel or roast pork with dumplings and cabbage.

Dorfstrasse 1, 82487 Oberammergau. ☏ **08822/9-23-30.** Fax 08822/9-23-333. 32 units. 66€–100€ double. Rates include buffet breakfast. AE, DC, MC, V. **Amenities:** Restaurant; lounge; pool; sauna; room service; solarium. *In room:* TV.

10 Mittenwald ★

106km (66 miles) S of Munich, 18km (11 miles) SE of Garmisch-Partenkirchen, 37km (23 miles) NW of Innsbruck

The year-round resort of Mittenwald has often been called the most beautiful town in the Bavarian Alps. In 1996, it underwent a face-lift, a restoration that has made it more attractive than ever. The village is noteworthy for its photogenic painted houses with their intricate carved gables—even the baroque church tower is covered with frescoes. It's also noted as a center for the highly specialized craft of violin making. On the square stands a monument to Matthias Klotz, who introduced violin making to Mittenwald in 1684.

In the countryside around Mittenwald, the Wetterstein and Karwendel ranges offer constantly changing scenic vistas. In the winter, the town is a skiing center, and in the summer, an even more popular range of outdoor activities invites the visitor.

ESSENTIALS
GETTING THERE
BY TRAIN   Mittenwald is reached by almost hourly train service, since it lies on the express rail line between Munich and Innsbruck (Austria). From Munich, trip time is 1½ to 2 hours, depending on the train. It is about 5 to 6 hours by train from Frankfurt. Call ☏ **01805/99-66-33** for information.

BY BUS   Regional bus service from Garmisch-Partenkirchen and nearby towns is frequently provided by **RVO Regionalverkehr Oberbayern at Garmisch.** Call ✆ **08821/94-82-74** for schedules and information.

BY CAR   Access by car is via the A95 Autobahn from Munich.

VISITOR INFORMATION

For tourist information, contact the **Kurverwaltung und Verkehrsamt,** Dammkarstrasse 3 (✆ **08823/3-39-81**), open Monday to Friday from 8am to noon and 1 to 5pm and Saturday from 10am to noon.

Horse and carriage trips or coach tours from Mittenwald to nearby villages are available; contact the tourist office for information.

SIGHTS & ACTIVITIES

Some 129km (80 miles) of hiking paths wind up and down the mountains around the village. Chairlifts make the mountain hiking trails readily accessible. Of course, where there are trails, there is mountain biking. A cycling map is available through Mittenwald's administration office. Besides hiking or biking through the hills on your own, you can take part in organized mountain-climbing expeditions. You can also take a cable car to the top of the Karwendel mountain for superb views.

Swimming in the brisk waters of the Lautersee and Ferchensee is a good way to cool off on a hot summer's day. However, for those who find the waters too cold, Mittenwald has a heated adventure pool.

Mittenwald also has good spa facilities, with large gardens landscaped with tree-lined streams and small pools. Concerts during the summer are held in the music pavilion.

Geigenbau-und Heimatmuseum   This fascinating museum traces the history of violin making in Mittenwald and the development of the violin and other stringed instruments, from their invention through various stages of evolution. There is also a violin workshop.

Ballenhausgasse 3. ✆ **08823/25-11**. Admission 2.50€ adults, 1.50€ children. Tues–Fri 10am–1pm and 3–6pm; Sat–Sun 10am–1pm. Closed Nov 1–Dec 20.

SHOPPING   Mittenwald is internationally known for its classical stringed instruments, which have supplied professional musicians for centuries. Prices may be steep for the amateur violinist, but if you are interested in browsing, visit **Geigenbau Leonhardt,** Mühlenweg 53A (✆ **08823/80-10**), for an educational and interesting experience. If you're ambitious to traipse about in a dirndl, embroidered blouse, or lederhosen, head for **Trachtenstubön,** Obermarkt 35 (✆ **08823/85-55**).

WHERE TO STAY
MODERATE

Hotel Post ★★   The Post is the most seasoned and established chalet hotel in the village—it's been here since 1632, when it was a stop for stagecoaches carrying mail and passengers across the Alps. Although it doesn't offer the tranquility or the scenic views of other Mittenwald hotels, it nevertheless is the city's finest address. Guest rooms are furnished in a comfortable although standard way. All units contain neatly kept bathrooms with shower-tub combinations. A delightful breakfast is served on the sun terrace, with a view of the Alps. On a cool day, take time out to enjoy a beer in the snug lounge/bar with an open fireplace. For a night of hearty Bavarian specialties, head for the wine tavern (Poststüberl), which is full of alpine charm from its deer antler collection, low beams, and wood paneling.

Obermarkt 9, 82481 Mittenwald. © 08823/10-94. Fax 08823/10-96. www.posthotel-mittenwald.de. 80 units. 95€–135€ double; 140€–150€ suite. Rates include buffet breakfast. No credit cards. Parking free outside or 5€ inside. **Amenities:** Restaurant; bar; lounge; pool; sauna; room service; massage. *In room:* TV, minibar, hair dryer, safe.

Rieger Hotel   The Rieger is attractive, whether snow is piled up outside or the window boxes are cascading with petunias. After the Post, the Rieger ranks number two in town. The living room has a beamed ceiling, wide arches, and a three-sided open fireplace. Guest rooms are pleasant and comfortable, with a well-kept bathroom with shower and a certain amount of Bavarian charm.

Dekan-Karl-Platz 28, D-82481 Mittenwald. © 08823/9-25-00. Fax 08823/925-0250. 45 units. 80€–120€ double. Rates include buffet breakfast. Half board 15€ extra. AE, DC, MC, V. Parking 5€. Closed Oct 21–Dec 19. **Amenities:** Breakfast room; lounge; pool; sauna; massage. *In room:* TV, hair dryer.

INEXPENSIVE

Alpenrose ⟨★⟩   A particularly inviting place to stay is this inn in the village center at the foot of a rugged mountain. The facade is covered with decorative designs; window boxes hold flowering vines. The inn's basic structure is 14th century—it was once part of a monastery—although additions and improvements have been made over the years. The present inn is comfortable, with suitable plumbing facilities. The hotel's rooms are divided between the Alpenrose and its annex, the Bichlerhof; they're modernized but often with Bavarian traditional styling. All units have small, well-kept bathrooms with shower units.

The tavern room, overlooking the street, has many ingratiating features, including coved ceilings (one decoratively painted), handmade chairs, flagstone floors, and a square tile stove in the center. In the Josefikeller, beer is served in giant steins, and musicians entertain guests in the evening. The dining room provides excellent meals, including Bavarian specialties.

Obermarkt 1, 82481 Mittenwald. © 08823/9-27-00. Fax 08823/3720. 18 units. 66€–95€ double; 100€ suite. Rates include buffet breakfast. AE, DC, DISC, MC, V. Free parking. **Amenities:** Restaurant; bar; lounge; room service; laundry. *In room:* TV, minibar, hair dryer.

Gästhaus Franziska   When Olaf Grothe built this guesthouse, he named it after the most important person in his life—his wife, Franziska. Both have labored to make it the most personalized guesthouse in town, with sympathetic attention given to their guests' needs. Rooms and suites are furnished tastefully in traditional Bavarian style. All have bathrooms with shower-tub combinations and balconies opening onto mountain views. Breakfast is the only meal served, but there are plenty of restaurants nearby. Note that it's extremely difficult to obtain bookings between June 20 and October 2.

Innsbruckerstrasse 24, D-82481 Mittenwald. © 08823/9-20-30. Fax 08823/3893. www.franziska-tourismus.de/. 18 units. 62€–78€ double; 82€–92€ suite. Rates include buffet breakfast. AE, V. Closed Nov 11–Dec 13. Free parking. **Amenities:** Breakfast room; lounge; room service. *In room:* minibar, hair dryer.

Gästhaus Sonnenbichl   One of the more modest hostelries in town, this inn nevertheless offers good value and comfort. Lodged in a hillside, the chalet has a view of the village set against a backdrop of the Alps. The rooms have been freshly decorated in vivid natural colors. The guesthouse is often completely booked, so reserving well in advance is a good idea. All rooms have well-kept bathrooms with shower-tub combinations. Breakfast is the only meal served.

Klausnerweg 32, 82481 Mittenwald. (C) **08823/9-22-30.** Fax 08823/58-14. www.sonnenbichl.de. 20 units. 62€–92€ double. Rates include buffet breakfast. No credit cards. Closed Nov–Dec 15. **Amenities:** Breakfast room; lounge; room service. *In room:* TV, minibar, hair dryer.

WHERE TO DINE

Restaurant Arnspitze ✿ BAVARIAN   Housed in a modern chalet hotel on the outskirts of town, the Restaurant Arnspitze is the finest dining room in Mittenwald. Although you can also eat well at the inns previously recommended, over the years we've found the menus at this place more enticing. The restaurant is decorated in the old style; the cuisine is solid, satisfying, and wholesome. You might order sole with homemade noodles or veal steak in a creamy smooth sauce, then finish with one of the freshly made desserts. There's an excellent fixed-price lunch.

Innsbruckerstrasse 68. (C) **08823/24-25.** Main courses 12€–21€. AE. Wed 6–9pm, Thurs–Mon noon–2pm and 6–9pm.

11 Neuschwanstein & Hohenschwangau

The 19th century saw a great classical revival in Germany, especially in Bavaria, mainly because of the enthusiasm of Bavarian kings for ancient art forms. Beginning with Ludwig I (1786–1868), who was responsible for many Greek revival buildings in Munich, the royal house ran the gamut of ancient architecture in just three short decades. Its culmination was the remarkable flights of fancy of Ludwig II (see "The Fairy-Tale King" box on p. 186). In spite of his rather lonely life and controversial alliances, both personal and political, he was a great patron of the arts.

In 1868, after a visit to the great castle of Wartburg, Ludwig wrote to his good friend, composer Richard Wagner: "I have the intention to rebuild the ancient castle ruins of Hohenschwangau in the true style of the ancient German knight's castle." The following year, construction began on the first of a series of fantastic edifices, a series that stopped only with Ludwig's untimely death in 1886 after he was deposed because of alleged insanity.

ESSENTIALS
GETTING THERE
BY CAR   From Munich, motorists can take the E533 toward Garmisch-Partenkirchen. At the end of the Autobahn, the road becomes Route 95 for its final run into Garmisch. From Garmisch, continue west on Route 187 to the junction with Route 314, at which point you cut north to Füssen, where the castles are signposted.

BY TOUR BUS   Panorama Tours offers an 8½-hour day tour from Munich to Neuschwanstein and Hohenschwangau that also includes Linderhof and a brief stopover in Oberammergau. For information see "Sightseeing Tours," in chapter 6.

VISITOR INFORMATION
Information about the castles and the region in general is available at the **Kurverwaltung,** Rathaus, Münchnerstrasse 2 in Schwangau ((C) **08362/8-19-80**). It's open Monday to Friday from 8am to 5pm.

VISITING THE ROYAL CASTLES
The name "Royal Castles" is limited to the castles of Hohenschwangau (built by Ludwig's father, Maximilian II) and Ludwig's Neuschwanstein. Ludwig's other

A Rococo Masterpiece

Füssen is not of major interest to tourists, except that it makes a good base for exploring Neuschwanstein, Hohenschwangau, the Wieskirche, and Lechfall, or Lech Falls, where the River Lech cascades down from an alpine ledge into a rock-studded gorge right near the border with Austria. (A footbridge spans the falls, giving you a dramatic up-close view.) From Füssen, you can take a fascinating side trip to the **Wieskirche** ★★, (✆ **08862/5-01**) one of the most extravagant and flamboyant rococo buildings in the world, a masterpiece by Dominikus Zimmermann. Wieskirche is a noted pilgrimage church, drawing visitors from all over the globe. It's located on the slopes of the Ammergau Alps between Ammer and Lech, in an alpine meadow just off Route 17 near Steingaden. Inquire at the tourist office for a map and the exact location before setting out. Also, confirm that the church will be open at the time of your visit.

With the help of his brother, Johann Baptist, Zimmermann worked on the building from 1746 to 1754. It's amazing that such rich decoration could be crowded into so small a place. The great Zimmermann was so enchanted with his creation that he constructed a small home in the vicinity and spent the last decade of his life here. A bus heading for the church leaves Füssen Monday to Saturday at 11:05am and on Sunday at 1:05pm. You can return on the 3:50pm bus from the church. The trip takes 1 hour and costs 5€ round-trip.

extravagant castles, Neues Schloss (Herrenchiemsee) and Schloss Linderhof (near Oberammergau), are described in sections 5 and 9, earlier in this chapter.

There are often very long lines in summer to these popular attractions, especially in August. With 25,000 people a day visiting, the wait in peak summer months can range from 4 to 5 hours for a 20-minute tour. There is no way of beating the system other than arriving very early in the morning to avoid the long lines that have already begun to form by 8am.

NEUSCHWANSTEIN ★★★

This is the fairy-tale castle of Ludwig II. Construction went on for 17 years until the king's death, when all work stopped, leaving a part of the interior incomplete. Ludwig lived in the rooms on and off for a total of only about 6 months from 1884 to 1886.

The doorway off the left side of the vestibule leads to the king's apartments. The study, like most of the rooms, is decorated with wall paintings showing scenes from the Nordic legends (which also inspired Wagner's operas). The theme of the study is the *Tannhäuser* saga, painted by J. Aigner. The only fabric in the room is hand-embroidered silk, used in curtains and chair coverings, all designed with the gold and silver Bavarian coat-of-arms.

From the vestibule, you enter the throne room ★★ through the doorway at the opposite end. This hall, designed in Byzantine style by J. Hofmann, was never completed. The floor is a mosaic design depicting the animals of the world. The columns in the main hall are the deep copper red of porphyry. The circular apse where the king's throne was to have stood is reached by a stairway of white

Carrera marble. The walls and ceiling are decorated with paintings of Christ in heaven looking down on the 12 apostles and 6 canonized kings of Europe.

The king's bedroom ✿ is the most richly carved in the entire castle—it took 4½ years to complete this room alone. Aside from the mural depicting the legend of Tristan and Isolde, the walls are decorated with panels carved to look like Gothic windows. In the center is a large wooden pillar completely encircled with gilded brass sconces. The ornate bed is on a raised platform with an elaborately carved canopy. Through the balcony window you can see the 150-foot waterfall in the Pollat Gorge, with the mountains in the distance.

The fourth floor of the castle is almost entirely given over to the Singer's Hall, the pride of Ludwig II and all of Bavaria. Modeled after the hall at Wartburg, where the legendary song contest of Tannhäuser supposedly took place, this hall is decorated with marble columns and elaborately painted designs interspersed with frescoes depicting the life of Parsifal.

The castle, at Neuschwansteinstrasse 20 (⌀ **08362/8-10-35**), can be visited year-round, and in September, visitors have the additional treat of concerts in the Singer's Hall. For information and reservations, contact the tourist office, **Verkehrsamt,** Schwangau, at the Rathaus (⌀ **08362/8-19-80**). The castle is open (guided tours only) April to September, Friday to Wednesday from 9am to 6pm and Thursday from 10am to 8pm; off-season, daily from 10am to 4pm. Admission is 6€ for adults, 4.50€ for students and seniors over 65, and free for children 15 and under.

Reaching Neuschwanstein involves a steep half-mile climb from the parking lot for Hohenschwangau Castle (see below). This is about a 25-minute walk for the energetic, an eternity for anybody else. To cut down the climb, you can take a bus to Marienbrücke, a bridge that crosses over the Pollat Gorge at a height of 305 feet. From that vantage point you can, like Ludwig, stop and meditate on the glories of the castle and its panoramic surroundings. If you want to photograph the castle, don't wait until you reach the top where you'll be too close to the edifice to photograph it properly. It costs 2€ for the bus ride up to the bridge or 1.50€ if you'd like to take the bus back down the hill. Marienbrücke is still not at the castle. From the bridge it's a 10-minute walk to reach Neuschwanstein. This footpath is very steep and not easy to negotiate for anyone who has trouble walking up or down precipitous hills.

The most traditional way to reach Neuschwanstein is by horse-drawn carriage, costing 4.50€ for the ascent, 2.50€ for the descent. Some readers have objected to the rides, though, complaining that too many people are crowded in.

HOHENSCHWANGAU ✿

Not as glamorous nor as spectacular as Neuschwanstein, the neo-Gothic Hohenschwangau Castle, nevertheless, has a much richer history. The original structure dates back to the 12th-century Knights of Schwangau. When the knights faded away, the castle began to do so too, helped along by the Napoleonic Wars. When Ludwig II's father, Crown Prince Maximilian (later Maximilian II), saw the castle in 1832, he purchased it and in 4 years had it completely restored. Ludwig II spent the first 17 years of his life here and later received Richard Wagner in its chambers, although Wagner never visited Neuschwanstein on the hill above. (Many visitors wrongly assume that the king and Wagner had their meetings in the "Fantasy" castle of Neuschwanstein, when in fact they were here in Hohenschwangau.)

The rooms of Hohenschwangau are styled and furnished in a much heavier Gothic mode than those in the castle built by Ludwig. Many are typical of the halls of knights' castles of the Middle Ages in both England and Germany.

Moments The Dream King

In 2000, the **Musical Theatre Neuschwanstein,** a state-of-the-art theater, opened on the shores of the Foegensee, at the foot of famed Neuschwanstein Castle, near Füssen. It launched a five-act spectacular musical production, *Ludwig II,* based on the life of the "fairy-tale" king. To find out what's happening there at the time of your visit, check the Web at **www.ludwigmusical.com.** For tickets and more information, contact Ludwig Musical Project at Maximilianstrasse 52, D-8538 München (**© 89/4-11-89-00**).

There's no doubt that the castle's style greatly influenced young Ludwig and encouraged the fanciful boyhood dreams that formed his later tastes and character. Unlike Neuschwanstein, however, this castle has a comfortable look about it, as if it actually were a home at one time, not just a museum. The small chapel, once a reception hall, still hosts Sunday Mass. The suits of armor and the Gothic arches here set the stage for the rest of the rooms.

Among the most attractive chambers is the Hall of the Swan Knight, named for the wall paintings depicting the saga of Lohengrin—before Wagner and Ludwig II. Note the Gothic grillwork on the ceiling with the open spaces studded with stars.

Hohenschwangau, Alpseestrasse 24 (**© 08362/8-11-27**), is open March 15 to October 15, daily from 8:30am to 5:30pm; October 16 to March 14, daily from 10am to 4pm. Admission is 7€ for adults and 6€ for children 6 to 15; children 5 and under enter free. There are several parking lots nearby where you can leave your car while visiting both castles.

WHERE TO STAY & DINE NEARBY

Hotel Lisl and Jägerhaus   This graciously styled villa, with an annex across the street, was seemingly made to provide views as well as comfort. Both houses sit in a narrow valley, surrounded by their own gardens. Most rooms have a view of at least one of the royal castles. Each has a compact shower-only bathroom. In the main house, two well-styled dining rooms serve good-tasting meals. The restaurant features international as well as local cuisine.

Neuschwansteinstrasse 1–3, 87645 Hohenschwangau. © 08362/88-70. Fax 08362/8-11-07. www.lisl.de. 47 units. 110€–180€ double; 200€–230€ suite. AE, DC, MC, V. Free parking. **Amenities:** 2 dining rooms; lounge; room service. *In room:* TV.

Hotel Müller Hohenschwangau   The location of this hospitable inn, near the foundations of Neuschwanstein Castle, makes it very alluring. The rooms are comfortable and have lots of rustic accessories. Bedrooms are inviting and have a bit of Bavarian charm. All units contain a bathroom with a shower stall. On the premises, you'll find a well-maintained restaurant lined with burnished pinewood and a more formal evening restaurant with views over a verdantly planted sun terrace. Nature lovers especially enjoy hiking the short distance to nearby Hohenschwangau Castle.

Alpseestrasse 16, 87645 Hohenschwangau. © 08362/8-19-90. Fax 08362/819913. www.hotel-mueller.de. 44 units. 120€–155€ double; 170€–215€ suite. Rates include buffet breakfast. AE, DC, MC, V. Closed Jan 1–Feb. Free parking. Füssen bus. **Amenities:** Restaurant; lounge; room service. *In room:* TV.

Appendix A:
Munich in Depth

While you will find reminders of the past all around you in the Altstadt or Old Town of Munich, the city is by no means standing still or living off its past. The city has embarked on a building program that will transform its 20th-century skyline into a 21st-century look with lots of new office and commercial buildings. However, the historic core, which has zoning rules that forbid any building to rise higher than the spires of the city's symbol, the Frauenkirche cathedral, will remain relatively unchanged. The sections below provide some know-before-you-go background before you actually descend on Munich.

1 History 101

THE BRIDGE OVER THE ISAR

Munich is a young city compared to some of its neighbors. It had its origins in 1156 in an unpleasant struggle between two feudal rulers over the right to impose tolls on the traffic moving along the salt road that stretched between the cities of Salzburg, Hallein, Reichenhall, and Augsburg. Up to that time, Bishop Otto von Freising had controlled a very lucrative toll bridge across the Isar River, directly on the salt route.

The ruler of the Bavarian territory, Guelph Heinrich der Löwe (Duke Henry the Lion), was in need of cash. So, with the customary ferocity that had earned him his nickname, he simply burnt down the bishop's bridge and built his own bridge a few miles upstream, pre-empting the profitable tolls. Emperor Frederick Barbarossa was called upon to settle this dispute between his cousin Henry and his uncle, Bishop Otto. However, the bishop's fully justified rage did little to influence the faraway emperor, who was too busy with more important problems to worry about than a minor clash between church and state (Duke Henry represented the state, the bishop the church. The battle over the

Dateline

- 1156 Feudal warlord Henry the Lion demolishes the local bishop's toll-collecting bridge and builds one nearby. The city of Munich is born near the new bridge. The collection of tolls helps Munich grow from the revenues.
- 1158 When the local bishop complains about his loss of toll revenues, Holy Roman Emperor Barbarossa validates Henry's actions, siding with the secular, rather than the ecclesiastical, power. Triumphantly loosened from the economic stranglehold of the Catholic bishops, Munich is officially established as a trade zone and as a city.
- 1173 Fortified behind walls and watchtowers, Munich's population swells to 2,500.
- 1180 Henry the Lion defies the emperor in a commercial squabble and is banished. Freising's bishop, still furious at the loss of his toll revenues, tries to destroy the settlement and redivert toll-paying trade through routes controlled by the bishops.
- 1240 The Wittelsbach dukes extend their influence to Munich.
- 1250–1300 Munich's population increases fourfold and new fortifications are built.

continues

tolls was whether the money would go to the state or to the church). This particular squabble, however, was to have far-reaching consequences.

Henry's new bridge was adjacent to a tiny settlement of Benedictine monks, a small community on the banks of the Isar River that was referred to as *zu den Münichen*—"at the site of the little monks." The name stuck—though it was later shortened to *München,* and the little monk, or *Münichen,* remains the symbol of the city of Munich even today.

Henry the Lion had already had successful experiences in founding trading centers. With this knowledge, he granted Munich the right to mint its own coins and to hold markets, basic tools that any city needed for survival. Tolls from his new bridge, which now funneled the lucrative salt trade across the Isar, went directly into Henry's coffers.

Within a few months, Barbarossa validated the crude but effective actions of his duke, legitimizing the establishment of Munich on June 14, 1158, the date that is commemorated as the official debut of the city. Henry, however, had to accept a price: Barbarossa ordered that a third of all tolls generated by the new bridge be paid to the bishop of Freising, whose bridge Henry had destroyed.

MEDIEVAL PROSPERITY

The first of the city's fortifications, a stone wall studded with watchtowers and five gates, was built in 1173 and enclosed 2,500 people. One of the most important survivals from this period (most of the wall was long ago demolished) is the Marienplatz—then and now the centerpiece of the city and the crossing point of the Salzstrasse (Salt Route), a crossroads that is still marked on the city map today. During its early days, the Marienplatz was simply known as the "Marketplace" or the "Grain Market."

- **1285** A pogrom burns 150 Jews (the elite of the Jewish community) within their synagogue.
- **1300s** Munich's population grows to 10,000, becoming the most-populated (and richest) city of the Wittelsbachs.
- **1314** Duke Ludwig IV, Munich's ruler, is elected head of the Holy Roman Empire. Munich is now the most important city in the German-speaking world.
- **1319** Frederick the Handsome attacks Munich, but the Wittelsbachs prevail, capturing the Habsburg ruler. In retaliation, the Pope excommunicates Munich's ruler, Duke Ludwig IV.
- **1322** Munich prospers through the salt trade and becomes the center of a loose association of German kingdoms.
- **1327** Fire devastates much of Munich's eastern district.
- **1346** Ludwig IV is killed in a bear hunt. The new emperor strips Munich of its honors.
- **1385** Citizens of Munich rebel against the Wittelsbach dynasty and execute a representative of the family. However, their attempt to overthrow the rulers fails.
- **1403** Power reverts back to the Wittelsbachs after their armies lay siege to Munich's walls.
- **1492** A mountain pass is carved through the Alps to expedite trade with Italy.
- **1516** Munich passes Europe's first law governing food and beverages, which set standards for weights, measures, and hygiene.
- **1517** Martin Luther sparks the Protestant Reformation. Munich's leaders order their city to remain Catholic.
- **1560** The Wittelsbach dynasty makes Munich its official seat and launches a massive rebuilding program.
- **1583** Wilhelm IV bans all religion other than Roman Catholicism, making Munich the German-speaking centerpiece of the Counter-Reformation.
- **1608** Non-Catholics are persecuted in Munich.

continues

In 1180, Duke Henry quarreled with Emperor Barbarossa and was banished forever from Munich and the rest of Bavaria. Gleefully, Henry's nemesis, the bishop of Freising, attempted to eradicate the upstart young city and reroute the salt trade back through his stronghold of Ober-föhring. By this time, however, Munich was simply too well established to succumb to his efforts.

ENTER THE WITTELSBACHS

By 1240, a new force had arisen in Munich, the Wittelsbach family. They were part of a new generation of merchant princes, and through a shrewd imposition of military and economic power, their family patriarch, Otto von Wittelsbach, succeeded in having himself designated as the ruler of Bavaria shortly after the banishment of Henry the Lion. Thus began the longest and most conservative reign of any dynasty in Germany. The Wittelsbachs ruled in Munich and the rest of Bavaria until the forces of socialism swept them away during the final days of World War I. Today, they are still viewed by the Bavarians with a kind of nostalgic affection.

Between 1250 and 1300, the population of Munich increased fivefold, the result of migration from the countryside and a period that was relatively free from plagues. Members of at least three religious orders established monasteries, convents, and hospitals within the city walls.

SOCIAL UNREST

As the population grew, the city's encircling fortifications were enlarged to protect new suburbs. Although predominantly Catholic, the city fostered a small population of much-persecuted Jews as well. The worst pogrom against them occurred in 1285, when Munich's Jews were accused of the murder of a small Catholic child, and 150 of them were burned alive inside their synagogue,

- **1618–48** The Thirty Years' War leads to the siege of Munich and devastates the city's economy, as Protestant forces defeat Catholic Habsburgs. Also, a plague claims a third of Munich's population.
- **1643** Wittelsbachs strip Münchners of the right to elect their own mayor.
- **1674** The Residenz catches fire, but resentful Münchners take their sweet time in putting out the flames.
- **1705** Austria invades and occupies Bavaria. Bavarian peasants marching on Munich in protest are massacred.
- **1758** The porcelain factory at Nymphenburg becomes a resounding success.
- **1759** The Academy of Sciences, by acknowledging some of the humanistic tenets then sweeping across Europe, marks the influence of the Enlightenment, thereby weakening the stranglehold of medieval ideas still endorsed by the Catholic church.
- **1771** King Max III Joseph makes some aspects of public education a legal requirement.
- **1777** Max III Joseph dies, ushering in the much-hated regime of Karl Theodor, who tries to trade Bavaria for the Netherlands.
- **1789** The outbreak of the French Revolution causes Munich's rulers to fear for their throne.
- **1799** Armies of Napoléon invade Munich. Napoléon makes Bavaria a kingdom and extends its territory.
- **1807** Maximilian I and Crown Prince Ludwig embark on a building program to beautify the city.
- **1818** Liberal administrative reforms, including more liberal laws about land use and ownership, inheritance rights, taxation, and military service, are put in place.
- **1821** Marienkirche is designed as the city's official cathedral (Dom).
- **1826** Munich gets its own university.
- **1848** Ludwig I's scandalous affair with Lola Montez leads to revolt and the king's voluntary abdication. Maximilian II then ascends the Bavarian throne.
- **1855** Maximilian II erects the Bavarian National Museum.

continues

which was, at the time, just behind the present-day location of the Neues Rathaus (New Town Hall). Two years later, other groups of Jews came to Munich, but ironically, the handicaps the city imposed upon them (exclusion from all trades except moneylending) led to a modest if precarious degree of prosperity. Pogroms were repeated throughout the rest of the Middle Ages, and in 1442, the Jews were banished from Munich altogether.

Just before the dawn of the 13th century, the artisans and merchants of Munich staged a revolt against the Wittelsbach family that revolved around the debased coins that were being issued by the dukes' mint. A mob destroyed the mint and killed its overseer and were fined for it by the dukes, as punishment and for reimbursement for the loss.

IMPERIAL MUNICH

During the 1300s, Munich was the richest of the several cities ruled by the Wittelsbachs. Grains, meats, fish, and wine were traded within specifically designated neighborhoods (a medieval form of zoning thought to lead to greater efficiency). The collection of tolls from the roads leading in and out of the city continued to help make their controllers (in this case, the Wittelsbachs) very rich.

In 1314, a Wittelsbach, Duke Ludwig IV, later to be known as Ludwig the Bavarian, was elected (by a tribunal of secular and ecclesiastical authorities called the Electors) as the German kaiser, thanks to his status as the least threatening choice among a roster of more powerful contenders. The election suddenly threw Munich into the center of German politics. Ludwig traveled to Rome for his coronation and brought back from his visit one of the treasured religious icons of medieval Munich—the severed arm of St. Anthony, which still can be seen in the church of St. Anna in Lehel.

- 1857 Weisswurst makes its debut in the city's beer halls.
- 1860–90 Munich takes over about a half-dozen small townships on its periphery, vastly expanding its city limits.
- 1864 Maximilian II dies. King Ludwig II ascends to the throne at the age of 18.
- 1864–65 Wagner, in Munich, creates some of his major operas before falling out of favor with young Ludwig, causing him to lose his financial backing in addition to the king's support, both of which were necessary to continue his work.
- 1871 Bismarck, ruler of Prussia, unites the quarreling principalities of Germany. The Bavarian king then becomes a figurehead.
- 1882 Munich electrifies its streets and houses.
- 1886 "Mad" King Ludwig is stripped of power and shortly thereafter drowns mysteriously.
- 1892 An artists' secession movement based on some of the tenets endorsed by the Impressionists in France, is founded in Munich as a protest against traditional perceptions and restrictions of Bavarian art.
- 1896 The curvaceous sinuousness of Art Nouveau, a decorative and architectural movement whose craftsmanship was made partly possible by the machinery of the industrial Revolution, reinforces its grip on Munich. Many of the tenets and presuppositions of the new movement are defined and articulated within the immensely influential Jugend magazine, which launched the architectural style known as Jugendstil.
- 1902 Lenin spends time in Munich, publishing an incendiary magazine.
- 1911 Klee and Kandinsky found *Der Blaue Reiter* school to promote modern and abstract art.
- 1914–18 World War I throws Munich into bloodshed and disillusionment, climaxed by the bitter Treaty of Versailles, which Germany is forced to sign, thereby accepting the responsibility for starting World War I.

continues

In 1319, one of the Wittelsbachs' most vindictive enemies, the Habsburg family in the person of Frederick the Handsome, attacked Munich and laid siege to its walls. Against expectations, the Wittelsbachs prevailed, eventually capturing the Habsburg leader and holding him prisoner. However, the pope sided with the Habsburgs and excommunicated Ludwig. Despite this serious handicap, Ludwig retained his throne. Consequences of the excommunication were enormous and were widely viewed as an example of a pope overplaying his cards. (Two hundred years later, when various German princes were forced to choose between allegiance to Rome and allegiance to the new Protestant order, the meddling of the popes in the secular affairs of Germany was widely remembered, often with disdain, a fact that played into the hands of the Protestants.) To reward Munich for its loyalty (and also to line his own pockets), Ludwig created a lucrative monopoly for the city in 1322 by ordering that all the salt mined within Hallein or Reichenhall must pass directly through Munich.

Although Bavaria remained Catholic, and continued to be Catholic even after the Protestant Reformation, Munich had positioned itself as a centerpiece of resistance to papal authority. Along these lines, Ludwig offered shelter to William of Occam, a brilliant scholar trained in the monasteries of both England and France and persecuted as a heretic by the pope. Occam spent the last years of his life in Munich, striving for reform of the Catholic Church. His presence helped to define Munich as a hardheaded Catholic city that catered only reluctantly to the whims of the faraway religious potentate.

While hunting bear in the Bavarian forest in 1346, Ludwig the Bavarian was accidentally killed. His enemies

1918 Social unrest prevails as 10,000 workers demonstrate in front of the Residenz. Ludwig III flees, marking the end of the Wittelsbach dynasty.

1919 Kurt Eisner, leader of a short-lived socialist regime, is assassinated. An army sent from Berlin evicts the revolutionary government.

1923 Hitler's Beer Hall Putsch, a rightist revolt against the Weimar government, fails in Munich.

1933 Munich, along with Germany, is swept by Nazi victories. A swastika flies atop city hall.

1934 Hitler consolidates power and crushes archrival Ernst Röhm. Munich falls under the Nazi yoke and all opposition to Hitler is suppressed.

1938 *Kristallnacht*—government-sanctioned vandalizing of Jewish-owned homes and businesses—descends on Munich and elsewhere.

1939 Assassination attempt against Hitler takes place in Munich's Bürgerbräukeller.

1942 The most intense Allied bombing of Munich.

1945 American troops enter Munich on April 30 to find 45% of the city's buildings in rubble and its population reduced by 250,000.

1949 Munich is redefined as the capital of the Federal Land of Bavaria.

1957 Immigrants, mainly from southern Europe, the Baltic, Turkey, and the Middle East, flood Munich, bringing the population to 1 million, and allow themselves to be hired as cheap labor for Bavarian industry.

1972 Summer Olympic Games in Munich are marred by a terrorist attack that kills 11 Israeli athletes.

1985 The Gasteig Center for Performing Arts opens.

1991 Munich becomes part of a reunified Germany.

1995 The Bavarian Beer Garden Revolution (see p. 150) draws 20,000 angry protesters.

2002 Germany abandons its longtime currency, the mark, and falls under the euro umbrella, leaving Münchners (along with the rest of the country) to struggle to cope with the new euro.

joked that he was killed "just at the right time" to escape big trouble from those who wanted to overthrow or assassinate him. His unbridled ambition and his successful defiance of the pope in Rome had earned Ludwig enemies, notably some of the most powerful German princes who were poised to attack him and overthrow him. Although he escaped battle with his powerful enemies, Ludwig's death signaled the end of Munich's role as the headquarters of the German-speaking empire.

During Ludwig's tenure, the city experienced explosive growth, and a new wall was built in 1327, so spacious that it encompassed the city throughout the next 400 years. Despite a strong temptation to alter Munich's central core, the Marienplatz was never changed from its original form—which it more or less retains today.

BEER, PIGS & PROSPERITY

Throughout the 1400s, Munich became a boomtown. More than 28,000 four-wheeled carts bearing marketable goods passed through the city gates every year in addition to the vast number of two-wheeled carts and people on foot. In response to this traffic, some of the town's main avenues, narrow though they were, were paved. Between 1392 and 1492, the city's increasingly prosperous merchant class built or altered into their present form many of the city's centerpieces, including the Ratsturm, the Altes Rathaus (Old City Hall), the Frauenkirche, and St. Peter's Church. Munich had graduated from a dependence on the salt trade, and was now reaping most of its profits from trade with Italy, especially Venice. In the same year Columbus stumbled upon his landfall in the New World, the Münchners opened a mountain pass over Mt. Kesselberg to speed up trade routes to the "Queen of the Adriatic."

By 1500, Munich boasted a population of almost 14,000 persons, 400 of whom were beggars, and 750 of whom were priests, nuns, or monks. It also included about three dozen brewers whose products were quickly becoming associated with the town. Pigs were engaged to eat the garbage strewn in the streets, and about two dozen innkeepers supplied food, drink, and lodgings to the medieval equivalent of the business traveler. The city's core (but not the surrounding fields that kept it fed) was protected from invasion by an ever-expanding ring of fortifications and towers. The most serious dangers were plagues and fires, both of which devastated the city at periodic intervals.

In 1516, the city adopted laws that later helped confirm its role as beer capital of the world. Known as the Bavarian Beer Purity Law, it was the first law in Europe to regulate the production of any food or beverage by setting minimum standards for quality and cleanliness in production.

RENAISSANCE EXPANSION

The showy and sometimes pompous building boom associated with the Counter-Reformation marked the debut of the Renaissance in Munich. The lavish building programs as well as the entertainments of the Wittelsbach rulers became legendary, both for their grandeur and extravagance (some feasts lasted for 3 weeks) and for the burdens they imposed on the citizenry who had to pay for them.

Munich blossomed with the appearance of Michaelskirche (St. Michael's Church), begun in 1583. The largest Renaissance-style church north of the Alps, it was conceived as a German-speaking response to St. Peter's Basilica in Rome. It took 14 frenetic years to build, and its construction costs almost bankrupted the Bavarian treasury. Despite the grumbling of the taxpayers who financed them, other buildings of equivalent splendor soon followed, including the Wittelsbach family stronghold, the Residenz.

Munich was also becoming a cultural center. By the late 16th century, the city was regarded as an artistic beacon. Credit for this must go to the reigning Wittelsbachs, founders of the art collection that eventually became the Alte Pinakothek, and the book collections that eventually became the Bayerischen Staatsbibliothek (Bavarian State Library).

Despite the prestige all these endeavors conveyed, virtually every trades-man and merchant in town complained of the burden such acquisitions and improvements placed upon the treasury, evidence of a fundamental conser-vatism that has demarcated Munich ever since.

THE THIRTY YEARS' WAR

Beneath the city's newly acquired glitter were other, darker tendencies. In the early years of the 17th century, witches were hunted down and burned, flagellants paraded through the town, and foreboding sermons predicted an apocalypse. At least the spirit of those predictions was fulfilled during the Thirty Years' War (1618–48). This struggle, between the Protestant princes and the Catholic League, swept across Europe, bringing devastation in its wake.

Munich wasn't directly affected until 1632. At that time, the Protestant king of Sweden, Karl Gustav Adolf, laid siege to "the German Rome." Munich sur-rendered almost immediately, since the city's rulers and citizens were worried about being hopelessly outnumbered and having their city destroyed. The terms of surrender included payment of a huge ransom; in exchange, the city was spared being sacked and burned. The war, however, wasn't the only problem faced by the Münchners—at about this time, the Black Plague killed 7,000 peo-ple, more than a third of the population. After the disease had run its course, Maximilian I ordered the construction of the Mariensaule (Virgin's Column—a statue dedicated to the Virgin) on the Marienplatz as a votive offering to God for having spared the city from total destruction.

In 1643, the authority of the town's merchants was greatly undermined by the removal of their right to elect the mayor of Munich. The Wittelsbachs were now able to place in power anyone who would cater to their interests.

BAROQUE CASTLES & BAROQUE DREAMS

The legacy of the Thirty Years' War left Munich demoralized and shattered. Although Bavaria was not to play a vital role in European politics during the next century, this period saw a building boom and the development of baroque architecture.

The flamboyant, richly gilded, free-flowing but symmetrical baroque style was used not only by the city's architects to the glory of God but also in secular construction. Notable are Nymphenburg Palace, Munich's answer to the palace at Versailles; the Green Gallery within the Residenz; ornate theaters; and count-less villas, pavilions, and garden structures. Funds for the construction of these buildings were derived, as in the past, from sometimes crippling taxes imposed on the citizenry and the forced sale of farming land to wealthy aristocrats who wanted to build ever-larger palaces for their own use.

Deep resentment was felt by the townspeople. In 1674, when the seat of the Wittelsbach family, the Residenz, accidentally caught fire, the town sullenly and deliberately postponed a response to calls for help for at least an hour, a vital delay that contributed to more enormous rebuilding costs and an increased mistrust among the various levels of society.

Part of the public resentment against Munich's leaders lay in the aristocracy's often disastrous meddling in international affairs. Among these were Bavaria's murky role in the War of the Spanish Succession, which resulted in the occupation of Bavaria between 1705 and 1715 by Austrian soldiers. The first year of this occupation witnessed one of the cruelest massacres in 18th-century history: Led by a local blacksmith, an army of peasants, craftsmen, and burghers, armed only with farm implements and scythes, marched upon Munich to protest against the Austrian regime. A short march from Munich's city walls, near the hamlet of Sendling, the entire army was betrayed (one of its members sold information to the enemy), then obliterated. The *Sendlinger Mordweihnacht* ("Sendling's Night of Murder") has ever since been the source for sculptures, plays, and popular legend.

In 1715, Max Emanuel was able—with the help of the French—to evict the Austrians. Aftereffects of these fruitless conflicts included countless deaths, a profound national disillusionment, and a national debt that historians assess at around 32 million guilders, a burden imposed upon an already impoverished population.

REFORM & REFORMERS

The tides of liberalization slowly spread to Bavaria. Newspapers were founded in 1702 and 1750, and in 1751, some vaguely liberal reforms (involving issues dealing with land use, penal codes, taxation, indentured labor, military service, and more) were made in the Bavarian legislature. An Academy of Sciences, whose discoveries sometimes opposed traditional Catholic teachings, was established in 1759.

To recover from the disasters initiated prior to his reign, Prince Elector Max III Joseph, one of the most enlightened Bavarian rulers, attempted to introduce economic reforms. He inaugurated new industries, including workshops for tapestry making and cloth making. Few of them worked out; the noteworthy exception was the outfit that manufactured Nymphenburg porcelain, founded in 1758, which consistently made a profit, and still does today.

In 1771, he revised the school system, making some aspects of public education a legal requirement. During his regime, the city opened its doors to playwrights, composers, and conductors from all over Europe. Munich was the site of the inaugural performance of one of Mozart's early operas (*Idomeneo*) in 1781, but it wasn't particularly well received, and Mozart's request for an ongoing creative stipend from the Wittelsbach family was rejected.

THE REBIRTH OF CONSERVATISM

When Max III Joseph died in 1777, his branch of the Wittelsbach dynasty died with him. The new Wittelsbach, from an obscure family branch in the Palatinate, was Karl Theodor, one of the least popular of all the Wittelsbachs. Caring little about Bavarian national destiny, he rather amazingly negotiated to cede Munich and all of Bavaria to Austria in exchange for the Habsburg-dominated Netherlands. Relief from this plan came in the form of the French Revolution.

Ironically, although he was despised as a ruler, Karl Theodor, as a builder, did many things well and skillfully, adding the Karlsplatz and the Englischer Garten to the roster of Munich's attractions. Politically, however, he continued to play his hand badly, outlawing most personal liberties and placing repressive measures on freethinkers. His death in 1799 was the cause of several days of drunken celebration throughout Munich.

THE AGE OF NAPOLEON

Except for distant rumblings on the western horizon and the hope it gave to Bavaria's liberals, the effects of the French Revolution of 1789 weren't immediately felt in reactionary Munich. All of that changed, however, with the rise of Napoléon. In 1799, French troops laid siege to the capital. The Bavarian court had already fled to the safety of their villas at Amberg, where they realized that they had to capitulate to Napoléon's overwhelming forces. Faced with little choice, they sided with the French dictator against their brethren in other parts of Germany. On the first night of occupation, in June 1799, French officers enjoyed a performance of Mozart's *Don Giovanni* in the Residenz's royal theater.

To reward his Bavarian vassal, Napoléon more than doubled the territory controlled by Bavaria (at the expense of Franconia and Swabia), thereby tripling the size of its population overnight. Bavaria was eventually made a kingdom, and in 1806, Napoléon personally conducted the coronation of Max IV Joseph as King Maximilian I.

A final irony was when the territory formerly controlled by the Bishop of Freising was swallowed up by the new Bavarian nation created by Napoléon, and the bishop's administrative headquarters—now no more than a ceremonial shadow of its former power—moved into the heart of its old "enemy territory" (the destruction of Freising's bridge over the Isar had led to the original founding of Munich)—downtown Munich.

TOWARD A MODERN STATE

The new king's son, Crown Prince Ludwig (later, Ludwig I), gets the credit for establishing what is now the most famous autumn festival in the world, *Oktoberfest*. Originally designated as a *Volksfest*, it was scheduled, along with some horse races, as a sideshow of the crown prince's wedding in 1810.

Beginning around 1820, with the gears of the Industrial Revolution already starting to turn, the first foundations of a modern state were established. A Bavarian constitution was drawn up, and Munich became the seat of a newly founded Bavarian Parliament, designed to afford the citizenry more clearly defined legal rights. Not all Münchners were happy, however—they were attached to their roster of religious holidays, complete with complicated processions and relief from workaday cares, which the new constitution swept away.

"THE ATHENS OF THE NORTH"

Crown Prince Ludwig, inspired by an idealized version of ancient Athens, made enormous changes to Munich. The old city walls were demolished, with the exception of a small stretch that still runs parallel to the Jungfernturmstrasse. The city moat was filled in and redesignated as the Sonnenstrasse, and new neighborhoods were designed with formal parks and gardens. The prince wanted the Munich equivalent of a triumphal promenade, and commissioned the street that has been known ever since as the Ludwigstrasse.

In 1821, the Frauenkirche became the official cathedral (Dom) of the archbishops of Munich and Freising. In 1826, the university was transferred from the town of Landshut to Munich, bestowing on the Bavarian capital the status of intellectual centerpiece.

BOURGEOIS MUNICH

By 1840, with a reported population of around 90,000 residents, Munich had been made into a neoclassical gem with a distinct identity. Munich's first railway line was laid in 1846—the foundation of a network of railways that soon converged on the city from all parts of southern Germany.

Initially a supporter of liberal reforms, Ludwig I gradually grew more and more conservative as his reign went on. In 1832, he began a campaign of censoring the press, repressing student activism, and stressing his role as an absolute monarch, casting himself in a romantic and heroic mold. Münchners considered his affair with actress and dancer Lola Montez even more odious than his rigid politics. All of this came to a head in the revolt of 1848. In a series of lurid events, Ludwig flaunted his affair with Lola so publicly that the fabric of the Wittelsbach dynasty itself was threatened. As the scandal raged out of control, Ludwig was forced to abdicate in favor of his son, Maximilian II.

Maximilian II continued the building programs of his father, established the Bavarian National Museum (1855), and played a role in encouraging writers to settle in Munich. One of these, Paul Heyse, was the first German to win the Nobel Prize for literature. Maximilian built an avenue (the Maximilianstrasse) in his own honor and held a series of competitions among architects for the design of such public buildings as the Regierung (Administrative Building) and the Maximilianeum (Bavarian Parliament Building).

Maximilian's role in the promotion of science, industry, and education made him one of the most enlightened despots of the 19th century. When he died in 1864, the administration of many of his programs was continued by what had developed into a massive governmental bureaucracy. The new king, Ludwig II, unfortunately, was not so beneficial to Bavaria.

ROMANTIC BAVARIA & THE DREAM KING

Rarely has the king of a nation so despised the citizens of his capital city as Ludwig II did the Münchners. Trouble began shortly after the new king ascended the Bavarian throne in 1864 at the age of 18. The king had become the patron of Richard Wagner, and four of Wagner's operas—*Tristan und Isolde* (1865), *Die Meistersinger von Nürnberg* (1867), *Das Rheingold* (1869), and *Die Walküre* (1870)—made their debuts in Munich. One of the many visions of the composer and his royal patron was the construction of a glittering opera house. However, this project, and its estimated cost of 6 million guilders, found little support and led to the collapse not only of plans for the hoped-for opera house but also of the friendship between the king and the composer. A spate of arrogant public outbursts by Wagner (newspapers published his statements that the citizens of Munich had no artistic imagination), led to the composer and his lofty romantic ideals leaving Munich forever.

Curiously, although viewed as hopelessly eccentric, a bizarre member of a family riddled with other mental aberrations, Ludwig seemed to captivate an age obsessed with romanticism. Although his mania for the building of neo-romantic castles and palaces far from the urban bustle of Munich helped bankrupt the treasury, he rarely meddled in the day-to-day affairs of his subjects and was consequently considered an expensive-to-maintain but relatively unthreatening monarch.

Actually, the lack of interest in politics on the part of Ludwig II is one of the factors that helped Bismarck, from his base in Prussia, arrange the unification of Germany in 1871. The unification transformed Berlin into the capital of a united Germany and stripped Bavaria of its status as an independent nation, a designation it had enjoyed since Napoléon's time. Some historians maintain that Bismarck helped induce the unstable king to give up his independent status by secretly subsidizing the building costs of his fairy-tale castles. Since the castles, especially Neuschwanstein, have brought billions of tourist dollars to the German nation ever since, he probably made a wise investment.

Fun Fact The Notorious Lola Montez

The sensational career of Lola Montez (1820–61) was hot copy in the newspapers all over the world during her lifetime, and she has even resurfaced more recently in a famous song by the Kinks. A woman who behaved as she pleased in the Victorian age, her liaison with Bavaria's king, Ludwig I, led to his forced abdication.

She was born in Limerick, Ireland, as Eliza Gilbert and grew up in India. An outstanding beauty with jet-black hair and alabaster skin, one admirer wrote of her, "Mrs. James looked like a star among the others." Her marriage to Lieutenant Thomas James had broken up in scandal (both she and her husband frequently cheated on each other, but she could never divorce him, since she couldn't find him to serve papers to), and she was forced to leave India. She went to Spain and then to London, where she reinvented herself as the dancer Lola Montez. Though she was a mediocre performer, her erotic "spider dance" catapulted her to notoriety. Subsequently, she went through dozens of lovers, including pianist Franz Liszt and novelist Alexandre Dumas.

When Lola arrived in Munich in 1846, she was refused an engagement at the Hof Theatre. Fighting her way past security guards, she stormed the palace of Ludwig I and demanded an audience with the king. Barging into his chambers, she slit the front of her dress open. Upon looking at her body, Ludwig asked his security guards and his chief aide to leave his chambers. Thus, began one of the most romantic and scandalous royal adventures of all time.

Although married to Princess Therese of Saxonia since 1810, the old, deaf, yet romantic, Ludwig came under Lola's spell. Ludwig indulged her every whim, bestowing the treasures of his kingdom upon her. In return, she catered to his sexual needs, including a foot fetish he had, as widely reported by his biographers. Lola was called "the Bavarian Pompadour," but Richard Wagner dubbed her a "demonic beast."

Ludwig gave her the titles of baroness of Rosenthal and countess of Lansfeld. Her enemies (Lola was deeply resented in Munich) suspected that she meddled in politics—it was rumored that she virtually ran the Bavarian government. Public sentiment against the king's infatuation and her outlandish behavior was so powerful that it contributed to the Revolution of 1848 and ultimately to the king's abdication.

Fleeing to London in the wake of the king's abdication, Lola settled into her next adventures. By July 19, 1849, she'd married George Trafford Heald, scion of a wealthy, aristocratic family. There was a problem, however: She'd never been granted a divorce from Lt. James. Learning that the state planned to arrest her on a bigamy charge on August 6, she fled first to Mexico, then to California, where she ended her days as a cigar-smoking, stage-strutting *artiste* who entertained miners during the California Gold Rush. An amazing life came to an end when she retired, found religion, and devoted the rest of her life to helping wayward women. She died in poverty in Brooklyn.

In 1886, the Bavarian cabinet in Munich stripped the 40-year-old Ludwig of his powers. A few days later, Ludwig's death by drowning in Starnberg Lake led to endless debate as to whether his death was prearranged because he planned an attempt at a royal comeback. His heir to the tattered remnants of the Bavarian throne was a mentally inept brother, Otto, whose day-to-day duties were assumed by a royal relative, Crown Prince Luitpold, who wore the much-diminished crown until 1912.

The only vestige of Bavaria's imperial past that remained was the designation of the local postal network and railways as "Royal Bavarian" (*Koeniglich-Bayerisch*). The Bavarian monarch was allowed to retain his position as figurehead during a transition period when real power slowly flowed toward Berlin.

Munich forged ahead in its role as an economic magnet within a unified Germany. In 1882, Munich began the process of electrifying its street lamps. Three years later, public transport was aided by a network of streetcars. And scientist Max von Pettenkofer, who discovered the source of cholera in contaminated water, was instrumental in the installation of a city water supply that was hailed as one of the best in Germany.

ARTISTIC FERMENT

Toward the end of the century, Munich became a center of creativity and artistic ferment. In 1892, the Secession movement was founded as a protest against traditional aesthetics. In 1896, the magazine *Jugend* helped define Munich (along with its closest rival, Vienna) as a centerpiece of the German Art Nouveau movement, *Jugendstil.* In 1902, a Russian expatriate, Lenin, spent a brief stint in Munich, publishing a revolutionary magazine called *Iskra.* Schwabing, once a farm village, then a summer retreat for the stylishly wealthy, became an icon for the avant-garde, the home base of satirical magazines whose contributors included Thomas Mann (who spent many years of his life in Munich), Rainer Maria Rilke, Hermann Hesse, and Heinrich Mann. In 1911, Franz Marc and Wassily Kandinsky, later joined by Paul Klee, founded the *Der Blaue Reiter* group to promote and define the role of abstract art.

WORLD WAR I & REVOLUTION

World War I (1914–18) led to more bloodshed and greater disillusionment than Europe had ever known. Hunger was rampant in Munich even in the early years of the war, and by 1918, social unrest was so widespread that a rash of demonstrations, burnings, mob executions, and brawls between advocates of the left and right became increasingly frequent. On the gray day of November 7, 1918, more than 10,000 workers mobilized for a mass demonstration, ending at the gates of the Wittelsbachs' hereditary stronghold, the Residenz. To the rulers' horror, even their guards were persuaded to join the revolutionaries, causing the dynasty's final scion to flee Munich under cover of darkness. The event marked the end of a dynasty that had ruled longer than any other in Europe.

The next day (Nov 8, 1918), Munich was declared the capital of the Free State of Bavaria (*Freistaat Bayern*), an independent revolutionary people's republic, led by the Revolutionary Workers Council. The conservative, so-called "legitimate" Bavarian government went into immediate exile, and Kurt Eisner, an articulate political leader who was much less radical than many of those who elected him, ruled briefly and tempestuously. Within a few months, he was assassinated on Munich's Promenadeplatz. Power shifted in a rapid series of events between centrists and leftists and ended in a horrendous bloodbath when troops, sent by Berlin in 1919, laid siege to the city as a means of restoring the status quo.

THE RISE OF HITLER

Conservative reaction to the near takeover of Munich by revolutionaries was swift and powerful, with long-ranging effects. After the events of 1919, and the humiliating terms of surrender imposed upon Germany at Versailles, Munich became one of the most conservative cities in Germany. Combine that with staggering inflation and a deep distrust of any Prussian interference from the despised city of Berlin, and Munich, unfortunately, became a kind of incubator for reactionary, anti-Semitic, and sometimes rabidly conservative political movements.

One of these was the NSDAP (National Socialist Workers Party of Germany), of which Adolf Hitler was a member. Hitler's early speeches, as well as the formulation of his ideas as written in *Mein Kampf* (*My Struggle*), were articulated in Munich's beer halls, including the famous Hofbräuhaus, where meetings were often held. Many members of Hitler's inner circle (including Heinrich Himmler and Hermann Göring) were from the region around Munich, and thousands of the dictator's rank and file originated from the city's long-suffering, endlessly deprived slums.

Under its reactionary civic government, Munich's cultural scene degenerated—anything racy or politically provocative was banned, and many creative persons (including Bruno Walter and Berthold Brecht) left Munich for the more sophisticated milieu of Berlin.

After Hitler came to power as chancellor in Berlin, there was little opposition in Bavaria to the National Socialists, whose candidates swept the city's elections of March 5, 1933, and whose swastika flew above city hall by the end of the day. By July of that same year, it was painfully obvious that anyone who opposed the all-Nazi city council would be deported to Germany's first concentration camp, Dachau, on Munich's outskirts.

The headquarters of the Nazi Party was established on the corner of Brienner and Arcis streets, later to be the site of the 1938 signing by Neville Chamberlain, Daladier, Mussolini, and Hitler of the Munich Agreement. Around the same time, a torture chamber was set up in the cellar of what had always been the city's symbol of power: the Wittelsbach Palace. Hitler himself even referred to Munich as "the capital of our movement," a statement heard then, as now, with great ambivalence.

Beginning in 1935, vast sums of money were spent on grandiose building projects that followed the Nazi aesthetic. In 1937, a Nazi-sponsored exhibition, permeated with anti-Semitic, xenophobic references, *Entartete Kunst* (*Denatured Art*), mocked the tenets of modern art.

Jews then began to be persecuted in earnest. The city's largest synagogue was closed in 1938, the same year that *Kristallnacht* ("Night of Broken Glass"; Nov 9, 1938) resulted in the vandalism of Jewish-owned homes and businesses across Germany. In spite of the ban on Jews, some 200 of them had managed to evade the Nazi net and were still alive at the end of World War II (though the city's pre-war Jewish population was over 10,000). After the war, Jews returned in very slow numbers to Munich since they were no longer persecuted and many still had long-rooted family ties with the Bavarian capital.

In 1939, a Marxist attempt to assassinate Hitler as he drank with cronies in a Munich beer hall (the Bürgerbräukeller) failed, and Germany (and Munich) continued the succession of aggressions that eventually led to World War II and the destruction of much of historic Munich.

WORLD WAR II & ITS AFTERMATH

Resistance to Hitler was fatal. Nonetheless, a handful of clergymen opposed the Nazi regime. One notable opponent was Father Rupert Mayer, who was imprisoned for many years at Dachau, Germany's first concentration camp. Built in 1933 in Bavaria, Dachau became a model for other death camps, as thousands upon thousands of "undesirables" were murdered, often in the most brutal fashion there. When Allied troops, in May of 1945, liberated the Oranienburg-Sachsenhausen concentration camp, they found that the priest from Munich had been transferred there and was still alive at the end of the war. Mayer has since been beatified by the Catholic hierarchy. Other heroic resistance came from the Weisse Rose (White Rose) coalition of university students and professors. At the risk of their lives, they published secret leaflets calling for the downfall of the Nazi regime. The White Rose Leaders, Hans and Sophie Scholl, Willi Graf, and Hans Huber, were later arrested and beheaded.

By the war's end, almost half of the city's buildings lay in rubble, many having been blown to pieces as early as 1942. Most of Munich's Renaissance and neoclassical grandeur had been literally bombed off the map, a fact that's easy to overlook by modern visitors who admire the city's many restored monuments.

Munich paid a high price in the blood of its citizens: 22,000 of its sons died in military campaigns, and the civilian population of the city was reduced by almost a quarter million before the end of the war.

THE POSTWAR YEARS & A FOLK HERO

The tone was set after the war by the city's mayor, Thomas Wimmer. He was much beloved by Münchners, and his weekly meet-the-people sessions, when anyone could talk to him personally, made the people in the street feel he was really their representative. His call to clean up the city met with overwhelming response—the rubble was assembled into decorative hillocks in the city's parks.

Unlike other German cities, Munich was able to unearth the original plans for many of the demolished buildings, which were tastefully restored, even if at astronomical expense, to their original appearance. Today, the city's historic core is surrounded by the same church steeples and towers as in the past.

As capital of the Federal *Land* (state) of Bavaria within the Federal Republic of Germany, Munich took up its new role as focal point for trade between northern and southern Europe. Manufacturers of computers, weapons manufacturers, publishing ventures, fashion houses, movie studios, and companies such as Siemens made Munich their base. The city boomed, with a population that numbered over a million before the end of 1957. As home to BMW (Bayerisches Motoren Werke), Munich is at least partly responsible for Germany's image as home to Europe's fastest drivers.

As the city's population exploded in the 1960s, sprawling masses of concrete suburbs were thrown up hastily, designed for ease of access by cars. Older buildings were demolished to make room for yet another Munich building boom.

The obsession for rebuilding and modernizing at any price was halted when the then-mayor of Munich paid an official visit to Los Angeles. Munich's press

---

Impressions

Bavarians say the difference between a rich farmer and a poor farmer is that the poor farmer cleans his Mercedes himself.

—J. W. Murray, *Observer*, June 17, 1979

gleefully reported that the automobile-dominated society of L.A. so horrified him that he introduced a new emphasis on historical preservation. Since then, active participation by historic-minded groups has encouraged careful renovations of older buildings.

The 1972 Summer Olympic Games were meant to show the entire world the bold new face of a radically rebuilt Munich from the premises of the innovative Olympic City. However, the terrorist attack on the Israeli athletes, and the collective murder of 11 of them, revived recollection of the recent past and left behind ambivalent memories.

MUNICH TODAY

Reunification has proved to be something of a mixed blessing to Bavaria. It brought business opportunities in the newly democratized eastern zone, but at the same time, there was an influx of new residents from the east, whose hopes for a share in western prosperity often aroused resentment and were frequently disappointed.

Social unrest has not disappeared either, although the latest incident, in 1995, had a trivial cause. "The Bavarian Beer Garden Revolution" started when residents in a prosperous neighborhood requested that the local beer garden be closed after 9:30pm because of noise and congestion. Picked up as a *cause célèbre* by thousands of beer drinkers who were afraid that such a rule might become the norm, the event provoked a raucous demonstration by 20,000 angry protesters. Although the owners of the beer garden in question, the Waldwirtshaft, had sown the seeds for the initial protest marches, the number of participants exceeded their wildest imagination. The incident was seen as a visible sign of stress between opposing political and social forces.

In the waning weeks of 1999, Germany signed a historic agreement that resolved one of the gravest injustices left over from World War II. It formally pledged to pay $5.2 billion in belated compensation to hundreds of thousands of Nazi-era slave workers and other victims of the Third Reich.

As Munich moves past the millennium, its citizens are rightly concerned about the impact of Berlin's re-establishment as the official capital of a reunited country and the possible shift of trade and power into the north and east of Germany.

2 Munich's Architecture: From the Baroque to the 21st Century

THE FLOWERING OF THE BAROQUE

The glory of Bavaria is its baroque and rococo architecture. The Gothic style never took hold in southern Germany as it did in England and France, although the style can be seen in the somber brick profile of the Frauenkirche, constructed from 1468 to 1525. Even Munich's oldest parish church, St. Peter's, whose foundations date from the early Middle Ages, has an interior overlaid with baroque decoration.

The most spectacular example of early baroque appears in the form of the massive St. Michael's Church, the largest baroque building north of the Alps. A symbol of defiance to the growing power of the Protestants farther to the north, it was begun in 1583 and finished in a record-breaking 14 years. When one of its towers collapsed during the 7th year of its construction, its royal patron,

Duke Wilhelm V, interpreted the accident as a sign of displeasure from God—the building wasn't impressive enough. Consequently, it was enlarged into the airy and soaring interior you'll see today. It was laboriously reconstructed as a symbol of civic pride after the damages of World War II.

High baroque style was an Italian import, whose influence in Germany began around 1660 and continued into the 18th century. The style swept southern Germany, especially Munich and Bavaria. As characterized by art historian Helen Gardner, baroque architecture was "spacious and dynamic, brilliant and colorful, theatrical and passionate, sensual and ecstatic, opulent and extravagant, versatile and virtuoso." This period saw the merging of painting, sculpture, and architecture into an integrated whole. Painting became illusionist, architecture pictorial. Visual impact and sensual delight characterized the movement, as stained glass gave way to floods of natural light. Altarpieces grew monumental, and baroque space provided multiple changing views. Sometimes a baroque building reached out to embrace an entire square and all the buildings surrounding it. The ceilings of baroque churches, with their painted scenes, were meant "to lift the viewer to heaven." Illusions like trompe l'oeil, with its whimsical style, often merged with stucco adornment in what one architect called a "form of 3-D trickery."

Outstanding among baroque artists and architects in Bavaria were two sets of brothers. The work of the Asam brothers, painter Cosmas Damian Asam and sculptor Egid Quirin Asam, are the best examples of the southern high baroque style. Their masterpiece is the Asamkirche in Munich, whose interior bursts upon the viewer in a riot of gold. Cosmas became particularly celebrated for his vast dome paintings of the heavens. Another pair of brothers, the architect Dominikus Zimmerman (1685–1766) and the fresco master, Johann Baptist Zimmerman (1688–1769), created the towering masterpiece, the Wieskirche near Landsberg. This church is a virtual fantasy, with cherubs and angels peeking out behind garlands of foliage (see "A Rococo Masterpiece," in chapter 11).

The towering figure of the movement, however, was Balthasar Neumann (1687–1753), whose architecture has been called "music frozen in time." Although he never worked in Munich, his Vierzehnhelligenkirche near Bamberg is Neumann at his most energetic and intricate.

The baroque movement eventually dipped its brushes into the flippant paint of the rococo and brought to the style even greater flamboyance and gaiety. The first rococo church in Bavaria was Johann Michael Fischer's St. Anna im Lehel. The great architect of this movement was François de Cuvilliés whose masterpiece is the Residenztheater (p. 103). He is also responsible for the facade of the Theatinerkirche (p. 107), built by Prince Elector Ferdinand Maria in 1662 in gratitude for the birth of his heir, Max Emanuel. Its construction was among the most complicated in Munich because it took a century before the building was finally completed.

NEOCLASSICAL GRANDEUR

By the 19th century, the baroque and rococo styles, with their connections to the *ancien régime,* had been swept away by the French Revolution. In their place, neoclassicism made reference to the grandeur of ancient Greece and imperial Rome. Between 1825 and 1848, Munich's transformation into a suitably royal capital of neoclassical splendor owed a great deal to the attempt by the autocratic

Crown Prince Ludwig (later Ludwig I) to transform Munich into a second Athens or Rome. The Alte Pinakothek was begun in 1826, and at the time it was the largest art gallery in the world. Ludwig himself is responsible for the collection you see today of early German masters, including Dürer and such early Italian painters as Giotto, Botticelli, and da Vinci. Other neoclassical examples of Ludwig's efforts are the Königsplatz, the Glyptothek, and, within the Residenz complex, the *Königsbau* (King's Building).

In the later 1800s, the Romantic movement, which looked back to a rose-colored interpretation of Germany's medieval history, myth, and folklore, introduced an architectural and decorative style sometimes termed *historicism*. This style is exemplified in Fredrich von Gartner's *Staatsbibliothek* (State Library), the university complex, and such focal points along the Ludwigstrasse as the Feldherrnhalle and the Siegestor. This movement, of course, also inspired Ludwig II, and no other building represents it so well as his palace, Neuschwanstein (see chapter 11).

TOWARD THE MODERN AGE

By the end of the 19th century, the Art Nouveau, or Jugendstil movement marked the distant beginnings of contemporary architecture, as architects began to use such materials as glass, steel, and concrete. In the aftermath of World War I, the influence of Walter Gropius's Bauhaus movement, whose primary aim was to unify arts and crafts within the context of architecture, began to be felt. Gropius stressed an idea of functional design that reflected the tastes of the postindustrial revolution.

Bauhaus ideas, however, did not suit the tastes of the rising National Socialists, and the Bauhaus was dissolved in 1933. By 1935, the so-called "Third Reich" style of architecture was the law of the land, with Munich (site of most of Hitler's earliest successes) providing the experimental background for many of its ideas. Under Hitler's favorite architect, Albert Speer, art and architecture became propaganda tools: pompous, monumental, and devoid of any real humanity. Postwar Munich did its best to conceal the Nazi roots of some of its buildings by skillfully transforming them into something more human. An example is the *Zentralministerium* (Central Ministry), a predictably pompous but anonymous building on the Von-der-Tann-Strasse, cutting through the otherwise orderly progression of the Ludwigstrasse. An even better example, recycled after the war into an art gallery, is the Haus der Kunst, which now houses the *Staatsgalerie Moderner Kunst* (State Gallery of Modern Art). Its angular Fascist architecture seems curiously appropriate for the starkly modern paintings it showcases today. Ironically, virtually everything inside would have been anathema to Hitler and outlawed as "degenerate" by its original builders.

RESTORATION & RENEWAL

One of the sad legacies of World War II was the virtual leveling of many of Germany's greatest architectural treasures by Allied bombing raids. On-site witnesses claim that, in Munich, the first 2 years after the end of the war were devoted almost exclusively to clearing away the rubble. Part of the past had been swept away, but visitors will find that many of the treasured landmarks have been carefully reconstructed in their original style.

New structures for the modern age, ever more innovative, can be seen in such sites as the stadium built for the 1972 Olympics and the performance center at Gasteig, begun in 1979 and opened in 1985.

3 A Taste of Bavaria
THE TRADITIONAL CUISINE

Bavarians like to eat, justifying their appetites with the very reasonable assertion that any type of human interaction operates more smoothly when it's lubricated with ample amounts of food and wine, or even better, food and beer.

Calorie- and cholesterol-conscious North Americans might recoil at the sight of meals made up of dumplings, potatoes, any of a dozen different types of *würste* (sausages), roasted meats flavored with bacon drippings, breads, and pastries. Munich, of course, has many restaurants that specialize in *cuisine moderne,* as well as *nouvelle* counterparts of the traditional cuisine. But the standard old-fashioned *kuchen* is still widely served and enjoyed.

The Bavarian affair with sausage is of ancient lineage, würst having been a major part of the national diet almost since there were people and livestock in the area. Bavarians tend to view their würst with some superstition, nostalgically adhering to such adages as "Never let the sunshine of noon shine on a Weisswurst," and the reservation of Rotwurst for consumption in the evening.

Every Bavarian professes a love for his or her favorite kind of würst (a choice that's often based on childhood associations). Many visitors' favorite is *Bratwurst,* which came originally from nearby Nürnberg and is concocted from seasoned and spiced pork. *Weisswurst,* Munich's traditional accompaniment to a foaming mug of beer, wasn't "invented" until 1857, a date remembered by Münchners as an important watershed. The ingredients that go into it are less appetizing than the final result—usually including veal, calves' brains, and spleen. Modern versions contain less offal and better quantities of veal, as well as spices and lemon juice to enhance the flavor. Two are usually considered a snack. Five or six are a respectable main course. Most aficionados try not to eat the skin, but some diehards wouldn't think of removing it.

Bauernwurst (farmer's sausage) and *Knockwurst* are variations of the Frankfurter, which, although it originated in the more westerly city of Frankfurt, achieved its greatest fame in the New World. While *Leberwurst* is a specialty of Hesse, and *Riderwurst* (beef sausage) and *Blutwurst* (blood sausage) are specialties of Westphalia, all of them are widely served and enjoyed in Munich. Regardless of which you choose, the perfect accompaniment for würst consists of mustard, a roll (preferably studded with pumpernickel seeds), and beer.

As savory as the würsts of Munich might be, they're considered too simple to grace the table at any truly elaborate Bavarian meal, unless accompanied by other dishes. From the long-ago repertoire of agrarian Bavarian cuisine comes *Züngerl* (pig's tongue) or *Wammerl* (pig's stomach), most often served with braised or boiled cabbage. Potato dumplings (*Klösse,* or *Kartoffelknödel*) and *Leber* (liver) dumplings are mandatory features. *Semmelknödel* (bread dumplings) generally accompany the most famous meat dish of Bavaria, *Schweinbraten* (roast pork). Also popular with many devotees are *Kalbshaxen* (veal shank) and *Schweinshaxen* (roasted knuckle of pork). Carp is prized by Munich's gastronomes, as is a succulent variety of trout, or *Forelle.*

Feeling hungry during your sightseeing promenades around Munich? Step into the nearest *Metzgerei* (butcher shop) and order such items as a *Warmer Leberkäs,* which has nothing to do with either liver or cheese, but instead with ground beef and bacon, baked like a meat loaf and sold in slices of about 100 grams each. It's best consumed with mild mustard and a roll. Another worthy choice is *Wurtzsemmel,* sliced sausage meat on a roll, or a *Schinkensemmel,* sliced ham served on a roll. You can carry it away for consumption where there's a view or take it into a *Bierkeller* or Biergarten (it's been legal for centuries to bring in your own food and order a small beer to go with it).

AND WHAT BEER SHOULD YOU DRINK?

No self-respecting Münchner will refuse a sparkling glass of wine, and will even praise highly the light, slightly acidic wines from the Rhineland. But the real glint enters a Münchner's eye when the relative merits of beer are discussed. You won't lack for variety within the beer halls of Munich—there are even beers available according to season.

Both because it's the law, and as a matter of pride, breweries make their beer with yeast, barley, hops, and water. Preservatives aren't usually added—in a city where a 200-liter cask of beer can be drained by a thirsty crowd in fewer than 12 minutes, the beer never lasts long enough to really need them. Legally required adherence to certain standards dates back to 1516—before the establishment of standards anywhere else in Europe.

Here's a rundown on what you're likely to need in your dialogues with a Münchner bartender.

"Normal" Bavarian beer, also referred to as light beer (ask for *ein Helles*), is slightly less potent than the brew consumed in North Germany, France, or England. Its relative weakness is the main reason why many visitors can consume several liters before beginning to feel the least bit giddy.

Don't think, however, that "normal" beer is the same as *Weiss* or (in Münchner dialect) *Weizenbier,* which is brewed with a high concentration of fermented wheat. In springtime, along with spring lamb and fresh fruits and vegetables, Munich offers *Bock* and *Doppelbock* (Double Bock), *Märzenbier,* and *Pils.*

Beck's dark is an example of dark beer (*ein Dunkles*) known to many North Americans. There's even a dark Weiss beer, which happens to be wheat beer brewed in such a way as to make it smoky-looking rather than pale. And in case you've forgotten a particularly unpleasant episode in Munich's civic history, there's even a beer named after the doomed socialists (the Red Guards) who forcibly took over the city's government for a few months in 1918, a *Russe,* which consists of Weiss (wheat) beer and lemonade.

What is the polite thing to ask for if you think you're too drunk to handle another liter of "normal" beer? Ask for a *Radlermass* (literally, "a mug for the bike"), composed of half "normal" beer, half lemonade.

The ideal place to go for consuming this amazing variety of fermented grains is any of the city's dozens of Bierkellers or Biergartens, which serve simple snacklike food items—sausages, white radishes, cheese, and the kind of salted pretzels that are guaranteed to make you thirstier. Munich's most historic drinking sites include the Hofbräuhaus and the Bürgerbräukeller (p. 150 and 149 respectively), both of which carry local associations of everyone from Adolf Hitler to the boy or girl next door.

Appendix B: Useful Terms & Phrases

GENERAL TERMS

Allee Avenue

Altes Rathaus Old town hall (kept as an historical monument, but no longer used as the headquarters of the city's officials)

Altstadt Old part of a city or town

Anlage Park area

Apotheke Pharmacy

Auf Wiedersehen Goodbye

Ausgang Exit

Bad Spa (also bath)

Bahn Railroad, train

Bahnhof Railroad station

Bau Building

Berg Mountain

Bitte Please

Brücke Bridge

Brunnen Fountain or spring

Burg Fortified castle

Danke Thank you

Dom Cathedral

Domplatz Cathedral square

Drogerie Shop selling cosmetics, sundries

Eingang/Einfahrt Entrance

Eintritt Admission

Fahrrad Bicycle

Fleet Canal

Flughafen Airport

Gasse Lane

Gasthof Inn

Gemütlichkeit (adj. gemütlich) Comfort, coziness, friendliness

GmbH German equivalent of "Inc."

Graben Moat

Gutbürgerliche Küche German home-cooking

Hallo Hello

Hauptbahnhof Main railroad station

Hotelgarni Hotel that serves no meals or serves breakfast only

Insel Island

Jugendstil Art Nouveau

Kapelle Chapel

Kammer Room (in public building)

Kaufhaus Department store

Kino Cinema

Kirche Church

Kloster Monastery

Kneipe Bar for drinking, may serve snacks

Konditorei Cafe for coffee and pastries

Kunst Art

Land State

Marktplatz Market square

Messegelände Exhibition center, fairgrounds

Neue Küche Cuisine moderne

Neues Rathaus New town hall (the seat of current city business)

Neustadt New part of city or town

Palatinate A region of Germany bordering France

Platz Square

Polizei Police

Postamt Post office

Rathaus Town or city hall

Ratskeller Restaurant in Rathaus cellar serving traditional German food

Reisebüro Travel agency

Residenz Palace

Schauspielhaus Theater for plays

Schicki-Micki A club-going Bavarian yuppie, an archetype whose aesthetic and social values are satirically referred to by some Germans as "Mickey Mouse chic."

Schloss Palace, castle

See Lake *(der See)* or sea *(die See)*

Seilbahn Cable car

Speisekarte Menu

Spielbank Casino

Stadt Town, city

Stadtbahn (S-bahn) Commuter railroad

Steg Footbridge

Strasse Street

Strassenbahn Streetcar, tram

Stübe A cozy room, usually outfitted with wood paneling and a sense of traditional German decor, that is used for dining.

Tankstelle Filling station

Tagesmenu The menu of the day

Teich Pond

Teller Platter

Tor Gateway

Turm Tower

Ufer Shore, riverbank

Untergrundbahn (U-bahn) Subway, underground transportation system in a city

Verkehrsamt Tourist office

Weg Road

Weinstube Wine bar or tavern serving meals

Zimmer Room

2 Menu Terms

MEATS AND POULTRY (WURST, FLEISCH & GEFLÜGEL)

Aufschnitt Cold cuts

Brathuhn Roasted chicken

Bratwurst Grilled sausage

Beefsteak or Rindfleisch Hamburger steak

Eisbein Pigs' knuckles

Ente Duck

Frankfurter Hotdog

Gans Goose

Geflügel Poultry

Hammel Mutton

Kalb Veal

Kassler Rippchen Pork chops

Lamm Lamb

Leber Liver

Ragout Stew

Rinderbraten Roast beef

Rindfleisch Beef

Sauerbraten Marinated beef

Schinken Ham

Schnitzel Cutlet

Schweinebraten Roast pork

Tafelspitz Boiled beef usually served with applesauce and horseradish—a famous staple of Austria.

Truthahn Turkey

Wiener Schnitzel Breaded veal cutlet

Wurst Sausage

FISH (FISCH)

Aal Eel

Forelle Trout

Hecht Pike

Karpfen Carp

Lachs Salmon

Makrele Mackerel

Muschel Mussel

Rheinsalm Rhine salmon

Schellfisch Haddock

Seezunge Sole

EGGS (EIER)

Eier in der Schale Boiled eggs

Mit Speck With bacon

Rühreier Scrambled eggs

Spiegeleier Fried eggs

Verlorene Eier Poached eggs

SANDWICHES (BELEGTE BROTE)

Aufschnitt mit Brot   Cold cuts sandwich (a sandwich Germans are more fond of ordering than a specific type, such as roast beef or bologna)

Brotaufstrich   Meat paste sandwich (a very popular sandwich in Germany)

Entebrot   Chicken sandwich

Eierbrot   Egg sandwich

Käsebrot   Cheese sandwich

Schinkenbrot   Ham sandwich

Schwarzbrot mit Butter Pumpernickel with butter sandwich

Speckbrot   Bacon sandwich

Tomatenbrot   Tomato sandwich

Wurstbrot   Sausage sandwich

VEGETABLES (GEMÜSE)

Artischocken   Artichokes

Blumenkohl   Cauliflower

Bohnen   Beans

Bratkartoffeln   Fried potatoes

Champignon   Mushroom

Erbsen   Peas

Grüne Bohnen   Green or string beans

Gurken   Cucumbers

Karotten   Carrots

Kartoffel   Potato

Kartoffelbrei   Mashed potatoes

Kartoffelsalat   Potato salad

Knödel   Dumplings

Kohl   Cabbage

Rettich   Radish

Reis   Rice

Rote Rüben   Beets

Rotkraut   Red cabbage

Salat   Lettuce

Salzkartoffeln   Boiled potatoes

Sellerie   Celery

Spargel   Asparagus

Spinat   Spinach

Steinpilze   Boletus mushrooms

Tomaten   Tomatoes

Vorspeisen   Hors d'oeuvres

Weisse Rüben   turnips

DESSERTS (NACHTISCH)

Apfel Reispudding   Apple rice pudding

Apfelstrudel   Apple strudel

Auflauf   Soufflé

Bienenstich   Honey almond cake

Blatterteiggebäck   Puff pastry

Bratapfel   Baked apple

Dolce di Castagne   Chestnut roll

Eis   Ice cream

Erdbeermeringue   Strawberry meringue

Kaffeecreme   Coffee mousse

Käse   Cheese

Kirschenstrudel   Cherry strudel

Kirschtorte   Black Forest cake

Kompott   Stewed fruit

Obstkuchen   Fruit tart

Obstsalat   Fruit salad

Pfannkuchen   Sugared pancakes

Pflaumenkompott   Stewed plums

Salzburger Nockerl   A light, creamy dessert made with beaten egg yolks and beaten egg whites, plus vanilla and sugar, cooked in a skillet with butter.

Schlagsahne   Whipped cream

Schokolademus   Chocolate mousse

Tarte Tatin   A tart filled with, most often, apples

Topfenpalatschinken   Cottage cheese pancakes

Torte   Pastry

Zwetschkenknodel   Plum dumplings

FRUITS (OBST)

Ananas   Pineapple

Apfel   Apple

Apfelsine   Orange

Banane   Banana

Birne   Pear

Erdbeeren   Strawberries

Himberren   Raspberries

Kirschen   Cherries

Pfirsich   Peach

Weintrauben   Grapes

Zitrone   Lemon

BEVERAGES (GETRÄNKE)

Bier Beer
Coca-Cola Coca-Cola (order a soda in Germany by its specific name: Coke, Pepsi, Dr. Pepper, etc.)
Ein dunkles A dark beer
Ein helles A light beer
Eine Tasse Kaffee A cup of coffee
Eine Tasse Tee A cup of tea
Eiskalt Chilled
Eistee Ice tea
Geist Brandy
Heisse Schokolade Hot chocolate
Kaffee Coffee
Kaffee mit Milch/Zucker Coffee with cream/sugar:
Kaffee mit Suss-stoff Coffee with artificial sweetener
Kaffee Schwarz Black coffee
Koffeinfrei Decaffeinated coffee
Kräutertee Herb tea
Leicht Light (wine)
Likör Liqueur
Limonade Lemonade
Milch Milk

Mineralwasser Mineral water
Mit Eis With ice
Mit Wasser With water
Ohne Eis Without ice
Ohne Wasser Without water
Pur Straight
Rotwein Red wine
Saft Juice
Schaumwein Sparkling wine
Schnaps Schnapps
Schokolade Chocolate
Soda Club soda
Soda mit gas Soda with gas (to make sure your club soda is carbonated, if that's what you want—the German word for carbonated is *Kohlensäure,* but Germans don't use this when ordering drinks)
Süss Sweet (wine)
Tee mit Milch Tea with cream
Tee mit Zitrone Tea with lemon
Tomatensaft Tomato juice
Trocken Dry (wine)
Wasser Water
Weisswein White wine

CONDIMENTS & TABLE ITEMS (WÜRZE & TAFELGESCHIRR)

Brot Bread
Brötchen Rolls
Butter Butter
Eis Ice
Essig Vinegar
Flasche Bottle
Gabel Fork
Glas Glass
Kalte pikante sosse Ketchup
Löffel Spoon
Messer Knife

Öl Oil
Pfeffer Pepper
Platte Plate
Sahne Cream
Salat Zubereitung Salad dressing
Salz Salt
Senf Mustard
Tasse Cup
Teller Platter
Tischzeug Napkin
Zucker Sugar

COOKING TERMS

Gebacken Baked
Gebraten Fried
Gedämpft Steamed
Gefüllt Stuffed
Gekocht Boiled
Geröstet Roasted
Gut durchgebraten Well done

Heiss Hot
Kaltes Cold
Mittep Medium
Nicht durchgebraten Rare
Paniert Breaded
Pochiert Poached

Index

See also Accommodations and Restaurant indexes, below.

GENERAL INDEX

Abbey Church (Stiftskirche) (Berchtesgaden), 174
Academy of Fine Arts (Akademie der Shönen), 128
Accommodations, 43–63. *See also* Accommodations Index
best, 8–10
what's new in, 1
Addresses, finding, 37
Ainmillerstrasse, 128
Airfares, 22
Airlines, 22
Airport, 35
accommodations near, 62–63
Akademie der Shönen (Academy of Fine Arts), 128
Alabama, 144–145
Albl, Josef, 203
Allerheiligenkirche am Kreuz, 126
Alois Dallmayr, 71–72
Alpamare (Bad Tölz), 163
Alpine hiking, 168. *See also* Hiking
Alpspitz cable car, 199
Alpspitz region, 199
Alte Pinakothek, 95, 98
Alte Residenztheater (Cuvilliés Theater), 103
Alter Hof, 120
Alter Simpl, 146
Altes Rathaus (Old Town Hall), 94
Altes Residenztheater (Cuvilliés Theater), 142
Altstadt (Old Town), 36, 37
Amalienburg, 104
American Express, 30–31
Ammersee, 116, 160–162
Andechs, monastery of (near Herrsching), 161
Andreas Huber, 138

Anglia English Bookshop, 130, 132
Antikensammlungen (Museum of Antiquities), 107
Antike Uhren Eder, 131
Antiques, 131–132, 139
Arabellapark, 40
Art gallery, 132
Asamkirche (St.-Johann-Nepomuk-Kirche), 105–106
Asamkirche and Haus, 126
Asamsaal (Freising), 166
ATMs (automated-teller machines), 16
Auer Dult, 17, 139
Augustinerbrau, 149
Automobilclub von Deutschland (AvD), 29
Axel Bar (Bad Reichenhall), 183

Backstage Club & Biergarten, 145
Badenburg Pavilion, 104
Bad Heilbrunn, 170
Bad Reichenhall, 170, 180–183
Bad Reichenhall Casino, 183
Bad Reichenhaller Saltmuseum, 181
Bad Tölz, 162–165, 170
Bad Wiessee, 186–190
Ballet, 142
Ballooning, 169
Bars, 146–149
Bau, 151
Baur, Tony, 203–204
Bavarian Alps, 2, 168–213
hiking, 198–201
natural world of, 200–201
outdoor activities, 168–169
scenic drives, 169–170, 172
Bavarian Association of Artisans (Bayerischer Kunstgewerbeverein), 134

Bavarian Film Studio, 107–108, 114
Bavarian National Museum (Bayerisches National-museum), 98
Bavarian Radio Orchestra (Bayerischer Rundfunk Symphonieorchester), 142
Bavarian State Ballet, 142
Bavarian State Library (Bayerische Staatsbiblio-thek), 130
Bavarian State Opera (Bayer-ische Staatsoper), 142
Bavarian State Radio Orchestra (Bayerischer Rundfunk Münchner Rund-funkorchestra), 142
Bayerischer Hof Night Club, 143
Bayerischer Kunstgewerbe-verein (Bavarian Associa-tion of Artisans), 134
Bayerischer Landes-Sportverbund, 116
Bayerischer Rundfunk Münchner Rundfunk-orchestra (Bavarian State Radio Orchestra), 142
Bayerischer Rundfunk Sym-phonieorchester (Bavarian Radio Orchestra), 142
Bayerischer Zehnschiffart GmbH, 158
Bayerisches Nationalmuseum (Bavarian National Museum), 98
Bayerisches Staatsschauspiel (State Theater), 142
Bayerische Staatsbiblio-thek (Bavarian State Library), 130
Bayerische Staatsoper (Bavarian State Opera), 142
Bayerische Zugspitz-bahn, 198
Bayernhalle (Garmisch-Partenkirchen), 197
Bayern München, 112

Beaches, 116
Beer, 150, 219, 232
Beer gardens *(Biergarten)*, 4, 90–92
Beer halls, 149–151
Bei Carla, 151
Benediktbeuren, 165, 170
Berchtesgaden, 170, 173–180
  accommodations, 175–176
  day trips from, 177–180
  organized tours, 175
  outdoor activities, 175
  restaurants, 176–177
  sights and attractions, 173–175
  traveling to, 173
Berchtesgaden Bahnhof, 173
Berchtesgadener Land, 169
Berchtesgaden Mini Bus Tours, 175
Berchtesgaden National Park, 26, 168–169, 172–173
Berg, 156
Berghof (Obersalzberg), 178–179
Berg Kolber (Mt. Kolber), 202
Berg Laber (Mt. Laber), 202
Bicycling, 25, 42, 116
  Berchtesgaden, 175
  tours, 115
Biebl, 139
Bike & Walk Company, outdoor activities, 116–118
BMW Museum, 113–114
Boating, 116–117
Boat tours and cruises
  Ammersee, 161
  Chiemsee, 183–184
  Lake Starnberg, 156
  Tegernsee, 158
Bogenhausen, 40–41
  accommodations, 60
  restaurants, 87–88
Bogner Haus, 136
Books, recommended, 30
Bookstores, 132
Botanischer Garten, 7, 111
Bourdalou Museum (Chamber Pot Museum), 110
Brauneck mountain, 163
Bräustüberl (Tegernsee), 158
Brienner Strasse, 41
Bucket shops, 22–23
Burgerbräu (Bad Reichenhall), 183
Bürgersaal, 124
Business hours, 31
Bus travel, 24, 36, 41

C abs, 42
Café Extrablatt, 146–147
Cafe Puck, 147
Cafes, 89–90, 146–149
Café Waldstein (Garmisch-Partenkirchen), 197
Calendar of events, 17
Canoeing, 163
Carl Jagemann, 132
Carl Jagemann's, 138
Carnival (Fasching), 17
Car rentals, 28, 42
Car travel, 28–29
Casino, Bad Reichenhall, 183
Cathedral of Our Lady (Frauenkirche), 106
Central Munich
  accommodations, 44–58
  beer gardens, 91
  cafes, 89–90
  restaurants, 67–83
  sights and attractions, 94–95
Chamber Pot Museum (Bourdalou Museum), 110
Chapel of St. Anton (Garmisch-Partenkirchen), 191
Chiemsee, 183–186
China (porcelain), 133
Chocolate and pastries, 134
Chocolates, 134
Christkindlmarkt, 18, 139
Christmas ornaments, 139
Christopher Street Day, 18
Churches, 105–107
Church of St. Kajetan (Theatinerkirche), 94, 102, 107, 122
Church of St. Martin (Garmisch-Partenkirchen), 191
Circus Krone, 114
Classical music, 4, 142
Climate, 16
Clocks, 138
  antique, 131, 132, 135
Club and music scene, 143–146
Confiserie Kreutzkann, 134
Consolidators, 22–23
Corpus Christi street processions, 17
Country music, 144
Crafts and folklore, 134–135
Credit cards, 16
Croccodrillo, 147
Cross-country skiing, 169
Curling (Eisstock), 175
Currency exchange, 31
Customs regulations, 14–15

Cuvilliés, François, 102, 104, 107, 122, 142, 167, 230
Cuvilliés Theater (Altes Residenztheater), 103, 142

D achau Concentration Camp, 153–154
Dallmayr, 138
Dance clubs and discos, 144–146
Denning, restaurant, 88
Dentists, 31
Department stores, 135
  Bad Reichenhall, 181
Deutsche Alpenstrasse (German Alpine Road), 169–170
Deutscher Alpenverein/ DAV (German Alpine Association), 201
Deutsches Museum, 98–100, 114
Deutsches Theater, 143
Deutsches Theater-museum, 108
Diessen, 161
Diözesanmuseum (Freising), 167
Dirndl-Ecke, 136
Disabilities, travelers with, 19–20
Doctors, 31
Dombibliothek (Freising), 167
Driver's licenses, 29
Driving rules, 29
Drug laws, 31

E agles Nest (Kehlstein) (Obersalzberg), 179
Easter Bunny Museum, 111
Eckbauer, 168, 198–199
Eibsee Seilbahn (Eibsee Cable car), 198
Eisstadion (Berchtesgaden), 175
Eisstock (curling), 175
Electricity, 31
Electronics, 136
Elisabethmarkt, 139
E-mail, 31
Embassies and consulates, 31
Emergencies, 32
Englischer Garten, 4, 36, 111, 116–118, 130
Engravings and postcards, 136
Entry requirements, 14
Escorted tours, 24–25

Ethnology Museum (Staatliches Museum für Völkerkunde), 110
Euro, 15–16
Expedia, 27

Families with children attractions for, 114
toys, 140
Fasching (Carnival), 17
Fashions (clothing), 136–138
Garmisch-Partenkirchen, 192
Mittenwald, 208
Fax machines, 32
Feierwerk, 145
Feldherrnhalle, 122
Fishing, 169
Food (cuisine), 138, 231–232
Forsthaus Graseck, 198
Frankonia, 136
Franz-Josef-Strauss International Airport, 35
accommodations near, 62–63
Franz Trinkl (Bad Wiessee), 188
Frauenchiemsee, 184
Frauenkirche (Cathedral of Our Lady), 106, 119
Freising, 166–167
Friedl Mandel (Bad Wiessee), 188
Frommers.com, 27
Full Stall (Berchtesgaden), 175
Furore, 137
Füssen, 211

Galerie für Angewandte Künst München, 132
Garmisch-Partenkirchen, 26, 172, 190–197
Gasoline, 29
Gasteig Kulturzentrum, 142
Gay and lesbian travelers, 20–21
clubs, 151–152
Geigenbau Leonhardt (Mittenwald), 208
Geigenbau-und Heimatmuseum (Mittenwald), 208
Geisel's Vinothek, 140
German Alpine Association (Deutscher Alpenverein/DAV), 168, 201
German National Tourist Board, 13
Gletscher Seilbahn, 197
Glyptothek, 108

Golf, 117
Golf Club Feldafing, 117
Golf Club Isarwinkel (Bad Tölz), 163
Golfclub Strasslach (Munich Golf Club), 117
Golfplatz am Buchberg (Bad Tölz), 163
Göring, Herman, 2, 178, 227
Graseck Seilbahn, 198
Graunke Symphony Orchestra, 142
Great Hall of Mirrors (Neues Schloss), 184
Grossmarkthalle, 139
Grünwald, restaurant, 88
Gulbransson, Olaf, 158

Haidhausen, 6, 37
accommodations, 59–60
Hang gliding, 169, 175
Hauptbahnhof, 36
Haus der 111 Biere, 147
Havana Club, 147
Health concerns, 19
Health insurance, 19
Heiliger Berg, 161
Heiliggeist (Holy Ghost) Church, 120
Heimatmuseum (Berchtesgaden), 174
Heimatmuseum (Oberammergau), 203
Hellabrunn Zoo, 111–112, 114
Hemmerle, 138–139
Henry the Lion, 166, 214–216
Herkulessaal, 142
Herrenchiemsee, 170, 184–186
Herrsching, 161
Hertie, 135
Hieber am Dom, 141
Hiking, 25–26
Bavarian Alps, 198–201
Mittenwald, 208
Hildebrand Haus, 108
Hirmer, 137
Hirschgarten, 6, 111
History of Munich, 214–228
Hitler, Adolf, 177–179, 226–227
Hochalm cable car, 200
Hofbräuhaus am Platzl, 8, 120, 149–150
Hofgarten, 103, 122
Hohenschwangau, 210–213
Hohenzollernstrasse, 128, 131
Holidays, 17

Holy Ghost (Heiliggeist) Church, 120
Holzschittschule (Woodcarving School) (Oberammergau), 203
Horse-drawn carriage rides, (Neuschwanstein), 212
Horse-drawn mail coach, (Garmisch-Partenkirchen), 192
Horse-drawn sled, (Garmisch-Partenkirchen), 197
Hospitals, 32
Hugendubel, 132–133

Ignaz-Günther-Haus, 126–128
Insurance, 18–19
Irish Pub (Garmisch-Partenkirchen), 197
Isar River, 214, 215
raft trips on, 117
Isartor (Isar Gate), 95
Itineraries, suggested, 93–94

Jadschloss Schachen, 191
Jakobidult, 18
Jazz, 144
Jazzclub Unterfahrt, 144
Jenner, Mt., 168, 169, 175
Jewelry and watches, 138–139
Jews, 216, 217, 226
Jogging, 117–118
Josef Mack Co. (Bad Reichenhall), 181
Jüdisches Museum München, 108
Jugendstil Museum (Stuck-Villa), 109
Just Pure Day Spa, 117

Kaffe Hause Reber, 134
Karlsplatz (Stachus), 36, 95, 124, 126
Karlstor, 95
Karolinenplatz, 123
Karstadt, 135
Kaufhaus Huhasz (Bad Reichenhall), 181
Kaufhof, 135
Kaufingerstrasse, 36
shopping on, 131, 137
Kaufmann (Garmisch-Partenkirchen), 192
Kayaking, 163, 169
Kehlstein (Eagles Nest) (Obersalzberg), 179

Kirchberg-Schlössel, 170
Kitchenware, 139
Kloster Ettal, 172, 205
Kloster Likör, 184
Knives, 139
Kolber, Mt.
  (Berg Kolber), 202
Königliches Schloss
  Berchtesgaden, 174
Königsplatz, 94, 123
Königssee, 170, 172, 177
Kulturzentrum Gasteig, 143
Kunstpark Ost, 145
Kunstring Meissen, 133
Kurpark Schlösschen
  (Herrsching), 161
Kurverwaltung
  (Bad Tölz), 162
Kutschen-Wagen-Schlitten
  Museum (Postal Carriage
  Museum) (Tegernsee), 158
KZ-Dachau (film), 154
KZ-Gedenkstätte
  Dachau, 154

L aber, Mt.
  (Berg Laber), 202
Langer Samstag, 131
Lehel, 37
Linderhof Palace, 204–205
Liquor laws, 32
Loden-Frey, 136–137
Loisachtaler (Garmisch-
  Partenkirchen), 192
Ludwig Beck am
  Rathauseck, 135
Ludwig I, King, 104, 222
Ludwig II (musical produc-
  tion), 213
Ludwig II, "Mad" King,
  104, 106, 138, 155, 172,
  186–187, 191, 204,
  223, 230
    Neues Schloss (Herren-
      chiemsee), 184–185
    Neuschwanstein and
      Hohenschwangau,
      210–213
Ludwig-Maximilian
Universität (University of
  Munich), 128
Ludwig Mory, 134
Ludwigstrasse, 37
Ludwig the Bavarian
  (Duke Ludwig IV),
  172, 205, 217–218

M aendler, 137–138
Magdalenenklause, 104
Mann, Thomas, 3, 7, 30, 40,
  127, 206, 226

Maps, 29, 37
Maria-Einsiedel, 116
Marienbrücke (near
  Neuschwanstein), 212
Mariendom (Freising),
  166–167
Marienplatz, 36, 94,
  119–120, 215
    walking tour, 124–127
Marionetten Theater,
  Münchner, 114
Markets, 139
Marstallmuseum, 104
Marzipan, 134
Master's Home, 147
Matthäuskirche, 105
Max Emanuel Brauerei, 145
Maximilian II, King, 8, 37,
  98, 123, 210, 212, 223
Maximiliansplatz, 123
Maximilianstrasse,
  36, 37, 40, 223
    shopping on, 131, 132,
      137, 139
Max-Joseph-Platz, 36, 122
Maxvorstadt, 41
Medical insurance, 19
Michaelskirche (St. Michael's
  Church), 106, 219
Mister B's, 144
Mittenwald, 170, 207–210
Monatsprogramm, 141
Money matters, 15–16
Montez, Lola, 224
Moorish Kiosk
  (Schloss Linderhof), 204
Morizz, 151
Moshammer Rudolph's, 137
Motorcycling, 26
Mountain climbing, 25–26
Müller's Public Baths, 8
München Tickets, 141
Münchner Kammer-
  spiele, 143
Münchner Marionetten
  Theater, 114
Münchner Philharmoniker
  (Munich Philharmonic), 142
Münchner Poupenstuben
  und Zinnfiguren
  Kabinette, 140
Münchner Stadtmuseum
  (Municipal Museum),
  108–109, 114
Munich Fashion Week, 17
Munich Film Festival, 18
Munich Golf Club (Golfclub
  Strasslach), 117
Munich Philharmonic
  (Münchner Philhar-
  moniker), 142
Munich Summer of Music,
  18

Munich Tourist Office, 13
Municipal Museum
  (Münchner Stadtmuseum),
  108–109, 114
Münzhof, 120
Museum of Antiquities
  (Antikensammlungen), 107
Museum of Scent, 111
Music
  classical, 142
  country, 144
  jazz, 144
Musical Theatre
  Neuschwanstein, 213

N achtcafé, 148
Nachtwerk, 145
Nationaltheater, 94
Neue Pinakothek, 100
Neues Rathaus (New Town
  Hall), 94
Neues Schloss (Herren-
  chiemsee), 170, 184
Neuhausen
  accommodations, 61–62
  café, 90
Neuhauserstrasse, 36
  shopping on, 131, 135, 138
Neuschwanstein, 186,
  210–213
Newspapers and
  magazines, 32
New York, 151
Night Flight, 143–144
Nightlife and entertainment,
  141–152
    beer halls, 149–151
    club and music scene,
      143–146
    current listings, 141
    gay and lesbian, 151–152
    performing arts, 141–143
Nil, 152
Nymphenburger Porzellan-
  manufaktur, 133
Nymphenburg
  neighborhood, 40
    accommodations, 62
    beer garden, 91–92
    cafe, 90
    restaurant, 88
Nymphenburg Palace
  (Schloss Nymphenburg), 7,
  40, 102, 103–105, 133
    park surrounding, 104, 118

O berammergau, 172,
  201–207
Obermenzing
  accommodations, 61
  restaurant, 89

Obersalzberg, 2, 177–180
Obletter's, 140
Ochsen Garten, 152
Odeonsplatz, 94
Oklahoma, 144
Oktoberfest, 6, 18
Olaf Gulbransson Museum
    (Tegernsee), 158
Old Town. See Altstadt
Olympiapark, 6, 40, 112, 118
    accommodations, 59
Olympiapark
    Sommerfest, 18
Olympia-Schwimmhalle
    (swimming pool), 116
Olympiasee, 117
Olympia stadium, 112
Olympia Tower, 112
Olympic Games (1972), 40,
    112, 113
Olympic Ice Stadium
    (Garmisch-Partenkirchen),
    190–191
Opera, 142
Opera Festival, 18
Orbitz, 27
O'Reilly's Irish Pub, 148
Osterfelderkopf, 199
Otto Kellnberger
    Holzhandlung, 134
Outdoor activities
    Bad Tölz, 163
    in the Bavarian Alps,
        168–169
    Berchtesgaden, 175
Outdoor Club
    Berchtesgaden, 169

P ackage tours, 24
Padlock Museum, 110–111
Pagodenburg, 104
Panorama Tours, 115
Paragliding, 169, 175
Parkcafé, 146
Parks and gardens, 111
Partnachklamm Gorge, 198
Passion Play
    (Oberammergau), 201–202
Passionspielhaus
    (Oberammergau), 202–203
Pedal-Car Museum, 110
Perchen Strand, 156
Performing arts, 141–143
Peterskirche (St. Peter's
    Church), 94, 106–107, 120
Pewter, 140
Pharmacies, 32
Philatelie und Ansichts-
    karten, 136
Philographikon Galerie
    Rauhut, 132

Philosopher's Walk
    (Garmisch-
    Partenkirchen), 191
Pilatushaus
    (Oberammergau), 203
Pinakothek der Moderne,
    2, 100
Porcelain (china), 133
Porzellansammlung, 105
Possenhofen, 156
Possenhofen castle (Schloss
    Possenhofen), 155, 156
Possenhofer Strand, 156
Postal Carriage Museum
    (Kutschen-Wagen-Schlitten
    Museum) (Tegernsee), 158
Post offices, 33
Priceline, 27–28
Prinoth, 134
Pusser's New York Bar, 148

Q ixo, 27

R adio, 33
Radius Tours & Bikes, 116
Rafting, 7–8, 163
Raft trips, 117
Rain, average, 17
Rattlesnake Saloon, 144
Red/Green of
    Scandinavia, 137
Residenz (Royal Palace), 94,
    100–102, 122
Residenz Museum, 102–103
Restaurants, 64–92. See also
    Restaurant Index
    best, 10–12
    by cuisine, 64–66
    what's new in, 1
Restrooms, 33
Richard Strauss
    Fountain, 124
Rosenthal-Studio-Haus, 133
Rosy Maendler, 138
Rottach-Egern, 157–160

S afety, 33
Sailing, 116
St.-Anna-Damenstift, 126
St. George's Parish Church
    (Freising), 166
St.-Johann-Nepomuk-Kirche
    (Asamkirche), 105–106
St. Martin, church of
    (Garmisch-
    Partenkirchen), 191
St. Michael's Church
    (Michaelskirche), 219

St. Peter's Church (Peter-
    skirche), 94, 106–107, 120
St. Zeno (Bad
    Reichenhall), 181
Salzbergwerk Berchtes-
    gaden, 174–175
Sankt Quirinus, monastery of
    (Tegernsee), 158
Saturn Electro Techno-
    center, 136
S-bahn, 35, 41
Schack-Galerie, 109
Schatzkammer, 103
Schellingstrasse, shopping
    on, 131–133
Schiffahrt Königssee, 177
Schloss Berg, 155, 156
Schloss Linderhof, 172,
    204–205
Schloss Nymphenburg
    (Nymphenburg Palace), 7,
    40, 102, 103–105, 133
    park surrounding, 104, 118
Schlossplatz
    (Berchtesgaden), 173–174
Schloss Possenhofen (Possen-
    hofen castle), 155, 156
Schultz, 148
Schumann's, 148
Schwabing, 7, 36, 40, 94
    accommodations, 58–59
    beer garden, 91
    restaurants, 84–87
    walking tour, 129–130
Schwabinger Ballhouse, 145
Schwabinger Podium, 146
Sebastian Wesely, 140
Sendlingertorplatz, 126
Seniors, 21–22
Shamrock, 149
Shopping, 131–140
    Bad Reichenhall, 181
    Bad Wiessee, 188
    Garmisch-Partenkirchen,
        191–192
    Mittenwald, 208
Singer's Hall
    (Neuschwanstein), 212
Sisi Museum, 110
Skiing, 118
    Bavarian Alps, 169
    Brauneck mountain, 163
Ski Stadium (Garmisch-
    Partenkirchen), 191
Soul City, 152
Special interest
    vacations, 25
Spielbank Garmisch-
    Partenkirchen, 197
Spielzeugmuseum, 114
Squirrel, 132

Staatliche Museum Ägyptischer Kunst (State Museum of Egyptian Art), 109
Staatliche Schiffahrt (Starnberg), 156
Staatliche Schiffahrt (Ammersee), 161
Staatliches Museum für Völkerkunde (Ethnology Museum), 110
Staatsbrauerei Weihenstephan (Freising), 166
Staatstheater am Gärtnerplatz, 142
Stachus (Karlsplatz), 36, 95, 124, 126
Stadtcafé, 149
Stadtische Galerie im Lenbachhaus, 109
Stadtpfarrkirche (Bad Tölz), 162
Starkbierzeit, 17
Starnbergersee (Lake Starnberg), 116, 154–157
State Theater (Bayerisches Staatsschauspiel), 142
Steck Segel-und-Surf Schule, 158
Stiftskirche (Abbey Church) (Berchtesgaden), 174
Strauss, Richard, Fountain, 124
Stuck-Villa (Jugendstil Museum), 109
Stummbaum (Herrsching), 161
Südbahnhof, restaurants near, 83–84
Summit Club, 201
Surf Tools, 156
Swimming, Bavarian Alps, 169
Swimming pools, 116
  Bad Tölz, 163

T axes, 33
Taxis, 42
Teddy-Bar, 152
Tegernsee, 157–160
Tegernsee Ducal Palace, 188
Telephone, 33–34
Television, 34
Temperature, average daytime, 17
Temple Club, 145
Tennis, 118
Theater, 142–143
  Bad Reichenhall, 183

Theatinerkirche (Church of St. Kajetan), 94, 102, 107, 122
Thirty Years' War (1618-48), 220
Tiffany Bar (Bad Reichenhall), 183
Time zone, 34
Tipping, 34
Tollwood, 18
Tomate Sports, 149
Tourist information, 13–14, 36
Tours
  Berchtesgaden, 175
  bike, 25, 115–116
  escorted, 24–25
  motorcycle, 26
  package, 24
  sightseeing, 115
Toys, 140
Trachtenstubön (Mittenwald), 208
Train travel, 23–24, 28, 35–36
Transportation, 41–42
Travelocity, 27
T.S.V. 1860 München, 112
Türkenhof, 151

U -bahn (subway), 36, 41
Uli Knecht, 137, 138
University of Munich (Ludwig-Maximilian Universität), 128
Untermenzing, accommodations, 60–61

V erkehrsamt der Kurverwaltung, 200
Viktualienmarkt, 7, 94, 120, 139–140
Visitor information, 13–14, 36

W agner, Richard, 7, 18, 76, 186–187, 210, 212, 223, 224
Wagner Festival (Garmisch-Partenkirchen), 197
Waldwirtschaft Grosshesselohe, 151
Walking tours
  historic center, 119–123
  Marienplatz, 124–127
  Schwabing, 129–130
Wallach, 134–135

Wallberg Road, 188
Wank, 198
Watches, 138–139
Watzmann Mountain, 168, 172
Websites
  travel-planning and booking, 26
  visitor information, 13–14
Weinhaus Moschner (Rottach-Egern), 160
Weisswurst, 6, 150
Wellenberg (Oberammergau), 202
Welser Kuche, 146
Werkraum, 143
Westpark, 41
White-water canoeing, kayaking, or rafting, 163, 169
Wieskirche (near Füssen), 211
Wildflowers, Bavarian Alps, 201
Wildlife, Bavarian Alps, 200–201
Windsurfing
  Ammersee, 161
  Munich, 116
  Tegernsee, 158
Wine, 140
Winter sports, 26
Wittelsbacher-Platz, 123
Wittelsbach family, 7, 40, 93, 95, 102, 103, 120, 122, 124, 155, 156, 174, 215–223, 226
WOM (World of Music), 141
Woodcarvings, 134, 188, 203
Woodcarving School (Holzschittschule) (Oberammergau), 203
Words'Worth, 133
World War I, 225
World War II, 120, 227, 230
Wristwatches, 138–139

Z AM, 110–111
Zimmerman, Johann Baptist, 103, 106, 167, 211, 230
Zimmermann, Dominikus, 211, 230
Zoo, Hellabrunn, 111–112, 114
Zugspitzbahn, 197
Zugspitze, 4, 6, 118, 172, 197–198
Zugspitzplatt, 169, 197
Zwink, Peter, 204

ACCOMMODATIONS

Admiral, 1, 45
Adria, 50
Advokat Hotel, 50
Alexandra (Bad Tölz), 164
Alpenrose (Mittenwald), 209
Alpina Hotel (Garmisch-
   Partenkirchen), 192
Alte Post
   (Oberammergau), 206
Am Markt, 54
Ammersee-Hotel
   (Herrsching), 161
Arabella Sheraton Airport,
   62–63
Arabella Sheraton Grand
   Hotel, 10, 60
Arabella Westpark-Hotel, 45
Asam Stadthotel, 1, 50
Bachmair-Alpina
   (Rottach-Egern), 159
Bachmair Hotel am See
   (Rottach-Egern), 158–159
Bayerischer Hof (Prien am
   Chiemsee), 185
Bayerischer Hof & Palais
   Montgelas, 9, 44
City Hotel, 50
Eden-Hotel-Wolff, 9–10,
   45, 48
Erzgiesserei Europe, 50–51
Europäischer Hof, 54–55
Excelsior Hotel, 48
Forum Hotel München, 48
Four Points Hotel München
   Central, 51
Four Points Hotel München
   Olympiapark, 9, 59
Gästehaus Englischer
   Garten, 9, 58–59
Gästhaus Franziska
   (Mittenwald), 209
Gästhaus Maier-Kirschner
   (Rottach-Egern), 159–160
Gästhaus Sonnenbichl
   (Mittenwald), 209–210
Gästhaus Trenkler (Garmisch-
   Partenkirchen), 194
Gasthof Fraundorfer
   (Garmisch-Partenkirchen),
   194–195
Golden Tulip Hotel
   Olymp, 63
Grand Hotel Sonnenbichl
   (Garmisch-Partenkirchen),
   192–193
Haltmair am See (Rottach-
   Egern), 159

Haus Lilly (Garmisch-
   Partenkirchen), 195
Holiday Inn Munich
   City-North, 59
Hotel An der Oper, 10, 51
Hotel Bayerischer Hof
   (Bad Reichenhall), 182
Hotel Biederstein, 51
Hotel Brack, 51–52
Hotel Bristol München, 55
Hotel Café-Restaurant
   Friedenshöhe
   (Oberammergau), 206
Hotel Carlton, 52
Hotel Concorde, 48
Hotel der Schilcherhof
   (Oberammergau), 206
Hotel Domus, 52
Hotel Exquisit, 52
Hotel Fischer
   (Berchtesgaden), 175
Hotel Germania, 52–53
Hotel Hilleprandt (Garmisch-
   Partenkirchen), 195
Hotel Jedermann, 55
Hotel Krone
   (Berchtesgaden), 176
Hotel Lederer
   (Bad Wiessee), 188
Hotel Leoni (Berg), 156
Hotel Leopold, 58
Hotel Lisl and Jägerhaus
   (Hohenschwangau), 213
Hotel Mirabell, 1
Hotel Müller Hohen-
   schwangau, 213
Hotel Olympic, 9, 53
Hotel Palace, 60
Hotel Pension Am
   Siegestor, 55
Hotel-Pension Beck, 55–56
Hotel-Pension Mariandl,
   1, 56
Hotel-Pension Schmeller-
   garten, 56
Hotel Post (Mittenwald),
   208–209
Hotel Promenade
   (Herrsching), 161–162
Hotel Reinbold, 53
Hotel Restaurant Böld
   (Oberammergau), 205
Hotel Rex (Bad
   Wiessee), 188
Hotel St. Paul, 1, 53–54
Hotel Schlicker, 56
Hotel Schloss Berg, 157
Hotel Wallis, 56–57

Hotel Zum Türken
   (Obersalzberg), 179–180
Intercity-Hotel München,
   48–49
Jagdschloss, 61
Jodquellenhof-Alpamare
   (Bad Tölz), 163
Kempinski Hotel Airport
   München, 62
Kempinski Hotel Vier
   Jahreszeiten München,
   8, 44
King's First Class Hotel, 49
Kolbergarten (Bad Tölz), 164
Königshof, 44–45
Kraft Hotel, 54
Kriemhild, 62
Kurhotel Eberl
   (Bad Tölz), 164
Kurhotel Edelweiss
   (Bad Wiessee), 189
Kurpfalz, 57
Landhaus Am Stein
   (Bad Wiessee), 189
Mandarin Oriental, 9, 45
Mercure München Königin
   Elisabeth, 1, 61
München City Hilton, 59
München Marriott Hotel,
   10, 58
München Park Hilton,
   8–9, 49
Obermühle (Garmisch-
   Partenkirchen), 193
Parkhotel Egerner Hof
   (Rottach-Egern), 159
Parkhotel Luisenbad (Bad
   Reichenhall), 181–182
Park Hotel Resi von der Post
   (Bad Wiessee), 189
Parkhotel Sonnenhof
   (Oberammergau), 205–206
Pension Stadt München, 57
Pension Westfalia, 57
Posthotel Kolberbräu
   (Bad Tölz), 164–165
Posthotel Partenkirchen
   (Garmisch-
   Partenkirchen), 193
Preysing, 59–60
Reindl's Partenkirchner Hof
   (Garmisch-Partenkirchen),
   193–194
Rieger Hotel
   (Mittenwald), 209
Romantik Hotel Clausing's
   Posthotel (Garmisch-
   Partenkirchen), 194
Romantik Hotel Insel Mühle,
   9, 60–61

Rotkreuzplatz, 61–62
Salzburger Hof (Bad
   Reichenhall), 182
Schlosshotel Linderhof
   (Oberammergau), 206–207
SKH-Trustee Parkhotel, 54
Steigenberger Axel-
   mannstein (Bad Reichen-
   hall), 10, 181
Torbräu, 49
Turmwirt
   (Oberammergau), 207
Uhland Garni, 9, 57–58
Vier Jahreszeiten
   (Berchtesgaden), 175
Watzmann
   (Berchtesgaden), 176
Wiesseer Hof (Bad
   Wiessee), 189
Wittelsbach
   (Berchtesgaden), 175–176
Wolf Restaurant-Hotel
   (Oberammergau), 207
Yachthotel Chiemsee (Prien
   am Chiemsee), 185

RESTAURANTS

Alba, 87
Alois Dallmayr, 12, 71–72
Alpenhof (Garmisch-
   Partenkirchen), 196
Altes Fahrhaus
   (Bad Tölz), 165
Am Marstall, 70
Andechser am Dom, 76
Andechser Hof
   (Herrsching), 162
Asam Schlössel, 84
Austernkeller, 12, 70
Bamberger Haus, 91
Bar-Restaurant Morizz, 72
Biergarten Chinesischer
   Turm, 91
Bistro Cézanne, 1, 85
Bistro Terrine, 11, 85
Boettner's, 10, 67
Bogenhauser Hof, 87
Buon Gusto (Talamonti),
   11–12, 72
Café am Beethovenplatz, 1,
   76–77
Café Dukatz in the Liter-
   aturhaus, 2, 77
Café Glockenspiel, 89
Café Luitpold, 89–90, 122
Café Roxy, 128

Casale, 88
Cohen's, 2, 77
Demming-Restaurant
   Le Gourmet
   (Berchtesgaden), 176
Der Katzlmacher, 85–86
Der Tisch, 1, 72–73
Deutsche Eiche (German
   Oak), 77–78
Dichterstube/Hubertus-
   Stüberl (Rottach-
   Egern), 160
Donisl, 78
Erstes Münchner
   Kartoffelhaus, 2, 78
Flösserstuben (Garmisch-
   Partenkirchen), 196
Freihaus Brenner (Bad
   Wiessee), 189–190
Garden Restaurant, 67
Gästhaus Glockenbach,
   83–84
Gästhaus Landbrecht
   (Freising), 167
Gaststätte zum Flaucher, 91
Geisel's Vinothek, 11, 78
Graffunder, 12, 79
Grüne Gans, 73
Grünwalder Einkehr,
   10–11, 88
Guglhupf, 90
Hackerhaus, 79
Halali, 73
Hard Rock Cafe, 73–74
Hirschgarten, 91–92
Hotel Am Wald
   (Bad Tölz), 170
Hubertusstube
   (Berchtesgaden), 176–177
Hundskugel, 79
Hunsinger's Pacific, 74
Käfer am Hofgarten, 12,
   79–80
Käfer-Schänke, 87–88
Kay's Bistro, 11, 70–71
La Galleria, 71
La Mucca, 86
Locanda Picolit, 12, 86
Mark's Restaurant, 11, 71
Mövenpick Restaurant,
   11, 74
Nürnberger Bratwurst Glöckl
   am Dom, 12, 80
Nymphenburger Hof, 88–89
Palais Keller, 11, 80
Panorama Restaurant
   (Berchtesgaden), 177

Park-Café Kitchen, 80
Pfalzer Weinprobierstube,
   80–81
Pfistermühle, 74
Posthotel Partenkirchen
   (Garmisch-
   Partenkirchen), 195
Prinz Myshkin, 81
Ratskeller München, 75
Reindl's Restaurant
   (Garmisch-Partenkirchen),
   195–196
Restaurant Arnspitze
   (Mittenwald), 210
Restaurant die Holzstube
   (Bad Reichenhall), 182
Restaurant Königshof, 67
Restaurant Lenbach, 75
Restaurant Mühlberger
   (Prien), 2, 12, 185
Restaurant Olympiasee, 113
Restaurant Posthotel Kolber-
   bräu (Bad Tölz), 165
Restaurant Promenade
   (Herrsching), 162
Restaurant Vier
   Jahreszeiten, 70
Riessersee (Garmisch-
   Partenkirchen), 196
Ruffini, 90
Sausalito's, 86–87
Schlosscafé im
   Palmenhaus, 90
Schweizer Stuben (Bad
   Reichenhall), 182–183
Spago, 86
Spatenhaus, 75–76
Spöckmeier, 81
Straubinger Hof, 81–82
Sushi & Soul, 82
Tantris, 11, 84–85
Tattenbach, 82
Times Square Online
   Bistro, 82
Tower Restaurant, 112
Weichandhof, 89
Weinbauer, 87
Weinhaus Neuner, 76
Weisses Bräuhaus, 82
Welser Kuche, 146
Wolf Restaurant-Hotel
   (Oberammergau), 207
Zum Alten Markt, 76
Zum Aumeister, 92
Zum Burgerhaus, 82–83
Zum Dürnbräu, 83
Zum Hofer, 83

FROMMER'S® COMPLETE TRAVEL GUIDES

Alaska
Alaska Cruises & Ports of Call
Amsterdam
Argentina & Chile
Arizona
Atlanta
Australia
Austria
Bahamas
Barcelona, Madrid & Seville
Beijing
Belgium, Holland & Luxembourg
Bermuda
Boston
Brazil
British Columbia & the Canadian
  Rockies
Budapest & the Best of Hungary
California
Canada
Cancún, Cozumel & the Yucatán
Cape Cod, Nantucket & Martha's
  Vineyard
Caribbean
Caribbean Cruises & Ports of Call
Caribbean Ports of Call
Carolinas & Georgia
Chicago
China
Colorado
Costa Rica
Denmark
Denver, Boulder & Colorado
  Springs
England
Europe
European Cruises & Ports of Call
Florida

France
Germany
Great Britain
Greece
Greek Islands
Hawaii
Hong Kong
Honolulu, Waikiki & Oahu
Ireland
Israel
Italy
Jamaica
Japan
Las Vegas
London
Los Angeles
Maryland & Delaware
Maui
Mexico
Montana & Wyoming
Montréal & Québec City
Munich & the Bavarian Alps
Nashville & Memphis
Nepal
New England
New Mexico
New Orleans
New York City
New Zealand
Northern Italy
Nova Scotia, New Brunswick &
  Prince Edward Island
Oregon
Paris
Philadelphia & the Amish Country
Portugal
Prague & the Best of the Czech
  Republic

Provence & the Riviera
Puerto Rico
Rome
San Antonio & Austin
San Diego
San Francisco
Santa Fe, Taos & Albuquerque
Scandinavia
Scotland
Seattle & Portland
Shanghai
Singapore & Malaysia
South Africa
South America
South Florida
South Pacific
Southeast Asia
Spain
Sweden
Switzerland
Texas
Thailand
Tokyo
Toronto
Tuscany & Umbria
USA
Utah
Vancouver & Victoria
Vermont, New Hampshire &
  Maine
Vienna & the Danube Valley
Virgin Islands
Virginia
Walt Disney World® & Orlando
Washington, D.C.
Washington State

FROMMER'S® DOLLAR-A-DAY GUIDES

Australia from $50 a Day
California from $70 a Day
Caribbean from $70 a Day
England from $75 a Day
Europe from $70 a Day

Florida from $70 a Day
Hawaii from $80 a Day
Ireland from $60 a Day
Italy from $70 a Day
London from $85 a Day

New York from $90 a Day
Paris from $80 a Day
San Francisco from $70 a Day
Washington, D.C. from $80 a Day

FROMMER'S® PORTABLE GUIDES

Acapulco, Ixtapa & Zihuatanejo
Amsterdam
Aruba
Australia's Great Barrier Reef
Bahamas
Berlin
Big Island of Hawaii
Boston
California Wine Country
Cancún
Charleston & Savannah
Chicago
Disneyland®
Dublin
Florence

Frankfurt
Hong Kong
Houston
Las Vegas
London
Los Angeles
Los Cabos & Baja
Maine Coast
Maui
Miami
New Orleans
New York City
Paris
Phoenix & Scottsdale

Portland
Puerto Rico
Puerto Vallarta, Manzanillo &
  Guadalajara
Rio de Janeiro
San Diego
San Francisco
Seattle
Sydney
Tampa & St. Petersburg
Vancouver
Venice
Virgin Islands
Washington, D.C.

FROMMER'S® NATIONAL PARK GUIDES

Banff & Jasper
Family Vacations in the National
  Parks
Grand Canyon

National Parks of the American
  West
Rocky Mountain

Yellowstone & Grand Teton
Yosemite & Sequoia/ Kings Canyon
Zion & Bryce Canyon

FROMMER'S® MEMORABLE WALKS

Chicago
London

New York
Paris

San Francisco
Washington, D.C.

FROMMER'S® GREAT OUTDOOR GUIDES

Arizona & New Mexico
New England

Northern California
Southern New England

Vermont & New Hampshire

SUZY GERSHMAN'S BORN TO SHOP GUIDES

Born to Shop: France
Born to Shop: Hong Kong,
   Shanghai & Beijing

Born to Shop: Italy
Born to Shop: London

Born to Shop: New York
Born to Shop: Paris

FROMMER'S® IRREVERENT GUIDES

Amsterdam
Boston
Chicago
Las Vegas
London

Los Angeles
Manhattan
New Orleans
Paris
Rome

San Francisco
Seattle & Portland
Vancouver
Walt Disney World®
Washington, D.C.

FROMMER'S® BEST-LOVED DRIVING TOURS

Britain
California
Florida
France

Germany
Ireland
Italy
New England

Northern Italy
Scotland
Spain
Tuscany & Umbria

HANGING OUT™ GUIDES

Hanging Out in England
Hanging Out in Europe

Hanging Out in France
Hanging Out in Ireland

Hanging Out in Italy
Hanging Out in Spain

THE UNOFFICIAL GUIDES®

Bed & Breakfasts and Country
   Inns in:
   California
   Great Lakes States
   Mid-Atlantic
   New England
   Northwest
   Rockies
   Southeast
   Southwest
Best RV & Tent Campgrounds in:
   California & the West
   Florida & the Southeast
   Great Lakes States
   Mid-Atlantic
   Northeast
   Northwest & Central Plains

Southwest & South Central
   Plains
   U.S.A.
Beyond Disney
Branson, Missouri
California with Kids
Chicago
Cruises
Disneyland®
Florida with Kids
Golf Vacations in the Eastern U.S.
Great Smoky & Blue Ridge Region
Inside Disney
Hawaii
Las Vegas
London

Mid-Atlantic with Kids
Mini Las Vegas
Mini-Mickey
New England and New York with
   Kids
New Orleans
New York City
Paris
San Francisco
Skiing in the West
Southeast with Kids
Walt Disney World®
Walt Disney World® for Grown-ups
Walt Disney World® with Kids
Washington, D.C.
World's Best Diving Vacations

SPECIAL-INTEREST TITLES

Frommer's Adventure Guide to Australia &
   New Zealand
Frommer's Adventure Guide to Central America
Frommer's Adventure Guide to India & Pakistan
Frommer's Adventure Guide to South America
Frommer's Adventure Guide to Southeast Asia
Frommer's Adventure Guide to Southern Africa
Frommer's Britain's Best Bed & Breakfasts and
   Country Inns
Frommer's Caribbean Hideaways
Frommer's Exploring America by RV
Frommer's Fly Safe, Fly Smart
Frommer's France's Best Bed & Breakfasts and
   Country Inns
Frommer's Gay & Lesbian Europe

Frommer's Italy's Best Bed & Breakfasts and
   Country Inns
Frommer's New York City with Kids
Frommer's Ottawa with Kids
Frommer's Road Atlas Britain
Frommer's Road Atlas Europe
Frommer's Road Atlas France
Frommer's Toronto with Kids
Frommer's Vancouver with Kids
Frommer's Washington, D.C., with Kids
Israel Past & Present
The New York Times' Guide to Unforgettable
   Weekends
Places Rated Almanac
Retirement Places Rated